D1360645

PLAYWRIGHTS / LYRICISTS / COMPOSERS
ON THEATER

110827

PLAYWRIGHTS LYRICISTS COMPOSERS ON THEATER

☆ ☆ ☆ ☆ ☆ ☆ ☆ ☆ ☆ ☆ ☆ ☆ ☆ ☆ ☆ ☆ ☆ ☆

*The inside story of a decade of theater
in articles and comments by its authors,
selected from their own publication,*

the *D*ramatists *G*uild *Q*uarterly

Edited by

Otis L. Guernsey Jr.

Drawings by Tom Funk

☆ ☆ ☆ ☆ ☆ ☆ ☆ ☆ ☆ ☆ ☆ ☆ ☆ ☆ ☆ ☆ ☆ ☆

DODD, MEAD & COMPANY   **New York**

Alverno College Library
Milwaukee, Wisconsin

792.0973
G933

Copyright © 1964 The Authors League of America, Inc.
Copyright © 1964, 1965, 1966, 1967, 1968, 1969, 1970,
1971, 1972, 1973, 1974 by The Dramatists Guild, Inc.
All rights reserved
No part of this book may be reproduced in any form
without permission in writing from the publisher

ISBN: 0-396-07008-6
Library of Congress Catalog Card Number: 74-11505

The type was set by Printworks, Inc., Norwalk, Connecticut
Printed and bound in the United States of America
by The Maple Press Co., Inc., York, Pennsylvania

Editor's Note

dram'a·tist, n. An author of a theatrical composition; a playwright; a librettist; a lyricist or composer of a work for the theater

This is a book written by dramatists in the sense of the word as defined above: playwrights (including librettists), lyricists and composers of the Broadway and off-Broadway plays and musicals, not just the dramas. By definition they are so distinguished individually and as a group that there's no one left outside these pages who could enhance this collection of their writings very much with an introduction. So these paragraphs are just what it says up there, the editor's factual footnote explaining how such a supremely authoritative inside story of our theater came to be.

The authors of the articles and comments in this volume, with a single exception, are members or ex-members of the Dramatists Guild, an organization which grew out of a committee of playwrights formed by Owen Davis in 1919 under the wing of the Authors League. It was established under its present name in 1922 and separately incorporated in 1964. It is a Guild, a professional association, formed and maintained to serve the economic and other interests of dramatists. Almost all American playwrights, lyricists and composers whose work has appeared on the professional New York stage are members of the Dramatists Guild, as are many U.S.-produced foreign authors (George Bernard Shaw, for example, joined in 1927). The roster includes not only those full members whose shows have actually been produced on or off Broadway (about 650) but also more than 1,500 associate members aspiring to such production with plays and musicals that have been staged elsewhere or are in hopeful circulation among play-readers.

The Guild's past presidents were: Edward Childs Carpenter, Arthur Richman, George Middleton, Sidney Howard, Robert E. Sherwood, Elmer Rice, Richard Rodgers, Moss Hart, Oscar Hammerstein II, Alan Jay Lerner, Sidney Kingsley, Frank D. Gilroy and Robert Anderson. Its leadership at the time of publication of this volume is composed of the following Council members and officers: Lee Adams, Edward Albee, Jerry Bock, Abe Burrows, Paddy Chayefsky, Betty Comden, Marc Connelly, Gretchen Cryer, Jules Feiffer, Bruce Jay Friedman, Ruth Goodman Goetz, James Goldman, John Guare, Sheldon Harnick (secretary), Lillian Hellman, John Kander, Garson Kanin, Arthur Kopit, Arthur Laurents, Jerome Lawrence, Richard Lewine (vice president), Terrence McNally, David Rabe, Mary Rodgers, Dore Schary (treasurer), Stephen Sondheim (president), Joseph Stein, Peter Stone, Jule Styne and Jerome Weidman.

In 1964 the Guild Council decided to set up a more expansive form of intercom among members than the mimeographed bulletin then being put out at intervals. A committee composed of Marc Connelly (a charter Councillor of the Guild) chairman, Robert Anderson and Jean Kerr was named to organize a more formal publication to be called the *Dramatists Guild Quarterly*. It was to be edited by the undersigned, a sometime journalist and still-aspiring playwright who was instantly transformed by the touch of the *Quarterly* committee's magic wand into the world's luckiest editor with more than 2,000 of its most articulate men and women as contributors. This luck has held in the large number of others who have done their utmost for the *Quarterly*: Councillors, members and aficionados (including the Guild's counsel, Irwin Karp) whose suggestions have led to some of the best features; the masthead personnel, past and present, including Camille Croce and Gail Bass who helped assemble this material; and the office staffs of the Guild and the Authors League under the executive secretaryships of David E. LeVine and Mills Ten Eyck Jr., respectively.

In these pages, then, are selections from the *Quarterly*'s first decade of publication: articles, comments, symposia, poems, sudden thoughts, etc., on every aspect of the musical and dramatic stage, addressed by dramatists to dramatists on a highly professional level and in virtually private circulation (though it's possible for a theater enthusiast to subscribe to the *Quarterly* by applying to the Dramatists Guild in New York City). With the one exception already noted (New York *Times* critic Clive Barnes), all authors of this volume are Guild members or ex-members who prepared their remarks for each other, so that this amazing collection of theater bylines, impossible to bring together on purpose within a single set of covers, came together in the spontaneous fusion of the *Quarterly*. A few of these articles were reprinted in publications of more general circulation following their initial appearance in the *Quarterly*—the comedy symposium in *Vogue,* Jerry Herman's in *Diplomat*, Jean Kerr's in her book *Penny Candy*, Arthur Miller's in the New York *Times,* for example—but in most cases their first extracurricular circulation is taking place in this volume. In only one case did an article originate elsewhere: much of John Kander's was first published in a TWA publication, *Adventures in Sight and Sound.*

The *Quarterly*'s pages are open to the whole Guild membership of dramatists and would-be dramatists, and likewise the authorship of this book represents every career phase from the renowned like Richard Rodgers and Edward Albee to the virtually unknown—as yet. Much of the material, like Stephen Sondheim's sparkling dissertation on theater lyrics or Neil Simon's adventurous exploration of Neil Simon, originated in the spoken rather than the written word, via question-and-answer sessions and conversations at Dramatists Guild headquarters or on such outside occasions as the lyricists' and playwrights' evenings at New York's 92d Street YM-YWHA, or discussions set up by the Eugene O'Neill Memorial Foundation. This is to be expected and even preferred editorially in the case of authors whose medium is dialogue, not prose. The spoken word is the dramatist's thing, but there are no "raw" tapes laid on the *Quarterly*. Each was gone over carefully by its author before publication, not to adjust or eliminate facts but to sharpen up the dialogue, as any playwright would insist on doing.

Some of the best *Quarterly* articles of the decade were attached too firmly to specific and now past events for inclusion here. We've tried to bring in as many points of view on as many general subjects as possible, however, in a "Soliloquys" chapter of short but well-aimed observations, many of them excerpts from larger contexts. A sampling of the *Quarterly*'s editorial comment on peripheral stage matters of recent years also appears in this chapter. The whole volume is flavored with Tom Funk's drawings of theater subjects and objects, selected from his ten years of drawings for the *Quarterly* and scattered pretty much at random through this book as through the pages of the magazine. In addition, a "Settings" chapter of Funk drawings preserves the 1970s look of the Broadway and off-Broadway environment, however wide the wrecker's ball may swing in future seasons.

In a comment in these pages, Tennessee Williams identifies the author's function as follows: "The playwright must be at once his own catharsis and that of the audience." In an effort to verbalize the dramatist's catharsis, the *Quarterly* asked all the produced dramatists of a couple of seasons which single word best described their feelings about the experience of having their work staged in New York. Here is the spectrum of their replies, from light to dark:

Joyous	Onward	Discouraged
Exuberant	Ambivalent	Ugh
Expansive	Unfulfilled	Pained
Accomplishment	Regret	Despair
Adventure	Frustration	Horrendous
Enlightening	Disappointment	Agony
Gratitude	Depressing	Help!

Obviously the dramatist's spirit takes heat from the theater as iron does from the fire; the emotional temperature of his catharsis, for better or for worse, equals the audience's. This volume escorts its readers out of the observer's traditional relationship to the theater, into the private world of the playwrights, librettists, lyricists and composers who make it all possible. A visit backstage can be disillusioning to an enthralled member of the audience encountering the struts and braces behind the contrived image, whose doors lead nowhere. Not so in the case of this book; here, behind the dramatist's illusion, we encounter an infinity of feeling, a sunshine of experience whose rays are focussed into burning concentration on the stage. Here is no borderline of artifice, but the true mind and heart of the dramatist, where the show goes on and on and the music never stops.

OTIS L. GUERNSEY JR.
Editor, *Dramatists Guild Quarterly*

Contents

I. On Playwriting.....

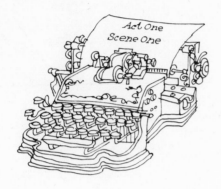

*This is a gift that I have, a foolish extrav-
agant spirit, full of forms, figures, shapes,
objects, ideas, apprehensions, motions, rev-
olutions; these are begot in the ventricle of
memory, nourished in the womb of the* **pia
mater,** *and delivered upon the mellowing of
occasion.*

—Love's Labour's Lost

The Playwright: A Commuter Between Heaven and Hell

By Marc Connelly

I have been trying to learn how to write plays for more than sixty years. During that time I've read at least two hundred books dealing directly or indirectly with the craft of playwriting. I can recall several written by successful playwrights in the hope that their experience might prove useful to others. Sometimes they made points about technical problems they had faced and solved. I admired the deftness of the solutions. It was encouraging to learn that they had not been licked by difficulties of a sort I so often had to face. Unhappily the instances cited gave me no more help in licking mine than the books by self-conscious esthetes whose ignorance of dramaturgy didn't restrain them from pronouncing godhead precepts. I am still grateful for the stimulation that came from handbooks, the names of most of which I'm sorry to say I've forgotten. I remember that when I was young, William Archer's *Play-Making* took me into a kind of surgery where engrossing dissections were performed before my pre-med eyes. From Archer and others I acquired something very valuable, the sense of the importance of plays to the world's well-being. It is also possible that in my reading I picked up a few carpentry lessons which affected, perhaps improved, the mechanics of my work. What I am certain about is that nothing I ever read showed me how to write a play.

Every time I begin one I know I am entering strange territory without a map. I may have some knowledge of the tools I'll be using—but will I hold them properly while working so much of the time in the dark? If I weren't so excited by the possibilities I'd probably give up the idea in despair. But I am excited, excited in an almost manic way, feeling somthing like the torment of

3

an infatuated suitor, fearful of being unworthy of his new love but hell bent on winning her.

I know that I'm going to use a few tricks of the trade which will be as important in plotting my play as they were to the Alexandrian Greeks who discovered them. The born playwright uses them instinctively, but it might be worth while to identify them. There are four, and I am aware that all must be employed in my play's architecture. The Greeks called them the Protasis, the Epitasis, the Catastasis and the Catastrophe.

The Protasis is what today we call the exposition. I know that when the curtain goes up the people who have come to see it will be like passengers approaching a kind of airplane they have never seen before, willing to climb aboard but uncertain that the flight will be pleasant. The first moments of my play must induce those spectators to become something vital to the play's life: an audience. My audience is not that group of individuals, some of whom during the Protasis are scanning their programs, resenting elbows prodding at their sides; or, should they be looking at the stage, considering costumes and scenery or trying to remember when they last saw this or that member of the cast. I know that during the Protasis I must gain their interest and then waste no time getting to the Epitasis, the quickening; the magical phase that begins when programs, elbows, hairdo's, actors and scenery disappear and up on the stage interesting people are present in a room, a garden or some other place that a minute ago was scenery.

My audience must come into being with no more awareness of birth than a baby. During its existence it must be a single, homogeneous creature in all its reactions. Like a baby it will have little knowledge of place and time, being familiar only with the stage's microcosm and those who inhabit it. An audience cannot deliberately cogitate; its thinking is at the most hypnoidal, conditioned by what it experiences from the stage. I know I must keep the audience happy and healthy by making it exercise its perceptions, not its reasoning powers.

From experience I know that should a voice in an audience say, "Wasn't that good!" whatever prompted the exclamation was not really good. Had the scene been functioning properly, its merit would have been only felt, not considered, and the speaker would have been unaware of the presence of a companion who could be addressed vocally. Both would have been sharing the pleasure of the scene through their perceptions. So something on the stage has gone wrong, and the fault may be mine. I've learned that an uninterrupted flow of perceptions is the blood stream that keeps the audience creature alive. In a truly fine play it is the ichor that relates the audience to divinity, enabling it to become an engrossed Olympian, concerned with a revelation of truth. And what is theater at its best but a means for hunting truth under pleasant circumstances?

I know, too, that the audience, in its serene unconsciousness of externalities, can become almost omniscient. Possibly its release from the restrictions of everyday individualities has sharpened its perceptions to an amazing acuteness. Whatever has caused it, I know that once the Epitasis is in progress I need only imply skillfully and the audience will swallow whatever I give it to eat. Of course the actors must serve the food. If they are competent they will be offering portions the audience can ingest easily in the

form of hints rather than statements. The good actor knows that economy of expression is imperative, that in theatrical cookery the difference between a fine actor and a poor one is that the poor one acts ten times as much as he should. So if the cast and I see that the audience is being nourished by inferences the play will be effective and the audience unaware that it, too, is working, happily but with inflagging industry.

I must remember that at no time can my audience have divergent responses to the play's incidents. If any two of the personally unacquainted people now parts of the audience witnessed strangers quarreling in the street they would most likely have different reactions. A. might assume X. was the aggressor, B. might think it was Y. There would be no such dichotomy if the A. and B. of the audience witnessed a similar quarrel on the stage because they know more about every character's personality than the characters themselves do—that is, if the godlike omniscience is at work.

By the time the Catastasis, the crisis, has been reached I must have the audience in such a state that its emotions are racing along in complete harmony with the action. And as I approach the Catastrophe, the conclusion, I know I must terminate it with words or an action as conclusive as the period at the end of a book's final sentence. If all has gone well when the curtain falls a spell will be broken and the audience will revert to people sitting in a theater, refreshed and satisfied.

I must remember as I start a play that there will be harmful temptations ahead that will not have diminished merely because I have encountered them before and consider myself a bit wiser than I used to be. There was that funny scene in *The Wild Man of Borneo* almost fifty years ago. I had already been fortunate enough to have written several hits with George Kaufman. I was again with another collaborator, a novice in the theater. His delight in a scene I had written dulled what editorial astuteness I may have had. It was meant to be a funny scene, and that's what it turned out to be. It was played by fine comedians. The audiences laughed their heads off. It was also completely out of key with what went before and what followed and contributed as much as anything to the play's failure. I thought I had learned to be on guard against the gratuitous scene when, years later, I wrote *The Green Pastures.* But it wasn't until I was examining the script just before starting rehearsals as its director that I discovered I'd done it again. I'd charmed myself into thinking the scene in which Little David killed Goliath was an integral part of the play.

A week or so after the play was in production Rowland Stebbins, who was financing it, asked when the scene was going to be rehearsed.

"Oh, that's out," I told him.

"What do you mean, 'it's out'? It's one of the things that made me want to produce the play."

I said that I thought it was a good scene, too, and if he could tell where it should be placed in the play I'd be happy to stage it. He admitted he couldn't, so the scene stayed out.

I don't mean to imply that in a college classroom the student playwright won't be warned against the irrelevant scene. An informed instructor may also caution him against the dangers of putting too much trust in facility and may fill his mind with other useful generalities. But it's going to be in the loneliness of his own creativity that he may really learn to avoid mistakes. If he is doing more than just listening he can get valuable things from a good drama class. He can learn something about proper approaches to the craft of playwriting and be helped to find his most suitable metier as a writer. The beginner who might waste time trying to fashion himself into writing comedies may be hastened into recognizing he has more potentials for serious drama. One preoccupied with social tensions may find his gifts can flower best in lyrical poetry. John Mason Brown was one of George Pierce

Baker's students of playwriting at Harvard. At the end of his second year a play Brown had presented for Baker's consideration caused Baker to say, "I think you have a great talent for writing, but I don't believe you have the makings of a dramatist. Have you ever given any thought to criticism?"

Yes, the good teacher can help the student appreciate and become familiar with tools and sometimes put windows into the student's workshop. But no one should expect to get more than guidance from a college or university course. Playwrights can no more be produced by schools than a geneticist can grow extra fingers on human hands.

The playwright learns eventually that he has to find himself empirically. Lord Dunsany in describing the compass of a play said, "A dewdrop is a little thing but it can reflect the whole sky." Achieving the dewdrop's reflection is more than any playwright should hope to do. He must be reconciled to the creation of small mirror-like facets in which his audiences can see glimpses of mankind in the act of living. And that should satisfy him. Later laws may be changed because of what he presented in terms of entertainment and the frontiers of civilization pushed back because of his comment on contemporary morals and manners. He may have the privilege of bringing hope and comfort, even delight, to those who hunger for them. So if you are being driven from within to become a playwright don't be afraid. You're going to make many trips between heaven and hell. But most of the journeying will be wonderful.

From Atlantic Beach to Broadway, A Playwright Grows in New York

By John Guare

This article was excerpted from Mr. Guare's comments at an informal talk on playwriting and prepared under his supervision.

My mother had two uncles who had a touring repertory company of 16 plays from 1880 until the act finally folded in 1925—plays like *The Old Toll House* and *Pawn Ticket 210*. My mother would act them out for me. Finally in my teens, through my cousins in Lynn, I tracked down copies of these 16 plays. It was miraculous that somebody had toured for 45 years in them——they had lines like, "It's a horrible night. My son left not knowing the money he took was rightfully his."

Then in 1949 my best friend Bobby and I were down at Atlantic Beach, Long Island, for the summer, and we read this story in *Life* about these 10-year-old kids who did a movie of *Tom Sawyer* with an 8 mm camera for kicks, on their summer vacation—and what were we doing with our summer? So I wrote three plays, knowing how to write them because I knew about plays. The week before we opened we called up *Time-Life* and told the operator there were these two boys doing these plays down at Atlantic Beach. She hung up on us. We kept calling. She kept hanging up. So we called up *Newsday* and told them there were these two kids putting on these plays and planning to give the money to charity. They wrote down the dates, and on the last day (we ran for a week) they came up and took pictures of us. We had a story in *Newsday*—"Atlantic Beach playwright." I was 11 years old. I was there. They had pictures. That was it; it was terrific.

From the time I was 12 I could go to see a play a week at the matinees—I guess that's the best part of growing up in New York City. All I remember of high school was waiting for Saturday afternoon to come. Then I went to Georgetown, and luckily they had, not a drama department, but people who liked theater (I was lucky, I always got to places when things were just starting). They were doing new plays, and I did one there every year.

I liked musicals best of anything, and I was always trying to figure out how they were put together. So I went through all the original cast albums and I realized—this is very primitive and banal, but when you are 17 it's an eye-opener—I realized that the second song of a musical is usually the "want" song. Eliza Doolittle sang, "All I *want* is a room somewhere." Tony in *West Side Story* can't put a name to what he wants, but he feels "Something's coming." Good shows have a *want* song, something to set up to pay off in the end—it was like knowing a secret, knowing something about form, why a play is not a book, why a play is not a movie. I read *Three Sisters* and realized they *wanted* to get to Moscow. It was like a revelation.

After Georgetown and Yale Drama School and the Air Force I had some plays done at Caffe Cino and the Eugene O'Neill Memorial Foundation and elsewhere. I had four plays done in 1965. Then I went to Europe and traveled around, I'd never been anywhere before. I finally got to

Rome—and then I looked at the paper and there was a picture of the Pope on Queens Boulevard, near where my family lived. I had got to Rome on the day the Pope had come to New York City. He came back the next day, but I left, and I went to Cairo, where I got my mail. All my mother and father were writing about was the day the Pope came to New York.

One reason why you start writing, I think, is that when you get very far away from yourself you write to get back. I was stuck eight hours in Alexandria waiting for a desert bus, and I started thinking about my parents. They had been through some difficulties; in the letter about the Pope they expressed what it meant to them, and suddenly you have those metal shavings all over you. You put a magnet underneath them and they all come up. That one day, that one episode of the Pope coming to New York suddenly pulled it all together. It would be fun to write about because I wasn't there. Also I was curious about *why* I wasn't there, why I was here so far away, and what I wanted to write about. You say you want to be a writer, but it's all a blur in your head. So I began writing *The House of Blue Leaves* that day; I came home, and the day I finished the first act of the play in 1966, my father died. It was like a bizarre revenge, all of the steam went out of the play. It took me five years to get the second act right (the trouble was not only emotional but also technical, I didn't have the craft to write that long a play). Oh, I didn't have any trouble writing—I can write by the yard—but it's shaping it up into a workable meaning on the stage that counts.

My work method is write, write, write—start from nothing and write speeches and sentences. You yourself have to discover what you're interested in doing, and always in the back of your head you're looking for some central incident that's going to hold it all together—whether it's the Pope coming to New York or those three women trying to get to Moscow. I still write plays like musicals, in a strange way. A good speech is very much like a song; you say to yourself, I really would like to use this song, this speech, in this play, so what do I have to do to arrive at the point to use it?

Hitchcock in the Truffaut book says he doesn't begin filming a picture until he has a certain number of bumps in the script. I recognize that. A play isn't in a book, a play is upon the stage, it's a mongrel, it's all raggle-taggle, it's Joseph's coat. You take whatever you can to protect any speech you want to use. Once, I had finished a play call *Muzeeka,* but it began all wrong. I started looking into things I'd written three years before, and I found a speech about "if I could have been born anybody I wanted to be, I would have picked to be an Etruscan." It was a long speech, and I just took it. It was as though that speech was *waiting* there to fit into the play. I'm always amazed when people say they are working on a play, and they are this far into it, I don't see how people can work that methodically. I write every day, I put it down without knowing when it's going to turn up. I don't know how it's going to be used. I mean, you may be working on a play but other things are going to happen too, and anything is grist for the mill. I put it down in the book, and I might go over it later and find I've forgotten I wrote it. I often write something without knowing who is saying it. I don't mean to sound mystical. I just write a speech, like a song, and then find the person who wanted to say that.

I wrote a play once in John Gassner's class at Yale Drama School in which there were three people: mother, father and son. The father shot the son, and then the same scene was repeated over and the son shot the father; and the same incident was repeated over and over again with different endings. Gassner wrote on it: "This is illogical. Didn't this person die in the previous scene?" It was like saying, before you break any rules you have to write an Ibsen play. Yes you have to know how, but you have to come to your Ibsen play in your own way. You can't say such-and-such is a model. I learned more about plays at Yale by taking set design courses from Donald Oenslager and finding out about the *light* that a play has to take place in.

I think one of the ways to write plays is to go to plays a lot. You have to be connected with the theater. What was wonderful about the Eugene O'Neill Playwrights Conference in Waterford, Conn. was that you met actors, designers, directors and other playwrights. Everybody suddenly got connected to others in the theater, and you found out that writing a play is not a mystery, not some kind of cabalistic incantation. It's co-working in the theater. When the Conference first started, they would say "O.K. John, July 18 is your day and that's when your play will be done." If I said, "But I don't have a play," they said, "Well, you'll have one by then." Everyone was assigned a day. After 1969 it got to be very showcasey, so they switched it around and said, "now we can no longer pick the playwright, we pick the play." So again something was killed. But I tell you, from 1965 through 1968 it was terrific. You could have your plays done by good people and if they didn't work, well, they didn't work, and if they did work it was *terrific*.

In 1964 when off off Broadway was starting, it was sensational too. I once wrote a play on Thursday and it was done the following Monday. Stuff was being done all the time, and it wasn't reviewed. Then after about two years scripts began filtering in from the O'Neill and from off Broadway, and the critics began covering it, and there's nothing like criticism to kill work. In the good days of off off Broadway your friends would come to see your play and tell you what was wrong with it. But when you start to review La Mama in the *Times* it makes everyone angry in the wrong way, nervous in the wrong way. Reviews are just consumer reports anyway, they don't have any artistic value whatever. Criticism makes audiences lazy, it pre-digests theater for them. There's no adventurousness, no saying "Let's go to La Mama tonight and see what's happening down there."

I got into *Two Gentlemen of Verona* because Mel Shapiro and I are good friends and we began talking about the problems of the script, and Mel asked me if maybe. . .The Shakespeare plot is a long, ungainly plot. It stops and starts and goes and drips all over. The play has lovely sections in it but it really meanders. Let me backtrack a little. When I had been in London in 1969 I saw Olivier do the Feydeau farce *A Flea in Her Ear* and I was just knocked out by it. I'd never read or known anything about Feydeau farces before. I started reading them, and it seemed to me that farce was an extraordinary form for today. Farce was that container I had been looking for. In writing a long play I had very naturalistic scenes with lines like "Excuse me, I have to pass the cigarettes," I always wanted to move faster. Farce had this bad name because of TV situation comedies but suddenly I just saw, and I read a lot of farces trying to get a strong sense of farce structure. The whole second act of *Blue Leaves* is cast entirely in farce form. When Mel Shapiro and I went to work on *Two Gentlemen of Verona,* we used a purely farce mode. We knew what we had to cut out, we knew that farce gave us a form in which to work. It was easy to write because Mel and I had the structure, we had this erector set we could work from.

I think that a play is about making the audience *crazy.* You want to get people off the streets into this dark room and give them that feeling of delight or laughter that makes them crazy. Farce is always being pushed toward hysteria. You are trying to get the audience to a point at which things can happen to them, where suddenly you can lift the covers off their heads, where they can all come together with laughter or some kind of delight. And there's something about music in plays that becomes an act of insanity.

I'm now working on a long play, and strangely enough I had a lot of songs in the first draft. After *Two Gentlemen* I went back and took them all out because I felt maybe I was just cheating. I said to myself well, maybe I am not going into that scene deep enough because I've got a song here. So that's it, I'm still writing plays, but you never know . . . you never know. At any time it might be the last time. Every time you finish a play there's always that frightening moment when you say to yourself, "Well, maybe that's it."

Comedy: A Sharp-Cornered Round Table Discussion

The scene is Dramatists Guild headquarters on 44th Street, a paper airplane glide from all the Broadway hits. The time is the present, a spring afternoon.

Grouped in a circle are five celebrated authors of stage comedy: Neil Simon, Jean Kerr, James Goldman, Jules Feiffer and Abe Burrows. They are seated on sofas and chairs near a tall marble mantelpiece whose single ornament is a tiny autographed snapshot of George Bernard Shaw. The playwrights are relaxed, freewheeling. . . .

JEAN KERR: Very few actresses bow correctly.

ABE BURROWS: The bow is supposed to be a court bow to the dress circle. The correct bow is directed up there—(*Pointing.*) Not down at the orchestra.

JAMES GOLDMAN: To the boxes.

JULES FEIFFER: Not to the applause?

BURROWS: No, shoot for the balcony rails.

NEIL SIMON: Art Carney would come out and bowl, he literally would bowl. . . .

Present with the five authors is the editor of the Dramatists Guild Quarterly, *Otis L. Guernsey Jr. He could not be called a moderator, for this discussion (without an audience) is clearly intended to be an immoderately expert consideration of the state of the comedy art. Rather, he is to act as a referee to make sure the ball stays in the court.*

Guernsey looks up at the Shaw photograph, then turns to the playwrights and speaks distinctly the word "Comedy." Instantly there occurs a taut silence, as of greyhounds among whom a live rabbit has just been flung. . . .

GUERNSEY: What is comedy? Why do you write comedy as you do? (*Pause.*) Why has comedy expanded to fill the whole theater nowadays, so that they can even change the point of view on *Hamlet* and present it in a comedy context?

MRS. KERR: I think comedy is disappearing under a seriousness posed as comedy.

GUERNSEY: Do you mean humor is disappearing, or comedy? Are comedy and humor the same thing? (*Glances again at the photo on the mantel.*) Shaw once said, "Comedy is the fine art of disillusion."

BURROWS: That's a terrible line.

GOLDMAN: I'll tell you what I think comedy is, because I had to consider it for a Sunday piece I once did for Walter Kerr. There was this awful pressure, asking myself, "Well, my God, what is it?" The best I could do is this: comedy doesn't have anything to do with laughter at all. It comes out of the author's general attitude toward life. One writes a comedy or a tragedy because one believes that existence is either a sad or a funny business. It's this that informs the kind of writing you do. Laughter in comedy is merely a part of style and device, just as tears have more to do with *The Winslow Boy*, or something like that, than they have to do with Shakespearean or Greek tragedy. What is *essentially* comedy comes out of whether or not you see our position in life and our endeavors and relationships with other people and to our environment as funny or sad.

> *Pause.*

The important point is, what lies underneath comedy isn't *serious*. What lies underneath is *funny*.

BURROWS: No, Goldman, no!

MRS. KERR: No! The thing underneath is *sad*.

GOLDMAN: No, I think it's funny.

GUERNSEY: What you're saying is, when smiling comedy takes off the smiling mask, down underneath—it's really funny?

GOLDMAN: Yes, I think so.

MRS. KERR: You can make anything funny just by duplicating it, as Walter pointed out in his book *Tragedy and Comedy*. If Oedipus on the way to Colonus met another king with his eyes out who had married his mother. . . .

GOLDMAN: Let me see if I can make what I'm trying to say clearer. I think the basic material in *Hamlet* is funny, because I see it that way. Now, Shakespeare saw it differently and wrote a tragic play. But to me Hamlet, a man who is as much driven as he is immobilized, is a funny guy. And his problem is a comic problem. Given that material, I'd have written a comic play. I also think the basic material in *King Lear* is funny.

BURROWS: Yeah, it's a show about a housing shortage.

GOLDMAN: I'm not talking about what the artist *did* with it, I'm talking about what he started with.

BURROWS: Still frame. The point is, comedy is successful and downgraded.

MRS. KERR: Now, we're not going to waste any time talking about critics who are patronizing, are we?

BURROWS No, but I don't think even Neil here gets the credit. . . .

GUERNSEY (*hastily*): What we're trying to get at is, are comedy and humor the same thing?

BURROWS: Let me answer you this way: when I give lectures, I always go dry early and ask for questions. The first question I'm always asked is, "Mr. Burrows, haven't you ever wanted to write anything serious?" My answer is, "I write very seriously. But it comes out funny."

SIMON: I don't understand what it is they're missing, why they think you have to write out-and-out seriously.

FEIFFER: When *are* you going to write a serious play, Abe?

BURROWS: What they mean is, they resent and suspect levity. We're a Puritan nation. I don't care how many immigrants have come over, we're still a Puritan nation. Comedy is levity. Somehow or other, they feel that a comedy writer isn't taking the world seriously. When they come into an Arthur Williams play. . . .

GOLDMAN: Tennessee Miller.

SIMON: That's the cable address.

BURROWS: An Arthur Miller or a Tennessee Williams play, they come in hushed . . . careful. . . .

SIMON: You don't want them to come in hushed and careful to your comedy.

BURROWS: No, I don't. But they come to a Miller or a Williams play, and they say to themselves, "This is going to be marvelous, it's going to be *about* something." Comedy is levity. But I say this: the belly laugh that Neil gets, that Jean gets, that I get is bigger than any tear. When you laugh, you're helpless. You're absolutely lost. Now, I defy you to show me any place in a serious play where an audience is shaken that way.

SIMON: It may not be an overt action, but. . . .

MRS. KERR: In a good production of *A Streetcar Named Desire*, something hits you as hard as anything can hit you.

GUERNSEY: Jim has defined comedy as a point of view, Abe says it's levity. Present company excepted, what's your all-time favorite comedy?

SIMON: I really, truthfully can't say, because I'm afraid it would indicate that I have a special attitude towards comedy, and I don't. I take them as they come. There isn't any one particular style of comedy that I like. I like anything that is particularly good.

BURROWS: If it's good it's funny. When I was a kid, before I went into show business, the thing that made me laugh the loudest was *Room Service*.

SIMON: If you ask me what are the *funniest* things that I recall, they are never plays, they are films. The funniest thing I ever saw in my life was *Modern Times*. I think my attitude has changed. Where I used to like verbal comedy, I don't like it as much now—but it has nothing to do with what I write, because I write verbally.

MRS. KERR: I would write *Summer and Smoke* if I could write it, but you can't necessarily do even bad copies of what you most admire.

SIMON: I think that I would like to write *Streetcar*. It's just my favorite play.

GUERNSEY: Jean, what's your favorite comedy?

MRS. KERR: *The Importance of Being Ernest,* and that's probably because I listen rather than look. I mean, physical comedy does not amuse me very much. You don't laugh *that* much at *Ernest*. It pleases your mind.

GOLDMAN: But it doesn't move you emotionally.

MRS: KERR: But to me it's magical, even though I wouldn't laugh a lot. Take Neil's *Plaza Suite*, for instance. I laughed out loud at the third play more than I have in a long time, convulsively with the visual stuff, the coming in and out of the rain. But I liked the first play about the marriage better, so the amount of laughter would not necessarily measure the degree of pleasure. *The Lady's Not for Burning* is a comedy I like, but I wouldn't ask: is it funny? It's the dancing syllables that delight me.

GOLDMAN: I like Chekhov's plays best, I like Giraudoux's plays a lot, and Anouilh's plays. They're not what I used to like best. I thought *The Man Who Came to Dinner* was the funniest thing I ever heard.

FEIFFER: The humor, I suppose, that I like best is material I can relate to directly, the kind of humor I identify with, meaning that it will have little to do with the theater and mostly to do with the night club and cabaret humor that came up in the middle and late fifties and the early sixties. Mort Sahl, Second City, Nichols and May, in particular Lennie Bruce. I like comedy that says something about the time I'm living in, and that has what an audience would consider to be an off-focus point of view that, in fact, places things within a more proper focus than the one we usually see.

GUERNSEY: When you insert humor, those belly laughs Abe was talking about, into whatever comedy you're writing. . .

BURROWS: No insert, I can't do it any other way.

GUERNSEY: That's what I was getting at? Is your use of humor instinctive or deliberate?

SIMON: Both.

MRS. KERR: I won't get paid if I don't do it that way, that's why I do it that way.

GOLDMAN: You should do it that way because you see life that way, that's all it is.

BURROWS: It's the way you work, it's how it comes out.

FEIFFER: I work at it.

SIMON: It comes out instinctively, but when I see I don't have it, I go back and do it deliberately.

GOLDMAN: Neil's answer is right. It comes out instinctively. But when it's not funny enough, you have to try and make it funny.

GUERNSEY: What's the biggest laugh you've had in the theater?

SIMON: From my point of view or the audience's?

GUERNSEY: The audience's. The biggest response.

GOLDMAN: The best laugh I ever got was in *The Lion in Winter*. There's that big horrendous scene in the bedroom when Queen Eleanor and King Henry say terrible things to each other. And finally the Queen asks, "What family doesn't have its ups and downs?" That got the biggest laugh.

SIMON: The strongest response I ever got happened purely by accident. The F.U. joke in *The Odd Couple*. The scene where Oscar finds the note from Felix under his pillow. And Oscar says to Felix something like: "I've asked you a million times not to leave me little notes like 'We're all out of cornflakes—F.U.' It took me three hours to figure out the F.U. was Felix Unger." It happened by mistake. I was just kind of writing it and saying to myself, what would Felix do that would annoy Oscar? Leaving notes. So I started to write a note. Then I tried to figure out how he would sign it. And it just came by accident, that Felix Unger's initials were F.U. I discovered it like a piece of gold lying there. I never thought it would get *that* big a response, but it was pretty big.

GUERNSEY: Abe, what's the funniest line you ever wrote?

BURROWS: I think one of the nicest lines I ever wrote was six weeks after *Guys and Dolls* opened. George Kaufman, he directed it, phoned me and said we have work to do. I said I thought we were done. He said "There's a dead spot in Sam Levene's part." Sam was playing Nathan Detroit. So I wrote Sam a line: "A guy has to have a doll. A doll is a necessity. When a guy walks into a restaurant it looks nice if there's a doll behind him." I always liked that, I don't know why.

MRS. KERR: The most explosive laugh I've had in the theater was a line in *King of Hearts*— when the child is invited to stay for lunch and calls up to ask his mother's permission, then turns from the phone to tell the others, "I *had* lunch." A child really said it at our house in New Rochelle. There are some things you can't invent because your mind doesn't operate that way. It happened, and I sent it right in to the *New Yorker*. They sent it back, and now I'm so glad, because it got a big laugh in the play.

GUERNSEY: Jules, how about *Little Murders*, what was your biggest laugh?

FEIFFER: It's very simple: "I've been shooting shit for a year now." The second time the character said it, when the audience knew that literally he meant it. The first time he's asked what he does, he answers "I take pictures of shit." The mother character says "Language, language." And he says, "I don't mean to offend you, Mrs. Newquist, but I've been shooting shit for a year now." He couldn't get out the rest of the sentence, which was a surprise to us in Boston. We had to break it for about thirty seconds so he could finish it. The rest of the line is, ". . . and I've already got a half dozen awards." I expected a laugh at the end of *that*. I didn't expect a laugh at the first part of the line, but that's where it all broke up.

SIMON: The most disappointing thing in my writing life is that very often I write lines and say to myself, oh, this is very moving, and they laugh at it. I can never understand what I'm doing wrong.

MRS. KERR: It's very embarrassing to say to an actor, please try *not* to get that laugh.

SIMON: In *Plaza Suite*, honestly, we kept cutting laugh after laugh in Boston and putting straight lines in that kept getting laughs. I finally said, well, they don't need me any more.

GOLDMAN: When they come in with certain expectations, it's hard to kill them.

MRS. KERR: I read a quote today from Max Beerbohm that I don't quite understand: "Laughter doesn't become extreme until it becomes consecutive." What exactly does that mean?

GOLDMAN: It must mean a lot of laughs in a row.

BURROWS: It means beat, beat, beat, bigger laugh, bigger laugh.

FEIFFER: I don't think laughter becomes consescutive until it becomes extreme.

MRS. KERR: It's maddening when a line has got to get a laugh, and it won't, and it won't no matter how many times you change it—but it's also irksome to get a laugh when you don't want it. To say something I've said before, a straight line is the shortest distance between two laughs. But you get to a point when you're writing when you don't know what's funny and what's not funny. And you're always wrong, especially in New Haven. When I first get a little idea, I think it's *so* funny. I think never since the world began did anyone ever get such a funny idea. By the time I've got it typed, not only do I *not* think it's funny, I've forgotten what was supposed to be funny about it. Then afterwards if one person, somebody at Gristede's, says she likes it, I'll go back and read it and say to myself, "It isn't so bad, not really so bad." But if the first person I meet says something like "Well, I thought your earlier work was more characteristic," then I can't look at it ever again.

BURROWS: Once when I brought George Kaufman a joke he told me, "You did this joke before." I said, well in radio we call this a running gag. He said, "Here they're paying $6.60, give them another joke." It really racked me up.

GUERNSEY: Neil, you've written for a larger theater audience than any playwright in modern times, I guess. What would you say your impact on them has been?

SIMON: I really have no idea. It's so diverse, some of them are moved and some just think it's terribly funny, they come away with what *they* want to come away with.

MRS. KERR: I think much more important than Neil's effect on the audience is his effect on other playwrights. He's doing his bit to make the world safe for garde plays—for plays and scenes with shape. Hail to him.

SIMON: Once after *Barefoot in the Park* had been playing for about a week I went back to see it, watching the audience, which was just falling over laughing except for one guy sitting on the aisle. I was transfixed. I said to myself, there seems to be no way to get to him. No one else would I watch except this one man. My wife joined me about twenty minutes later and asked me how it was going, and I said, terrible. I really meant it. There was no way to get to this man. It destroyed me.

MRS. KERR: Yes, I've noticed with other people's shows as well as my own, sometimes you'll get a holdout. He'll hold out . . . but if he finally laughs, he'll then laugh at everything. I very seldom laugh in the theater because I have this unfortunate situation of being with a critic, and critics do not laugh. But if I get caught once and laugh—if I have been caught off guard —then I laugh all through the show.

FEIFFER: I think, sadly, it would be accurate to say that the theater has less and less effect on the audience, on the times. Certainly this is true when you compare it with films, which really *do* strongly effect our style, the way we see things, in many ways the way we think. I'd guess that in another fifteen or twenty years there may not be any Broadway as we know it, because the audience that now goes to the Broadway theater will have been retired and dissipated.

SIMON: But still, when it comes down to it, as Walter Kerr said in a Sunday piece, the most provocative things come from the theater.

MRS. KERR: Jules, it's fair to say you're a satirist. More than a humorist. A satirist is also funny, but a satirist is by definition a little ahead of everybody. He's the first one to notice. But if you're doing that, you're not going to get as wide a reaction from a theater audience of the moment, because they are squarer. Right?

FEIFFER: It just seems to me that films are more tuned in, more connected. Maybe because they have a younger audience, I don't know.

GOLDMAN: I think satirists are essentially action people, as well as artists.

MRS. KERR: They want to get the job done.

GOLDMAN: They want to have some kind of ideological effect on the people who are exposed to their work. And I don't think that's the business of the artists. I think artists affect people differently. We're often misled because theater exists in words. We think, well, if we're saying words we can say what the intellectual content of a play is. But I don't think we can really do that, any more than we can in the case of a painting or a piece of music. When we're successful, we're saying something above and beyond what the words say, and that kind of communication is addressed to the souls or spirits—fancy words!—of our audiences. By moving them in one way or another, we can hope to change them. But if we want to change them in terms of "Well, let's all get out and vote for my candidate," then we don't write a play, we write a tract, we write a speech or a political pamphlet. I don't think this is the business of the arts—when they do it, they do it badly and end up with agit-prop.

BURROWS: We're all talking about humor, we're skirting the point. The point is, *why* do we say it funny? Why does Neil do it the way he does? Why does Jim, why does Jean, why does Jules? Why don't we say (*Nobly.*) "This was the noblest Roman of them all!" Why don't we say "Goodnight, sweet Prince."

FEIFFER: Somebody said it first.

MRS. KERR: You couldn't say "Goodnight, sweet Prince," your character's name was Detroit, Nathan Detroit.

BURROWS: Why do you answer me with a joke?

MRS. KERR: You're born with the equipment you have, that's all.

SIMON: I don't agree, I think it was those years right *after* you were born that made you what you are.

MRS. KERR: Wait till your children are a little older, Neil. You'll realize they are what they are at seven months. You just wait and watch it, you don't change it.

SIMON: As to why we say it funny, I think it's to attract attention to what you're trying to say. It's like a political speech—when you hear one filled with bromides that you've heard over and over again, you turn off. But if there's a bit of wit and humor injected into it, you might listen, and you still get the point.

MRS. KERR: You make it sound as though you have funny lines for openers so you can say the serious thing.

SIMON: No, but I hope underneath there is something to hang onto.

BURROWS: The point is, you say it with a joke. Why? Why do we do it that way? In my family, every Friday night my mother would make gefullte fish with chopped liver. And every Friday night she'd ask, "How's the fish?" And I'd say "Terrible." And she'd beam. It was a big laugh. And she knew it was my way of complimenting her. Why do we say it funny? Why has my son Jim now learned this knack? Jim's whole approach is to say it with a curve. When he gives it that twist, he's saying "I love you" to me. (*Pause.*) Tom Paine once said, "These are the times that try men's souls." Why didn't he switch it? Why does one man say it in polemics and another say it in poetry?

GOLDMAN: Why are there stars in the sky? I don't think the question is open to intellectual pursuit. It's an emotional question.

GUERNSEY: Speaking of emotion . . . (*Consulting notes.*) Horace Walpole said, "The world is a comedy to those who think, a tragedy to those who feel." Does that give us a clue as to why you write as you do? When you approach the world we're living in today. . . .

BURROWS: Oh, God.

GUERNSEY: *Not* in writing your plays, but just generally, do you react to it emotionally first, or intellectually?

GOLDMAN: Oh, emotionally, First one and then the other, same way I work.

FEIFFER: Is hate an emotion?

MRS. KERR: First he gets mad, then he gets cerebral.

BURROWS: Jules is the only one of us here who says what he feels about today's events. The rest of us . . . I'm sorry, I duck it.

MRS. KERR: I react to the times in a fury, in a rage. But not being cerebral, I'll never be able to handle it the way Jules does.

SIMON: I react emotionally to everything in life, and it has nothing to do with today's times.

BURROWS: Jules, you control your people, your people aren't theater. You've done theater, and very well. But the people you put on that strip are you. You control every bit of them, the way they look, the way they talk. In the theater, we generally don't have that control.

FEIFFER: I had a play that ran for seven glorious performances on Broadway.

MRS. KERR: I remember the opening night of your *Little Murders*. At intermission we all thought it was going to be a big hit. It was *in*.

FEIFFER: I knew it was all over then. I learned something in Boston: If the audience was happy at the end of the first act, if the actors started playing the jokes and didn't play the characters, we were finished. When they played the characters there was a kind of tension. At the end of the first act, if the audience was saying, "It's funny but I don't know what's going on," we were OK.

BURROWS: If they play the characters and don't play the jokes, you're dead too. I tell you, the only way to be truthful is to be funny.

GUERNSEY: Jules would hardly agree that comedy is levity per se. One of the things that went on in *Little Murders* was, snipers kept firing through the windows and one of the shots struck the heroine and killed her.

FEIFFER: Because of that, none of the critics except John Lahr understood that it was a play about things other than urban violence. I had to move the play to England for the critics to understand that it was a play about, among other things, the Kennedy assassination and Vietnam. There's a radically different style to the humor that's come out of Cold War America than any humor we've ever had.

GUERNSEY: What is it, a kind of gallows humor in the face of extinction of all values?

FEIFFER: I don't think that quite gets to it. It's simply this, that in these last twenty-five years this country has been breaking apart into small pieces, and in increasingly large pieces. The breaking-apart began, I suppose, with the Depression, but it came into its own after 1945 with the acceptance of a kind of Cold War ecclesiasticism. It involved affluence, the bomb, the death of Stalin and his whole influence on the American left, the death of liberalism in terms of a working philosophy, the death of all ideology, and a shifting around, looking for new values. A generation grew up within all this, a generation of haves, the first generation of middle-class haves in this or any other country—kids who grew up with affluence and found that the fulfillment of the American dream was not worth very much as far as they were concerned. And so they became hippies, acid-heads, protesters. On every level of society—which includes, of course, its art, its literature, its humor—we're disrupting, we're breaking apart. Now, whatever anybody writes, whatever anybody thinks must be part of this, if it is to have any relevance at all. It doesn't have to talk directly to the problem necessarily, but it must grow out of this atmosphere, because that's the name of the game right now.

GUERNSEY (*consulting notes again*): I found this by Albert Pike: "The sense of humor . . . is the strongest inducement to submit with a wise and pious patience to the vicissitudes of human existence." Is he saying that comedy is a means of glossing over unpleasantness, a kind of cop-out?

BURROWS: I've asked myself that, I've wondered whether in saying it with humor I'm choosing the safest way, the most acceptable way. The *Time* review of *How to Succeed in Business Without Really Trying* said that in his treatment of big business Abe Burrows instead of throwing vitriol painted a mustache on it. It sounded as though I'd gone for safety. It sounded as though I'd thrown a cream puff, copped out. Are we afraid? Are we incapable? Walter Kerr once spoke of the terrible nature of the world problems we have to deal with today . . .

MRS. KERR: *Walter* did?

BURROWS: . . . so difficult that perhaps humor is the only way we can deal with them.

SIMON: I just think the other way is too boring most of the time. You don't sit and tell yourself, maybe this is the way out of insanity, so I'll do it funny. You do it funny because the other way is just too boring. Unless you're brilliant.

MRS. KERR: Unless you're a real poet like Williams.

GUERNSEY: Isn't *black* comedy a way of accepting and dealing with terrible modern problems—like the breakup of society Jules was talking about?

MRS. KERR: I think black comedy is just another name for sick jokes. It's an effort to give status to what is neither serious material nor real wit. It's merely an inversion of the possible. It's merely preposterous.

GOLDMAN: No, there's good black comedy and bad black comedy.

MRS. KERR: Name me a good black comedy—and if you say *A Day in the Death of Joe Egg*, I claim it's not black comedy, it's genuine comedy. But I never saw a play that enraged me so much as *Loot*. When the dead mother's dentures were out, and they were using them as castanets—I can't handle it. I don't mind when characters have their eyes put out like Oedipus, but they've got to keep their goddam teeth in!

GOLDMAN: Well, I think the prevalence of black comedy is part of a search for new styles. You see, the set of circumstances Jules was talking about doesn't have to yield comedy. It would be much more likely to yield despair, gloom, Strindbergain discourses.

BURROWS: Jim, what makes you think comedy is not despair and gloom?

SIMON: Because there is a certain comedy that is *not* despair and gloom.

BURROWS: I say there can be more despair and gloom in comedy. . . .

GOLDMAN: I agree with you, it's the kind of comedy I tend to write.

BURROWS: A man can express pain in comedy.

GOLDMAN: No question about it. When I first came to New York I belonged to the New Dramatists, and I was the only playwright there who was writing comedy. The other thirty-five people, all my age or younger, were writing serious work. One of the reasons why we've chosen to treat everything comedically today, I think, is because we've just been through this very bleak and tedious period of socialist realism. It took place in the twenties and thirties—I thought it was dead fifteen years ago, but some people are still making great reputations writing it. Nevertheless a lot of the comedy we have today is appearing because the other tradition is dead. We have to find new ways of treating the situation.

FEIFFER: I think that's part of it, and I think the mass media have made us over-aware of all the emotional truths that serious drama and serious films once gave us. That's why the best films being made today are the shorthand films—Godard is the best example, I suppose—films that quickly clue you in on what's happening without giving an editorial comment. Because we know there's not a single editorial message we're not aware of, not a single emotional truth that by now we haven't heard over and over again.

BURROWS: There isn't a serious writer alive who could make us believe them.

FEIFFER: So the only way of going at it is to hit at it obliquely, to try to show up, whether through humor or other more abstract means, what's really happening—to make us go through the defense we have against emotional truths. Because we're so larded over with serious insight by now that we can't be reached by anything.

BURROWS: When you write it funny, you write it from the gut. G-U-T. When I'm asked for the best play of our times I come up frequently with *Waiting for Godot*. That was a very funny play. Hilarious. I play the record, and I fall down every time.

MRS. KERR: I stand up every time. I'm the last of the great squares. I'm a Lindsay-Crouse girl.

GUERNSEY: Jean, you said *Joe Egg* is not black comedy?

MRS. KERR: No, it's not, there are no ridiculous distortions of reality just for distortion's sake. Take *Entertaining Mr. Sloane*, where a sister and a brother are trying to seduce the same man. It's macabre, but it doesn't correspond to anything real. At least, it doesn't to the present audience. It will next year, but right now it doesn't. Anyhow, in *Joe Egg* the situation of that couple with the retarded child—you know it's true. You didn't just hear they had a child like that, you *know it*. It seemed so valid. Furthermore, you feel that their pain is so genuine, if they can make jokes about it they're privileged to.

SIMON: *Joe Egg's* main objective isn't to make us laugh. The laughter is a byproduct.

MRS. KERR: Yes, the laughter is how they got through it. Their genuine concern for the child is more real than the jokes.

GUERNSEY: Where do we go from here in American comedy? Towards formlessness, or back to structure?

BURROWS: Well, I'll tell you, we're up against something. All playwrights I respect are looking over this new stuff, maybe wondering if this is what they want. Maybe we're a little dissatisfied with our own material. We wonder if, after all, comedy is levity. We wonder, are we really writing about what's moving us? I look at this group of faces, and I don't think anybody disagrees with me. I think we're all asking ourselves, are we doing what we want to do, and is it any good by today's standards? Are we saying what we want to say?

GOLDMAN: If you're any good at all, you're dissatisfied with your own work. You don't want to write the last play over again. You always have to force yourself.

BURROWS: Let's talk from success. You say to yourself, I'm a big hit, right? Well, do I enjoy it as much as I should?

SIMON: It's not as exhilarating as it was, I can't lie about it.

GUERNSEY: You mean writing the play is not exhilarating or having a hit is not exhilarating?

SIMON: Success.

BURROWS: Success is a failure.

SIMON: I was more exhilarated, I had more sense of purpose after the opening night of *The Star-Spangled Girl* than ever before. I said, hell, I'm not going to do that again. It just didn't work, it wasn't good enough.

MRS. KERR: How were you exhilarated?

SIMON: I went back to work again feeling, I can do it better. It sounds terrible, but it's the truth, I feel that way.

BURROWS: Neil, we tell it funny, and then deep down we ask ourselves, why didn't we tell it for real?

SIMON: No.

MRS. KERR: No.

GOLDMAN: Absolutely no. I can't do anything else *but* comedy.

MRS. KERR: Well, *my* problem with the contemporary theater is its form-lessness. Recently I saw a revival of *The Little Foxes*, and I was so pleased. You know—you couldn't play the second act first. Isn't that nice? And you couldn't take out forty minutes and make it a lot better. I thought, "Good, good, this is the way plays were when I came in." (*A pause: no comment.*) I'm not a typical playwright. I'm not a professional playwright in the sense of keeping at it year after year. I don't. But what I find talking to other playwrights is, they're intimidated by the feeling that they are *out* of it. The kind of play being done is not the kind they used to admire or wish to write. Mostly, they're kind of mild about it, trying to find out what's in this new thing. I think they feel sort of betwixt and between. Particularly as they get older, they don't have the kind of energy that says, "This is the way I want it, and by God I'm going to write it this way and I'll bet somebody will like it."

No, they look at one of these new plays and they think, "I'm out of touch, I'm out of touch. I'm gone. Something else has taken over." That's why I love to see the success of a shapely play—because I think it will encourage other people to write them. I like form, I like shape, I like design. (*Pause.*) I like to think the playwright did *some* work before I got there.

GUERNSEY (*glancing once again at the photo on the mantel*): You know, Shaw in his time wondered, "Who cares for comedy today? Who knows what it is?"

MRS. KERR: *Yes*. Well, goodnight, everybody.

BURROWS: Goodnight.

SIMON: Goodnight.

GOLDMAN: Goodnight.

FEIFFER: Goodnight, all.

GUERNSEY: And thank you.

The greyhounds fall silent over their mangled rabbit. End of discussion.

Tragedy

By Israel Horovitz

If a stage play is a fiction, then a stage tragedy is a grand fiction. For tragedy alone can take its audience to the outer limits of human possibility. Great tragedy creates an artful microcosmic world that first illuminates life as it is, then life as it can be. There is no higher dramatic prose form than tragedy. As long as serious plays continue to be written, there will be dramatists struggling to wrestle authentic tragedy from the facts of modern circumstance.

The object, then, is to define *authentic tragedy,* to aid and abet the modern dramatist who might bless the 20th century with such a work of art. The center of a modern definition is still Aristotle's, from the *Poetics:* "Tragedy is a representation of an action, serious and complete, of a satisfactory length; it is expressed in speech made beautiful in different ways in different parts of the play; it is acted, not narrated; and by exciting pity and terror it gives a healthy relief to such emotions."

Aristotle's full definition of the tragic is far more detailed, and I shall attempt to summarize his *Poetics* briefly here in view of what might be useful to the modern tragedian. *Mimesis* is suggested in the representation of an action. Subjects for this imitative art seem to be defined in three forms: men as they are (life), men meaner than they are (comedy) and men finer than they are (tragedy). Narrative and acting are the two available methods of presenting poetry, the latter being recommended for tragedy, of course.

Next, in the *Poetics,* Aristotle suggests origins for poetry, tragedy, comedy and the epic. He concludes this section with a comparison of the epic's form to the form of tragedy. The origins of tragedy, by the way, are found in the Dithyramb, a choral ode which was sung in honor of the god Diorlysus. The next step in the development of tragedy was made by Aeschylus, who added more dialogue to the Dithyramb, reduced the role of the chorus and added a second character. Sophocles added the third character and made use of painted scenery.

Aristotle's definition of tragedy, as cited above, follows next and calls for serious complete action of satisfactory length. Language should be made beautiful. The text should be acted, not narrated. Each play should present moments of *catharsis*. Aristotle concludes that there are six important elements in tragedy: plot, character, thought, language, music and spectacle.

The concept of plot holds a considerable position in Aristotle's *Poetics*. He suggests that a plot must be balanced with a proper beginning, middle and end. The whole plot should be of logical proportions. The subject of the plot should present an ideal truth, holding that "Poetry is more philosophical than historical," but, Aristotle suggests, tragedy usually keeps to mythical figures. The worst kind of plot is defined as episodic, the best is defined as containing "the irony of fate." The three essential elements of plot are *peripeteia*, when a moment of action produces the opposite of what is intended; *anagnorisis* (discovery), recognition of a person, a thing or an essential fact of life; *catastrophe*, a conclusion of tragic suffering. An ideal plot is meant to be complex, leading to pity and terror in the audience's relationship to the stage characters' lives. The most ideal plot would seem to present a pretty good man coming to a bad end, as opposed to a very good or very bad man coming to the same end. Aristotle suggests that intricate stage scenic effects are cheap and that the interplay of a friend against a friend is the highest relationship.

The notion of character is played down to the notion of plot. Aristotle maintains the characterization should be true to type. The recognition scene is best motivated by logical inference. In composition, it is suggested that the play be outlined and detailed, that the intricacies of plot be worked out before the writing of the text. The best writing style is described as one clear, but not mean; lofty, but not obscure.

In a section presenting theories of criticism, Aristotle suggests that improbabilities may be justified as ideally true, in terms of what is actually true, true to tradition or poetically just. To be avoided are the immoral, the inconsistent, the irrational, the inartistic.

In comparing the epic to tragedy, Aristotle suggests that tragedy is the highest form of writing because tragedy embraces the most interesting aspects of the epic and adds to those music and spectacle. Aristotle concludes that tragedy is more *present* to its audience than the epic to its reader, that tragedy is more concise and concentrated than the epic and that tragedy presents the greatest unity.

I have bothered to summarize the *Poetics* for two essential reasons: the first is that such a summary is not easily found and seems to me useful; also, although I certainly don't feel the *Poetics* offers a modern writer an easy route to constructing a tragedy, there is in Aristotle a wonderfully complete structure within which the possibility of building a tragedy may be inspected.

Tragedy in the Modern Theater

Certainly, the paucity of tragedy in our contemporary theater is parallel to 20th-century man's diminishing faith in a cosmic order. It is difficult to extract responses of pity and terror from a modern audience completely resigned to man's limitations in the full universe. Yet there are some modern plays that fail as authentic tragedy but present many of the elements essential to such a work.

Yeats, in his short essay on the nature of tragedy, discusses a tragic result in which man's active will suffers and perishes. This notion is a good one for the modern writer of tragedy, as it seems central to a modern definition of a tragic event. Concern for the death of man's will is shown in plays of Beckett, Ionesco, Camus: *Happy Days, Exit the King, Caligula,* for examples. The central figure of each of these three plays undergoes one essential change during the course of the play: the active will perishes. As tragedy is fiction, it matters little whether a play's central character expresses a will to live or a will to die; either choice is quite acceptable. Winnie, the heroine of the Beckett play, wishes to remain. She adapts to each and every change around her. Buried first to her waist, then to her neck, she wishes to remain, until she does not. Berenger, Ionesco's naughty hero-king, wishes to continue because death, he feels, is not quite right for a man of his position, and doesn't precisely fit his style of living. All around Berenger call for his death: his doctor, his wives, his court. At the conclusion of the play, Berenger's will perishes, he feels himself old, he is resigned to die. Camus's Caligula is a true absurdist-tragic hero, as he wishes first to die, later to live. The expected is inverted.

While each of these plays serves as an example to Yeats's notion of man's shrinking will, each play also presents a hero defined in relation to his state. As there is rottenness in the Denmark-England of *Hamlet,* there is also a rotting state in *Exit the King, Caligula* and *Happy Days*. Caligula's Rome is instantly understandable, as is Berenger's double-queened France. Beckett's piece widens, from the bell that begins Winnie's day, to include a larger state, though no less rotten. In each instance the state is fictional, a stage metaphor: a backdrop against which a fictional stage hero may wrestle for a return to health, for sanity, for order. The imagination needn't strain to discover a contemporary rotten state in which to set a modern tragedy. Indeed, the contemporary climate seems nearly perfect for extraction of a credible setting, modern and in ill-health. Such an element I believe to be essential to the construction of modern tragedy.

Hegel has written that tragedy need not necessarily be stated in terms of good against evil, but possibly in terms of the opposition of conflicting goods. This notion would have been quite satisfactory to Aristotle and should aid the modern dramatist in his search for a hero who is not unnaturally good but instead merely pretty good. Beckett, Ionesco and Camus might easily argue that tragedy is possible within a construct of conflicting evils. Beckett could argue that tragedy is possible without conflict, that our natural state is tragic, that tragedy is omnipresent, the sole affirmation of Winnie's existence. Though Berenger's very name is a neat pun on the French word for insanity, for all Berenger's evil he is a lesser evil than the state of his creation. Most important, he, Berenger, wrestles as a mortal being to continue his existence, while the rotten state presents no such mortal longings. To invert Berenger's will is to recreate Camus's hero. If one is to accept basic Coleridgean doctrine, such an opposite is finally a match, but for purposes of setting down *ideal* rules for modern tragedy, the warring of two conflicting powers of non-evil seems most correct.

There are essential differences between classical and modern tragedies. The hero of classical tragedy discovers his mortality during the course of the play. The modern tragic hero will possess almost overwhelming knowledge of his mortality throughout the play. The modern hero will not long for immortality but for something, by contrast, almost superficial: comfort, perhaps. For in his knowledge of his mortality the modern tragic hero will possess a sense of his limitations that will distress, then weaken him. He will not strain against mortality *per se,* but against his sense of his own limitations. Thus there will be a conflict between what the modern tragic hero *senses* to be his limitations and what the play will *prove* to be his limitations. In the solution of this conflict the dramatist will find Aristotle's serious action.

The hero of classical tragedy embodied religious or near-religious myth. Simply, the classical tragic hero lays copyright to a specific force of nature. Antigone therefore doesn't merely believe that her brother should be buried; she is the force of nature that demands such behavior. While the ancient myths were available to the classical tragedian, the modern playwright, generally, is faced with the problem of mythmaking. Therefore a modern tragic hero has responsibility, in a sense, to both create problems and solve problems. In the working-out process, the dramatist will have to call upon a mythic structure from another area of literature, perhaps from a prior related play, or literally attend to the making of a mythic order within the boundaries of the one play in question.

Here I submit that the contemporary dramatist will be best advised to use forms other than tragedy, perhaps tragic-farce or melodrama, in the creation of the modern myth. The modern tragedy should be a separate play, related by the tragic hero as well as the total play. Thus, had *Antigone* not been written before, the author of a modern version would first have to create, for example, a melodrama about a prototypical Antigone. A totally new play would utilize what was learned from the former—Antigone's family structure, the literal working-out of her life—and place instantly into conflict what-we-know-must-be against what seems-to-be. In essence, what is different here from a standard classic trilogy is simply the realization that the creation of three related modern tragedies is virtually impossible. Instead, it is reasonable to hope that the third of three plays might qualify as authentic tragedy, while the first and second qualify as melodrama or tragic-farce.

Arthur Miller's Willie Loman fails to reach the status of tragic hero but does embrace some ingredients peculiar to authentic tragedy. *Death of a Salesman* presents such warring contraries in conflict in man-against-state, and there is an unsettling yield at the end of the play: the audience has an almost renovated faith *in the state.* Yet *Death of a Salesman* is a highly successful, highly crafted work. But the realized form is melodrama, not tragedy. Willie Loman is not made to live with the horror of his discovery, but is allowed actual release from his bondage. Indeed, if reversed, the play would still not qualify as authentic tragedy, since Loman's discovery is too minimal in nature to be satisfying. With Willie's succesful suicide, Miller has submerged any possibility that he had created an authentic modern tragedy. If anything, Willie is a hero who actually *fulfills* his deepest drives, yet within the course of the action, nothing really changes, nothing is really learned, the world is as it was when the play began. The classical tragic hero was made to effect change in his world and then live forever in the face of that very change.

Shakespeare and Tragedy

Shakespearean tragedy is finally a category unto itself, highly useful to inspect in the construction of rules toward a modern tragic form. *Macbeth*, as example, collides good against good with the play's protagonist trapped in the midst of that collision. Shakespeare adds supernatural characters to his play; the three witches have actual contact with both Macbeth and Banquo. Such construction, while familiar to Greek comedy, is not heard of in classical tragedy. Shakespeare represents a midpoint between Greek tragedy and modern tragedy. While for Shakespeare's audience there was an essential faith in a Christian God and, morally, attendance to the forces of the ancient gods, there were no literal gods upon whom a dramatist could call for rules (as there were evidently for the Greeks). Thus Shakespeare was, to a certain extent, concerned with mythmaking. Consider the "If I be . . . then you be . . ." of Anthony and Cleopatra. In this spirit of mythmaking, consider Cleopatra's immortal longings, not in metaphor but as just that: immortal longings. Shakespeare then had the extraordinary task of creating both the world and the other-world, all within the construct of one play. England, the real world, remained always in metaphor, even when

England herself was an actual setting. Also consider Shakespeare's frequent use of history as myth, during the many instances in which he used England as the actual setting for tragedy.

Kierkegaard, who has written so brilliantly on the absurd, has also written on tragedy. He suggests that the central concern of the tragic hero is a dread of that which is essentially good. Specifically, such a distinction should finally separate that which is tragic from that which is absurd. Ultimately, I believe, Kierkegaard claims too great an area for the absurd. While it is not possible to move Beckett or Ionesco from one camp to the other, it is imperative to note tragic elements in their work, elements that in structure seem mirror images of Sophoclean tragedy. Consider Hamm and Clov of *Endgame*. Their awful discovery, in a strong sense, is that they are bound to the play by their dialogue. While a neat pun on Platonic discourse, such a moment is also neatly mythic. What stronger control is there over a play's characters than the control (the hand) of the playwright? When characters are invested with knowledge (awareness) of that control, there is a reaching to a new kind of mythic order. But, more central to Beckett, his heroes want only to feel their existence. In the Beckett cosmos such desires are immortal longings. Man does not finally exist. There is nothing in the beginning, nothing at the end. Play and life are the same, all void, nothing. Yet in Kierkegaard's terms, Hamm and Clov are really tragic heroes, in dread of what Beckett presents as essential good: non-existence, indeed unconcerned nonexistence. Here we can conclude that the modern playwright can draw much from the absurd; that, for some, a certain existential order will aid and support a modern myth. Beckett's hopelessness might be a totally contemporary definition of what Kierkegaard deems dreadable as essential good.

Not surprisingly, Aristotle remains the true voice of moderation. His call for major action must hold for today as it did for Sophocles. Beckett's plays present anti-major action; finally, there is almost no physical action at all. These qualities which hold Beckett's plays from qualifying as tragedies do not in my opinion herald their failure as plays. To the contrary, problems of characters with minor concerns or lack of major action are not oversights but instead central to Beckett's vision. One suspects that Beckett suspects life is simply without major action. But the stage is not life. The stage exists for fiction; and fiction, as such, is capable of deceptions such as major action, existence, highly charged conflict and confrontation.

While one might look to known myth beneath a Greek tragedy, or historical recollections under a Shakespearean tragedy, one must look to a modern tragedian's imagination for an enacted vision of the future. While the playwright holds the real world still in metaphor, he must illustrate the change he has created in the world he has created. I believe that a contemporary tragic hero will have to take on that changed new world as his responsibility and, like it or not, he will have to continue to live in that changed world. One simple conclusion can be drawn here: the modern tragic hero should be made to stay alive at the conclusion of the play. Of course, the concept of conclusion may vary, to each playwright's advantage. Once the world has changed and the hero has been forced to live for a reasonable amount of time (time enough to suffer) in that world, he may die. Or he may not. In the acceptance of this new order there is an implicit separation between the tragic and the absurd.

The Unities Reconsidered

Unity of time and unity of place must be considered again in terms of what is feasible in this modern world. Travel in the present world is so common, it seems almost unnatural to limit a play to one location. But if the action is performed in one location, then it follows that it would seem even more unnatural to hold the time of the play to the span of a day. Therefore, while it is a worthy goal to consider evoking the traditional unities in the construction of modern tragedy, it is far more realistic to evoke either unity of time or unity of place, breaking one, specifically, to aid and abet the credibility of the other.

Hegel has written on the modern tragic hero's insistence on satisfaction of the inner, of the heart, which seems to me another way of structuring *hubris* into the personality of the tragic hero. Hegel, obliquely, suggests the possibility of a new distancing between hero and myth. For purposes of contemporary tragedy, it seems to me possible to construct a fresh myth and then draw a hero whose innermost drive puts him through conflict with the known outcome of the play (viewers' awareness of myth), adding a new dimension to a hero who, like his audience, also has awareness of the central myth. The explicit dangers are that the tragedy could fall to tragic-farce or, worse yet, collapse to naturalistic-melodrama. Whether or not the tragic hero is aware of his outcome through awareness of the central myth, the modern hero, like his ancient predecessor, must *be* that myth. He is not ever permitted the distance of believing in that myth as one who might follow a political doctrine. Qualities of credibility and naturalism must be held as distinctly different. Concerns of naturalism disallow any possibility of tragedy. Naturalism is too slow, too familiar, too much the stuff of satire. Details that create naturalism must be often eliminated from the drama for tragedy to grow, as each detail of tragedy must be large. The tragic hero must move with steps that are larger than those of life. While he needn't be a king, his needs must be of kingly proportions. In Beckett's insistence that Molloy literally stop all forward motion in order to suck stones, Beckett has reduced and thus removed Molloy from all possibility of tragic stature. In such an action, Beckett has presented a neat observation on the elitism of tragedy, that tragedy is the work of a highly selective artist joined by and to a highly selective hero.

Dramatists cannot possibly stumble into the form of tragedy without a plan to do so. And even with such a plan, history proves that failure occurs more often than not. Here we may conclude that Hegel's notion of a modern tragic hero's insistence on inner satisfaction is a workable idea, but the modern dramatist must be wary of distancing his hero from the created myth to a point of risking naturalism. We also must conclude that qualities of naturalism must be held apart from those realistic details that create credibility. Credibility in tragedy is caused by a stringing together of major details with the elimination of minor details (the latter being the stuff of naturalism) to the end of a larger-than-life protrayal of life, a larger world. Aristotle's qualification of major action still holds tragedy out of the form and style of naturalism as we have come to know it in contemporary melodrama.

Not surprisingly, a successful contemporary tragedy will, by and large, attend to most of the structural details of a tragedy by Sophocles or Shakespeare. Thus, the real differences between ancient tragedy and modern tragedy will not be drawn from the known, but instead from the ever-changing unknown. Twentieth-century man's view of the unknown is central to the problems of creating tragedy in this period. Modern man's faith in the cosmos has changed radically from the climate of faith in which Sophocles wrote his great *Oedipus* cycle. The modern playwright is of his own modern time. As his audience questions and constantly defies virtually all order perceived as *natural* order, so too does the modern playwright proceed to question and defy. Superficially, this circumstance would seem correct for the creation of authentic tragedy, yet, to the contrary, such a process leads a dramatist to conclusions within his play. There may not be conclusions drawn in tragedy. The tragedian must strive for great questions, not simple answers, certainly not answers in the traditions of those found heretofore in contemporary drama.

Thus far, it has been voguish for serious dramatists in this third quarter of the 20th century to conclude that the cosmos doesn't exist, that there is nothing. At first glance, this prevalent attitude would seem to herald the death of tragedy. Yet, to the contrary, such a phenomenon heralds a rebirth. The already heightened concern for tragedy that we *know* exists should, in itself, be taken as a hopeful symptom, but for the knowledge that such a concern was present straight through the 18th century, producing the extant tragedies of that period—plays that are decidedly unsatisfactory to us now. Consider, however, that the goal is to realize tragedy that is acceptable as authentic tragedy to contemporary audiences. Also recall that Dryden's *All for Love* was without question considered to be authentic tragedy during its own period. We cannot hope to create rules for all time, but we can create viable rules for our own period. It is most hopeful to note that this contemporary period of literature has been devoid of realized tragic drama. It has instead been a period of preparation. With renewed interest in Christian and Judaic myth, with new interest in the religion and culture of China and India, with the advent of exploration into space, with the awful presence of unmeasurable repression and violence now commonplace in the life of 20th-century man, it does seem reasonable to speculate that there has been more than adequate preparation.

Having observed the naturalistic melodrama of the early 20th century, and the more recent employment by contemporary dramatists of elements of the absurd, a correlative line can be seen from the Greeks through Shakespeare into the 18th century. The line continues through modern writers such as Camus and Beckett to the literal present. Indeed, the future of tragedy is hopeful: such is its nature and its condition.

What Comes First
In a Musical?
The Libretto

By Sheldon Harnick

Once, in an interview, Jerry Bock (the "Jerry" of all future references) and I were asked the inevitable question: "What comes first, the words or the music?" Jerry's unexpected answer was, "The book"—which now seems a very convenient way to get into this article. As far as Jerry and I are concerned the book is of primary importance and always comes first. It's true that we have occasionally written second-act songs while the librettist was still carving out the first act, but we were able to do this only because all of us were working from the same source material and we had agreed beforehand that certain scenes and material would of necessity appear in the final script. Even then we were running the risk that the "tone" of the songs we wrote would not match the "tone" of the dialogue that the librettist was evolving.

I have heard of situations in which a whole score was written and then a librettist hired to weave a book around the score. For all I know, some successful shows may have been written this way, but it would be difficult for me to believe that they were the "homogeneous" kinds of shows that I admire myself.

Jerry and I prefer to have a draft of the libretto first, so that we can write the type of song that (in addition to being entertaining) attempts to continue the flow of the story, to provide insight into character, to heighten climactic moments, or to enrich the feeling of time and place. This means working very closely with the librettist, and working out problems together.

In passing, let me mention something which I believe is *not* a problem for the librettist, namely, the institution of the divertissement, i.e., songs (or dances) which are actually extraneous to the book, no matter how entertaining. There's nothing wrong with divertissements, whether inserted as moments of sheer frolic, or as editorial comment, but they have little to do with the kind of collaboration between librettist, lyricist and composer that I am writing about. If all the parties agree that divertissements are desirable, then they constitute no writing problem for the librettist, as such. Various points in the show can be selected where the libretto will simply pause while some variety of musical interlude takes over. If the interlude is effective, well and good. If not, the interlude can always be cut and the only loss is that there will no longer be quite as much music in the musical as there was before. Of course, there is always the danger that the divertissement may prove so diverting that the audience may have some difficulty getting back into the story again; but I only wish to alert the potential librettist to the possible danger of the "show-stopper.".

To clarify further the point of view of this article, it strikes me that I should differentiate between two types of librettists. One type is the playwright who is hired by a producer to adapt a previously successful novel, play, movie or what-have-you, on the grounds that it will make a highly commercial musical property. The librettist may not even feel that the particular project is worthwhile or exciting; but, lured on by the glimmer of those astronomical musical grosses, he agrees. This article is not really intended for him (whether or not it contains anything of value for him) because he will presumably use a totally pragmatic approach, caring not about the unity or integrity of the piece, but grabbing at suggestions from anyone, latching on to any joke, applause-getter or theatrical device, so long as the end product works on any level.

No, this article is aimed at the other type of librettist: the writer who has a theatrical vision. His may be a comic vision, a poetic vision, a poignant vision, but whatever vision he has he knows that it requires music and lyrics and he also knows (or feels) that he himself is not competent to supply these elements. So he has to call on others to help achieve his vision; or he joins with others because he can see and share *their* vision. And this article may help make him aware of what he is letting himself in for.

One of the first things that occurs to me regarding any close collaboration between librettist and song-writer is the matter of generosity. And let me state right here that Jerry and I have been blessed with librettists of singular generosity. (Maybe *all* librettists are generous and noble, but we haven't worked with all of them yet.)

The word "generosity" has at least two connotations here. For one, each of our librettists has been extremely modest about suggesting where songs should fall within scenes. They have almost invariably prefaced each suggestion by mumbling: "Now, here is where I thought there might be a song about such-and-such, but feel absolutely free to disregard this suggestion if it doesn't stimulate you. Oh, yes, and please consider this tentative song

title a mere hint of what I feel might just possibly be appropriate here."
Whenever we *have* chosen to disregard such suggestions (which is much of
the time with song placement, and almost all of the time with song titles) the
various librettists, however wounded, have generously refrained from
sulking.

Another variety of generosity, and I would guess a much more difficult
thing for a librettist to tolerate, is the expropriation of ideas, jokes, lines of
dialogue, and occasionally entire scenes by the lyricist and composer. A
ready example of the lengths to which we lyricists will go springs immediately to mind.

One of Jerome Weidman's early drafts of *Fiorello* contained a scene in
which a number of ward-heelers were playing poker when they should have
been attending to the business of choosing a candidate to run for Congress
from their district. As written, it was an amusing scene which seemed
certain to play well. Now, I had long had a desire to write a lyric involving
poker terms which had struck me as especially colorful and tangy ever since

I had played a lot of it in the army. When I read Mr. Weidman's scene, I had an instant vision of an effective song which could incorporate much of the scene and to which I felt I could contribute a great deal. I asked him if he would mind if Jerry and I tried to "musicalize" his scene. Generously, he told us to go ahead and to feel free to use anything in the scene which we felt would be valuable. I then proceeded to construct the lyric for "Politics and Poker," rephrasing what I felt were the most valuable aspects of the scene, and adding to them my own notions. When we played the song for Mr. Weidman, he was genuinely delighted, which must have taken great generosity of spirit indeed, for he must have seen that he would get no credit for a number of funny notions in the song, including the notion for the punch line ("You idiot, that's me!")

I used to worry a bit about the vague feeling of dishonesty I felt when listening to the song "work" in the theater. I understood Mr. Weidman's generosity better after the reverse situation had occurred. That situation I can best illustrate with an incident which is still very fresh in my mind from *Fiddler on the Roof*. In this show, we had written a song for a certain scene, but everyone had such grave doubts about the song's potential effectiveness that we decided to discard it. There was one particular lyric in the song, however, a wry little joke which everyone felt would be quite appropriate as a line of dialogue. So it was added to the script. To this day, when that line comes along and "works," I don't feel "wronged" or feel that the audience is crediting Joseph Stein with a line of mine. Instead, I feel a sense of secret pride, both that the line gets its chuckle, and that I have added something valuable to the show. I assume that's how librettists feel when a scene or a line has been transmuted into a lyric and is effective.

My point, of course, is that any playwright turned librettist should be prepared to see his dialogue re-shaped and set to music. Just as often, he should be prepared to have entire sections of dialogue chopped away to be replaced by a song (entirely of the song writer's devising) in those places where the song writer feels that one song is worth a thousand words (of dialogue, that is). If the playwright has qualms about this (assuming that the lyricist is capable) he should think twice about attempting a libretto, or else provide his own lyrics (may he sprain his wrist in the attempt!).

I am suddenly reminded of a friend who is a painter. I once asked him if he had ever designed scenery. He was honest enough to admit that he was too much the prima donna to dream of creating work that was meant to be used as background for something else. He wanted the focus of attention on himself, and consequently he had never accepted any offers to do scenery.

Similarly, a fine playwright I know has also declined to write libretti. For him, a more important consideration was that he would have had to relinquish some control over his material, a thoroughly understandable reservation. For, make no mistake, that is what happens in a musical: absolute contol (if there is such a thing) gives way to compromise. At best, a musical can seem "seamless," with no jarring reminders that librettist and lyricist are two separate persons, but such homogeneity is achieved only after long, thoughtful discussions (not to mention argument) and endless rewriting. True collaboration is the essence, and not every playwright will want to subject himself to the necessity of abiding by group decisions (such group usually consisting of the librettist, lyricist, composer, director, often the producer, and sometimes the choreographer).

I hope the foregoing hasn't frightened any potential librettists away. If my comments have made any playwrights leery about entering the musical arena, perhaps I can remove an apprehension in a different direction.

When Jerry and I had our first meetings with Joe Masteroff on *She Loves Me,* it developed that Mr. Masteroff was diffident about how and where to start. He wasn't sure which parts of the original material (the film *The Shop Around the Corner* and the play *Parfumerie* on which it was based) he should adapt, and which parts he should skip, leaving gaps for us to fill with songs. Since this was the case, Jerry and I decided to try an experiment. We asked Mr. Masteroff to ignore the musical aspects entirely and simply to write a straight play. I don't remember whether or not he decided to write a shorter play than he would ordinarily have written, assuming it would expand with the addition of music and movement, but I do remember our urging him not to worry about over-writing. He was to let us worry about the songs. This meant, of course, that much of what he wrote would either be replaced by our material, or altered by us for musical purposes. He knew, also, that more of his material than usual would be so treated because we had all agreed that *She Loves Me* would benefit by more than the customary amount of music. He began to write after assuring us that not only would he not feel abused at our taking liberties with his script, but that the more of it we "musicalized" the happier he would be, surely the pinnacle of generosity.

So, without worrying about where and how the music would enter, he wrote his play; and later we found all the musical moments we could possibly have wanted. I suppose the original material, being essentially romantic and emotional, was inherently filled with music, and that not every musical book could or should be approached this way; but at least it illustrates one possible approach for the playwright launching his first libretto.

I have lately been brooding about styles of songs and, by implication, styles of musicals. The source of this brooding may very well come from a mystery I've never solved to my own satisfaction with regard to *The Apple Tree.*

Originally, Jerry and I started out to write three one-act musicals with librettist Jerome Coopersmith. The first musical, by common agreement and enthusiasm, was to be based on Mark Twain's short story *The Diary of Adam and Eve*. Since Mr. Coopersmith is an experienced librettist, we had a minimum of preliminary talks on this material; he felt he knew how to treat it, and he went ahead and wrote several drafts. Part of the mystery was this: Mr. Coopersmith created a libretto that we all found amusing, charming, and seemed theatrically sound, but Jerry and I couldn't find the songs in it. We came up with a few, but it took an astonishing length of time, and the rest of the songs proved stubbornly elusive. I'm not speaking of good songs or bad songs but of *any* songs.

Finally, Stuart Ostrow, our producer, suggested that the problem might lie in the one-act form itself. He suggested that in so short a form (shorter even than a first act of an average musical) the librettist and lyricist might be getting in each other's way. Eventually, on the supposition that Mr. Ostrow was right, Mr. Coopersmith graciously stepped aside after it had been decided that I was to attempt a libretto using his as a basis. I had never attempted one before, except for a few long musical sketches. The rest of the mystery (to me) lies in the fact that I don't feel that I changed Mr. Coopersmith's libretto that much and yet by making what I consider to be minor changes, cuts, additions, and transpositions, suddenly the hitherto elusive score materialized.

After thinking about this for many, many months I'm *still* not sure why the songs were so elusive in Mr. Coopersmith's version and why they came so easily in mine. Because, as I say, I feel that with all the changes I made, the end product was still *essentially* his libretto. Possibly Mr. Ostrow's surmise was right. And, possibly, underlying that surmise was some very subtle difference in the way we each "saw" the Twain material, a difference so subtle as to remain hidden from me still.

I believe that the point that can be drawn from all this, for you librettists, is the necessity of making certain that you see eye to eye with your lyricists and composers. It means, among other things, probing discussions as to the style of dialogue, the nature of the events in the scenes, the intent of the libretto (what the show is really *about*). It means coming to terms with the style of the show itself: are the characters to be naturalistic, realistic, satiric, poetic, caricatures, just-plain-old-fashioned-song-and-dance—what? If seemingly trivial but real differences in approach and viewpoint exist, then minor or major damage to the show will inevitably reveal itself somewhere along the line. I imagine this point should seem almost too obvious to mention here; but all too often such discussions are neglected, or skimmed over by writers who should know better, including myself.

I have an image in my mind of two parties laying sections of railroad track, each starting from different locations, but with the intention of joining their respective tracks at some mid-point. One can well imagine the consternation if there has been some minor miscalculation and the tracks are half a mile away from each other at the point where they should meet! I have experienced some such rough parallel as this at points in shows where songs and text should meet. Of course, if there has been a genuine meeting of the minds between librettist and lyricist then there's no problem. The librettist (or lyricist, if the librettist has no objections) can supply a sentence, a phrase, or even a word that makes for the smoothest possible transition between speech and song. However, if the collaborators have been subtly veering away from each other it can be exasperating. The text seems to be saying something very clearly. The song seems ready to pick up where the dialogue leaves off. And then maddeningly, there is a mystifying gulf between the two! A clever, facile librettist (or lyricist) can find words to bridge this gulf in what *seems* like a meaningful way, yet as often as not the song will not sound as convincing or as effective as it seemed when sung out of context. The audience may not even know why they feel dissatisfied with the song, but they will "feel" the lack of a true connection and respond accordingly. The real solution, if the writers have the time (and too often they don't, if they're on the road facing imminent deadlines) is to try to go back in the script to the point at which the divergence began to take place; but this is work that should really be done long before a show goes into production.

Reading over what I've written, I can only hope that I haven't made the collaborative process between librettist on the one hand and lyricist/ composer on the other sound too complicated, or too conducive to wearisome analysis or unsettling arguments. If a librettist is prepared to be somewhat generous in the ways I have touched upon, and is willing to spend the necessary hours making sure that he and his collaborators are traveling the same road together, then I believe he can experience at least two great satisfactions. There is the distinct probability that the playwright will find himself, when stimulated by creative collaborators, entertaining ideas and developing concepts that would not have occurred to him if he were working by himself. And there is the possibility of creating a rich theatrical work, heightened and deepened by the incorporation of music and movement, which could only have been created in collaboration. And to me those two reasons seem sufficient.

The Widening Circles Of Children's Theater

By Frank Gagliano

Several years ago, George White, president of the Eugene O'Neill Theater Center, commissioned me to write an original play for children in conjuction with a Connecticut-wide experiment call "Project Create." At the time I had written a number of off-Broadway plays which, while not what C. Barnes would call "14-carat hits," gave me the reputation of being a serious American playwright.

I mention this because, at the time, I approached the children's play commission, if not with condescension, then with the attitude of a vaguely inferior assignment. After all, I was a "serious" playwright and, as far as I knew, Tennessee Williams, another serious playwright, had never written a children's play (though *Camino Real*, I now realize, would be, with some obvious tightening and excisions, a possible play for older children). No, I was aiming for the street of dreams and children's theater had nothing to do with Broadway's kind of dreams.

What the commission did have to do with, however, was Lloyd Richards as the director of the play, Peter Larkin as the designer, a cast headed by then unknown Raul Julia, and a $2,500 fee. I didn't know it at the time, but this marked a revolution of sorts as a children's theater project. All I did know was that it was a quality setup and I was hard-up for money.

The resulting play was called *The Hide-and-Seek Odyssey of Madeleine Gimple* and the joyous experience of that one play has helped change my attitude toward the entire area of children's theater. As I got into the writing, I made my first pleasant discovery: I could deal with, and render for children, themes that I had been exploring in my adult plays—the crisis of individual identity, for example; also the problems of a polluted society (to

45

me, a metaphor for mass suicide); the question of indivdual reponsibility in a corrupt world which God has abdicated and within which one is constantly facing violence—and other such areas of modern angst. And since my adult plays are Moralities and Everyman journeys of one sort or another, the odyssey format suggested itself as the central technique. I even borrowed the setting (a playgound) from one of my earlier plays. In short, since I was on familiar ground, it never occurred to me to write down to the audience, and the creative juices flowed.

And since I liked being told stories when I was a child, I automatically assumed that narrative was an essential part of a play for children and that archetypal characters and situations were also necessary components. It also seemed natural to add songs, a dash of slapstick, a bit of magic, humor and extravagant imagery; though I must admit I was afraid of this last ingredient.

A school in a disadvantaged area (a euphemism at the time for "poor" and "black") in New Haven was chosen to house the first production of my play. And so, with a lowly children's play I was able to achieve what I could never achieve with my adult plays: open in New Haven. And what an opening! We did two shows that day in a very large auditorium. Hundreds of kids were (you'll pardon the expression) bussed in from all over the area. And my first shock was seeing an audience with a good deal of openness and exciting expectation. Not that they came of their own free will; they *were* a captive audience. But from 9 to 3 they would be captive anyway, and this theater-going junket at least had the novelty of a good old-fashioned get-together bash with one's peers. And something might—just might—involve and captivate them up there on the stage.

Well, that audience captivated me. No—they more than captivated me (second shock); they made me have respect for them. Remember, I had been used to New York audiences, many of whom went to the serious theater (at least back when New Yorkers were going to serious theater) because they were told to go by reviewers and/or who went with a "show me" attitude or were angry at having to pay so much money and who often went to see you fail. It was the rare audience that entered with an expectant buzz and seemed open, relaxed, honest, positive, and who could think for itself.

Well—here it was; the "up," no-ax-to-grind kind of audience you wanted. And they were brutally honest. When something wasn't holding on that stage, the kids simply turned off and began talking to their friends or punching each other on the arm (each punch became a rewrite, and I did so many rewrites after that first performance that I anticipated an arm paralysis epidemic in that school). But if things *were* working, you were rewarded with the kind of total involvement and focus that playwrights dream about and that children do so naturally and purely.

I was to discover over the years that this kind of open, honest reaction was to continue from children-audience to children-audience. The problems came—if they came at all—from the grownups in the crowd. And there are always grownups accompanying the kids. Unfortunately, it's the grownup who usually insists on the one-millionth version of *Snow White*; not the kid. It's the grownup who objects to certain themes, subjects and/or words being used; not the child. And it's the grownup who will dutifully sit through a mediocre show and force his child to sit still even though the child knows better and would rather punch the kid next to him in the arm.

The *Hide-and-Seek Odyssey of Madeleine Gimple* raised many a grownup eyebrow. The play doesn't break any new gound as to form, but it does have a scene in a place call Litterville where everyone is urged by the evil character chasing Madeleine to buy more and more of everything in order to create more litter and pollution. As a result, everyone in Litterville wears breathing gizmos on their noses and the noise pollution has made them deaf. The scene was criticized by some of the educators because it would be over the childrens' heads. And I was worried about it until I visited some of the libraries in these same schools and discovered that, in fact, the children had materials on the subject and had been into the pollution situation all along. As usual, the children were ahead of some of the teachers. Today, my scene is more easily accepted—even by grownups. But the final scene in which Madeleine journeys to a land where everyone has "puppetitis" and the dreaded Puppetmaster turns out to be a machine being run by other machines, is still attacked, on occasion, as being Commie-Nazi treason.

And there is also an event in the play where a boy, through an heroic act, dies. This upset, and still upsets, many a grownup, and I have seen productions of the play where this scene has been so accelerated by the adult directors as to be almost a blur. And yet, when it's done honestly, this scene never fails to move and absorb the children who can, just as I suspected, deal with a serious theme like death.

Royalties for *Gimple* have been steadily increasing over the years (in fact, I get most of my royalties from this children's play—playwrights, please note!), which means that more enlightened groups are doing the play, which means that a new attitude toward the contemporary play for children may be developing. Historically in this country, children's theater has been left to the amateurs. It's been the communities, high schools and universities that have kept children's theater alive over the years. And it has been university drama departments, in particular, that have taken the lead in presenting quality plays written specifically for children; especially in recent years when younger creative dramatics faculty have been joining drama departments.

The quality of these university productions is usually very high. The acting, of course, is done by student actors who make up for their lack of experience with talent and enthusiasm. The physical productions are usually quite stunning. In fact, I doubt if professional companies (with the possible exception of the Minneapolis Children's Theater Co., the Goodman Theater in Chicago and a few others) could ever afford to mount the kinds of productions the universities can mount. One problem children's theater directors in the university do face is the problem all creative faculty face at a university; their energies are often dissipated because of teaching loads, conferences, committee assignments, publishing and the like—and these duties continue even when in rehearsal. And dissipated energies often tend to confuse priorities so that, in the rehearsal crunch, technical values are emphasized at the expense of exploring the nuances of script and ensemble.

The serious professionals (those who were interested in going beyond the usual cutsey-pie productions of *Cinderella*) began entering the children's theater field in larger and larger numbers within the last decade. I'm not quite sure why. A good portion, of course, probably always wanted to work with serious material for children and current circumstances make it all possible. But I suspect that some just couldn't hack it in the adult theater. And since, in recent years, hardly anyone can hack it in the adult theater, more and more have been turning to children's theater simply to find a place to work (which is also why so many professionals are entering the academic world; the audiences are there, standards are high and getting higher and the academic theater plants are the best in the country). Also, foundation, state and national subsidies are available for children's theater—even for professional children's theater—which makes it all attractive. And there *are* those wonderful, exciting audiences I mentioned above.

In any case, professional interest has grown to such an extent that at a recent O'Neill Theater Center Playwrights' Conference at Waterford, Conn., a three-day symposium was held during which professional children's theater practitioners confronted a number of leading newspaper reviewers and said, in effect, "It's time you took us seriously." Whereupon the critics said, "We'll take you seriously when you deserve to be taken seriously." And before the three days were over there were productions, demonstrations and discussions all over the place.

The New York-based Merry Mini Players were there, and their theory is to have a cast of talented children give finished, almost Broadway-glossy-mounted performances. The New York-based New York City Center's Young People's Theater was there, and its theory is to combine performance with workshop exercises that ultimately involve the audience of children. Both these groups collaboratively devise their shows with, as I understand it, writers on hand to help shape the material.

The Little Theater of the Deaf (LTD) was also there, and David Hayes, its artistic director, seems to have no *one* theory. He chooses material he likes and has that material presented by a beautifully trained ensemble. In fact, the LTD along with its parent company (The National Theater of the Deaf) is probably the only real ensemble company we have in the U.S. What is of interest here is that the LTD, according to David Hayes, came into being when the main company "played by accident for children and realized that the combination of the spoken and visual word was very rich—it was very thick in image for the children." But while the LTD was undoubtedly the best-trained ensemble there, what came out of that symposium was the feeling that all the professional children's theater companies seem to be attempting to upgrade their ensemble techniques.

The symposium at the O'Neill Conference missed one major opportunity. It failed to specifically include the 11 contemporary American playwrights who were at Waterford to show their adult wares. I also was showing a new adult play, but I went to the symposium because I had written a children's play (vested interest). The other playwrights were aware of the meetings, too, and could have attended, but the whole area of children's theater is a foreign one to playwrights. They've got to be approached, seduced—whatever.

Most of the leaders in the field of children's theater are performance-oriented and tend to be group-devisers of scripts. But children's theater will not come of age until a sizable dramatic literature in the genre is built.

Devising a play by group is not the way to build that literature. The vision of an individual playwright-artist is needed.

It's true that what differentiates the playwright-artist from the prose or poetry-artist is that once that vision has been shaped into a playable script, the playwright-artist becomes one of the collaborators (along with actor, director, technical creative artist, etc.) who go about the business of making that vision work. But the collaboration does begin with the playwright-artist's vision. And so it must be with the playwright-artist of children's plays. One of the most moving pieces the LTD does is a little story about a tree who unselfishly allows itself to be literally truncated to help a child grow into manhood. It's one of the few narrative pieces in the LTD repertory. And yet, it is this little narrative that seems to render the kind of compressed, archetypal, shaped, directly-communicative narrative essence that is at the heart of the play-work-of-art for children. And one would hope that David Hayes will develop more such pieces (perhaps evening-long such peices) to enrich the literature. This will probably mean training and encouraging deaf playwrights to write for their medium.

I mentioned at the top of this piece that I really plunged into the writing of a children's play because of one factor: loot. George White had said: "Frank here's $2,500. Write a children's play and we'll do it with the best professional talent around."

Since it does not seem natural for playwright-artists to turn to children's theater or for the leaders in the field to naturally think in terms of the individual playwright-artist, I'm convinced that the only way to get the playwright-artist to turn to writing a children's play is to commission him to do so. And I don't mean a $100 or $250 commission, I mean a $3,500 to $5,000 commission. Such a commission will make it worthwhile for the skeptical playwright-artist to take the time needed to write somthing of value. And even if only a handful get hooked, that might be enough to get the literature started. In England Robert Bolt was commissioned by the Royal Shakespeare Company to write *The Thwarting of Baron Bolligrew* and London's Unicorn Theater commissioned Mary Melwood to write *The Tingalary Bird*; two substantial additions to the literature of children's plays in England.

What the new awareness in children's theater *has* done is to upgrade the level of performance, thus attracting audience and skilled theater practitioners to the movement. The Theater of the Deaf and O'Neill Theater Center have in the works a Showboat floating professional children's theater of very high calibre around the boroughs of New York (and may you have a bundle of commissions at the ready, David). In Minneapolis, a $3 million complex devoted entirely to children's theater is a permanent home for John Donahue's much-acclaimed Children's Theater Co. (may the edifice complex not overwhelm you, John). Many of the regional theaters have, or plan to have, children's theater as part of their new complexes (may their dismal record of producing contemporary adult American plays change regarding worthwhile original children's plays). And the O'Neill confrontation between critics and children's theater professionals left most of the critics favorably inclined toward recognizing the movement (may you critics re-learn from the children what an honest, open reaction to a play is). What this upgrading and awareness now need is the literature that can be published and disseminated to all parts of the country, that will really stretch the re-creative artist and make fine ensemble companies. Great written roles help make great actors. Devised group-plays, even by great actors, rarely make transcendent plays.

As I've been trying to point out, not only can the writing and making of a play for children be artistically rewarding and fulfilling, but also there is a large, serious audience of children out there (possibly the last serious theater audience left!) ready to experience an honest dramatic vision. But if the theater practitioners give them less than the best in the way of contemporary dramatic literature, this last serious audience will turn from the stage and start punching their buddies in the arm. And for those of us who still want to work in and/or see live theater continue in this country, those punches may be the last body-blows for us all.

The Journal of a Virgin Playwright on the Primrose Path of Production

By Simm Landres

I am a professional actor and I've been a secret writer ever since I can remember. My spelling stinks and even though the Army tried to teach me touch typing I never concentrated much, preferring to write letters to whatever girl I was pining for at the time. I have devised a two-and-one-half-finger method of typing that gets satisfactory results. I have three or four manila envelopes stuffed with pithy ideas, poetic opening lines and provocative startling scenes of never-completed plays and scenarios; mostly written on the back of envelopes and old letters and the inside of matchbook covers that have not promised instant $ and/or success for selling shoes in your spare time or warning of VD.

I am now a Playwright. A produced Playwright. I was probably watching a game show, waiting for the Muse to call me, when the phone rang and my agent's secretary's voice was heard: "They want to do your play" . . . "Terrific," blase me says, "who?" She told me who and when and for how much. I was no longer blase. My strong fantasy life, my insatiable need to role-play, took over at once. Who was I? Gregory Peck? Glenn Ford with tweeds and pipe? Woody Allen? Who? I'm still too much of an actor to be able to erase entirely images of other actors' portrayals, but my name spelled properly on the check, the subsequent publicity and the program helped dispel those fantasies. I am a Playwright. I have a production. I can prove it because I decided to keep a daily journal, primarily to prove to myself that the event was really taking place and for a record to look back upon when I'm selling shoes.

The first day: The Director and I meet for the first time and talk. His circumlocution is wondrous to behold, and he has no idea whatsoever as to what my play is about. (I have to say that the Director has been thrust upon me . . . *fait accompli*.) The Designer is all meat and potatoes practical, in contrast to the Director. This makes me fantasy a putsch, calling a friend in New York to come and direct and if that fails (as it would undoubtedly due to lack of funds) directing it myself. But what would that serve? I want to be here as the Playwright and have good fights with the Director and learn from him. I don't want to direct. I want to see what works and fix what doesn't. I don't want any diluted TDR rhetoric. I want the play to be served.

The essential bizarre phenomenon of having my characters and my words and my thoughts and my jokes come back to me slowly becomes more objectified as rehearsals progress. I am inevitably losing my virginity.

A *new feeling:* In acting, a character comes to me either as a quick flash impression or is slowly built and understood. But ultimately I "become" the character or vice versa. I could talk and explain and justify any and all motivations and actions and relationships. I work within a form; within a structure.

Now as a Playwright watching the actors rehearse and work to some end (that they may not fully know as yet), I learn subtleties, nuances. They are fleshing out, truly giving birth to an essentially intellectual concept. The Actor, with, by and in his craft, completes the Playwright's work. So what I am learning as a Playwright in rehearsal is simply re-learning, and subsequently re-enforcing, my love and respect for the Actor. Now as a Playwright I must be open to this. And of course the Director contributes, and I swear that I'm open to it. But this guy doesn't know; all his instincts vis-a-vis my play are wrong.

Now as a Playwright I think: I am *finding* my own Play. The actors are showing me things good and heretofore unknown; things bad and heretofore unknown. The latter I cut or redo. Generally speaking I'm not loathe to cut, and I find rewriting simple. The rehearsals and the cast help me to find those places. At certain times during the day, I can relate to my words, jokes, characters and situations objectively. My stardust and subjectivity disappear. I'm simply working on problems, solving theatrical problems. So far, I've been good at that, and I like it. My 11 years' professional acting experience is serving, and I'm a Playwright now.

From time to time I feel jealous of the actors. I'm still an actor and I don't forget the joy of working on a part and of the discoveries. I hope these actors feel the same. I hope my text doesn't let them down, and I hope they tell me if it does. If it does, I'll try to fit it. My pleasure.

A *week into rehearsals:* It's been going badly. The Director runs the gamut from pretentious exercises to complicated ugly blocking. There is no discovery, but one hell of a baptism. So I talk to the Director once again: "The Play dictates the way. Serve the Play; not me or you or some vision or some style or some abstract in the sky," and on and on and on . . . He looks at me as if I were a Martian. I am not a Martian. The actors have been coming to me for help, so I guess that in one way or another I'm going to direct. I'm sorry, because I wanted to bounce ideas back and forth with the Director. I wanted my vision to be pruned and refined, I wanted to suggest and change. I wanted to be the Playwright studying his Play to see the mistakes and mend them. I wanted to learn my new craft by doing . . . But there is no optimum situation. I count my blessings and bite on a bullet.

I'm doing minor cuts and rearranging. The actors are a fine bunch, willing to work and, as always, wanting to. They are all as new as hell but with lovely instincts and a considerable amount of talent. They are all "right" for their parts.

Talk to the Director again. Talk to him for an hour and more. Talk to him and try to explain the practical logic and the organic reasons for decisions. He ultimately throws up his hands and "capitulates." He doesn't agree he says. "But if that's what you want . . ." I don't care if he agrees or not. The fact is that he doesn't understand . . . I *am* a Martian.

A few days later: There is a great deal of trouble with the pivotal section in the second act. What I want I can only express in result terms, and the Director doesn't know how to achieve it. I don't know either. I talk to the cast and I blow it. I make bad stupid choices out of my frustration; and I talk like a writer, not a director. It creates barriers. I must now go home and think of the problem in acting terms for each of the characters. Now I'm an actor again.

Run-through that evening: I begin madly taking notes. Dammit, these are directing notes of the most rudimentary kind. There is one difficult transition for "Will," and looking at it I can't solve it either from a playwright's or actor's point of view. Dammit, I'm split too many ways. My attention is too fragmented.

After a few more run-throughs I'm losing interest! I've heard it and I've seen it too much. I need to be away from rehearsals a bit, but I'm afraid to be. I'm getting paranoid. I rewrite "Will's" transition . . . it's all coming together but I have yet to solve the big problem.

Dress Tech: Very few and minor things to be worked out. The tech people are on top of it and I feel secure with them . . . It starts. People wander in for the first ten minutes of the run. Who are they? "Floy" and "Emily" are not thrown as I thought they might be. As the audience settles down, the laughs begin and continue throughout. It's great and weird to hear laughter for the first time and the actors are to be credited. It serves the cast wonderfully well. They are very "up" after the show. I know that my play is funny, but I never thought that it would be a "laff-riot," and I'm not convinced that it should be one. The emphasis is all lopsided. I love the laughs but too much has been sacrificed. I fully blame the Director for this and am doubly frustrated because I was unable to make it what it should be.

Opening night: It's the hottest day of the year, and my wife and I are swimming in our clothes and our eyes are burning. Shower and shave and go over to the theater to stage the curtain call . . . (Last night before I left, the Workshop Director, the man who chose my play as the recipient of a Grant, suggested softly and with no strings that one of the characters should wind up differently. I said, "Let me think about it," I did. It is true that "He" isn't fully resolved, but I haven't thought through the alternatives sufficiently, and to fix it now, hurriedly, would not serve.) . . . We got there too soon. There is too much time to wait around. My stomach really feels full of butterflies; just like in the movies. My picture is out front with the other playwrights and directors. Nice picture. I see people buy tickets. "Are you faculty?" asks the ticket seller. "No, just civilians," says a white-haired couple. Civilians! Jesus! I pace and smoke and drink water and coke and breathe the warm fresh air outside. My wife looks beautiful and is bemused by my antics; albeit sympathetic.

It's time. I sit next to my wife; front row, center, highest rise. The house is pretty full. The bird sounds are nice; the speakers have plenty of treble. These are country birds no doubt, not pigeons or sparrows. House to half. House down and out. Here we go. Stage up. TV sound go. "Emily" in place. "Floy" enters . . . Merde to all . . . Floy and Emily a bit nervous and slow and tend to force; and there are no laughs . . .

I see all these people; young, middle and old, and I check their faces for the first of many times. Everything, it seems, makes me squirm; the actors, the audience, my Play. Whose Play? Look there, a smirk. It's beginning. The audience is warming up to those people on stage. They know who Floy is. There's a titter. An explosion of noise . . . it's, I think, a girl sound. Will it be infectious? Catch, dammit! Don't be afraid, people. It's a sorta, kinda comedy . . . Floy, relax, you'll be fine. Real fine. Emily settles in first . . . Some snickers . . . a tiny snort again from the girl on the left. Was it a girl? Maybe it wasn't. Was it young, middle or old? Faculty or civilian? OK, you did it, Floy, you're there. Keep it going. You're home free, Floy boy, home free. Now just relax and do it . . .

What was that line? What was that move? What happened that was funny? Hey, that was the first laugh!!! A full-audience complete laugh. An honest-to-goodness laugh. No one unsure or holding back. I didn't even know why. What was funny, anyway? Was it one of the "coffee" lines? I don't know. I don't remember now. But we—no, it's They now, dummy, They. I'm not in it any more . . . They lost an awful lot. Can they regain? Can they be consistent?

Here comes "Lizzie." Speak up, Lizzie, she doesn't. Don't be scared, they're all set up waiting, needing to like you. Relax. Relax. Good girl; a moment. Have faith in yourself. Don't slouch and speak up. Here comes "Will"—great entrance. Strong, clean, purposeful action. Lots of laughs right away. He's milking them. Not too much too soon, Will, there's plenty of time. Quick establishing scene and then off. Just enough. An appetizer. The second scene works well and gets applause! The third scene with Will and Lizzie doesn't work; they both seem to have gone back to their earlier ways . . . My agonies. What can I do? Nothing! Plotz! . . .

Who am I? A Playwright watching an event that I invented? An event that is no longer mine? Part mine? What part? An Actor empathizing when lines are dropped or ad-libbed? An audience? Partly. I've seen the Play before in some dream . . . A Director? Yes, quite a bit. I directed it a lot . . . dammit

. . . It's going slowly tonight. Or is it? I don't know. I didn't time it. It's slow because my mechanism is functioning so many ways and so differently . . . The act is over. The last scene was rotten. The points weren't made. The audience applauds politely. I have a cigarette. I hate cigarettes. I'm totally disoriented. Some stranger who is seeing the show tells me that he too is a playwright and then simply stares at me. I think that all I do is smile and then mercifully it's time to go back for the second act . . . I feel very peculiar.

Act Two: The laughter begins right away. Will is the favorite. He's creative and flashy, and the laughs keep coming and coming in clusters. There's no stopping them and . . . Oh my God "Lode's" wig is slipping! Does he know? Do the other Actors? Does the audience? Is it that apparent? Is it simply my educated eye? Lode knows. Be cool, Lode. He is. Floy knows and so do the others. Floy is terrific. In the action he pats, fondles and cuffs Lode and helps secure the wig. Whew! Good man, Floy. Good man, Lode. The act is going well, all the points are being made and the laughs are honest. I still check the house. Young and old and what do they respond to? . . . There goes the wig again. Will Lode leave? Can he leave? What if it comes off entirely? And on and on and on . . .

Afterwards: There are a few sequences (not due to this production) that do not work. Some of it is too cutesy, too arch; some overwritten and some underwritten, and there is a character that needs to be resolved. I found these things out because of the Workshop. The Workshop served. That's what it was all about.

Very lucky me. A first Play and it had a production. A production made possible by the enlightened desire of the University of Texas Drama Department, Professor Webster Smalley and the Rockefeller Foundation; a happy marriage of Academia and the professional theater; an educational experience for all, for the students, the new wet-behind-the-ears professionals, full of piss and vinegar and desire; and an education for me. A new Playwright. A now produced Playwright. A once and future virgin.

II. On Theater Lyrics.....

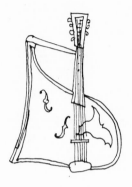

And be you blithe and bonny,
Converting all your sounds of woe
Into Hey, nonny, nonny.
  –MUCH ADO ABOUT NOTHING

Theater Lyrics

By Stephen Sondheim

This article was first presented as an informal talk by Stephen Sondheim and later prepared for publication under Mr. Sondheim's supervision. We extend our thanks to the music publishers and their representatives who have given us permission to print Mr. Sondheim's quotations from lyrics.

I am just going to talk and I am just going to ramble. Some of the thoughts will be incomplete, some will be pontifical. And contentious and dogmatic and opinionated.

I'm going to talk only about theater lyrics, lyrics in a dramatic situation on a stage in terms of character—not pop lyrics. Most of the examples are going to be from my own work simply because I know it best; and from Oscar Hammerstein II and Cole Porter because they are among the few lyricists who have been deemed worthy of having their lyrics published in book form. I'll quote some others, but a lot will be from Hammerstein and Porter also because I like them a lot. Many of the examples from my own work will be songs you've never heard, cutouts from shows. Generally they are songs I like, and I seldom get a chance like this to lay them on people.

Sinclair Lewis once began a talk to some writers by asking, "How many in the audience want to write?" When a few people raised their hands, he asked, "Then why aren't you all at home writing?" Well I don't think he was entirely right. I think there is something to learn. I learned most of what I know from Oscar Hammerstein, and maybe some of the things I have to say, even though they are just random thoughts, will help those of you who want to write. I think most of what has to be said about the principles of lyric writing—when to follow rules and when to break them—can be said in a very short time. There are in fact only one or two principles from which I think all lyric writing springs, and I will get to those shortly.

To start off with a little history: I first got into lyric writing because when I was a child of 11 my parents were divorced and we moved to Pennsylvania. I moved there with my mother, and among her friends were the Hammerstein family. They had a son my age and we became very close. Oscar Hammerstein gradually got me interested in the theater, and I suppose most of it happened one fateful or memorable afternoon. He had urged me to write a musical for my school (George School, a Friends school in Bucks County). With two classmates I wrote a musical called *By George*, a thinly disguised version of campus life with the teachers' names changed by one vowel or consonant. I thought it was pretty terrific, so I asked Oscar to read it—and I was arrogant enough to say to him, "Will you read it as if it were just a musical that crossed your desk as a producer? Pretend you don't know me." He said "O.K.," and I went home that night with visions of being the first 15-year-old to have a show on Broadway. I knew he was going to love it.

Oscar called me in the next day and said, "Now you really want me to treat this as if it were by somebody I don't know?" and I said, "Yes, please," and he said, "Well, in that case it's the worst thing I ever read in my life." He must have seen my lower lip tremble, and he followed up with, "I didn't say it wasn't talented, I said it was terrible, and if you want to know why it's terrible I'll tell you." He started with the first stage direction and went all the way through the show for a whole afternoon, really treating it seriously. It was a seminar on the piece as though it were *Long Day's Journey Into Night*. Detail by detail, he told me how to structure songs, how to build them with a beginning and a development and an ending, according to his principles. I found out many years later there are other ways to write songs, but he taught me, according to his own principles, how to introduce character, what relates a song to character, etc., etc. It was four hours of the most *packed* information. I dare say, at the risk of hyperbole, that I learned in that afternoon more than most people learn about song writing in a lifetime.

He saw how interested I was in writing shows, so he outlined a kind of course of study for me which I followed over the next six years, right through college. He said, "Write four musicals. For the first one, take a play you admire and turn it into a musical." I admired a play called *Beggar on Horseback* by George S. Kaufman and Marc Connelly, and we actually got permission to do it for three performances at college. Next, Oscar told me: "Take a play that you don't think is very good or that you liked but you think can be improved and make a musical out of it." I chose a play called *High Tor* by Maxwell Anderson—I couldn't get permission to put it on in college because Anderson wanted to do a musical of it with Kurt Weill (they never got around to it), but it taught me something about playwriting, about structure, about how to take out fat and how to make points.

Then Oscar said, "For your third effort, take something that is non-dramatic: a novel, a short story." I landed on *Mary Poppins* and spent about a year writing a musical version. That's where I first encountered the real difficulties of playwriting, which is one of the reasons I am not a playwright. It was very hard to structure a group of short stories and make a play out of them, and I wasn't able to accomplish it. Finally Oscar said, "For your fourth, do an original," so right after I got out of college I wrote an original musical whose first act was 99 pages long and the second act 60-odd. Oscar had recently given me a copy of *South Pacific* to read and the entire show was 90 pages long, so when I sent him my script I got it back from him with a circle around 99 and just a "Wow!" written on it.

By that time, though, I had learned something about the craft of writing musicals, and I happened to meet Lemuel Ayers, one the best set designers ever, who had produced a number of shows including *Kiss Me Kate*. Lem had a property called *Front Porch in Flatbush* by two Hollywood screen writers, Julius J. and Philip G. Epstein, twin brothers who won an Academy Award for *Casablanca*. Phil had died, but this, their last play together, was about their third brother and a group of kids in Flatbush in 1928 all investing in the stock market. Lem wanted to make a musical out of it. He had approached Frank Loesser because it was very New York and Loesser had turned it down because he was busy on something else and Lem heard some of my stuff from these four apprentice musicals and hired me on spec to write three songs—which I did, and which he and Julie Epstein liked. We went into supposed production on this show, which was now retitled *Saturday Night* (this was the first professional work I had done, and I was prepared to do professional work only because of what Oscar had made me go through).

During the course of the backers' auditions Lem died, and the show never got anywhere. But it was my portfolio, and as a result of it I got *West Side Story*. In the course of auditioning for producers around town, I was taken to Martin Gabel's apartment; he was going to co-produce a musical of James M. Cain's *Serenade* with a book by Arthur Laurents and was looking for song writers, so that's the first time I met Arthur and he heard my work. About six months later I was at an opening night party, and I saw one familiar face, Arthur Laurents, and I went over to make small talk with him. I asked him what he was doing, and he said, "I'm about to begin a musical of *Romeo and Juliet* with Leonard Bernstein and Jerry Robbins." I asked "Who's doing the lyrics?"—just idly, because I didn't think of myself as a lyric writer, I thought of myself as a song writer, I was composing all the time. Arthur literally smote his forehead (I think it's the only time I have ever seen anybody literally smite his forehead). He said, "I never thought of you and I liked your lyrics very much. I didn't like your music very much, but I did like your lyrics a lot." (Arthur is nothing if not frank.) Arthur invited me to meet Leonard Bernstein and play for him. Lenny liked what he heard and asked me if I would do the lyrics for the show. I didn't want to do just lyrics, but I went to have a talk with Oscar who was my guide and mentor all through my career. He said, "I think it will be very valuable for you to work with professionals of this calibre. The project sounds very exciting so I think you ought to do it."

That was my first show. It had one unfortunate consequence: I got typed as a lyric writer, which I didn't want. Obviously, the best thing about writing is to keep writing, and that applies to music as well as words; if you don't compose for a while, you tend to become rusty. However, that's the history.

Two Principles

It's hard to talk about lyrics independently of music, but I will try. Obviously, all the principles of writing apply to lyrics: grace, affinity for words, a feeling for the weight of words, resonances, tone, all of that. But there are two basic differences between lyric writing and all other forms, and they dictate what you have to do as a lyric writer. They are not even rules, they are just principles. First, lyrics exist in time—as opposed to poetry, for example. You can read a poem at your own speed. I find most poetry very difficult, and there are a few poets I like very much. Wallace Stevens is one, but it takes me a good 20 minutes to get through a medium-length Wallace Stevens poem, and even then I don't understand a lot of it, yet I enjoy it and can read it at my own speed. That's the point. On the stage, the lyrics come at you and you hear them once. If there's a reprise you hear them twice, if there are two reprises you hear them three times, but that's all. Quite often you've had the experience, or you've heard friends say, "Gee, I didn't get the lyric until I heard the record." Well that's the problem, you only get it once. The music is a relentless engine and keeps the lyrics going.

This leads to the second principle. Lyrics go with music, and music is very rich, in my opinion the richest form of art. It's also abstract and does very strange things to your emotions. So not only do you have that going, but you also have lights, costumes, scenery, characters, performers. There's a great deal to hear and get. Lyrics therefore have to be underwritten. They have to be very simple in essence. That doesn't mean you can't do convoluted lyrics, but essentially the thought is what counts and you have to stretch the thought out enough so that the listener has a fair chance to get it. Many lyrics suffer from being much too packed.

I'll give you some samples of my own later, but my favorite example is "Oh, what a beautiful mornin'/Oh, what a beautiful day*." I would be ashamed to put it down on paper, it would look silly. What Hammerstein knew was that set to music it was going to have an enormous richness. It did, it's a *beautiful* lyric—but not on paper.

*Copyright © 1943 by Williamson Music, Inc., New York, N.Y. Copyright renewed. Used by permission. All rights reserved.

I have a book of Hammerstein's lyrics and one of Cole Porter's. Hammerstein's you fall asleep reading, while Porter's is an absolute delight, like reading light verse. "Oh, what a beautiful mornin' " is not anywhere near as much fun to read as to hear. An imitation Hammerstein lyric that I did is "Maria" in *West Side Story*, a lyric I am not terribly fond of except for one good line: "Maria, I've just kissed a girl named Maria*." I remember when I wrote that I thought, "I can't do anything that bland and banal but I'll fix it later." Of course when it went with the music it just soared, it was perfect. The fancier part of the lyric "Say it loud and there's music playing/Say it soft. . ." etc., etc. (I'm too embarrassed to quote it) is a very fruity lyric, too much, overripe.

Serious poets make very bad lyric writers. Auden, for example; his lyrics for *The Rake's Progress* read brilliantly, they are sharp and witty but so packed and so full of reverberations and resonances that they are impossible to get, they are wearing, they are exhausting. It's an opera that should be read—or, as with most operas, you can hear it without having to hear the words anyway because of the singers—but the point is that the lyrics are too packed.

I've always thought of lyric writing as a craft rather than an art. It's so small. There are how many words in an average lyric? I'm tending to write long songs these days, but the average lyric has maybe 60 to 80 words, so each word counts for a great deal. Now, any novelist or short story writer takes as much pains as he can over each individual word, but they are not as important as in a lyric, not even as important to a playwright because each lyric line is practically a scene in itself. If there are 12 lines in a song, this is like 12 scenes in a play, and if one word is off it's like an entire section of the scene.

The opening line of *Porgy and Bess* by DuBose Heyward, who wrote all the lyrics for the first act, is "Summertime and the livin' is easy**"—and that "and" is worth a great deal of attention. I would write "Summertime when" but that "and" sets up a tone, a whole poetic tone, not to mention a whole kind of diction that is going to be used in the play; an informal, uneducated diction and a stream of consciousness, as in many of the songs like "My Man's Gone Now." It's the exact right word and that word is worth its weight in gold. "Summertime *when* the livin' is easy" is a boring line compared to "Summertime *and*." The choices of "ands" and "buts" become almost traumatic as you are writing a lyric—or should, anyway—because each one weighs so much.

Oscar Hammerstein once told me how astonished he was to learn that the sculptor of the Statue of Liberty had carved the top of the head as carefully as

*Copyright © 1957 by Leonard Bernstein and Stephen Sondheim. Reprinted by permission.
**Copyright © 1935 by Gershwin Publishing Corp. Copyright renewed. Used by permission of Chappel & Co., Inc.

the rest of the statue, even though he couldn't possible have known that one day there would be airplanes. That's what you have to do in a lyric, too —every word counts, whether the audience hears it specifically or not. In "Everything's Coming Up Roses" there was very little to say in the lyric after the title was over, so I decided that I would give it its feeling by restricting myself to images of traveling, children and show business, because the scene was in a railroad station and was about a mother pushing her child into show business. Now that may be of no interest except to somebody doing a doctorate in 200 years on the use of traveling images in *Gypsy*. But the point is, it's there, and it informs the whole song.

On one level, I suppose, lyric writing is an elegant form of puzzle, and I am a great puzzle fan. There's a great deal of joy for me in the sweat involved in the working out of lyrics, but it can lead to bloodlessness, and I've often been capable of writing bloodless lyrics (there are a number of them in *West Side Story*).

Anyway, all the principles extend from this one, which is lyrics existing in time. They also help shape the music, just as the music shapes them. The rigidity of lyric writing is like sonnets, and onstage this rigidity makes creating characters difficult, because characters, if they are to be alive, don't tend to talk in well-rounded phrases. But on the other hand, the power that is packed into the rigid form can give it enormous punch and make the characters splat out at you. An example from my own work is "The Ladies Who Lunch" in *Company* which is so packed that it gives out a ferocity, mainly because I chose a fairly rigid form, full of inner rhymes and with the lines in the music almost square—not that it's sung square, I mean the lines are very formed.

Three Influences: Hammerstein, Shevelove, Laurents

I would like to talk next about influences. Oscar I have told you about. The main thing he taught me was that it's content that counts. It's what you say rather than how you say it, and clarity of thought, making the thought clear to the listener (that has to do with the lyrics existing in time again). Oscar also said, "Say what you feel, not what other song writers feel." When I started out writing love songs I would write about stars and trees and dreams and moonlight, the usual song writer's vocabulary. That's fine if you believe it, but I didn't. Oscar also stressed the opening of a show: "The first lyric the audience hears, the first song, is what really makes or breaks a show. If you start with the right opening, you can ride for 45 minutes on the telephone book. On the other hand, if you start off with a wrong one it's an uphill fight all the way."

I would like to tell you about an opening problem that cost Hal Prince, Bobby Griffith and their backers $100,000. *A Funny Thing Happened on the Way to the Forum* with a *brilliant* book by Burt Shevelove and Larry Gelbart was maybe the funniest musical ever written and certainly the best farce. I prefer it to Feydeau. But we opened out of town and it was a disaster, the critics hated it. It was baffling, because usually when you have a show in trouble you can sense what's wrong and why it's not working when you stand in the back. In this case we were totally baffled. Even George Abbott, who had been connected with more farces than anybody, said, "I don't know what to do. I like it. They don't like it. I don't know what to do, you've got to call in George Abbott."

Well, of course the trouble was up front. The opening song, "Love Is in the Air," was a perfectly charming song which preceded a not-charming evening. The evening was low comedy, a celebration of 2,000 years of burlesque comedy, of farce situational comedy. What you were led to believe at the beginning was that it would have, I don't know, all the grittiness of *The Fantasticks*. The song was so delicate and charming. About a month before rehearsals began, Burt, Larry and I smelled trouble coming, so we decided on another song which told the audience essentially what the evening was about. George Abbott didn't like the second one, however, so we stuck with the first one, which was originally sung by Davey Burns, then by Zero Mostel.

Finally when we got to Washington we called in Jerome Robbins whose first comment was: "Everything's fine, *please* change the opening number. You've got to tell the audience what the evening is about." That's what led to "Comedy Tonight." I can remember a matinee in Washington when we played to 50 people—that's how disastrous the show was. We put the new opening in the first New York preview, and it was cheers and laughter throughout the entire evening at the same lines the audiences had received in silence four days earlier in Washington. That's the difference an opening can make—of course, it's also an advantage to have one staged by Jerry Robbins—but at least this one told the audience what the show was going to be about.

Here are two opening songs tried in *Forum*. This first was sung by Prologus (who is an actor, not a character in the play) and the Proteans, and it developed into sort of a soft shoe.

Love is in the air
Quite clearly.
People everywhere
Act queerly.
Some are hasty, some are halting,
Some are simply somersaulting,
Love is going around.
Anyone exposed
Can catch it.

Keep your window closed
And latch it.
Leave your house and lose your reason,
This is the contagious season:
Love is going around.
It's spreading each minute
Through the whole vicinity,
Step out and you're in it:
With all the fun involved,
Who can stay uninvolved?
Love is in the air
This morning,
Bachelors beware,
Fair warning:
If you start to feel a tingle
And you like remaining single,
Stay home, don't take a breath,
You could catch your death
'Cause love is around.

Copyright © 1962 by Stephen Sondheim. Burthen Music Company Inc.,
owner of publication and allied rights for the world.
Used by permission of Chappell & Co., Inc.

As you can see, that was fine but it did not prepare you for Davey Burns coming on and doing the kind of things he did. The following song is what I wanted to replace it with. I had written it a month before rehearsals began, but George didn't like it. It involved the whole cast, the whole company of actors coming out bearing braziers, led by Prologus (Zero Mostel) as they offered an invocation to the gods. In the middle it gets into a canon, a sort of round, but anyway here they are coming at you with their braziers.

Gods of the theater, smile on us,
You who sit up there stern in judgment, smile on us.
You who look down on actors (and who doesn't?),
Bless our little company and smile on us.
Think not about deep concerns.
Think not about dark dilemmas.
We offer you rites and revels,
Smile on us for a while.

And then they all faced front towards the audience:

Gods of the theater, smile on us.
You who sit out there stern in judgment, smile on us.
Think not about deep concerns,
Think not about dark dilemmas.

We offer you rites and revels,
Bless our play and smile.

Forget war, forget woe,
Forget matters weighty and great,
Allow matters weighty to wait
For a while.
For this moment, this brief time,
Frown on reason, smile on rhyme.
Forget pomp, forget show,
Forget laurels, helmets and crowns,
Receive lovers, liars and clowns
For a while.
For this brief moment, this brief span,
Celebrate the state of man.
Forget war, forget woe,
Forget greed and vengeance and sin
And let mime and mockery in
For a while.
Gods of the theater, smile on us.
Gods of the theater, bless our efforts, smile on us.

This part of the song is the canon:

We offer you song and dance,
We offer you rites and revels,
Grace and beauty,
Joy and laughter,
Sly disguises,
Wild confusions,
Happy endings.
If we please you,
Bless our play,
Smile our way,
Smile this moment, then at length
Go, and with a new-found strength
Resume war, resume woe,
Resume matters weighty and great,
Resume man's impossible state,
But now smile.
For this moment,
This brief stay,
Bless these players,
Bless this play!

Copyright © 1971 by Stephen Sondheim.

The next major influence in my lyric-writing life was Burt Shevelove. He's a man who has written lyrics; he doesn't write them any more, which is a great loss. He was once a sort of white-haired boy on Broadway because he wrote some of the sketches and lyrics and directed a show called *Small Wonder*, which was a *succes d'estime*. He then spent two years of his life writing a show called *A Month of Sundays* based on a play called *Excursion*, and it flopped. For a number of years he wrote industrial shows and worked in television. After *West Side Story* I approached Burt and asked him if he felt ready to write another musical, and he had this idea for a Roman comedy, something he had always wanted to do and in fact had fiddled around with while he was at Yale. I got to be good friends with Burt. We've talked ever since, endlessly, and one of the things he taught me was that clarity of language was important as well as clarity of thought. He believes that the best art always seems effortless—maybe not true of something like *Guernica*, but true of lyric writing, I think. Burt advised me, "Never sacrifice smoothness for cleverness. Better dull than clumsy." I agree. An awful lot of lyrics suffer from the lyric writer having a really clever, sharp idea which he can't quite fit into the music, so it sits there clumsily and the actor is stuck with singing it. The net result always is that it doesn't land with the audience. It has to be smooth if you are going to make the point.

Burt writes conversational lyrics. Here's one from *Month of Sundays*, one that I admire very much. It has a very simple tune sung by a girl in a story about a group of New Yorkers who go on an excursion on a ferry and the ferryboat captain decides to take off to the South Seas. Instead of going up to the Bronx, the passengers end up on an island in the South Seas. One of them is a New York secretary, and she meets a guy on board the ship, and they fall in love. She sings a lyric that goes as follows:

> I'm in trouble, Lord above,
> I'm in trouble, I'm in love.
> Is the problem ever solved?
> I'm in trouble, I'm involved.
> Who can fight it, who can win,
> Who can say what should have been?
> But this kind of trouble,
> If there must be trouble,
> Is the nicest trouble to be in.

Copyright © 1951 by Burt Shevelove.

Now, that's a simple and terrific lyric. The use of the word "involved" is what lyric writing is all about.

The third major influence on my lyrics is Arthur Laurents. We have done four shows together—*West Side Story, Gypsy, Anyone Can Whistle* and *Do I Hear a Waltz?*—and I hope we will do more. Arthur taught me mostly playwriting principles about lyrics, much deeper and subtler than Oscar because Arthur writes deeper and subtler plays than Oscar. The major thing I got from Arthur was the notion of sub-text. Now, this is a word that I had heard tossed around by Actors Studio types for a long time and really rather sneered at; but what it means simply is, give the actor something to act. I think this is a real secret; if I had to sell secrets about lyric writing I would sell this secret about sub-text. Watch how even some Broadway lyrics that you admire just sit there, with nothing for the actor to play. They just play the next logical step. A playwright when he writes a scene always gives some sub-text, or it's a very shallow scene. Well, that happens with lyrics. They may be very good, but if they're just on the surface, if there's no pull, there's a kind of deadness on the stage.

This concerns dramatic lyric writing, of course, I'm not talking about the Cole Porter kind of lyric writing which I'll get to later. I'm talking about the texture of a play where you are really dealing with character. There's a song in *Follies* called "The Road You Didn't Take" which on the surface is a man saying, "Oh, I never look back on the past, I mean, my goodness, it just wouldn't be worth it." He's doing it to con himself as well as the lady he is with; in point of fact, he is ripped to shreds internally. Now, the actor has the ripped-to-shreds that he can play. There's also a stabbing dissonance in the music, a note in the music that tells you, the audience, that something is not quite Kosher about what this guy is saying. But more important, it gives the actor something to play.

Follies contains a lesson in sub-text, a song called "In Buddy's Eyes." It's a woman's lie to her former lover in which she says that everything is just wonderful and she's having a terrific time at home, she's so happily married. Nothing in the lyric, nothing, not a single word tells you that maybe it isn't true. Nothing in the music tells you, although there's something in the orchestration. The actress has to tell you, and if you watch her deliver that song with intense anger because she feels she has been had, because she was jilted by Ben (the former lover) 30 years before, the whole song takes on a very peculiar quality. It isn't quite what it seems to be, and yet there's nothing in the lyric or music that tells you this. Incidentally, Jonathan Tunick, the orchestrator, also understands something about sub-text because every phrase in that song which refers to Buddy, her husband, is dry, it's all woodwinds. Whenever she refers to herself it's all strings again. Not one person in a thousand would get this, but like the top of the Statue of Liberty's head it's there and it helps in forming the song.

There's a song in *Gypsy* called "Some People" that Arthur Laurents had given me the idea for. I was afraid it was going to be just a list song about a woman's anger—about how some people settle for this and some for that but as for me, I've got to get out of here—and it seemed to me to just be on the surface. What Arthur had wanted her to play, which I hadn't realized, is that she wants a plaque that's hanging on the wall behind her father's head. It is worth $88, which is what she needs. She is using the entire song as an excuse for borrowing money from him, and when he doesn't fall for the song she goes and takes the plaque. Here again, the sub-text gives the actress something to play. She can play the money and the plaque.

Arthur is the collaborator with whom I've worked the closest. He's taught me a great deal about matching diction with ideas and continuity of content. He also is terrific on titles as any good book writer-collaborator had better be if he works with me, because I steal from them all the time. "I Feel Pretty" is a title of Arthur's and "Some People" and "Something's Coming." Anyway, Oscar, Burt and Arthur have been my three major influences.

The Genesis of Songs

I go about starting a song first with the collaborators, sometimes just with the book writer, sometimes with the director. We have long discussions and I take notes, just general notes, and then we decide what the song should be about, and I try to make a title. If I am writing the music as well as the lyric I sometimes try to get a vamp first, a musical atmosphere, an accompaniment, a pulse, a melodic idea, but usually the tone comes from the accompaniment figure, and I find that the more specific the task, the easier. If somebody says write a song about a lady in a red dress crying at the end of a bar, that's a lot easier than somebody saying write a song about a fellow who's sorry. I would like to quote Oscar on this subject, in a marvelous introduction to a book of his called *Lyrics*: "There is in all art a fine balance between the benefits of confinement and the benefits of freedom. An artist who is too fond of freedom is likely to be obscure in his expression." So what you want is something specific, but not too specific.

Then I usually make a list of useful rhymes related to the song's topic, sometimes useful phrases, a list of ideas that pop into my head. Then I try to make a prose statement to the point, so that it won't get lost. James Goldman once said in a lecture at the New Dramatists that when he goes out of town he posts a piece of paper on his dresser or bathroom mirror so he can see it every morning. It says "What is the play about?" so that in all the terrible rewriting, where you suddenly have to write for the actress to make a costume change, you don't lose the point. I find it useful to write at the top of the page a couple of sentences of what the song is to be about, no matter how flimsy.

To illustrate another thing I do, I remember I played "Maria" for Jerome Robbins, and he liked the song fine but got very angry about the pauses. He said, " 'Maria, I've just met a girl named Maria, and suddenly that name will never be the same to me*,' and then there's this bar-and-a-half pause. What am I supposed to do there?" I said, "Well, I mean, he's just standing there on

*Copyright © 1957 bu Leonard Bernstein and Stephen Sondheim. Reprinted by permission.

the stage." Jerry said, "But how am I supposed to direct him?" I said, "Well, can't he just stand there?" Jerry said, "You've got to give me something for him to do, or do you want to stage it?" Choreographers and many directors don't like pauses, but he had a point there that's very important. You should stage your numbers when you are writing them. Never just write a love song and give it to the director and the choreographer, expecting them to invent. That's not their job. That's their job *after* you've invented. When you've invented the staging they can do anything they want with it, completely change it, but they have to have at least a blueprint, some idea of the theatrical use of the song. "Company" I staged in my own head all the way through to the second chorus including the use of the long word "love,"

which was to get the cast off the elevators and down to the main level. I wanted that to be the first time the elevators moved, but we couldn't work that out specifically. But I knew where Bobby was standing, I knew in *my* head where all the people were. This had nothing to do with what Michael Bennett eventually did with it, except that he was delighted to receive a general blueprint which helped him over certain hurdles. He was able to invent freely because he never felt he would be hung the next day in rehearsal by having to wonder what to do about a blank space. For example, "Who's That Woman?" in *Follies* was a number designed for a lady named Stella Deems who hasn't performed the number in 30 years. The six girls who used to perform the number with her are all 30 years older except for one who is dead. The number was to be for Stella Deems and five girls with a hole in the line. I thought that would be macabre and touching. The number ended with a challenge dance between the two leading ladies who were at the ends of the line—I had the whole thing worked out carefully in my head, including tap dance sections. Michael came along and threw the whole thing out and changed it entirely.

In the genesis of a song, another important principle that I've always believed in is: content dictates form. There's a song in *Company* called "Getting Married Today." In content, it is about this hysterical girl who doesn't want to get married except that she's forced to in her own head, so it suggested the counterpoint and the contrast between a serene choir and a hysterical lady, between the slow and the fast and the serene and the hysterical.

Looking back at the first page of notes I ever made about *Company*, I see that we sat around and talked about how to turn these one-act plays into a musical. We talked about the central character, and Hal Prince said it would be nice to have a number called "Company." Well, "company" is a word you can't rhyme—except Lorenz Hart rhymed it with "bump a knee," which is not my kind of rhyme—so it would be a little hard to do it as a title refrain. Then Hal said, "And also I would like it to introduce the various styles of the show, the way we are going to cut back and forth; also I would like it to introduce the main character and include all the other characters; also I would like it to use the set . . ." So I replied in my usual grudging way, "Well I am not sure if I can, well, let me see if I can do it and maybe I can write the score, I don't know."

I have my sketch sheets here. Let me read you some of the notes I put down:"Everybody loves Robert (Bob, Bobby) . . ." the idea of nicknames had already occurred to me. Then I had Robert say, "I've got the best friends in the world," and then the line occurred to me, "You I love and you I love and you I love," and then, talking about marriage, "A country I've never been to," and "Who wants vine-covered cottages, marriage is for children." It's all Bob's attitude: "Companion for life, who wants that?" And then he says, "I've got company, love is company, three is company, friends are company," and I started a list of what's company. Then I started to expand the lines: "Love is what you need is company. What I've got as friends is company. Good friends, weird friends, married friends, days go, years go, full of company." I started to spin free associations, and I got to "Phones ring, bells buzz, door clicks, company, call back, get a bite," and the whole notion of short phrases, staccato phrases, occurred to me. By the time I got through just listing general thoughts, I had a smell of the rhythm of the vocal line, so that when I was able to turn to the next page and start expanding it I got into whole lists of things: "No ties, small lies. So much, too much. Easy, comfy, hearts pour, the nets descend, private jokes," all short phrases—but what came out of it eventually was the form of that song, which worked out better than I had expected.

Clarity and Synthesis

How the lyrics work with the music affects their clarity of expression. When a phrase of music comes to an end the lyric should come to an end, otherwise it sets up a conflict in the listerner's ear. The lyric should match the music with a comma, a semicolon, a period or just the completion of a phrase. Here's a song I wrote for *Saturday Night* that violates it (it's also a song I like). It's called "So Many People" and it was the ballad in the first act between the young girl and the young man, with the verse sung by the girl. This girl has always been ambitious, she's always wanted to be rich, and she thinks this guy is rich or had thought he was and just found out to her horror that he isn't but she is in love with him anyway.

> I said the man for me
> Must have a castle.
> A man of means he'd be,
> A man of fame.
> And then I met a man who hadn't any,
> Without a penny
> To his name.
> I had to go and fall
> For so much less than
> What I had planned from all
> The magazines . . .

There's the violation, in those last few lines.

> . . . I should be good and sore,
> What am I happy for?
> I guess the man means more than the means
>
> Copyright © 1973 by Stephen Sondheim. Used by permission of Chappell & Co., Inc.

When you come to that "so much less than . . ." and think it must be the end of a sentence, well, that's what I mean about periodicity. I remember that the tune of "One Hand, One Heart" (Bernstein had originally written that tune for *Candide*) had only a dotted half-note to each bar, just that steady motion. I realized I couldn't set any two-syllable words to the song, it had to be all one-syllable words. I was stifled, and down in Washington after my endless pleas Lenny put in two little quarter notes so that I could put in "make of my" and "make of our" as in "Make of our . . . hearts . . . one . . . heart*," not a great deal but at least a little better.

Words have to sit on music in order to become clear to the audience. I am talking about clarity, remember, and clarity has to do with that thing I talked about, time. You don't get a chance to hear the lyric twice or to read it, and if the lyric doesn't sit and bounce when the music bounces and rise when the music rises, it isn't just a question of mis-accents, which are bad enough, but if it is too crowded and doesn't rise and fall with the music, the audience becomes confused. There's a song in *West Side Story* called "America" and thank God it's a spectacular dance because it wouldn't get a hand otherwise. It has 27 words to the square inch. I had this "wonderful" quatrain that went "I like to be in America/O.K. by me in America/Everything free in America/For a small fee in America*." The "For a small fee" was my little zinger— except that the "for" is accented and the "sm" is impossible to say that fast, so it went "For a smafee in America." Nobody knew what it meant, and I learned my lesson: you have to consider an actor's tongue and teeth. I have gotten better at it. Towards the end of rehearsals of *Company* I wrote "Getting Married Today" which has a lot of words in it. It was fast because, as I said, the character is a hysteric. The lyric was written quite carefully; I did the second draft in Boston (and it really needs a third draft, but we had other problems and because I was late in writing the score, as I always am, I never got a chance to polish it). By comparing the two drafts, I can show you a little bit about how you alternate vowels and consonants. The song is to be sung in one breath, though Beth Howland didn't do it all in one breath on the stage. In the recording, where the microphone was right up close and she wasn't anxious about projecting, she did it all in one breath with no problem. The character is a bride treating the audience like the guests at her wedding in church:

*Copyright © 1957 by Leonard Bernstein and Stephen Sondheim. Reprinted by permission.

First Draft

Wait a sec, is everybody
Here? Because if everybody's
Here, I want to thank you all for
Coming. I'd appreciate your
Going even more. I mean, you
See, we aren't coming to the
Wedding, me and Paul.
                                    Remember
Paul? You know, the man
                            I'm gonna
Marry, but I'm not because I
Wouldn't ruin anyone as
Wonderful as he is, but I
Haven't even told him, so I
Thank you all for the gifts
                    and the flowers,
Thank you all, now it's back
                    to the showers.
Don't tell Paul, but I'm not
            getting married today!

Revised Version

Pardon me, is everybody
There? Because if everybody's
There, I want to thank you all for
Coming to the wedding. I'd ap-
Preciate your going even
More. I mean, you must have
                            lots of
Better things to do, and not a
Word of it to Paul. Remember
Paul? You know, the man
                            I'm gonna
Marry, but I'm not because I
Wouldn't ruin anyone as
Wonderful as he is, but I
Thank you all for the gifts
                    and the flowers,
Thank you all, now it's back
                    to the showers.
Don't tell Paul, but I'm not
            getting married today!

Copyright ©1970 by Valando Music, Inc. and Beautiful Music, Inc.
All rights administered by Music of the Times Publishing Corp., New York, N.Y.
Used by permission.

The second version is much easier to sing. Just the effort in forming the
"w" in "wait," the first word of the first draft, does something to the jaw;
right away a little effort is wasted, and she is just that much weaker for the
rest of the song. I decided to start with something easier, the "p" in
"pardon." You don't sing "Pardon" with a strong "P," you just do "pardon" with a soft "p" and save some strength, some of the strain on the jaw
muscles. All the changes from the first to the second draft are essentially
about that. I had a second verse to this song that had some nice jokes in it,
but I could never solve it in terms of the viability of the words. Hal always
liked it, but it bothered me because poor Beth was stuck there every night
with her lips over her teeth and everything getting all tangled. It went
like this:

Isn't this a tacky little
Chapel? I apologize, we
Thought of Presbyterian, but
Paul, you know, is Jewish and my
Mother is a Catholic, so
Synagogues were out, which is ir-

Relevant since anyway the
Whole thing is ridiculous, con-
Sidering we've lived together
Nearly seven years, and very
Happily, so what's the point of
Marrying and spoiling it? . . .

Copyright © 1970 Valando Music Inc. and Beautiful Music, Inc.
All rights administered by Music of the Times Publishing Corp., New York, N.Y.
Used by permission.

And so forth. Anyway, it's your job as a lyric writer for the theater to consider the singer's problems, to be careful of consonants. Some very odd things happen when you string words together with music, because actors can't play with rhythm an awful lot. For example, the first time I heard "I Could Write a Book" the last line sounded to me like "How to make two lovers a friend" because of the two "f's in "How to make two lovers of friends*." The way to sing it is to take space between the two "f's, but that kills the melodic line.

I went out of town to see *Carousel* when I was 15. I was thrilled by it, and then I heard something that shocked me. A character named Nettie came out to sing "June Is Bustin' Out All Over" just after Julie Jordan had discovered she was pregnant. Nettie was played by Christine Johnson, a lady with a good deal of operatic training, and many opera singers never say the word "is". They use it as an "e" sound. And so I suddenly heard "Julie's bustin' out all over." I thought, "In a Rodgers and Hammerstein show?"

If audiences would concentrate more on lyrics, a lyric writer's job would be easier—but we live in an era of miked theaters. You ought to hear Hal Prince on the subject. Nobody listens in the theater any more, and it's because everybody is so used to miked sound that they don't have to concentrate. Since they don't have to concentrate they not only talk among themselves but they are not into the play. Hal says that one of the reasons he is so involved with the theater is that when he was young he used to get tickets for a dollar or two at the top of the second balcony in a Broadway theater. He would lean forward, and it would take him about five minutes to adjust his ear to what the actors on the stage were saying. Always at the end of about five minutes the entire audience could hear everything. Remember, it's not that Ethel Merman had this great clarion voice that allowed her to do all those musicals without mikes, it's that people were used to listening. Microphones are a relatively recent invention, and we are stuck with them.

Favorite Lyric Writers

Picking a favorite lyricist is a tricky if not impossible business. When the *Dramatists Guild Quarterly* asked me to name my favorite lyric writer, I made

*Copyright © 1940 by Chappell & Co. Inc. Copyright renewed. Used by permission.

this comment: "There are too many good ones and no perfect ones. Therefore let me list some preferences, rather than favorites. Among present lyricists I especially like Frank Loesser. Any man who has the nerve to set the line 'Some irresponsible dress manufacturer*, the way he did in *How to Succeed* deserves an award." He never was afraid of setting anything, no matter how peculiar it was, and it always came out funny. My favorite groups of lyrics are those from Hammerstein's *Carousel,* Loesser's *Guys and Dolls,* E.Y. Harburg's *Finian's Rainbow* and Cole Porter's *Kiss Me Kate.* These pretty well determine my favorites, although I would like to add to them Dorothy Fields. Among the younger lyricists I especially like Sheldon Harnick and Carolyn Leigh.

I'll tell you a little bit about what I like about them. The best thing about Porter, the most astonishing thing to me is not his facility with words —facility with words is fairly common. He *believed* what he wrote, that's what kills me. Oscar did too. Oscar was able to write about dreams and trees and grass and stars because he *believed* in them, and what Porter believed in was gossamer wings. No man on earth can write "gossamer wings" except Cole Porter, and nobody has been able to imitate Porter successfully because they don't believe what he believed.

Frank Loesser's ideas are what kill me about him. "Fugue for Tinhorns" is a sensational idea for a song . . . it was also written out of town, which is even better (you get a lot of good ideas out of town). Where Loesser wasn't very good was when he was imitating Oscar Hammerstein as in *The Most Happy Fella.* He's got a pair of lines in there that I just wouldn't believe he would ever write: "Warm all over, warm all over/Gone are all the clouds that used to swarm all over**"—real imitation Hammerstein, and it doesn't work. What I like best about Dorothy Fields is her use of colloquialism and her effortlessness, as in "Sunny Side of the Street," which is just perfect as a lyric. Hammerstein—clarity; the terribly simple statement of a song like "What's the Use of Wond'rin'?" It's a song he couldn't end, as he often complained, but it goes:

> What's the use of wond'rin'
> If he's good or if he's bad
> Or if you like the way he wears his hat?
> Oh, what's the use of wond'rin'
> If he's good or if he's bad?
> He's your feller and you love him—
> That's all there is to that.

Copyright © 1945 by Williamson Music Inc. Copyright renewed.
Used by permission of T.B. Harms Company—sole selling agent.

*"Paris Original" by Frank Loesser copyright © 1961, 1962 Frank Music Corp. Used by permission.
**"Warm All Over" by Frank Loesser copyright © 1956 Frank Music Corp. Used by permission.

"Yip" Harburg is a master of whimsy, and I suppose "When I'm Not Near the Girl I Love" is one of the five or ten best lyrics ever written. What's most extraordinary about it, you listen to the first eight lines astonished at the clever ins and outs of the idea, and then every successive verse has one twist you don't expect, on and on, endlessly inventive until, exhausted, he stops. He is also a master of the arch rhyme. There's a couplet in "The Wizard of Oz" that nobody else could get away with, when the Cowardly Lion in "If I only Had a Heart" sings: "I would demonstrate my prowess/Be a man and not a mow-ess.*"

Sheldon Harnick I admire for grace and charm and perfection of setting. He is an impeccable lyric writer. I wrote a private joke into *Follies* for him, but it got cut during rehearsals. He wrote a show called *The Body Beautiful*, and I was very impressed with the lyrics, particularly with one rhyme of "feminine" with "lemon in (my tea)". In colloquial speech that's O.K., but that "i" in "feminine" is just that much off the "o" in "lemon," and I decided some day I would improve on it. The original version of the song "Beautiful Girls" that introduces the ladies as they come down the stairs in *Follies* went like this:

Painters have tried with all of their skill
To catch the grace
Of the feminine
Form and face.
Poets have tried, but try as they will,
They waste their time
Painting them in in-
Ternal rhyme.

Copyright © 1971 Valando Music, Inc. Beautiful Music, Inc. and Burthen Music Company, Inc. All rights administered by Music of the Times Publishing Corp., New York, N.Y. Used by permission.

I guess my favorite set of lyrics ever is DuBose Heyward's for *Porgy and Bess*. He wrote all the ones in Act I including "Summertime" and "My Man's Gone Now" and about half the others. Some lyrics he wrote in collaboration with Ira Gershwin, some Gershwin wrote himself and some Heyward wrote himself in the last two acts. It's a tiny body of work, a dozen songs, but every one is perfect, not a single improvement to make. I can hardly believe how brilliant these lyrics are, how they accomplish exactly what they set out to do, how emotional they are.

And as I also said in the *Quarterly*, my favorite single lyric line is "Yip"

*Copyright © 1938, renewed 1966, by Metro-Goldwyn-Mayer Inc. Rights throughout the world controlled by Leo Feist Inc. Used by permission.

Harburg's from *The Eagle and Me*: "Ever since the day when the world was an onion*." I don't know how an idea like that ever occurs to somebody, it's too good.

Last Lines

I find it useful to write backwards, and I think most lyric writers probably do too when they have a climax, a twist, a punch, a joke. You start at the bottom of the page, you preserve your best joke to the last, the ideas should be placed in ascending order of punch. And another thing, the last word ought to be singable. It always bothered Oscar that the last line of "What's the Use of Wond'rin'?" is "And all the rest is talk,**" and he always claimed that the number never became as popular as it should have because "talk" is not a word that is graceful for a singer to hold. The "k" cuts it off, closes the sound. It's best to end with an "ow" or "ah," open sounds that the singer can go with. Two of the most useful words in the language are "me" and "be," but unfortunately they have pinched sounds.

I tried desperately to fix the end of "The Road You Didn't Take" in *Follies*. The line I wanted to use was "The Ben I'll never be, who remembers him?***" but "him" is a terrible sound for a singer to hold and expect to get any kind of applause. I think "talk" is O.K. for "What's the Use of Wond'rin'?" and "him" is O.K. for my song, but it's best to have a more singable word. Of course, I love twists, I love punchy last lines. One of my favorites is the end of a Rodgers and Hart song called "He Was Too Good to Me." It starts out "He was too good to me/How can I get along now?/So close he stood to me/Ev'rything seems all wrong now.****" It goes on and on, seeming to be a blues, but the last line is "He was too good to be true." I also like a lyric of mine, the end of "Little Lamb" in which she sings, "I wonder how old I am*****." Another I like was cut out of *Forum* in New Haven, "The Echo Song," (which we put back in the show in the 1972 revival). It uses using a specific technique that isn't often taken advantage of on the stage. Philia is asking her gods whether she should go off with Hero, or keep her promise to marry someone else. She believes she is hearing the genuine reply of the gods

*Copyright © 1944 by The Players Music Corporation. Copyright renewed, assigned to Chappell & Co., Inc. Used by permission.
**Copyright © 1945 Williamson Music, Inc. Copyright renewed. Used by permission of T.B. Harms Co.—sole selling agent.
***Copyright © 1971 by Valando Music, Inc., Beautiful Music, Inc. and Burthen Music Co., Inc. All rights administered by Music of the Times Publishing Corp., New York, N.Y. Used by permission.
****"He Was Too Good to Me" (Lorenz Hart) copyright © 1930 by Harms, Inc. Copyright renewed. All rights reserved. Used by permission of Warner Bros. Music.
*****Copyright © 1959 by Norbeth Productions, Inc. and Stephen Sondheim (Williamson Music, Inc. and Stratford Music Corp. owners of publication and allied rights for the world). Chappell & Co., Inc., agent. Used by permission.

only when it comes back in the form of an echo. Hero rigs it so that he himself, concealed, is providing the echoing answers (which appear below in parentheses) to Philia's questions as she sings:

> Tell me, (Tell me.)
> Dare I ask it? (Ask it.)
> Should I love him? (Love him.)
> Shall I leave with him? (Leave with him, leave with him.)
> Tell me, (Tell me.)
> Should I leave right now? (Right now.)
> I hear my heart say, "Let him live with me."
>   (Live with me, live with me.)
> Should I hear my heart and go? (Go! Go! Go!)
> Or should I, worthy, wait here
> Till I meet my fate here?
> Tell me, tell me, I must know. (No! No! No!)
> Tell me, (Tell me.)
> Should I hold him (Hold him.)
> Or forget him (Get him.)
> And forego my love? (Go, my love, go, my love!)
> Thank you, (Thank you.)
> I believe now! (Leave now!)
> I must hurry (Hurry!)
> So I'll say goodbye. (Say goodbye! Say goodbye!)
> Only one more question please, (Please, please, please!)
> Does he want me? (Does he!)
> Would he miss me? (Would he!)
> Must I pay the debt I owe? (Oh . . . oh . . . oh . . .)
> Or may I go with Hero,
> My beloved Hero,
> Tell me yes so I may know.
> (No—Ye—N—Yes!)

Copyright © 1971 by Stephen Sondheim. (Burthen Music Company, Inc. owner of publication and allied rights for the world.) Used by permission of Chappell & Co., Inc.

Another song with a last line I like is from *Anyone Can Whistle*, called "A Parade in Town." Angela Lansbury sang it as the mayoress of the town who had lost all her voters and they were carrying somebody else around on their shoulders. She sings the first chorus, the parade comes on and runs right over her. Then she sings this second chorus:

> I see flags, I hear bells,
> There's a parade in town.
> I see crowds, I hear yells,

There's a parade in town.
I hear drums in the air,
I see clowns in the square,
I see marchers marching,
Tossing hats at the sky. . . .

Did you hear? Did you see?
Was a parade in town?
Were there drums without me?
Was a parade in town?
'Cause I'm dressed at last, at my best,
And my banners are high.
Tell me, while I was getting ready,
Did a parade go by?

Copyright © 1964 by Stephen Sondheim (Burthen Music Co. owner of publication
and allied rights for the world). Used by permission of
Chappell & Co., Inc.

Rhyme

Many lyric writers don't understand the difference between rhymes and
identities. In a rhyme, the vowel sound is the same but the initial consonant
is different, as in "way" and "day." In identity, both the vowel and the
consonant that precedes the vowel sound are exactly alike, as in "consternation" and "procrastination." That is not a rhyme, it is an identity. It's not
that identities are outlawed, it's just that they don't prick the ear the way
rhymes do. They don't point up the words, so if you are going to use an
identity you have to use it carefully. They can be monochromatic but very
useful. Oscar not only liked to use identities, he liked to repeat words where
ordinarily you might rhyme, as in "Younger than springtime am I/Gayer
than laughter am I*," using the exact word as a little refrain. I did it in
"There's a place for us/Somewhere a place for us**" (every time I see that
phrase what comes to mind is that it goes "There's *a* place for us," the word
"a" is clearly the most important word in the line, it's one of the most
embarrassing lyric lines ever written).

You try to make your rhyming seem fresh but inevitable (I guess it's what
you try for in all kinds of writing), you try for surprise but not so wrenching
that the listener loses the sense of the line. Larry Hart is full of that kind of
wrenching, that's why I'm down on him. The hardest kind of word to rhyme
is "day" because it makes you concentrate on the content. "Day" is when I
use my rhyming dictionary, going down the list of all the "a" rhymes to find
something that will express the vague thought in my head; whereas if you

*Copyright © 1949 by Richard Rodgers and Oscar Hammerstein II. Williamson Music, Inc.,
New York, N.Y. owner of publication and allied rights for all countries of the Western
Hemisphere. Used by permission. All rights reserved.
**Copyright © 1957 by Leonard Bernstein and Stephen Sondheim. Reprinted by permission.

are going to rhyme a word like "orange" it restricts your thought about content greatly. In a way, it makes it easier for you. By the way, I was quoted in *Time* as saying that "orange or" and "porringer" rhyme. They don't, unless you happen to be in certain sections of the country, or unless the lyrics are very fast—but I would never rhyme "orange *or*" and "porring*er*," so I was a little embarrassed to see it. It's much more fun to try to rhyme words like "month," because then you have to invent a character who lisps words like "wonth" or "dunth" or you have to rhyme it as part of an inner scheme like *"unthinking."*

The function of a rhyme is to point up the word that rhymes—if you don't want that word to be the most important in the line, don't rhyme it. Also, rhyme helps shape the music, it helps the listener hear what the shape of the music is. Inner rhymes, which are fun to work out if you have a puzzle mind, have one essential function, which is to speed the line along. Examples are to be found in Cole Porter's "Where Is the Life That Late I Led?" Porter is a master on inner rhymes which make the line not only funnier but also speed it up, as "Where is Venetia who loved to chat so?/Could still she be drinking in her stinking pink palazzo?*" The inner rhyme speeds it, makes it funnier, gives it a shine. "And lovely Lisa, where are you, Lisa?/You gave a new meaning to the leaning tow'r of Pisa*"—the inner rhyme makes this a superb joke with the "leaning" and the "meaning." Inner rhyme can also be used for strength. "Our love was too hot *not* to cool down**"—the "not" makes that rock solid. I use it myself a lot in "The Ladies Who Lunch," where the inner rhymes are kind of hidden, to give the lines a tautness so the listener would feel what the lady is feeling. "Here's to the girls who play wife—/Aren't they too much?/Keeping house but clutching a copy of *Life*/Just to keep in touch***" The "clutch" is hidden, there's no musical pause there, no way of pointing it up, but it's there to help make the line tense, the way the character is. It's very bad, I think, to use rhymes when you bend the sense for them, which is my major objection to Lorenz Hart's lyrics.

Another function of rhyme is that it implies education. One of the most embarrassing moments of my life as a lyric writer was after a runthrough of *West Side Story* when some of my friends including Sheldon Harnick were out front. I asked Sheldon after the show, "What do you think?" knowing he was going to fall to his knees and lick the sidewalk. But he didn't, and I asked him to tell me what was wrong. "There's that lyric 'I Feel Pretty' " he said. Now, I thought "I Feel Pretty" was just terrific, I had spent the previous year of my life rhyming "day" and "way" and "me" and "be," and

---

*Copyright © 1949 by Cole Porter. Sole selling agent T. B. Harms Company. International copyright secured.

**Copyright © 1935 Harms, Inc. Copyright renewed. All rights reserved. Used by permission of Warner Bros. Music.

***Copyright © 1970 Valando Music, Inc. and Beautiful Music, Inc. All rights administered by Music of the Times Publishing Corp., New York, N.Y. Used by permission.

with "I Feel Pretty" I wanted to show that I could do inner rhymes too. So I had this uneducated Puerto Rican girl singing, "It's alarming how charming I feel.*" You know, she would not have been unwelcome in Noel Coward's living room. Sheldon was very gentle, but oh! did it hurt. I immediately went back to the drawing board and wrote a simplified version of the lyric which nobody connected with the show would accept; so there it is, embarrassing me every time it's sung, because it's full of mistakes like that. Well, when rhyme goes against character, out it should go, and rhyme always implies education and mind working, and the more rhymes the sharper the mind.

It's nice to find rhymes that have been lying around all the time with nobody using them. I think I found one in "Love Will See Us Through" in *Follies*, the rhyme of "soul-stirring" and "bolstering." I don't think anybody's used it, and when you find one like that you feel very proud.

When you have nothing to say, there are lots of techniques available and rhyme is one of them. I offer in evidence "Lover" by Lorenz Hart which starts out "Lover, when I'm near you/And I hear you/Speak my name/Softly in my ear you/Breathe a flame.**" Surely if that thought has any validity at all it can be stated better than that. My guess is that he had this amount of music to fill out, or a situation too simple for him to apply any kind of wit or feeling,

*Copyright © 1957 by Leonard Bernstein and Stephen Sondheim. Reprinted by permission.
**Copyright © 1932 & 1933 by Famous Music Corporation. Copyright renewed 1959 & 1960.

so it's all inner rhyme. As for alliteration, my counterpoint teacher had a phrase "the refuge of the destitute." That's my attitude toward alliteration. Any time you hear alliteration in a lyric, get suspicious. For example, when you hear "I Feel Pretty" and she sings "I feel fizzy and funny and fine*," somebody doesn't have something to say. On the other hand, I used a line very much like it in *Gypsy* in the song "Small World" where she sings "Small and funny and fine**." Well, here the alliteration is accidental, but it's O.K. because "funny" is the song's key word; it starts out "Funny, you're a stranger who's come here**." "Funny" works as the theme of the song, so "small and funny and fine" is quite different. But I would have been a fool if I had used an "f" word in place of "small," it would have killed the lyric with alliteration. Ideally, the third word shouldn't have an "f" in it either, it should be "Small and funny and nice," maybe, because the almost-alliteration hurts the line. Of course if you use alliteration subtly, it can be terrific. "It was just one of those fabulous flights***," says Porter. Those two "f's" are a lot more effective than "It was just one of those glorious flights," they give the line a little breath, a little shine. When you hear words like "just" and "I know" it's usually to fill out a line, unless really used as intensifiers. When Porter in "Let's Do It" writes "Electric eels, I might add, do it/Though it shocks them, I know****," you wonder what is that "I know" doing there? "Though it shocks them"—that's the end of the thought. "I know" is there because he gets to a perfect joke: "Why ask if shad do it?/Waiter bring me shad roe****." But I would like him to have worked a little harder because that "I know" doesn't lend anything to the song.

Humor

It's always better to be funny than clever, and a lot harder. Porter vs. Loesser for example: "Where Is the Life That Late I Led?" vs. "Adelaide's Lament." I'd like to sign my name to both songs, but if I were pushed to the wall to pick one or the other, I would rather have signed it to "Adelaide's Lament" because even though the jokes run out as the song goes on, it is truly very funny and there are very few times when you laugh out loud in the theater at a lyric joke. One laugh per score is a lot for me, anyway, and I think most of my shows have one laugh. In *West Side Story* there's the section in "Gee Officer Krupke" which uses a favorite technique of mine, parallel lines where you just make a list:

*Copyright © 1957 by Leonard Bernstein and Stephen Sondheim. Reprinted by permission.

**Copyright © 1959 by Norbeth Productions Inc. and Stephen Sondheim. (Williamson Music Inc. and Stratford Music Corp. owners of publication and allied rights for the world.) Chappell & Co., Inc., agent. Used by permission.

***Copyright © 1935 Harms, Inc. Copyright renewed. All rights reserved. Used by permission of Warner Bros. Music.

****Copyright © 1928 Harms, Inc. Copyright renewed. All rights reserved. Used by permission of Warner Bros. Music.

My father is a bastard,
My ma's an S.O.B.
My grandpa's always plastered,
My grandma pushes tea.
My sister wears a mustache,
My brother wears a dress.
Goodness gracious, that's why I'm a mess!

Copyright © 1957 by Leonard Bernstein and Stephen Sondheim.
Reprinted by permission.

That's not exceptionally funny on its own, but it brought down the house every night because the form helps make it funny. It was a genuine piece of humor because it depended not on cleverness but on the kids' attitudes, and that is what humor is about: character, not cleverness. There's one big laugh in *Gypsy* when Rose, who's trying to book her act, changes from fierce one second to smiling good nature the next when she finds out that the act is finally booked, and she sings, "Have an eggroll, Mr. Goldstone*." Incidentally, the trouble with that song is that once that line was stated and there was a big laugh it was all over, there was nothing else to say, and I had to fill out two or three minutes of plays on words. If you could stop that song after the first line it would have brought down the house.

The funniest line in *Forum* is "I am a parade," the only direct translation from Plautus in the whole show. In *Company*, the funniest lyric line isn't even rhymed, it is just shoved in there during the scene where Bobby is in bed with the stewardess. All the wives are singing "Poor Baby," knocking the girl he's in bed with, and Elaine Stritch comments, "She's tall enough to be your mother**." It doesn't rhyme, it's not rhythmically like anything else, but it is again a character observation and that's what makes it funny, it consistently gets a laugh.

The problem with the one-joke song is that as the song goes on and on the joke becomes less funny. Here's one that was cut from *Follies*, written as a throwaway for Carlotta, who was played by Yvonne De Carlo. It was supposed to be done by a lady standing at the piano with a drink in her hand. She's talking about a number she had in the Follies, a college number in which she was queen of the prom and looking for a partner, but they all disappointed her.

I know this grocery clerk,
Unprepossessing.
Some think the boy's a jerk,

*Copyright © 1959 by Norbeth Productions Inc. and Stephen Sondheim. (Williamson Music Inc. and Stratford Music Corp. owners of publication and allied rights for the world.) Chappell & Co., Inc., agent. Used by permission.
**Copyright © 1970 by Valando Music, Inc. and Beautiful Music, Inc. All rights administered by Music of the Times Publishing Corp., New York, N.Y. Used by permission.

They have my blessing.
But when he starts to move,
He aims to please,
Which only goes to prove
That sometimes in a clerk you find a Hercules.
He hasn't much that's plus,
You might describe him thus:

A false alarm,
A broken arm,
An imitation Hitler and with littler charm,
But oh, can that boy fox trot!
His mouth is mean,
He's not too clean.
What makes him look reptilian is the brilliantine,
But oh, can that boy fox trot!
Who knows what I saw in him?
I took a chance.
Oh yes, one more flaw in him:
He can't dance.
As dumbbells go,
He's rather slow,
And as for being saintly, even faintly, no,
But who needs Albert Schweitzer when the lights are low?
And oh boy, oh boy,
Can that boy fox trot!

Copyright © 1971 by Valando Music, Inc., Beautiful Music, Inc. and Burthen Music
Co., Inc. All rights administered by Music of the Times Publishing Corp.,
New York, N.Y. Used by permission.

The problem with the one-joke song is, the laugh meter drops about 50
points with each verse. I wasted some time trying to build the number into a
large piece by using a whole trick middle section. We opened with it in
Boston, and Yvonne did it very well; she has a very large register. The
number always started up slam bang and ended up with a nice hand, which
is why we replaced it with "I'm Still Here" out of town.

Writing Habits

I write lying down so I can go to sleep easily. That's true. I write about ten
minutes and sleep for two, on the average. I write on legal pads in very small
writing, partly for frugality—I used to write on both sides of the page, and
Leonard Bernstein got annoyed because he would be constantly trying to
find lyrics and turning the pages over and over, so I don't do that any more. I
find it very useful to use a separate pad for each section of the song.

I do lots of recopying—that's like pencil-sharpening. I get a quatrain that's *almost* right, so I tear off the sheet and start at the top on a clean one with my nice little quatrain which I know isn't right—but this makes me feel I've accomplished something. I use a rhyming dictionary, the Clement Wood, which is the only one I would recommend because it's the only one with lists of words where the eye goes up and down the columns. You don't use a dictionary for trick rhymes, of course, you won't find them in there. I also use a thesaurus, and I find "The Dictionary of American Slang" very useful in writing contemporary stuff.

I use soft lead pencils, very soft. Supposedly that makes the writing easier on your wrist, but what it really does is allow you to sharpen it every five minutes. I am very undisciplined, though most of the writers I've worked with have been disciplined. Arthur Laurents, James Goldman, George Furth—they always meet deadlines. They work steady hours; they get up at a certain time in the morning and they knock off at five. I have to have somebody pushing me constantly to get it in by Tuesday, and then Monday night I start to work on it.

Curiously enough, some of the best songs are written out of town, and I think this is because pressure is good for all writers. "Little Tin Box" was written out of town by Jerry Bock and Sheldon Harnick. Rodgers and Hammerstein wrote "Getting to Know You" out of town. In my own case, "Being Alive" and Yvonne's "I'm Still Here" were written out of town. Writers respond very well to that kind of pressure, and certainly I find it almost necessary.

Book Writers

The most important thing for a lyric writer is to have a good book writer. I wrote a TV musical with James Goldman in 1966, a horror story based on John Collier's *Evening Primrose* about a group of people who live in department stores all over New York, hiding during the day and coming out at night, mostly old people with the exception of a poet who comes into their midst because he wants to get away from the world and a girl about 18 who came in with her mother when she was six years old and fell asleep in the hat department, and nobody found her. She's never seen the outside since. She meets the poet, and in their first long scene together she tells him her story in a song called "I Remember."

I remember sky,
It was blue as ink
Or at least I think
I remember sky.
I remember snow
Soft as feathers,

Sharp as thumb tacks,
Coming down like lint
And it made you squint
When the wind would blow.
And ice like vinyl on the streets,
Cold as silver, white as sheets.
Rain, like strings,
And changing things, like leaves.
I remember leaves,
Green as spearmint,
Crisp as paper.
I remember trees,
Bare as coat racks,
Spread like broken umbrellas.
And parks and bridges,
Ponds and zoos,
Ruddy faces,
Muddy shoes,
Light and noise
And bees and boys
And days.
I remember days,
Or at least I try,
But as years go by,
They're a sort of haze.
And the bluest ink
Isn't really sky
And at times I think
I would gladly die
For a day of sky.

Copyright © 1966 by Burthen Music Company, Inc.
Used by permission of Chappell & Co., Inc.,

Jim Goldman and I had talked about this song, and Jim wrote a sketch for it as follows: "I remember snow. It's white as bed sheets and as cold as frozen food. It comes down from the sky. I remember sky. It's blue as ink and very far away, as far away as Mommy. I remember her a little. She was big, as tall as trees. Oh, trees with leaves green as spearmint. Leaves rustle when the wind blows. I can hear them. Nothing in the store sounds like leaves in the wind. I remember rain. It comes down from the sky like shower water and makes the grass grow tall and soft like carpet. But grass is lovelier than carpet and a shower isn't rain and thirteen years of ink aren't like one minute of the sky. Oh, I'd do anything for snow. I'd even die I'm so unhappy here."

Now you see, everything was there. Everything. All it required was making it into a song. With the kind of book writer who has the poetic invention and the sense of music's function that Jim does, that's the closest I've ever come in my career to simply taking everything my collaborator had done (he didn't write that speech to be spoken in exactly that way, he wrote it to put down ideas for this whole section including the song). Jim started out with this lovely phrase, "I remember snow," and I kept trying to work with it, and I knew that at the end I wanted to use the word "die." After some hours, the light went on; I thought, "It's called 'I Remember Sky,' then I can repeat it at the end and rhyme it with 'die.' " The light flashed on, and I was able to go ahead with it.

Books are what the musical theater is about, it's not about songs, and I'm not being modest. It annoys me deeply (and I'd like to use stronger language than that) when I read those reviews that say *Follies* was good "in spite of the book." The show was good *because* of the book. A book is not only the dialogue, it's the scheme of the show, the way the songs and the dialogue work together, the style of the show. Very few directors superimpose a style. For example, Hal Prince was struck when he read the book of *Follies:* something flashed in his imagination, and he saw that picture of Gloria Swanson standing in the rubble of the Roxy Theater. It gave him an entire approach to the show as a director. He'd seen that picture many times—why did it strike him? Because this book suggested it, suggested the style.

I don't know of a musical since the 1930s that is good or successful in spite of its book, which is the seed from which a collaboration grows. I've just given you an extreme example of stealing from a book writer, but any book writer I work with knows what I'm going to do, and I try to help him out wherever I can, too, that's the only way you make a piece, make a texture. I keep hearing about people who write books and then give them to composers or composers who write scores and then get a book writer. I don't understand how that works. The piece *can't* have a texture unless it's all blended. It is right that you should steal from each other—maybe not as wholesale theft as "I Remember," but you should steal. The interrogation in *Anyone Can Whistle*, the long section called "Simple"—Arthur wrote some paradoxical sketches, I wrote some lyric syllogisms. We sat together at a piano and sort of ad libbed our way through it because we knew this mixture of dialogue and song was going to go on for 12 minutes. It had better sound as though one writer wrote it, or it would be terrible.

The important thing about the book is the characters, the essence of what dramatic song writing is about. Wilson Mizner said something I like to repeat: "People beat scenery." That's what the musical theater is about. When you are writing songs for a dramatic piece you must ask yourself always, "Why are the songs necessary to the play?" Not why are they enhancing, or fun, but why are they necessary? Is the play a poorer thing without them? I happen to be a big fan of *My Fair Lady* as a show. I had a wonderful time with it, but I liked the movie of *Pygmalion* better. The movie was an improvement on the play *Pygmalion*, and I don't think the songs were necessary to it. I *loved* seeing the musical, but I enjoyed the movie apart from its songs *more*.

A musical collaboration is more than just with a book writer. We have now what is commonly called a director's theater, usually a pejorative term but not when you are working with people like Jerry Robbins, Hal Prince and Michael Bennett. I'm sure there are others, but they're the ones in my experience. I believe in the supremacy of the writer, but you can get many helpful ideas from a director or choreographer. Also, you get abrasion. *Anyone Can Whistle* has acquired a kind of following who are always asking why it failed. Well, one of the reasons is that Taubman and Kerr hated it. But another, I think, is that Arthur and I worked so closely as a team, with Arthur directing the show (and I think he did an excellent job), but there was nobody to fight us. We were a team, there was nobody making us question our own work except our own intelligence, and that just isn't enough.

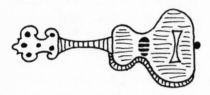

The abrasion can be very annoying sometimes. Out of town with *Company* we had a lot of trouble with the ending, and there was a song called "Happily Ever After" that Robert (Dean Jones) sang. It was the character's climactic self-discovery. It struck a number of people as being too bitter, and Hal Prince kept using the word "negative" to me all the time. It was through the abrasion with Hal that I came to write "Being Alive" rather against my will.

I'd like to refer to all four of the endings we tried for *Company*, because they are all songs that for different reasons I like. The first one was one of the first songs I wrote for the show and it was called "Marry Me a Little." In this version and for the purposes of the next song, Amy did not get married at the end of the first act, and Robert came to her in the second act and asked her to marry him. This is an excerpt from the song where he suddenly realizes he wants to get married:

Someone
Marry me a little,
Love me just enough,
Cry but not too often,
Play but not too rough,
Keep a tender distance
So we'll both be free,
That's the way it ought to be.
I'm ready!
Marry me a little,
Do it with a will,
Make a few demands
I'm able to fulfill.
Want me more than others,
Not exclusively,
That's the way it ought to be.
I'm ready,
I'm ready now!
You can be my best friend,
I can be your right arm.
We'll go through a fight or two—
No harm, no harm.
We'll look not too deep,
We'll go not too far,
We won't have to give up a thing,
We'll stay who we are,
Right?
I'm ready! . . .
Oh, how gently we'll talk,
Oh, how softly we'll tread.
All the stings,
The ugly things,
We'll keep unsaid.
We'll build a cocoon
Of love and respect.
You promise whatever you like,
I'll never collect,
Right? O.K. then,
I'm ready!
I'm ready now!
Amy, I'm ready!

Copyright © 1970 by Valando Music Inc., and Beautiful Music, Inc. All rights
administered by Music of the Times Publishing Corp., New York, N.Y.
Used by permission.

We decided that this was in a certain sense too knowing a song and the the audience might not *get* the lie that Robert is telling himself. So I wrote another song for him preceding his proposal to Amy. In this version, Robert was to take a tour through the rooms after singing the first chorus. This is a song in which he thinks he is finally in love with Amy.

Multitudes of Amys
Crowd the streets below.
Avenues of Amys,
Officefuls of Amys,
Everywhere I go.
Wonder what it means,
Oho, I wonder what it means!
I see them waiting for the lights,
Running for the bus,
Milling in the stores,
And hailing cabs
And disappearing through
Revolving doors.
Multitudes of Amys
Everywhere I look,
Sentences of Amys,
Paragraphs of Amys
Filling every book.
Wonder if it means
I've gone to pieces.
Every other word I speak
Is something she says.
Walls hang with pictures of Amys,
Galaxies of Amys dot the night skies,
Girls pass and look at me
With Amy's eyes.
I've seen an audience of Amys
Watch a cast of Amys act in a play.
Seems there are more of her every day.
What can it mean?
What can it mean?
I've caught a stadium of Amys
Standing up to cheer,
Choruses of Amys,
Symphonies of Amys,
Ringing in my ear.
I know what it means—

Hey, Amy, I know what it means—
Oh wow!
I'm ready, I'm ready,
I'm ready now!

Then he started to wander through the rooms taking something from each of the couples—maybe a boutonniere or something like that—to show how they'd affected him. Then he sang:

All that it takes is two, Amy,
Me, Amy, you, Amy.
I know what it means.
Hey, Amy, I know what it means—
Oh wow!
I'm ready, I'm ready,
I'll say it: marry me now!

Copyright © 1970 by Valando Music, Inc., and Beautiful Music, Inc.
All rights administered by Music of the Times Publishing Corp.,
New York, N.Y. Used by permission.

Here is the ending we did for Boston, "Happily Ever After" (below at left), the "bitter" or "negative" song—I think of it not that way but as a scream of agony. (Editor's note: at right below is "Being Alive," the song actually used to end *Company*.)

"Happily Ever After"
Someone to hold you too close,
Someone to hurt you too deep,
Someone to love you too hard,
Happily ever after.
Someone to need you too much,
Someone to read you too well,
Someone to bleed you of all
The things you don't want to tell—
That's happily ever after.
Ever, ever, ever after
In hell.
Somebody always there
Sitting in the chair
Where you want to sit—
Always, always.
Somebody always there
Wanting you to share
Just a little bit—

"Being Alive"
Someone to hold you too close,
Someone to hurt you too deep,
Someone to sit in your chair,
To ruin your sleep . . .

(Dialogue insert: Robert's friends advise him that there's more to marriage than he imagines; besides, with all his reasons for *not* getting married, he hasn't come up with a single reason for being alone.)

☆

Someone to need you too much,
Someone to know you too well,
Someone to pull you up short
And put you through hell . . .

"Happily Ever After" (Cont'd)
Always, always.
Then see the pretty girls
Smiling everywhere
From the ads and the TV set,
And why should you sweat?
What do you get?
One day of grateful for six of regret!
With someone to hold you too close,
Someone to hurt you too deep
Someone to bore you to death
Happily ever after.
Someone you have to know well,
Someone you have to show how.
Someone you have to allow
The things you'd never allow—
That's happily ever after,
Ever, ever, ever after
Till now.
So quick,
Get a little car,
Take a little drive,
Make a little love,
See a little flick,
Do a little work
Take a little walk,
Watch a little TV
And click!
Make a little love
Do a little work,
Get a little drunk.
You've got one little trip,
Seventy years, spread it around!
Take your pick:
Buy a little here,
Spend a little there,
Smoke a little pot
For a little kick,
Waste a little time,
Make a little love,
Show a little feeling,
But why
Should you try?

"Being Alive" (Cont'd)
(Dialogue insert: Robert's friends advise him not to fear imperfection, but to keep thinking about marriage along positive lines.)

☆

Someone you have to let in,
Someone whose feelings you spare,
Someone who, like it or not, will
                    want you to share
A little a lot . . .

(Dialogue insert: Robert's friends assure him marriage looks different from the inside; Robert cannot know much about it without having tried it; they advise him to add up its benefits.)

☆

Someone to crowd you with love,
Someone to force you to care,
Someone to make you come through,
Who'll always be there,
As frightened as you
Of being alive,
Being alive, being alive, being alive.

(Dialogue insert: Amy urges Robert to *want* something—want *something*.)

☆

Somebody hold me too close,
Somebody hurt me too deep,
Somebody sit in my chair
And ruin my sleep
And make me aware
Of being alive, being alive.
Somebody need me too much,
Somebody know me too well,

"Happily Ever After" (Cont'd)	*"Being Alive" (Cont'd)*
Why not, sure, feel a little lonely,	Somebody pull me up short
But fly,	And put me through hell
Why not fly	And give me support
With no one to hold you too close,	For being alive.
No one to hurt you too deep,	Make me alive,
No one to love you too hard	Make me alive,
Happily ever after?	Make me confused,
No one you have to know well,	Mock me with praise,
No one you have to show how,	Let me be used,
No one you have to allow	Vary my days,
The things you'd never allow—	But alone is alone, not alive.
That's happily ever after,	Somebody crowd me with love,
Ever, ever, ever after,	Somebody force me to care,
For now!	Somebody let me come through,
Ever, ever after,	I'll always be there,
Ever, ever, ever, ever after,	As frightened as you,
Ever, ever, ever, ever,	To help us survive
ever, ever after . . .	Being alive, being alive, being alive!

Copyright © 1970 by Valando Music, Inc. and Beautiful Music, Inc.
All rights administered by Music of the Times Publishing Corp.,
New York, N.Y. Used by permission.

I had a bow-off line, it's a quote from *Company*. It's when April says, "I don't have anything more to say." I have a lot more to say, but I don't have anything more to say. Thank you.

A Composer
Looks at His Lyricists

By Richard Rodgers

In many ways a song-writing partnership is like a marriage. Apart from just liking each other, a lyricist and a composer should be able to spend long periods of time together—around the clock if need be—without getting on each other's nerves. Their goals, outlooks and basic philosophies should be similar. They should have strong convictions, but no man should ever insist that his way alone is the right way. A member of a team should even be so in tune with his partner's work habits that he must be almost able to anticipate the other's next move. In short, the men should work together in such close harmony that the song they create is accepted as a spontaneous emotional expression emanating from a single source, with both words and music mutually dependent in achieving the desired effect.

I've been lucky. During most of my career I've had only two partners. Lorenz Hart and I worked together for 25 years; Oscar Hammerstein II and I were partners for over 18. Each man was totally different in appearance, work habits, personality, and practically anything else you can think of. Yet each was a genius at his craft, and each, during our association, was the closest friend I had.

I met Oscar before I met Larry. I was 12 and he was 19 when my older brother, Mortimer, a fraternity brother of Oscar's, took me backstage to meet him after a performance of a Columbia Varsity Show. Oscar played the comic lead in the production, and meeting this worldly college junior was pretty heady stuff for a stagestruck kid.

I met Larry about four years later. I was still in high school at the time, but I had already begun writing songs for amateur shows, and I was determined even then to make composing my life's work. Although I had written the words to some of my songs, I was anxious to team up with a full-fledged lyricist. A mutual friend, Philip Leavitt, was the matchmaker who introduced us one Sunday afternoon at Larry's house. I liked what Larry had written, and apparently he liked my music. But most important, we found in each other the kind of person we had been looking for in a partner—our ideas and aims were so much alike that we just sensed that this was it. From that day until I wrote *Oklahoma!* with Oscar, the team of Rodgers and Hart was an almost exclusive partnership.

I say "almost exclusive" because Oscar also figured in my early career. We had collaborated on a couple of songs (if you must know, they were called "Can it" and "Weaknesses") for an amateur show, *Up Stage and Down,* for which I had written most of the lyrics and all of the music. Oddly enough, when we rewrote the show and gave it a new title, *Twinkling Eyes,* Larry Hart came in as director. The following year, a Rodgers and Hart score for the Columbia Varsity Show also contained an interpolated Rodgers and Hammerstein effort, "Room for One More." Oscar, incidentally, had been on the panel of judges that had selected our musical, *Fly with Me,* as the Varsity Show. A few years later he even collaborated on the book for a musical, *Winkle Town,* with a score by Larry and me, but we never could sell it. The show, however, did have a song in it, "Manhattan," that later became our first hit.

Larry Hart, as almost everyone will agree, was a genius at lyric construction, at rhyming, at finding the offbeat way of expressing himself. He had a somewhat sardonic view of the world that can be found occasionally in his love songs and in his satirical numbers. But Larry was also a kind, gentle, generous little guy, and these traits too may be found in some of his most memorable lyrics. Working with him, however, did present problems since he had to be literally trapped into putting pen to paper—and then only after hearing a melody that stimulated him.

The great thing about Larry was that he was always growing—creatively if not physically. He was fascinated by the various techniques of rhyming, such as polysyllabic rhymes, interior rhymes, masculine and feminine rhymes, the trick of rhyming one word with only part of another. Who else could have come up with the line, "Beans could get no keener re-/Ception in a beanery,"* as he did in "Mountain Greenery"? or "Hear me holler/I choose a /Sweet Lolla-/Paloosa/In thee,"** in "Thou Swell"? Or "I'm wild again/Beguiled again/A whimpering simpering child again,"*** in "Bewitched"?

* © 1926 Harms, Inc. Copyright renewed. All rights reserved. Used by permission of Warner Bros. Music.

** © 1927 Harms, Inc. Copyright renewed. All rights reserved. Used by permission of Warner Bros. Music.

*** Copyright © 1941 by Chappell & Company., Inc., New York, N.Y. Copyright renewed. Used by permission.

Yet Larry could also write simply and poetically. "My Heart Stood Still," for example expressed so movingly the power of "that unfelt clasp of hand," and did it in a refrain consisting almost entirely of monosyllables. Larry was intrigued by almost every facet of human emotion. In "Where or When," he dared take up the psychic phenomenon of a person convinced that he has known someone before, even though the two people are meeting for the first time. As the years went on, there was an increasingly rueful quality in some of Larry's lyrics that gave them a very personal connotation. I am referring to such plaints as "Nobody's Heart," with its feigned indifference to love, and "Spring Is Here," a confession of one whose attitude about the season is colored by his feeling of being unloved.

Oscar Hammerstein's view of life was more positive, more optimistic. He had a wonderful family. He was a joiner, a leader, a man willing to do battle for whatever causes he believed in. He was not naive. He knew full well that man is not all good and that nature is not all good; yet it was his sincere belief that someone had to keep reminding people of the vast amount of good things that there are in the world. He was as meticulous a craftsman as Larry, and he was extremely versatile. As a partner he was completely dependable; about 70 per cent of the time I wrote the music only after Oscar handed me a lyric.

As far as his work with me was concerned, Oscar always wrote about the things that affected him deeply. What was truly remarkable was his never-ending ability to find new ways of revealing how he felt about three interrelated themes—nature, music and love. In "Oh, What a Beautiful Mornin'," the first song we wrote together for *Oklahoma!*, Oscar described an idyllic summer day on a farm. In "It's a Grand Night for Singing," he revealed that the things most likely to induce people to sing are a warm, moonlit, starry night and the first thrill of falling in love. In "You Are Never Away," he compared a girl to a song, a rainbow, a spring morning. In our last collaboration, *The Sound of Music,* just about everthing Oscar felt about nature and music and love was summed up in the title song.

Oscar believed that all too often people overlooked the wonders to be found in the simple pleasures of life. We even wrote two songs together, "A Hundred Million Miracles" and "My Favorite Things," in which Oscar enumerated some of them. To him there was no greater contentment that two people in love being close together as the day ends—a feeling that is found in, among other songs, "Oklahoma," "A Fellow Needs a Girl" and "An Ordinary Couple." It should not be overlooked, however, that Larry Hart was also attracted to the simple life. Remember his paean to rustic charms in "There's a Small Hotel." Or his attitude in "My Romance," in which he dismissed as unnecessary all the conventional romantic props when two people find themselves really in love.

After Oscar's death in 1960, I was faced with the dilemma of finding a new lyric-writing partner. I knew that I was not ready at that time to cope with another personality after having had so rich and close a working relationship. I had already had some experience updating a few of Larry's lyrics for revivals of our musicals, and I felt confident that I had assimilated the techniques of writing lyrics through my long association with two of the giants in the field. So I decided to go to it alone, to write the words as well as the music for my next stage production, *No Strings*. I also did double duty for additional songs written for the remake of the film, *State Fair*, and the movie version of *The Sound of Music*, and I have also written music and lyrics for a TV *Androcles and the Lion*.

Creating my own lyrics has given me a new perspective on the problems of song-writing collaboration. It is, I well know, more difficult to write words than to compose the melodies. In musical composition, I work in wide, broad strokes. Lyrics are more like little pieces in a puzzle that must be carefully put together. But creating both words and music does have certain advantages. Geographically, it couldn't be better; I'm always there whenever I want to meet me. As far as personal satisfaction is concerned, I find that there is nothing more exhilarating than to work on a complete song when I want to, and nothing matches the satisfaction of taking full responsibility for the complete product. There is a strange conflict—part loneliness, part fulfillment—that I feel in becoming my own partner. If I am successful at it, I know full well that it's because some of the talents of Larry Hart and Oscar Hammerstein must have rubbed off on me.

The Lyric in Politics

Here is a Jerry Herman lyric that joined a political party to the tune of "Hello, Dolly!" and became President Lyndon B. Johnson's 1964 re-election campaign song:

Hello, Lyndon
Well, hello, Lyndon
We'd be proud to have you back where you belong
You're lookin' swell, Lyndon
We can tell, Lyndon
You're still glowin'
You're still crowin'
You're still goin' strong
We hear the band playin'
And the folks sayin'
That the people know that you've got so much more . . . so
Flash that smile, Lyndon
Show us that winning style, Lyndon
Promise you'll stay with us in '64!

We hear the band playin'
And the folks sayin'
"Let's all rally round the one who knows the score" . . . so
Be our guide, Lyndon
Ladybird at your side, Lyndon
Promise you'll stay with us in '64!

©1963 Jerry Herman; all rights controlled by Edwin H. Morris & Company, Inc. Used by permission.

Memorable Lyric Moments On Broadway Selected by Authors of Shows

Lyricists, librettists and composers were asked to name their favorite Broadway lyricist past or present, and to send in quoted examples. Here are the replies—the selections and comments of lyric writers and their closest collaborators—listed in alphabetical order of the repliers. Our warmest thanks and admiration are extended to the many who created this collection of memorable theater lyrics. We are especially grateful to Richard Lewine for his help and advice in all phases of this project, and to the many music publishers who gave us permission to quote lyrics.

☆

I have several favorites. Of the older group, I have always particularly enjoyed the work of Oscar Hammerstein II and Alan Jay Lerner. It seems to me that the imagery of Hammerstein and the choice of language of Lerner are unsurpassed.

Of the younger lyricists, I am a great admirer of my friend Sheldon Harnick, both for his deftness and his choice of the amusing angle in his lyrics.

—LEE ADAMS

☆

I would like to tell you how difficult is your question, "Who is your favorite Broadway lyricist, past or present?" I admire so many—Lorenz Hart, Frank Loesser, Irving Berlin, Stephen Sondheim, Sheldon Harnick, Bob Merrill, to name a few. Then there are certain lines in lyric writing that remain in my memory, such as Larry Hart's twisting a rhyme into a universal thought:

You sew your trousseau
And Robinson Crusoe
Is not so far from worldly cares
As our blue room far away upstairs!

—"The Blue Room" from *The Girl Friend*
©1926 Harms, Inc. Copyright renewed. All rights reserved.
Used by permission of Warner Bros. Music.

And then, of course, there is the simple eloquence of and also the universal love thought as expressed by Cole Porter:

You'd be so nice to come home to,
You'd be so nice by the fire!

—"You'd Be So Nice To Come Home To" from
Something to Shout About (film)
Copyright © 1942 by Chappell & Co., Inc. Copyright renewed. Used by permission.

Those fifteen words say everything that every lonely lover thinks and feels.

Or the series of questions Mr. Berlin writes in "How Deep Is the Ocean?" I would love to go on and on, but being a lyricist myself, I understand the value of brevity.

—RICHARD ADLER

☆

Thank you for the chance to say that my favorite Broadway lyricist is Lee Adams. I could quote many fine lyrics from *Bye Bye Birdie, All American, Golden Boy* and *Superman*, but I will settle for one:

All scrubbed and shiny,
What a sight without her makeup,
But a sight I'd like to wake up and see!

—"I've Just Seen Her" from *All American*
©1962 Lee Adams and Charles Strouse; all rights controlled
by Edwin H. Morris & Company, Inc. Used by permission.

—ROBERT BENTON

☆

My pet peeve is idiotic lyrics that through haste, carelessness or plain ignorance in writing make a shambles of the English language. My leading contender for the sable-lined dunce cap in this department is none other than the late, Great Master, Oscar Hammerstein II. Example:

Tote dat barge! Lift dat bale!

—"Ol' Man River" from *Show Boat*
Copyright © 1927 by T. B. Harms Company, Copyright renewed. Used by permission.

To "tote" is to pick something up and carry it. A "barge" is a large non-self-propelled boat used usually for the marine transport of bulk cargos. Nobody in the long history of the Mississippi, including Mike Fink, has ever picked up and carried a barge. As a Licensed Pilot on the Mississippi and one who has spent years working at every conceivable job on the Mississippi from cook, deckhand and coal passer to Mate and Pilot, I can never hear these words without a fierce twinge of embarrassment. It's the kind of thing that the late genius Ring Lardner so loved to parody.

Too many song writers feel that they are "poets" (which they are not) and therefore working under a special dispensation permitting them to put down anything that happens to sound O.K., whether it makes sense or not. Examples would fill several shelves in the New York Public Library.

Cheerfully submitted,

—RICHARD BISSELL

☆

I cite Sheldon Harnick as my favorite lyricist. There, I said it and I'm glad.

I cite the next five lines as an example of his eloquent economy, the beginnings of a lyric that blossoms into a joyful lamentation, a celebration of human hope, an ironic litany of love and life:

> If I were a rich man
> Daidle deedle daidle
> Digguh digguh deedle daidle dum,
> All day long I'd biddy biddy bum,
> If I were a wealthy man.

—"If I Were a Rich Man" from *Fiddler on the Roof*

©1964 Sunbeam Music Corp. All rights administered by The New York
Times Music Corporation, New York, N.Y. Used by permission.

There, I said it and I'm sorry.

I'm sorry, but I hope I've made the point. Citing Harnick's lyrics on the printed page (or anyone's for that matter) is both a disservice and self-defeating. It's separating the inseparable. Lyrics are interwoven with music to make the fabric of something to be sung. I'll never forget my surprised disappointment when first I read a compilation of lyrics in book form by Oscar Hammerstein II. Those sensitive, romantic, sweetly singing treasures became dry, academic curiosities, awkward to the eye where once they soared to the ear.

Lyrics should be heard not seen. Take my word for it. No, better yet, take Sheldon Harnick's.

—JERRY BOCK

☆

My favorite lyricist, although I admit he runs a close first with other fine artisans, is Frank Loesser. My favorite lyric, although it runs a close first with other fine phrases, is:

Like a perfumed woman
Smellin' of where she's been. . . .

—"Joey, Joey, Joey" from *The Most Happy Fella*
©1956 Frank Music Corp. Used by permission.

I must say, however, that a sentimental favorite is a lyric never used, from a show that hardly ran at all. Paul Nassau wrote a verse to "Lord, You Sure Know How to Make a Sunday" for *A Joyful Noise*. The song was changed to "Lord, You Sure Know How to Make a New Day," and this lyric was dropped:

Lord, You sure know how to make a Sunday,
Lord, You sure know how to make a Sunday.
It sure smells sweet with the grass so green,
And the sky such a beautiful blue,
It sure smells sweet, and it's such a shame,
Everyone's in church,
Everyone, but me and You.

Irreverent? No.

—Oscar Brand
TRO—© 1966 & 1967 Devon Music Inc., New York, N.Y. Used by permission.

☆

Probably like everybody else, I think Lorenz Hart was the best; he influenced me the most (too much so). He had a sound that was elegant and yet human, and very frail. Most of all, he put us into the magical world of lyrics—where songs *did* things to you.
I love the endings of these two verses:

Thine arms are martial; thou hast grace;
My cheek is partial to thy face;
And if thy lips grow weary
Mine are their resting place.

You are so graceful, have you wings?
You have a faceful of nice things.
You have no speaking voice, dear. . . .
With every word it sings.

—"Thou Swell" from *A Connecticut Yankee*
©1927 Harms, Inc. Copyright renewed. All rights reserved. Used by
permission of Warner Bros. Music.

S **T** ephen Sondheim

Cole P **O** rter

L **O** renz Hart

Oscar Ha **M** merstein

Lee **A** dams

Caroly **N** Leigh

E. **Y** . Harburg

Be **T** ty Comden

and Ad **O** lph Green

Johnny Mer **C** er

H oward Dietz

O gden Nash

Frank L **O** esser

Ira Ger **S** hwin

Alan L **E** rner

Dorothy **F** ields

I **R** ving Berlin

All the **O** thers I haven't listed,

and **M** e.

—MARTIN CHARNIN

☆

Now to go on—this is outrageously incomplete *but*—there are others who, through their lyrics, have made my life happier in the musical theater: E. Y. Harburg, "Something Sort of Grandish" and "When I'm Not Near the Girl I Love" from *Finian's Rainbow*; Cole Porter, "Where Is the Life That Late I Led?" from *Kiss Me Kate*; Frank Loesser, "Adelaide's Lament" from *Guys and Dolls*; Oscar Hammerstein II, "Soliloquy" from *Carousel*; and Stephen Sondheim, "Officer Krupke" from *West Side Story*.

—MATT DUBEY

☆

For perception, originality, technique and production value, nobody but nobody can touch Frank Loesser. All of "Adelaide's Lament" illustrates this so well:

> The female remaining single, just in the legal sense
> Shows a neurotic tendency—see note.
> *(Looks at note.)*
> Chronic, organic syndromes, toxic or hypertense
> Involving the eye, the ear, the nose and throat.
> In other words, just from wondering whether
> The wedding is on or off,
> A person . . . can develop a cough.
> You can feed her all day with the vitamin A and the bromo fizz,
> But the medicine never gets anywhere near where the trouble is.
> If she's getting a kind of a name for herself, and the name ain't his,
> A person . . . can develop a cough.

—"Adelaide's Lament" from *Guys and Dolls*
©1950 Frank Music Corp. Used by permission.
—NORMAN GIMBEL

☆

Since time immemorial, "love" has been the main concern of lyricists and composers. The operatic aria always concerned itself primarily with love. Since the turn of the century, the pop song has taken over this subject with songs like "Will You Love Me in December as You Did in May?" by Jimmy Walker and Ernest R. Ball, "Let's Fall in Love" by Ted Kohler and Harold Arlen, "Love for Sale" by Cole Porter, "Love Is Sweeping the Country" by Ira and George Gershwin and many others.

In the last three decades the love lyric has become more sophisticated, and "love" is still interpreted with much *sentiment* but with much less *sentimentality*. Instead of crooning, "As my beloved wends her way/Along the highway/E'en the birds warble carols/To extol her sweetness," Jimmy McHugh, Irving Mills and Gene Austin wrote: "When my sugar walks down the street/All the birdies go 'tweet-tweet-tweet.' "*

*©1924 Mills Music, Inc. © renewed 1952.

But not all song writers have given up on sentimentality in their approach to love—not even the rock 'n' rollers. Sentimentality is still hit-producing. The public still buys it, and the royalties keep pouring in. Sentiment, it is said, is the cake itself; but sentimentality is the gooey icing.

Here's a challenge to the reader: which of the following hit songs express pure sentiment and which wallow in sheer sentimentality?

Harlan Thompson said it positively:

"I love you, I love You"
Is all that I can say.
I love you, I love you,
The same old words
I'm saying in the same old way.

—"I Love You" from *Little Jesse James*
©1923 (renewed 1951) by Leo Feist Inc. Used by permission.

But Cole Porter expressed it more poetically:

"I love you" hums the April breeze
"I love you" echo the hills.
"I love you" the golden dawn agrees
As once more she sees daffodils.

—"I Love You" from *Mexican Hayride*
Copyright © 1943 by Chappell & Co., Inc., New York, N.Y.
Copyright renewed. Used by permission.

Oscar Hammerstein II said it with negative positivism:

Don't throw bouquets at me
Don't please my folks too much
Don't laugh at my jokes too much
People will say we're in love!

—"People Will Say We're in Love" from *Oklahoma!*
Copyright © 1943 by Williamson Music, Inc., New York, N.Y.
Copyright renewed. Used by permission. All rights reserved.

But Buddy DeSylva and Lew Brown told the story of a broken-hearted lover quite succinctly:

> There she is—my old gal
> There he is—my old pal,
> And here am I—broken hearted.
> Mine in May—his in June
> She forgot mighty soon,
> And here am I—broken hearted.
> The last time that we said "goodby,"
> I knew that she was through,
> It's bad enough that I lost her,
> I had to lose *him* too.
>
> —"Broken Hearted" (popular song)

Copyright © 1927 by DeSylva, Brown & Henderson, Inc. Copyright renewed, assigned to Chappell & Co., Inc. Published in the U.S. by joint agreement of Chappell & Co., Inc. and Anne-Rachel Music Corporation. Used by permission.

Shall I go on? . . . Sentiment or sentimentality? The new sexy generation of rock 'n' roll song writers are cool, groovy and on the beat. What's their future, baby? Cake or icing? Or just the pill?

—JAY GORNEY

☆

Lyrics that grow out of character are the kind that appeal to me. Johnny Mercer wrote one to the music of Harold Arlen that never fails to move me. In it, a woman now living the high life sings about her childhood:

> It seems like yesterday I heard the grownup laughter
> The clink of dishes and the sound I loved the best
> And watched the kitchen lamp swing gently from the rafter
> As I lay half asleep against my mother's breast
> There with my head on her shoulder
> The troubles of the world seemed far away
> A million years, a million miles have come between us
> And yet it seems like only yesterday.
>
> —"Lullaby" from *St. Louis Woman*

Copyright © 1946 by A-M Music Corporation. Copyright renewed. Used by permission.

Every song in *St. Louis Woman* is wonderfully written. The score, in my opinion, is one of the finest ever written for the theater.

—IRVIN GRAHAM

☆

As a practising, professional composer, put myself on record as to my *favorite* lyricist? No, that I cannot do. But I *will* cite some examples of what is, in my opinion, perfection in lyric writing.

By Howard Dietz:

Dancing in the dark till the tune ends,—
We're dancing in the dark, and it soon ends.
We're waltzing in the wonder of why we're here;
Time hurries by, we're here
And gone.

—"Dancing in the Dark" from *The Band Wagon*
©1931 Harms, Inc. Copyright renewed. All rights reserved.
Used by permission of Warner Bros. Music.

By Ira Gershwin:

Embrace me,
My sweet embraceable you.
Embrace me,
You irreplaceable you.
Just one look at you—my heart grew tipsy in me;
You and you alone bring out the gypsy in me.

—"Embraceable You" from *Girl Crazy*
©1930 New World Music Corporation. Copyright renewed.
All rights reserved. Used by permission of Warner Bros. Music.

By Lorenz Hart:

I greet you
With a song in my heart.
I behold your adorable face,
Just a song at the start,
But it soon is a hymn to your grace. . . .

—"With a Song in My Heart" from *Spring Is Here*
©1929 Harms, Inc. Copyright revewed. All rights reserved.
Used by permission of Warner Bros. Music.

By Alan Jay Lerner:

I've grown accustomed to her face!
She almost makes the day begin.
I've grown accustomed to the tune
She whistles night and noon.
Her smiles. Her frowns.
Her ups, her downs
Are second nature to me now. . . .

—"I've Grown Accustomed to Her Face" from *My Fair Lady*
Copyright © 1956 by Alan Jay Lerner and Frederick Loewe.
Used by permission of Chappell & Co., Inc.

By Cole Porter:

My story is much too sad to be told,
For practic'lly everything leaves me totally cold.
The only exception I know is the case

When I'm out on a quiet spree,
Fighting vainly the old ennui,
And I suddenly turn and see
Your fabulous face!

—"I Get a Kick Out of You" from *Anything Goes*

©1934 Harms, Inc. Copyright renewed. All rights reserved.
Used by permission of Warner Bros. Music.

By P. G. Wodehouse:

But along came Bill,
Who's not the type at all.
You'd meet him on the street and never notice him,
His form and face,
His manly grace
Are not the kind that you
Would find in a statue.

—"Bill" from *Show Boat*

Copyright© 1927 by T. B. Harms Company. Copyright renewed. Used by permission.

And I could go on and on quoting from the *great pros*, past and present, writers of words with a deep *feeling* for the three basic elements of music —melody, rhythm and even harmony—the right word on the right note; writers who have added to this gift the mastery of an elusive and difficult technique, writers to whom discipline and form are a boon, not a prison; poets who have been able to endow song words with the beauty and stature of poetry.

—JOHN GREEN

☆

There have been so many fine lyricists contributing to the American musical theater that I find it next to impossible to select a favorite. If I have one, I suppose it's Stephen Sondheim, for the following reason: while there are a number of lyricists whose new work I look forward to, I invariably anticipate a new Sondheim score with special excitement because I know it will have a particularly high level of invention, wit, meticulous craftsmanship, taste and content.

No one lyric can convey a writer's range, but I've chosen a verse which I think illustrates at least some of the aforementioned qualities:

Feel the roll of the playful waves,
See the sails as they swell.
Hear the whips on the galley slaves
Pretty little picture? Well,
Let it carry your cares away,
Out of sight, out of mind,
Past the buoy and through the bay

Soon there's nothing but sea and spray,
Night descends and the moon's aglow.
Your arms entwined, you steal below,
And far behind at the edge of day
The bong of the bell of the buoy in the bay,
And the boat and the boy and the bride are away!
It's a pretty little picture to share
As the little boat sails to sea.
Take a little trip free as air,
Have a little freedom on me!

—"Pretty Little Picture" from *A Funny Thing Happened*
on the Way to the Forum
Copyright © 1962 & 1964 by Stephen Soundheim. Used by permission
of Burthen Music Company, Inc.
—Sheldon Harnick

☆

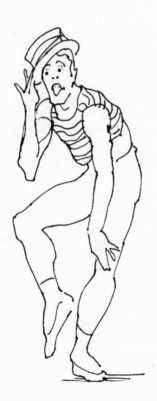

Among the old masters, I prize Lorenz Hart and Cole Porter over the
equally gifted Messrs. Oscar Hammerstein II, Irving Berlin and Ira Gershwin because they had such fabulous wit and style. I also thank heaven for E.

(. Harburg, Harold Rome and Dorothy Fields. Currently, Alan Jay Lerner, Stephen Sondheim and Sheldon Harnick are who I'd like to be when I grow up. Conceivably, Hart and Porter get my nod because the songs you fall in love with are the songs you fell in love to.

—ARNOLD HORWITT

☆

Without question, the best Broadway lyricist past or present is Stephen Sondheim. Any lyric he has written can be quoted to illustrate this contention. I think Sondheim is the only lyricist who almost always writes a lyric which could *only* be sung by the character for which it was designed, who never pads with unnecessary fillers, who never sacrifices meaning or intention for a clever rhyme and who knows that a lyric is the shortest of one-act plays, with a beginning, a middle and an end. Moreover, he knows how the words must sit on a musical phrase.

I am not his agent.

—ARTHUR LAURENTS

☆

I am a lyric-buff. With the possible exception of W. S. Gilbert, America has had a corner on this art form. And art form it is, an important element of musical comedy, the musical play, which is truly the people's art of this century—invented and perfected in the United States.

I am a great verse-lover, and one of my favorite parlor games is trying to guess a song from its verse. I also collect and cherish obscure second choruses. Reprises in a show are always a joy to me, especially when the original situation is "punned"—when the song ties back into context and is performed in a different tempo or by a different character. Often, a deft lyric writer can convey more in eight bars that a playwright can in eight pages.

But my favorite? I have too many. Lorenz Hart, certainly. "Funny Valentine" and "Glad to Be Unhappy" are only two of his many memorable lyrics. Oscar Hammerstein II made me cry, especially with this lyric:

Hush, you bird, my baby's a-sleepin'!
Maybe got a dream worth a-keepin'
Whoa! you team, and just keep a-creepin' at a slow clip clop
Don't you hurry with the surrey with the fringe on the top!

—"The Surrey With the Fringe on Top" from *Oklahoma*!

Copyright © 1943 by Williamson Music, Inc. New York, N.Y. Copyright renewed. Used by permission. All rights reserved.

Ira Gershwin is a better poet than even the Man-behind-the-cigar himself will admit. Examples include the third chorus encore (what ever happened to encores?) of "I Can't Get Started":

When J. P. Morgan bows, I just nod;
Green Pastures wanted me to play God. . . .
—"I Can't Get Started" from *Ziegfeld Follies* (1936

Copyright © 1935 by Chappell & Co., Inc. Copyright renewed. Used by permission

My list is endless. I have infinite admiration for Frank Loesser, Col
Porter, Howard Dietz, Alan Jay Lerner, E. Y. Harburg, Dorothy Fields, John
LaTouche, Stephen Sondheim—and who can argue with an Irving Berlin
lyric like:

The photographers will snap us
And you'll find that you're
In the rotogravure.
—"Easter Parade" from *As Thousands Cheer*

©1933 Irving Berlin. © renewed 1960

I think Johnny Mercer has been underrated on Broadway, for he seems to
have saved his best work for the flicks. But there is one exception: the
almost-forgotten *St. Louis Woman*. It contains "Any Place I Hang My Hat I
Home," from which the line "Howdy stranger, so long friend" is one I can'
get out of my head.

With pure prejudice, I lean on our two collaborators for my final salute
Hugh Martin and Jerry Herman. I think "Everytime," which Martin wrote
for *Best Foot Forward,* is an exquisite lyric. And "I'm the First Girl in the
Second Row in the Third Scene of the Fourth Number" from *Look, Ma, I'm
Dancin'!* is one of the best "point numbers" I've ever head in the theater.

The total lyric of Jerry Herman's "If He Walked Into My life" is a particular
favorite. But for me, the high spot lyrically in *Mame* is the slow reprise of "It's
Today" now directed to a person, the new little boy in Mame's life. So she
sings:

Someone gave me a wonderful present,
Something I needed and yet never knew
So start the whistling and clapping,
'Cause under the wrapping
Was you.
—"It's Today" from *Mame*

©1966 Jerry Herman; all rights controlled by Jerryco Music Company. Used by permission.

Lyric writers? I sing their praises.
—JEROME LAWRENCE

☆

My favorite lyricist, past or present? I have three: Irving Berlin . . .

Angels come from ev'rywhere with lots of jack
And when you lose it, there's no attack
Where could you get money that you don't give back?
—"There's No Business Like Show Business" from *Annie Get Your Gun*
©1946 Irving Berlin. © renewed 1974.

. . . Lorenz Hart . . .

My romance doesn't need a castle rising in Spain,
Nor a dance
To a constantly surprising refrain. . . .
—"My Romance" from *Jumbo*
Copyright © 1935 by T. B. Harms Company. Copyright renewed. Used by permission.

. . . and Cole Porter.

Is it for all time
Or simply a lark?
Is this Granada I see
Or only Asbury Park?
—"At Long Last Love" from *You Never Know*
Copyright © 1938 by Chappell & Co., Inc. Copyright renewed. Used by permission.
—RICHARD LEWINE

☆

I believe, along with most songwriters of my acquaintance, that Lorenz Hart and Johnny Mercer are the best lyric writers, although the latter has not done his best-known work for the theater.

Aside from these two, whose personal styles have had so much influence, I would like to mention E. Y. Harburg, who has put together some memorable word combinations. Two typical fine examples:

Even the rabbits
Inhibit their habits
On Sunday in Cicero Falls.
—"Sunday in Cicero Falls" from *Bloomer Girl*
Copyright © 1944 by The Players Music Corporation. Copyright renewed, assigned to Chappell & Co., Inc. Used by permission.

When I can't fondle the hand that I'm fond of,
I fondle the hand at hand.
—"When I'm Not Near the Girl I Love" from *Finian's Rainbow*
Copyright © 1946 by The Players Music Corporation.
Copyright renewed, assigned to Chappell & Co., Inc.

I would also like to mention the lyrics by Robert Wright and George Forrest for *Kismet*, which are among the best I have ever heard. The ideas, rhymes and alliteration are all wonderful, and they have that subtle combination of musical sound and color and mood that constitutes good lyric writing. One of many examples:

> Let peacocks and monkeys in purple adornings
> Show her the way to my bridal chamber,
> Then get you gone 'till the morn of my mornings
> After the night of my nights.

> —"Night of My Nights" from *Kismet*
> ©1953 Frank Music Corp. Used by permission.
> —JAY LIVINGSTON

☆

My favorite Broadway lyricist is Oscar Hammerstein II. I think there are three extremely important abilities which a good lyricist should have. One: he should be able to make a simple basic statement. Two: he should use words on occasion in a "poetic," or, more correctly, "lyrical" fashion. And three: he should be able to make a good joke. I think Hammerstein functioned brilliantly in all these areas.

Simple basic statement (Bloody Mary's advice to Lt. Cable):

> You got to have a dream
> If you don't have a dream
> How you gonna have a dream come true?

> —"Happy Talk" from *South Pacific*
> Copyright © 1949 by Richard Rodgers and Oscar Hammerstein II. Williamson Music, Inc.,
> New York, N.Y. owner of publication and allied rights for all countries of Western
> Hemisphere. Used by permission. All rights reserved.

Lyrical:

> You are the promised kiss of springtime
> That makes the lonely winter seem long.
> You are the breathless hush of evening
> That trembles on the brink of a lovely song.

> —"All the Things Your Are" from *Very Warm for May*
> Copyright © 1939 by T. B. Harms Company. Copyright renewed. Used by permission.

Joke (Anna's imagined beratement of the King):

> In your pursuit of pleasure, you
> Have mistresses who treasure you
> They have no ken
> Of other men
> Beside whom they can measure you

A flock of sheep, and you the only ram—
No wonder you're the wonder of Siam!
> —"Shall I Tell You What I Think of You?" from *The King and I*

Copyright © 1951 by Richard Rodgers and Oscar Hammerstein II. Williamson Music Inc., New York, N.Y. owner of publication and allied rights for all countries of Western Hemisphere. Used by permission. All rights reserved.

> —WALTER MARKS

☆

I take pleasure in nominating E. Y. Harburg, for two reasons: (1) he is a poet and (2) he has a social conscience. He thus ranks, by my estimate, above the many who have settled for the surface slickness favored by producers and critics.

An example of (1) which he wrote to Harold Arlen's music:

Little smiles of hope,
Little drops of tears,
Make this thing called love
Go dancing down the years.
> —"Little Drops of Rain" from *Gay Paree* (film)

©1961, 1962 Harwin Music Corporation. All rights controlled by Edwin H. Morris & Company, Inc. Used by permission.

I don't know why that moves me, and I'm not sure I want to know; its appeal is as unreasoning and unreasonable as that which I get from Keats's "Silent upon a peak in Darien."

An example of (2) which he wrote to Jay Gorney's music:

Once I built a railroad, made it run,
Made it race against time.
Once I built a railroad, now it's done.
Buddy, can't you spare a dime?
Once I built a tower to the sun,
Brick and rivet and lime.
Once I built a tower, now it's done
Brother can you spare a dime?
> —"Brother Can You Spare a Dime" from *Americana*

©1932 Harms, Inc. Copyright renewed. All rights reserved. Used by permission of Warner Bros. Music.

This has become, and deserves to be, a classic. In it, Harburg and his collaborator show their genuine concern for the humanity of which they are a part.

> —HENRY MYERS

☆

I am delighted at the chance to choose my favorite Broadway lyric writer because it gives me an opportunity to put on paper what I've been saying for years—that is, that Lee Adams is the best there is. Although the fact that we worked together on *Superman* would seem to influence my choice, the fact is that back when I was still in college and had no dreams of show business, I still was a big fan of Lee's.

Choosing representative lyrics is harder; I could go on all day citing favorites. But if I had to mention what I think is Lee Adams's special strength, it would be his ability to *simply* evoke large emotions and *simply* convey the essence of his characters by the precise way in which he selects just the one word that will make it all work. Examples of this abound in all his shows:

> One boy to laugh with,
> One boy to joke with and have Coke with. . . .

—"One Boy" from *Bye Bye Birdie*
©1960 Lee Adams and Charles Strouse; all right controlled by Edwin H. Morris & Company, Inc. Used by permission.

I find this one of the most artful and evocative stanzas of modern song, and it's all done so economically:

> Lots of dates,
> And no one to scold you!
> Loop the loop . . . and laugh at the view!
> Moonlight swims,
> And someone to hold you!
> Yeah! We got a lot of livin' to do!

—"A Lot of Livin' to Do" from *Bye Bye Birdie*
©1960 Lee Adams and Charles Strouse; all rights controlled by Edwin H. Morris & Company, Inc. Used by permission.

And, from *Golden Boy*, one of Adams's best and most typical lyrics:

> House at the beach,
> First cabin all the way . . .
> How sweet the song
> When you belong.

—"This Is the Life" from *Golden Boy*
©1964 Lee Adams and Charles Strouse. All rights controlled by Morley Music Co. Used by permission.

There are many others, in *All American* and *Superman* as well, but your space requirements and my disinclination to plug my own show prevent my going further. In any case, I think that the work of Lee Adams, in collaboration with the equally brilliant work of composer Charles Strouse, represents Broadway music or *any* music at the top of its form, and I'm glad of the chance to say so.

—David Newman

☆

How about Stephen Sondheim:

> . . .'Cause I'm dressed at last, at my best, and my banners are high
> Tell me, while I was getting ready,
> Did a parade go by?

—"A Parade in Town" from *Anyone Can Whistle*
Copyright © 1964 by Stephen Sondheim. (Burthen Music Co. owner of publication and allied rights for the world.) Used by permission of Chappell & Co. Inc.

Or any lyric in *Gypsy* or any lyric in *A Funny Thing Happened on the Way to the Forum.*

—MARY RODGERS

☆

I don't need to look far for the names of favored lyricists; I have had long and fruitful collaborations with two of the best in the history of Broadway, Lorenz Hart and Oscar Hammerstein II. They would doubtless win my vote hands down. But I would like to add the name of a man who will always have my personal and professional admiration: Cole Porter. Any one of dozens of lyrics could amply illustrate my reasons for choice, but I find particularly apt the words to "It's All Right With Me" from Porter's 1953 hit *Can-Can.* The imagery in these lyrics illustrates the special genius of Cole Porter:

> It's the wrong time and the wrong place
> Though your face is charming, it's the wrong face,
> It's not her face but such a charming face
> That it's all right with me.
> It's the wrong song in the wrong style
> Though your smile is lovely, it's the wrong smile,
> It's not her smile but such a lovely smile
> That it's all right with me.
> You can't know how happy I am that we met,
> I'm strangely attracted to you.
> There's someone I'm trying so hard to forget.
> Don't you want to forget someone too?
> It's the wrong game with the wrong chips,
> Though your lips are tempting, they're the wrong lips,
> They're not her lips, but such tempting lips
> That if some night you're free,
> Dear, it's all right, it's all right with me.

Copyright © 1953 by Cole Porter. Used by permission of Chappell & Co., Inc.

Porter's urbanity and wit combined with a wonderful heart and naivete appeal to me—probably because these were outstanding combined qualities of Hart and Hammerstein. "It's All Right With Me" somehow says it all.

—RICHARD RODGERS

☆

I think first of Irving Berlin, Ira Gershwin and Lorenz Hart. Berlin is the old master whose songs I was humming in high school, and still champion.

And for deftness, I'll take a song Berlin wrote for *Coconuts*. The Marx Brothers dwarfed every song writer, but "Five O'Clock Tea" remains in my memory as an especially felicitous example of excellent rhyming.

Everybody has his favorite, of course, when it comes to Gershwin. My own are (1) the couplet he wrote for his brother's inspired march:

> He's the man the people choose—
> Loves the Irish and the Jews.
>> —"Wintergreen for President" from *Of Thee I Sing*
>>> ©1932 New World Music Corporation. Copyright renewed.
>>> All rights reserved. Used by permission of Warner Bros. Music.

And (2) the "Union Square" lyric in *Let 'Em Eat Cake* with the refrain that satirized not only Karl Marx but our present New Left.

I'd known Lorenz Hart at college and ran into him and Richard Rodgers one day in the 1920s, and they asked me to write a few sketches for a revue they had in mind. The sketches (one on Coolidge and one on Bryan) became part of the first *Garrick Gaities*, which put the great team of Rodgers and Hart on the map. One vote for "Manhattan" in that delightful score.

As for the other greats, I'd pick Frank Loesser's score for *Guys and Dolls* because it was so integrated into the book that it was hard to tell where the dialogue left off and the music began. I go for that unforgettable opening that so superbly set the stage:

I got the horse right here
The name is Paul Revere
And here's a guy that says if the weather's clear,
Can do, can do. . . .

I'm pickin' Valentine
'Cause on the morning line
The guy has got him figured at five to nine. . . .

But look at Epitaph.
He wins it by a half
Accordin' to this here in the *Telegraph*. . . .
                    —'Fugue for Tinhorns" from *Guys and Dolls*
©1950 Frank Music Corp. Used by permission.

Oscar Hammerstein II was perhaps the best poet of them all. Even in his flops there were always great lyrics (but his books never equaled them). My favorite was *Oklahoma!* and again a great opening number, "Oh, What a Beautiful Mornin'."

Cole Porter was perhaps the most ingenious rhymer of all. "You're the Top" is my favorite:

You're the top, you're Mahatma Gandhi,
You're the top, you're Napoleon brandy,
You're the purple light
Of a summer night
In Spain,
You're the National Gallery,
You're Garbo's salary,
You're cellophane!
                    —"You're the Top" from *Anything Goes*
©1934 Harms, Inc. Copyright renewed.
All rights reserved. Used by permission of Warner Bros. Music.

There were lyrics in Alan Jay Lerner's *Brigadoon* that belong in any good anthology; and—need I say?—*My Fair Lady*. And, back in my salad days, there were the lyrics of P.G. Wodehouse in those delightfully intimate musical shows—and, of course, the immortal W.S.Gilbert verses.

There are other good ones—but the above are the lyricists I'd want to be stranded on a desert island with most.
                    —MORRIE RYSKIND

☆

My favorite older lyric writer is E. Y. Harburg, a wizard with words (the brilliant variants in "When I'm Not Near the Girl I Love" are a good example). Far and away the best of the new lyric writers is Stephen Sondheim. Beside wit, ingenuity, and warmth, he brings a sense of the character to every word that is sung. He is the first and perhaps the only true *theater* lyricist we have. There is no need to cite examples—any of his songs proves the point.

—Burt Shevelove

☆

I find it impossible to name a "favorite lyricist, past or present"; there were too many excellent ones.

But of the lyricists with whom I have had a working relationship, I wouldn't hesitate to name Sheldon Harnick, particularly for his work in *Fiddler on the Roof*. Sheldon's lyrics are not only bright and pointed they are consistently, conspicuously, completely true to character and situation.

And if I had to choose only one of his many superb lyrics in that show, I suppose I would pick one that was written under pressure, out of town. We were looking for a musical finish to a scene between Tevye and his wife, a song that would illustrate their very special relationship. I remember Sheldon coming into my hotel room and reading the lyric of "Do You Love Me?" He asked me what I thought of it. I could have hugged him. I think I did.

That's the duet that ends:

GOLDE: Do I love him?
        For twenty-five years I've lived with him,
        Fought with him, starved with him.
        Twenty-five years my bed is his.
        If that's not love, what is?
TEVYE: Then you love me?
GOLDE: I suppose I do.
TEVYE: And I suppose I love you, too.
TEVYE and GOLDE:
        It doesn't change a thing,
        But even so,
        After twenty-five years,
        It's nice to know.

—"Do You Love Me?" from *Fiddler on the Roof*
©1964 Sunbeam Music Corp. All rights administered by The New York
Times Music Corporation, New York, N.Y. Used by permission.

—Joseph Stein

☆

Either Cole Porter . . .

> Flying too high
> With some guy
> In the sky
> Is my i-dea of nothing to do. . . .
>
> —"I Get a Kick Out of You" from *Anything Goes*
> ©1934 by Harms Inc. Used by permission

. . . or Lorenz Hart:

> It was never
> My endeavor
> To be too clever or smart. . . .
>
> —"I Could Write a Book" from *Pal Joey*
> Copyright ©1940 by Chappell & Co., Inc. Copyright renewed. Used by permission.
>
> —PETER STONE

☆

I guess you know it's a hopeless task you set. But of lyricists living I would choose Lee Adams. Warmth, a great felicity to musical demands, humility (by that I mean a desire that the "song" itself, the medium, so to speak, be the message), and simplicity are among the traits I admire in his work.

As an example I'll cite the opening of this song. It would seem the mood is set almost artlessly: Harlem, lonesome boy . . .

> Summer,
> Not a bit of breeze,
> Neon lights are shining
> Through the tired trees. . . .
>
> —"Night Song" from *Golden Boy*
> ©1964 Lee Adams and Charles Strouse. All rights controlled
> by Morley Music Co. Used by permission.

No clever rhymes here; bare bones, lyrically speaking, but not many others do it. Not that he lacks in the intricate rhyme department, to wit:

> Take off the gloomy mask of tragedy
> It's not your style!
> You'll look so good that you'll be glad ya de-
> Cided to smile. . . .
>
> —"Put on a Happy Face" from *Bye Bye Birdie*
> ©1960 Lee Adams and Charles Strouse; all rights controlled
> by Edwin H. Morris & Company, Inc. Used by permission.

I can't compare artists. That is the task of committees. I can only add that I admire many of these traits in many others, which should go without saying, and that among the non-living lyricists (again with the arbitrary distinction of being "Broadway-produced") my favorite remains that man of urbanity and warmth, of passion and detachment, Cole Porter—and when you start getting around to favorite composer questionnaires, he's going to be there, too.

—CHARLES STROUSE

III. On Theater Music.....

The man that hath no music in himself,
Nor is not moved with concord of sweet sounds,
Is fit for treasons, stratagems and spoils.
THE MERCHANT OF VENICE

The American Musical: Still Glowin', Still Crowin', Still Goin' Strong

By Jerry Herman

In this edited version of a taped discussion, the questions have been swept out of your way so that Mr. Herman speaks directly to the reader in his answers to questions about the American musical theater, prepared for publication under his supervision, as follows:

Aside from being a songwriter, I'm a composer-lyricist for the musical theater. No, that's not being redundant. There's an enormous difference.

The title song from *Mame* is songwriting. "If He Walked Into My Life" is musical playwriting. The first song may lift the spirit, may even move the emotions, but exists solely as entertainment. The second probes a character, and informs and enlightens us . . . is actually a substitute for dialogue . . . is playwriting in the form of music and lyric.

God knows, I'm not knocking songwriting! I believe passionately in melody, simplicity, and giving the audience something to hum on the way out. Songwriting is what has made our musical theater great, and I'm proud that I can be listed in that category. But for me, the great satisfaction comes from taking over from the playwright and heightening an emotion that might not be reached by the spoken word alone. It is this rollercoaster between dialogue and song, this homogenization of the spoken and the sung word, that makes a career in the American musical theater so fascinating.

A good example of particularly effective homogenization in a work of mine is the "Dancing" sequence from *Hello, Dolly!* Mike Stewart, Gower Champion and I tried to blend completely our specific contributions, and it is for me the most effective segment of the show . . . Dance, music, dialogue and lyric truly became one.

Other examples? . . . "I Won't Send Roses" from *Mack and Mabel**, and the entire "We Need a Little Christmas" sequence from *Mame*.

The lovely thing about the relationship I've had with all my collaborators (Don Appell, Lawrence and Lee, Mike Stewart) is this joy of collaboration I've bakeen talking about. We gleefully accept each other's criticism, because we're sure that it isn't really criticism at all, but another step toward our mutual goal . . . the show . . . the single-minded vision we collectively have.

. . . . . In working on a score, my mind works with the *total*. In my thoughts, music and lyrics are inseparable, because I know of no other way to work. I almost never write a piece of music and then set it to lyric or write a lyric and then set it to music. I'll get the music idea and the lyric idea simultaneously and build them together.

I don't think lyrics will necessarily become more poetic as the musical theater progresses, but I do think they'll become more *important*. In the last few decades the lyric has advanced light-years ahead of what has happened musically. If you ask me what is the best single lyric ever written, I would

*A new musical by Jerry Herman, in preparation as we went to press.

have to say that the one that comes first to mind is Stephen Sondheim's "Some People" from *Gypsy*. It's perfectly metered and rhymed, it's a lyric in the Larry Hart sense of a *song* lyric, and at the same time it is a piece of dramatic literature, poetry that defines the character of Madam Rose as clearly as three scenes of dialogue. You *know* this woman after hearing it. It's harsh, it's bitter, it's unrelenting, it's skillful, it works on, like, three levels for me, and I admire it enormously. In fact, I admire the *Gypsy* lyrics and score more than any other I can think of at this moment.

. . . . .Few lyricists are fine poets (Oscar Hammerstein II was one exception). Most people don't realize that lyric-writing is a specific and unique art form. It has nothing to do with poetry. It serves a totally different function. Lyrics are one-half of Siamese twins. For example, in "Some People" when Sondheim writes "But *I* at least gotta try"* that "I" falls on a triumphant high note that tops the previous sixteen bars.

"I at least gotta try"? Not particularly brilliant, you might say. If it were spoken in dialogue I would have said to myself, the man's lost his mind. But the use of "But *I* at least gotta try" with those particular notes knocked me out of my seat. Lyric-writing is an art form that is unique and differs from poetry in that it must be attached to a piece of music and rises or falls with it.

Lyrics aren't meant to be read—I loathe seeing lyrics in print separated from their music. The notes that accompany "You're still glowin', you're still crowin', you're still goin' strong"** turn those words into a sincere, warm expression of welcome home. Say them, and I don't believe a word. Sing them, and you know what happens!

. . . . .You also have to know what *not* to musicalize. There are things in *Hello, Dolly* that are better spoken than sung. I thought a lot about musicalizing Thornton Wilder's famous line: "Money is like manure—it's not worth a thing unless it's spread around." I once had it in a lyric, but I decided that it was much more effective as spoken word.

In the musical version of *Auntie Mame*, one of Mame's famous speeches is: "Life is a banquet and most poor sons of bitches are starving to death." I tried to use it in a lyric. No matter what I did with it, it simply was not as effective as the marvelous spoken statement. Rhymed, it isn't as strong. Again, I had to decide what *not* to musicalize. . . . . .My own best lyric so far? "If He Walked Into My Life" from *Mame* and "I Don't Want to Know" from *Dear World* second.

. . . . .The musical is the American theater's major claim to fame. We are masters of the musical. Possibly we're behind in drama, or in set design, but constructing a musical is what we do better than anyone else in the world.

*Copyright © 1959 by Norbeth Productions, Inc. and Stephen Sondheim. Stratford Music Corporation and Williamson Music, Inc., owners of publication and allied rights. Used by permission of Chappell & Co., Inc.

**© 1963 Jerry Herman; all rights controlled by Edwin H. Morris & Company, Inc. Used by permission.

This is America's own art form, this is not what we have copied from anybody else, this is *ours*.

I resent anyone saying, "Imagine, a musical won the Pulitzer Prize." What's wrong with that? Why should the musical take second position, why isn't it proudly heralded as our art form, the top of our theater—even culturally?

. . . . .As to how I got started on this kind of a career, I have a very strange musical background. I started playing by ear as a four-year-old. My mother dragged me off to Juilliard. You know, what do you do with a kid that sits down at the piano and picks out the right chords for his own version of "Claire de Lune"? I was encouraged to develop my ear, and I play fluently.

College really got me started in the direction of *Hello, Dolly*. I went to the University of Miami because they had an experimental drama department with student productions which would give me a chance to try my craft. I got rid of all the pretentious ideas, you know, that a young man wants to try. Then I did a varsity revue called *I Feel Wonderful*. A group of Miami businessmen liked it and gave me $15,000 to produce it off Broadway at the Theater de Lys, where it ran for only two months. But it got me an agent and the kind of notice it sometimes takes a decade to acquire. I kept on sharpening my tools with television writing. Then I did a cabaret revue called *Nightcap* which really started a chain reaction. The producer of *Parade* did *Parade* because he saw *Nightcap*; the producer of *Milk and Honey* had seen *Parade*; and David Merrick, who produced *Hello, Dolly*, had seen *Milk and Honey*. You might call me a college kid with a great dream who kind of forced his way into a cabaret on 4th Street and made it happen.

. . . . .Subsidy? No. I lived on the very tiny income from my musical work. I don't think a direct subsidy would have helped me at all. In fact, if I'd had a subsidy at that point I might have been tempted to sit back and write what I was not ready to write. I *had* to start the way I started. And I might have been tempted to ignore that whole, necessary phase of my career and gone immediately to work trying to write a *Hello, Dolly* at a point when, first of all, I wasn't ready, and, second, there would have been no takers. I'm not sure I know any *other* composer who would have been helped by a subsidy, either.

The only way to get a David Merrick to accept your work is to function, to do something he can *see*. He's not going to accept you because you go into his office and play four pretty songs which you might have written if you were on some kind of a subsidy. You have to go out and work off Broadway, in television, you have to put something out there that a Merrick can see and *trust*. Of course, when I was just starting out I would never have spoken this way. I would have grabbed the subsidy and gone home and tried to write the Great American Musical.

Milk and Honey was a marvelous springboard for me. I was nominated for a Tony Award, and after an Actors Fund benefit performance, David Merrick stopped back and said he wanted to talk to me about something, which turned out to be *Hello, Dolly.*

. . . . . Adaptations? I wish I knew why that seems to be a dirty word. I *love* adaptations. Is *Carousel* any less of a classic because it's based on another work? And don't try to tell me *Dolly* isn't a new piece of theater. *The Matchmaker* is its skeleton. But Gower Champion, Mike Stewart, Carol Channing and I have given it flesh and blood of its very own. *Hello, Dolly* is not *The Matchmaker* with a few fancy feathers. It is a brand new baby whose grandfather happens to be Thornton Wilder. If the baby resembles its grandfather, that's all to the good. It's easier to write a good score if you love the material you're working from. Some of my best things have been written because of a line of dialogue; for example, "Ribbons Down My Back" and "Put on Your Sunday Clothes" are lines of dialogue from Thornton Wilder. Those few words express the whole character of Mrs. Malloy when she's awakening again, a widow ready to go back into the world. Those beautiful words of Wilder's really mean, "I'm ready to go out, and I hope some man notices me again." "Ribbons" would never have been written without the Wilder original, and neither would "Sunday Clothes". I might have written a song that said "Come on, we're going to New York," but it would not have had that hook, that title, that *feeling* (of course, *Milk and Honey* and *Mack and Mabel* are originals).

. . . . . What's going to happen next? Every decade or so, we say the musical has gone as far as it can go, and yet it keeps on developing. In its infancy and for a while afterwards, the Broadway musical was synonymous with girls and smutty jokes and legs. This is no longer true, there is no sex in *Hello, Dolly,* not one line that could be considered blue. Neither is there in *Fiddler on the Roof,* and yet these two were the hottest tickets in years. The bases of both shows are important works of literature.

Oklahoma was the breakthrough of all time in 1943, but it's an old fashioned musical today. Its dream ballet, its use of counterpart figures, its book and score not really blended, all these and other details are twenty years apart from a homogenized folk musical like *Fiddler on the Roof.* In *Fiddler* you aren't especially aware of the songs, the ballets, the dialogue as such, you are captivated by all the arts blended into one piece of theater. You can remove a song, a ballet, a scene or even a character from *Oklahoma,* and nothing much would happen to the rest of it. But you can't remove anything from *Fiddler.* It is a concept of homogenized musical that is entirely new and is the result of a slow and subtle progress over the years. *The Most Happy Fella* was an attempt at a brand new kind of blending of opera and musical theater. For some people it was not successful; for me it was. *West Side Story* was far advanced from *Oklahoma* in its homogenization. Here the big break-through was the subject matter. Until *West Side Story* no one would have dreamed of doing a musical about gang war.

Getting back to Jerry Bock and Sheldon Harnick, who did *Fiddler*, I admire their work very much. *She Loves Me* may not go down in history as their most successful show, but in it they did a little thing—I have to call it a thing because it's not a song, it's not recitative, I don't know what to call it. It was a greeting to each customer who came into the perfume shop. The sales people sang it, something about "Good afternoon, madam" . . .eight or sixteen bars and they trailed off and then the dialogue began. Bock and Harnick blended the elements of the musical as they have never been blended before

. . . . .Yes, I know what failure feels like. *Dear World* was a big smash failure on every level, critical and box office. But you pick yourself off the floor the next morning, if you have your wits about you, and you start working on something else.

As for success, I think that its most important result, for me, is that it has made me trust my instincts. I trust myself as a creative person more than I ever did before. I was always quite ready to doubt any new piece of material that I did. I don't mean that success has made me think that everything I write is perfection, or that I won't throw a song out in Philadelphia. But now if I *believe* in something I will talk up for it. Success has helped me get rid of some of the insecurity that the struggling artist has got to have. When you're living in a little one-room apartment and going to the producers' offices where *nobody* wants you, day after day, you *have* to develop a slight artistic insecurity. Even though, way down deep inside, you believe in what you are carrying in your briefcase, the fact that nobody in the world wants it *must* have an effect on you. The acceptance of my work over the past decade has made the new work easier for me. My working habits are the same, I haven't changed my methods or my style, but I've gotten rid of a lot of emotional problems, and now the work is the joy it should be. Success has helped me to *function*.

Theater Music: Seven Views

George Abbott
Jerry Bock
Micki Grant
E. Y. Harburg
Richard Rodgers
Harvey Schmidt
Jule Styne

On various occasions, distinguished musical authors (composers, lyricists and librettists) have complied generously with requests to call on their experience and contribute their thoughts on theater music in such aspects as: What makes a good show tune? What is the function of music in the theater? What are your favorite show tunes? What is the state of the art of theater music, and quo vadis? *Here is a sampling of their views.*

George Abbott:

A good show tune has to be of use to the show it is in. It is meant to be sung—or danced.

"The Rites of Spring" is an exciting piece of music, but I don't believe that it has any great future as a Broadway musical.

Name the best show tunes? I couldn't—it would have to be 200.

I know what I like. I like songs that move me. I like woman songs like "Love for Sale" or "Falling in Love With Love" or "Summertime." I like the man songs like "The Birth of the Blues" or "Sunrise, Sunset." I like nostalgic songs like "White Christmas." And I also think that the new rock music is very effective in the theater—as for instance, *Hair*. And then, of course, everybody has to like "Tea for Two." And for dancing, give me good old "Slaughter on Tenth Avenue."

So those are some random thoughts, but they are superficial. I need the 200.

Jerry Bock:

First off, where are we right now in the American musical theater?
Betwixt and between. Holding on and reaching out. Stumbling.

Now stumbling is not the worst thing that could happen to a person or a
musical theater. I mean it may shake you up, but half the time you catch
yourself and half the time you fall without mortal harm. The scrapes
smoothen, the bruises blend and the wounds wizen. And, more often than
not, you discover in passing that you've stumbled forward. But back to
"Where are we?"

I think holding on is beginning to make us weary. I think the trio of
tympani roll into overture into cheerful opening number is a succession of
musical theater events that needs tending to. I think the sound that usually
emanates from the orchestra pit too often lulls rather than excites, comforts
rather than exhilarates and ultimately becomes a two-and-a-half-hour
soporific that causes us to tune out rather than tune in. I think we are
discontented when frequently faced with the too pretty, too antiseptic, too
predictable two-in-lovenicks that proliferate on the musical scene. I think
we tire of sets and costumes that are just up there without speaking to the
point or helping the heart or contributing to the charisma of the musical
play. And finally, I think, if we were not restless we'd be in danger of
becoming tone deaf, astigmatic and halt from the assault of the conventional. But we are restless. And we are beginning to reach out or, perhaps
more appropriate, step out.

We are not always hearing overtures these days. Or, when we hear them,
they are sometimes unique, occasionally specific and now and then oddly
quiet. We are not always seeing fairyland show curtains that hide the
opening scene. These days we often walk into the theater with the curtain
already up revealing the opening scene, making us feel that the actors are
waiting for us to sit and settle rather than vice versa, as before. And we are
also hearing musical sounds inside the theater that we normally expect to
hear outside. Sounds of pop-rock, hard and cool. Sounds of high
amplification. Sounds of electrified plectrums accompanying the sight of
fresh faces against the background of startling visual projections. These are
sights and sounds of new contributors stepping out on the American musical theater's parade ground to the airs of *Sergeant Pepper's Lonely Hearts Club
Band* for *Hair* raising ceremonies. It is their own thing, and the theater
should welcome it or be justifiably accused of outrageous snobbery, dusty
isolationism, potential decadence. Welcome the wunderkind. They may not
be the only step, but at least they've taken one. And if they resist locking in
their innovations so that they, too soon, become conventions and avoid
trapping their freshness in repetition so that it, too soon, becomes stale,
their steps will be high, wide and handsome. And more important, helpful.

There are creative brothers who don't have much to say but say it brilliantly. Their style supersedes their content. There are other creative brothers who mean to say a great deal but say it awkwardly. Their content supersedes their style. That gap is what we all try to fill. But I confess to this. I favor the second set of brothers. That's the area I search for and root for. That's the underdog. And that's where the next step is always poised.

Tell us to be restless, annoyed, angry. Ask us to stretch and struggle, to reject and reflect. But don't encourage us to join the fold if we can't baaaah. Make us bristle and burn and yearn, but don't frame our reference in a trend. Implore us to do our own thing, what we will, better each time. Censor repetition, resignation and rut. But don't insist we join the union of organized popularity, for tomorrow it may be a closed shop.

An artist named Segonzac has been quoted as follows: "We never know what painting we will work on next. It all depends on the light." I imagine the American musical theater's next step is in the same bind. And when it's taken we probably won't know it. Dramatic steps are often imperceptible to those who take them. Those who take them are simply trying to walk on. It may be the most we can ask of each other. And ourselves.

Micki Grant:

For me, two good show tunes can be as unlike as a quiet pond and a rushing river, both of which are water and both of which are songs.

A good show tune can be one which has the definitive purpose of advancing the plot and nothing more. It can be simple or too musically complex for the average theatergoer to find himself humming as he leaves the theater. It should never be too complex lyrically for the theatergoer to grasp even as it is delivered, however. After all, when one sits down to a good meal one wants to taste and enjoy it then and there and leave the digestion for later.

Another good show tune, while forwarding the action, can be universal enough in what it has to say to become a separate entity outside the context of the show, i.e.: most of the numbers from *West Side Story*, a good deal of Rodgers and Hammerstein; melodically appealing, yet uncomplex enough to get a good hum going.

Neither one should be guilty of slowing down or halting the action simply because it is a great song. If one has to go back in one's mind to pick up the action from where it was before the song began, it probably didn't belong there. Being "a show-stopper" and stopping the show are not necessarily the same.

Being a lyricist as well as a composer, I'm afraid I've been guilty, in writing this, of being unable to separate the two. Here are a few of my favorite songs:

"Glitter and Be Gay" from *Candide* is, musically, exactly that, gay and glittering. At the same time, it depicts the irony of Cunegonde's situation.

"Aquarius" from *Hair* fairly soars with the exuberant spirit and expectation of a bright new age.

"Hello, Dolly" has that light, casual, almost conversational feeling of old friends greeting each other.

"A Sleepin' Bee" from *House of Flowers* is as wistful and elusive as the ideas expressed in its lyrics.

"And This Is My Beloved" from *Kismet* contains the mystery and wonder of the Beloved it describes. "Stranger in Paradise" is another of my favorites.

I could go on and on: Weill's "Pirate Jenny" and "Surabaya Johnny," Gershwin's "My Man's Gone Now," Berlin's "Show Business;" practically all of Bernstein, Rodgers and Brel; the satirical musical wittiness of Sondheim; "The Eagle and Me" among others of Arlen; Coleman's "Big Spender" and Newley's "What Kind of Fool Am I?"

Mind you, this is only a very tiny list of the show tunes I've enjoyed listening to, just off the top of my head. No doubt I've failed to mention some that are very important to me, probably because they have become entities within themselves. Mind you also, as a relative neophyte in the business I do not assess any of these as being "the best" show tunes. They are a tiny fraction of a long list of show tunes I've enjoyed, some of which are from shows I never had the privilege of seeing.

E. Y. Harburg:

A song is a song is a song . . . but a song in a stage musical is something special. It is a scene . . . an extension of the libretto . . . a development of character. The function of the music is to heighten the emotional quality of the scene and to make you empathize with tears or laughter, depending on the situation.

A song demands more of an audience than its interest and attention. It demands applause, the toughest achievement in the theater. This is what makes songwriting for the stage a mysterious and unique art form.

There are many fine composers, but few who could adapt to the histrionic demands of the stage.

No matter how perfect the lyric may be for the situation or how excellent the tune, unless the music provides the right emotional atmosphere, the happy souffle becomes the sad pancake.

George Gershwin's music was so completely wedded to the theater that the tune gave you the humor, satire or mood of the song almost without the words. Listen to "Bidin' My Time," "It Ain't Necessarily So," "Wintergreen for President." In the space of a blackout, he could break your heart with "Bess, You Is My Woman Now", melt you with the tenderness of "Summertime" or rouse you with "Strike Up the Band." The breathless range of his outpourings was amazing. But what is more astounding is that these melodies had a life of their own outside the theater. Although they were innovative, they were always infectious. They had the power of drama and the grandeur of simplicity. This is what every good composer knows, feels and tries to evoke.

Before the Rock of Ages hit the golden age of musicals, the period glittered with many shining talents who have left their echoes in the hills of time. The guitar pluckers of today cannot find the living melody or hear the witty phrase through the mad thunder of their percussion instruments. They have substituted noise for emotion, frenzy for drama, beat for melody, euphoria for humor and sentimentality for sentiment. These can never make theater music, or communicate mature emotion.

Among the myriad of great songs that emerged from the glory that was Broadway and that still sets my adrenalin dancing are "Ol' Man River," "September Song," "Bess You Is My Woman Now," "Without a Song" "My Funny Valentine," "Night and Day," "Bill," "Blues in the Night," "Mack the Knife," the entire score of "Porgy and Bess" and more in that category. What was great about all the above songs is that they were not only indigenous to the theater, but they were literate, fresh, moving and musical. The words gave destiny to the music and the music gave wings to the words. They were meticulously constructed for long-distance flight.

Then, of course, there are the bang-up show stoppers that were particularly pertinent to the libretto, like "Bongo on the Congo," "Show Business," "Sam and Delilah," "The Begat," "Comedy Tonight," "Diamonds Are a Girl's Best Friend," "Friendship" (from *Dubarry Was a Lady*), "When I'm Not Near the Girl I Love," "Fugue for Tinhorns," "T'morra, T'morra," "The Rain in Spain." I'm afraid it will take many a decade before the cultural atmosphere will again induce that sort of creative exuberance, wit and discipline.

Yes, times were a-changin' in 1960, but "The Great Songs of the Sixties" ain't blowin' in the wind of the 1970s. The youngsters who have been building that bridge over the troubled Watergate must still look to the rainbow that bridges man's hope to the heaven of his imagination.

Richard Rodgers:

When I studied music at Juilliard, I was told that music is composed of three elements: melody, harmony and rhythm. To an enormous degree, what they were hearing at Fillmore East includes only one-third of these: it has rhythm. It has very little in the way of harmony and nothing in the way of melody. You can, I suppose, tear up the old definition and say that rhythm is music. But I don't believe it. I don't think that anybody else does either.

Both *Hair* and *Promises, Promises* as scores try to be hard rock. Whether they succeed in this respect or not, I am not expert enough to know. But I know where I would place my money, if there were some way of betting on it. I would bet that the song "I'll Never Fall in Love Again" from *Promises* will be around when everything in *Hair*, and all of the hard rock portions of *Promises*, are forgotten. That's a song song. It's the only thing in the score that anybody knows and I think the reason is that it has melody and harmony, and the rhythm falls naturally. It's a lovely rhythm, but this isn't what it's based on. It is a very good song.

People are intimidated, mystified by the business of writing music. They can't imagine how you do it. They are sure that you wake up in the middle of the night and grab for a pencil—which has never happened to me in my life. I do it in all sorts of ways. I don't usually finger a melody, I usually get the approach sitting in a chair or walking around outdoors. Then I'll do the tune on a piece of paper, or at the piano. If it is on a piece of paper, I'll eventually take it to the piano to hear it.

I give the orchestrator a piano part so full that it cannot be played by one person, very often with further suggestions: a flute should do this, etc. I make a three-staff piano part, melody and the two lower ones for harmony and rhythm. The staves are very full, and this procedure works out very well because when I get the orchestration there are no surprises.

Music is my medium—my language. A painter's medium is color, in a composition on canvas. I use sounds. A good example is a thing I did for television a number of years ago called *Victory at Sea*. I had to write themes for all sorts of activity. There were no lyrics—no words. But there were pictures, which made it the same as having words. How do you make a noise like a submarine? Well, you make it your way. You've got your tool—which is sound—and you come up with sounds that, to you, are appropriate to a submarine.

I think *Carousel* is my best score. It isn't easy to explain why I think so. I have more respect for it; I think the music has more to say, and that the book has more to say. Maybe I like it best because to me it was the most important—in terms of quality. It dug deeper.

I like the actual work. I like being given a lyric, and taking it and trying to work out the problem, trying to get a good idea for a song—the music—that pleases me. Rehearsals please me. I enjoy the transfer from my head to somebody else's throat—the whole process. I like the whole process.

Harvey Schmidt:

If I try to conjure up the ideal Broadway show score, or imagine myself sitting in a theater listening to the kind of songs I'd like to hear coming at me from a stage, I find it difficult to get above or beyond the score for *Gypsy* by Jule Styne and Stephen Sondheim. Others may be more musically brilliant (*Candide*), more bewitching in style (*House of Flowers*), more comedic (*Guys and Dolls)* or more moving (*The King and I*), but *Gypsy* manages a very satisfying mixture of all these qualities wrapped up together and served on a traditional hard-edged-show-biz-Broadway platter that is thrilling in that special way that has made the form continue to work over the decades when the combination is right.

There is something about musical theater that demands a certain strength and boldness to cross the distance from the stage to the head and heart of the viewer, to connect in time before the next beat crushes it underfoot. It is a place for big outlines and absolute clarity of intent. The songs that communicate the most directly have very strong profiles and usually appear on the first encounter to be likeable, understandable and knowable.

I don't necessarily mean that one need be able to turn right around after the first hearing and re-render it intact, since, at its best, it will also have some uniquely mysterious quality that tantalizes the ear and sets it apart from the norm. In fact, it may, in purely technical terms, be a very complicated piece of musical machinery. Yet it is instantly clear what business it is about, and you are free to respond accordingly. You quickly read its own special personality, characteristic, and color. It stands alone and is unlike any other song in the show. If the entire score is successful you end up with a whole family of such individual musical statements, each very personal and different, yet joining together to form an entire mountain range of strong profiles joined at the base in a common landscape of musical style.

Gypsy manages all this like gangbusters, but its real distinction is in the fact that at its heart it is a "serious" musical dealing with deep human drives and needs. And it manages to avoid the pitfalls that work against most attempts at "seriousness" in musicals: sentimentality and pretentiousness. Each song is strongly rooted in character and story, yet bounces off the stage with artful simplicity, never once violating its premise to "Let Me Entertain You."

Whatever the word "entertainment" exactly may or may not mean (and to me it often means simply keeping me awake), it seems to have been slipping out of the musical theater a little more with each passing year. First we had shows with entertaining songs; then we had entertaining songs that also contained deeper subject matter; now, increasingly, we seem to have only subject matter with little or no entertainment. Traditionally, "entertainment" is what the musical theater is about, and if we change that hat for another, we end up with the academic musical, the personal musical or the statement musical, any of which may have valid things to say but may never find a large enough audience because they are unable to engage the attention by also being entertaining.

I have always felt that one should be able to do a musical about any subject and somehow make it entertaining. The fact that *Gypsy* also happens to have a show-business background doesn't make it any easier to pull off successfully. The dead-center rightness of the score to its subject matter should conceivably work just as well in transferring Admiral Byrd's polar expedition to the musical stage. And though *Gypsy* is a definitive big Broadway musical, the same attention to direct communication is just as necessary for the smaller off-Broadway situation. Having worked for both, I find there is absolutely no difference in their needs. They both demand music that strives to enlighten, illuminate and enlarge the material at hand in as bright, bold and seductive a way as possible; and whenever this happens, I not only manage to stay awake, I actually get excited (and so does the audience around me).

Jule Styne:

In 1929, after writing my first popular song, titled *Sunday,* and after my father was positive that my song was a big hit, he proudly announced to the family that I had become a "songwriter."

In recent years the word "composer" has been substituted for "songwriter." I don't know whether this has anything to do with the difference between eating at Downey's where a fellow who writes popular songs or lyrics is called "songwriter"; and eating at Twenty-One, where the same fellow becomes a "composer" and the lyric writer becomes the "lyricist."

Whether the song is *Some Enchanted Evening, Maria, True Love, People, Swanee,* all big hits are a result of a good lyric set to a good popular tune. This combination makes a good song, and the ones mentioned above were written by good songwriters. I'll never forget what my father said, after reading the reviews of my first Broadway show, "What's this?" he asked angrily. "The critics are calling you a composer, better you should be a songwriter. You'll write a song and get paid right away."

I don't mean to say that songwriters cannot compose. Richard Rodgers's *Slaughter on Tenth Avenue,* George Gershwin's *Rhapsody in Blue, American in Paris,* his wonderful *Piano Concerto in F,* Leonard Bernstein's inspiring dance music for *West Side Story* are all memorable compositions. For myself, I recall the *Cops and Robbers Ballet* for *High Button Shoes,* the dramatic scoring in *Gypsy* and *Funny Girl* as composition efforts.

But Rodgers, Cole Porter, Gershwin, Frank Loesser, will always be remembered for their popular songs in the theater and movies. A while back, in a discussion of theater music, Dick Rodgers reminded me, "There is no substitute for a hit song in a show." To the public, this means tunes to whistle as they leave a show, albums and records to remind them of what they've seen and much *more* communication with their young ones, who after all are the real critics these days.

Of course the drama cannot be neglected in writing a musical play. That is the songwriters' (meaning lyric and tune writers) first obligation to the venture. But there is a new and better way to write the "specifics," those numbers which must advance the story. The songwriters have found a subtler way to express the drama through words and music. The specific soliloquies have been replaced by a more general song—making musical and lyrical entertainment by themselves and at the same time furthering the story—as in the case of *Hello, Dolly!, Gypsy, West Side Story, My Fair Lady, No strings* and *Funny Girl.*

Today, more than ever before, it is important for Broadway songwriters to write songs with popular appeal. If a show has hit songs, the albums sell, and the show benefits by the "spiel" the disc jockeys make about that particular hit song from that particular hit show. And the new songwriter owes it to himself to strive to write popular songs. This eventually will help him build a standard catalogue. Just glance through the standard hits of Rodgers, Porter, Loesser, Harold Arlen, Vincent Youmans, Johnny Mercer, Irving Berlin. These kids wrote popular hits.

I recall another anecdote about my father. One day he asked me, "How come melody writers are called composers, and a lyric writer is never called a poet?"

"Well—"I said.

He said, "I'll tell you what a composer is—Bach, Beethoven and Mozart. Better you should be a songwriter."

Some of my fellow ASCAP members, including those mentioned above, may be composers. But all, including yours truly, are really songwriters.

Musical Theater Has Always Been a Theater Of Adaptations

By John Kander

I ran into that fellow again yesterday. You know the one I mean. He's at all the cocktail parties, and before he's halfway through his first pink gin he's off and running on his favorite topic—the peculiar condition of the American musical theater.

"Adaptations!" He announces scornfully. "Everything today is an adaptation. What's happened to our creative people? They're just taking all the old stories and putting music to them, hoping to turn a fast buck."

What he really wants to say (and would if it weren't such a cliché) is, "It's not like the good old days." His point is partially valid, of course. *Fiddler on the Roof, Mame, Cabaret, The Apple Tree, Promises, Promises, Your Own Thing, Applause* and *A Little Night Music,* to name some recent examples, are, in one way or another, "adaptations" of previously-conceived material. How did this happen, anyway? When did our musical theater craftsmen run out of steam and become so dependent on stories which had already proven their "commercial" value?

In 1597 an interesting theatrical evening was presented in Florence; interesting because the characters sang of their feelings, problems and aspirations. It was quite a novelty; no one had seen anything quite like it. It was (or is generally accepted as being) the first musical play, the first opera—and a solid hit. It was, of course, an adaptation. It was called *Dafne* and retold the ancient tale of one of Apollo's less successful attempts at

Copyright © 1967 by Trans World Airlines, Inc. Used by permission.

145

girl-chasing. Everyone in the audience knew the story, but music seemed to add another dimension, and the possibilities of this strange new art form, combining music and drama, seemed endless.

Jacopo Peri, the composer, knew a good thing when he found it, and three years later he produced what is probably the second musical play, the second opera. Another hit, and another adaptation. It was called *Euridice* and was so successful that a few years later a younger contemporary, Monteverdi by name, came along and wrote another version of the same story—and adaptation of an adaptation, if you will. Under the name of *Orfeo*, this version is still performed all over the western world. There are dozens of musical versions of this story in existence, composed in all periods of history since then, and the end is certainly not in sight as yet.

The history of musical theater from *Dafne* to *A little Night Music* is primarily made up of adaptations of already-existing material. Not that there aren't many exceptions, but oddly enough it's the adaptations which make up the great proportion of permanent or repertory pieces in opera, operetta or musical comedy.

Let's take a look at the operatic repertory for a moment. Of the four most often-performed Mozart operas, certainly *Don Giovanni* and *The Marriage of Figaro* are the most popular with the general public—both, of course, based on earlier dramatic pieces. With one or two exceptions, the entire Verdi repertory, including *Rigoletto* and *La Traviata,* is adapted from novels or plays. All of Richard Wagner's works are imaginative retellings of legends or, in the case of *Die Meistersinger,* history. Puccini and Massenet, practical theater men that they were, often musicalized the current hits of their own times. And so on down the line. The only real exception that comes to mind is Gian Carlo Menotti who, as far as I know, has written *only* original dramatic material for the libretti of his musicals. There are other exceptions, certainly—*Der Rosenkavalier* or *Aida,* for example—but the point is they *are* exceptions.

The same situation exists in lighter musical theater. In 1796 what one might consider the first American "musical" was premiered. There was song and dialogue and dance. It was called *The Archers* and was another version of the story of William Tell. Earlier in the century *The Beggar's Opera* had set the style for this newer, perhaps looser theatrical form. That was an adaptation in reverse, however. The story was original, but the music was adapted from already-existing popular melodies of the day.

Offenbach's operettas were often "original," but far and away the most permanent of his work are the two "adaptations"—*Orpheus* (remember him?) *in the Underworld* and *La Belle Hélène.* Of all Strauss's operettas, the most memorable and frequently performed is *Die Fledermaus,* again an adaptation. In our own century it's true that many, many musicals of the teens, 1920s and 1930s were not adaptations (except, perhaps, that they were constant variations on each other). But practically none of these is performable today except in a satirical manner actually deprecating the material at hand. Jerome Kern, my own personal hero from that period, is survived by dozens of perfectly gorgeous songs. Everyone knows them, and I suspect they will be sung for a very long time. But most of them were from musical comedies, "originals" if you will, that have disappeared, probably forever. Only one Kern musical is played today—in fact has never lost its popularity: *Show Boat,* from the novel of the same name.

From the 1940s up to the present time the situation is even clearer, because the book to a musical became an equal partner in the collaboration, rather than simply a series of cues for songs, interrupted occasionally by a comedy routine: *Oklahoma!, Kiss Me Kate, The Pajama Game, South Pacific, West Side Story, Carousel, Wonderful Town, Damn Yankees, My Fair Lady.* You may have additional favorites of your own, but the chances are that they too were based on a story or a play or an historical character.

There are exceptions, of course, like *Of Thee I Sing*, an original which won the Pulitzer Prize, or the recent Sondheim musicals *Company* and *Follies*. All the Gilbert & Sullivan operettas are original (or at least based on Gilbert's own material). But once again, the point is that these are exceptions, the minority of successful repertory pieces. Most of what has lasted in the musical theater is "adaptation."

So if my gin-drinking prophet of theatrical doom would just stop to think a minute, he would realize that when Jerry Herman writes *Hello, Dolly!*

based on *The Matchmaker* and follows it with *Mame* based on *Auntie Mame*, or when Jerry Bock and Sheldon Harnick put their talents to work telling the story of Fiorello H. LaGuardia or the Rothschilds, or retelling stories by Sholom Aleichem or Mark Twain, they are simply following in the long-established tradition of this strange conglomerate form of theater called the musical.

In conclusion, the safe thing is to draw no conclusion. Some people say that adaptations prevail because few really first-class writers are willing to work in the form (on the whole, though, in this article I have been viewing the subject of material as a composer, on a musical rather than literary slant). Others say that the musical theater only wants to play it safe and so only makes use of already-proven success. Personally, I suspect that there are actually very few stories to tell—only new people to tell them and new moments in social history from which to look back at the same old stories. And, in a way, that's as it should be since we're all really variations on a theme, versions of each other—adaptations, really.

Theater Music: A Discussion

This state-of-the-art discussion of theater music took place in a closed session (no audience) at Dramatists Guild headquarters for the purpose of taping and editing for publication in the **Quarterly.** *The participants were the* **Quarterly's** *editor and three composers whose produced musicals span the whole developmental area of regional, off-off-Broadway and off-Broadway theater, overlapping onto Broadway.*

The speakers are Jeff Sweet, a critic-composer-librettist whose **Winging It!** *was produced at the Milwaukee Repertory Theater under the auspices of the Office for Advanced Drama Research; Al Carmines of the Judson Poets' Theater, a prolific off-off- and off-Broadway composer-librettist; and Nancy Ford, composer of the long-run off-Broadway hit* **The Last Sweet Days of Isaac** *and of* **Shelter** *on Broadway. Their subject is theater music. Spurred on by an occasional question from the editor or one of the composers, uninhibited by any formality of audience presence, and edited for the printed page, here is the dicussion which followed the first question: Do you feel that you have here in New York a modern musical theater that is worth your talents, that satisfies you?*

NANCY FORD: Sometimes the result is unsatisfying, but I don't think it's because of limitations put on us. I think it's because of our own limitations. The theater does stimulate me to write, to keep trying.

AL CARMINES: Do you mean, do we have a real rep of performers we can depend on? I never worry about whether I will find an artist who can do my work, it's a problem that never occurs to me. I write often for the people who are *there.*

JEFF SWEET: You have an ideal situation putting on your own shows with

149

your own people at the Judson Poets' Theater. I don't know anybody else in musical theater who has that kind of situation, with this huge repertory of talent.

CARMINES: Yes, but there are obvious limitations. There are times when none of our people are paid, so I can't work eight hours a day with them—and there are times when it takes them eight hours a day to learn something I write. There are times when I want scenery but we don't have the money for scenery because we don't charge for tickets. Once you accept those limitations—that you aren't going to have the time you want, that you are not going to have any money for scenery or costumes—then there are no *other* limitations, and that is very exciting. Once you've accepted the situation, you can go ahead. I like to work under the kind of pressure you get when you set a rehearsal for tomorrow knowing that you have to write the material for it tonight. It gets up the steam to do it.

FORD: My writing is so much sparser. It comes along only when the spirit moves me and when we are actually working on a project. You do a different kind of thing. You must write all the time. You must write something every day.

CARMINES: I write a lot, yeah. I'll often write half the score after the show is cast. I like to write for individual people, for their voices and personalities. The more unusual, human and personal a performer is, the more interesting he is.

One of the things I dislike about the Broadway musical theater is its blandness in choral singing. There's a standard sound and a standard look that is boring.

FORD: It's true that in a Broadway show, where the book and the acting are extremely important, composers sometimes have to compromise on the singing voice. I've always felt, though, that the acting of the material would put it across as well as the singing of it. Beautiful tone production doesn't necessarily make a song sound better or reach people any better than, you know, a really fine actor poking out a tune.

CARMINES: No one sings "September Song" like Walter Huston. You would never cast him . . . but when he sings the song you would cast him in anything. You are absolutely right, sometimes the acting qualities are so personal and important that it's worth sacrificing sheer musicality.

I've noticed also that the quality of commitment you get from a cast to a work influences the feeling about the work that the audience finally has, and it's always puzzled me how widely that quality differs. From some you get an enjoyment, a belief, a kind of enthusiasm. From others you get an attitude they describe as "professional," which I think means just building your own career. I've heard the word "professional" bandied about so much that I almost hate it now, because people use it as a way of avoiding the commitment of excitement about a work. They are afraid to say, "I like this play I am in," or even "I don't like this play I am in," instead they say "It's a job," I find it very troublesome and I don't know how to deal with it. Even if I know you don't like it, at least we've got something. But when someone treats it like a plumbing job, I find it kind of hurts. and it takes away some of the good things that happen in reherarsal.

Are there kinds of music you wouldn't try as a theater composer?

CARMINES: I think people are terrified of opera. Even off off Broadway I don't call some of my shows "operas" because I think the public is scared of the word.

SWEET: But sometimes you call a show an "oratorio," which is almost as scary.

CARMINES: Right.

FORD: If you were doing it on Broadway I guess you'd have to be more careful about what you call it.

SWEET: When you get to the point where 95 per cent of the show is music as in Galt MacDermot's *Via Galactica,* how do you differentiate between musical theater and opera? Where do you draw the line?

CARMINES: There isn't any, opera is a form of musical theater. Musical comedies are the roots of an American opera that will come in the future, but neither music critics nor theater critics are ready for that kind of opera yet.

SWEET: I've always had this feeling that Nancy is kind of a perfectionist and keeps working until everything is right on and Al is kind of a rough sketch artist. I find pleasure in both, in something done as well as it can be done, and in the rough sketch. And both of you are using really unusual subject matter for musical theater, as in *Christmas Rappings* or *The Last Sweet Days of Isaac.*

FORD: With *Isaac* we decided we definitely would not have any songs that didn't have real justfication, like the use of a tape recorder. It was exactly opposite to what you were talking about, it was never sung dialogue—it was always *a* song. Once in a while the characters put something on the tape recorder for people to remember them by, but there's never any place where somebody is talking along and then all of a sudden starts to sing instead of speaking.

SWEET: Producers and publishers are very concerned about the commercial possibilities of a score. They always ask "What are the hit songs, what tunes could be taken out?" and they are very obviously interested in the rock sound. I doubt that there are many producers around who will take a chance on a conservatively-scored show, a score without guitars and drums. When was the last conservatively-scored show that wasn't written by an established Broadway professional? Rock has really taken over. It's one thing we can both thank and curse *Hair* for.

FORD: Are you now writing a conservatively-scored show?

SWEET: I am rewriting a show called *Hitch* which has a contemporary sound—some rock, some folkish, a little old-fashioned show-biz razzamatazz. But then the characters in my show are mostly young people, and that's the kind of music I feel expresses them best. The style I use on a project is very much dictated by the music appropriate for the characters. For instance, if I were doing a musical version of *Arsenic and Old Lace,* I wouldn't write the old ladies' songs in a rock vein. One major factor in the way I compose, however, is that I compose at the piano, and I'm not really a very good pianist. I don't usually compose what I can't play. It's a technical limitation which can only be overcome by study, and that's something I want to do more of.

CARMINES: One of the real limitations of the musical theater has a lot to do with the stupidity of producers. They get it into their heads that because something is a success every show that follows has to be like it. All of a sudden every producer wanted to do a rock musical like *Hair* and there have been forty since *Hair* opened in 1967 that have been absolute flops. It's terribly boring for the public and the critics and everyone else. It has to do with a lack of imagination and an enormous amount of greed. It has to do with the feeling that if a rock musical is a hit, therefore any rock musical is better than any non-rock musical; and if it's religious, let's go for a *religious* rock musical. I find it so funny that in the late 1960s and early 1970s I got several calls from producers who told me, "You'd be the perfect person to write a religious rock musical—after all, you're both a minister and a composer, and look how successful these religious rock musicals are now." I just wanted to hit them on the head. I loved *Hair,* I thought it was marvelous, but there was only one *Hair* and you don't create that kind of thing a second time unless you're a composer like Richard Rodgers who continues a certain style of his own.

Another Broadway limitation is the producers' incredible timidity about what the public will take. I'm sure that ninety producers out of a hundred wouldn't have touched *Hair* because they thought it would offend everybody. They would have changed it, taken out words, eliminated nudity. Producers are so condescending toward the public.

FORD: We never called *Isaac* a rock musical, I was always opposed to calling it that. The producers promised not to, and they never did in the advertising prior to opening night. But the critics called it "a rock musical," and then of course that's what it became when we picked up their quotes for the ads.

SWEET: And people came expecting a rock musical.

FORD: It was a *different* musical, not a rock musical, even though there was a rock group in the second part.

SWEET: The rhythms weren't rock.

FORD No.

SWEET: I wonder how much public expectation and taste limits what you want to do in musical theater. To a large part of the audience, you say the word "musical" and what comes to their minds is lightweight entertainment with a big chorus and dancers and a lot of flash and dazzle. They don't expect to have to deal with subtext and serious concerns at a musical, and when faced with them they either overlook these elements, because their expectations make them blind to them, or they get upset because you haven't given them the escapist entertainment they came for. Stephen Sondheim's *Company* and *Follies* were critical successes, but they weren't huge box-office successes. Some audiences were upset by them or came out missing the point. People would come out of *Company* debating whether the show was pro- or anti-marriage. I mean, if nothing else, all you have to do is listen to the lyrics of "Being Alive" and that question's laid to rest. The same people might come out of an Albee or a Pinter play with a much clearer understanding of what was going on in the subtext and the like. But that's because they've brought their serious-play heads. They've gone in expecting to have to work a little. But, because musicals have a tradition of being trivial and lightweight and obvious, they may go to a musical in that frame of mind and be unresponsive if the show tries to do something more. I think that kind of thing can discourage innovation.

CARMINES: I don't blame that on the public, I blame it on the producers—and the critics, too, as long as a critic like Walter Kerr will review *Company* in the same way he reviews *Hello, Dolly!*, say, with the same standards, the same point of view. One of the responsibilities of a critic is to say, finally, what he thinks is important and what unimportant, what profound and what trivial. One of the critic's duties is to help and educate the public in that way, even when he's giving only his own personal opinion. I suppose every major critic agrees that *Waiting for Godot* is one of the masterpieces of the twentieth centruy. But if you go back and read the reviews of *Godot* when it first opened in New York, you will find that some critics reviewed it the way they would review the work of some television hack, and I think that's a mistake.

Are the critics who write about your musicals really equipped to judge them?

FORD: I think it's strange that the same critics review both plays and musicals, yet there are separate music critics for other musical events. I think it would be a good idea to have special critics for musicals.

CARMINES: As long as you call it musical theater, I guess you must have theater critics review it. I think it's helpful sometimes to have both a theater and a music critic reviewing, as was done in the case of Leonard Bernstein's *Mass*, with Clive Barnes reviewing theatrically and Harold Schoenberg musically. But finally, I don't think that anybody who writes for the musical theater changes what he does because of what the critics say, good or bad. Critics hurt or help your ego, but they have very little to do with your artistry. Learning to keep those two things separate is very important if you are going to continue to work in the theater.

FORD: When they have such widely divergent opinions it's who you listen to, anyway, isn't it? Sometimes the critics say exactly opposite things, and naturally you listen to the one you want to listen to. You don't change the way you write, but sometimes they do exert an influence. When we opened *Isaac* the second part wasn't really ready and we had to cut three or four numbers that needed work. Most of the critics liked the first part better than the second, which confirmed our feeling, so that we continued to work on the second part and gradually put the songs back in.

It would be hard to say which specific critics would be equipped to judge our work and which not. As an audience member myself, I always appreciate a score more as I listen to it. I don't always get the whole thing the first time.

SWEET: Do you think it's the responsibility of a theater score to communicate itself immediately? I remember Clive Barnes said in one of his follow-up reviews of *Isaac* that he had been playing the score and had begun shaving to it. When he was reviewing Stephen Schwartz's *Pippin* he said he had been listening to Schwartz's *Godspell* score and was kind of changing his mind on that. He's said something along the line that he wishes producers would send out tapes or records of the score before a show opens so that he has a chance to prepare for it. I think it's a good idea.

FORD: Yes, I wish I'd remembered that, but I don't know. *Ideally*, the composer should reach his audience on the first hearing.

CARMINES: I wonder if there aren't sacrificial lambs in musical comedy, so to speak—shows that don't make it but nevertheless make it possible for someone else, or the same person three years later, to do something very similar and make it because the first show changed the consciousness of the critic.

SWEET: How about *Anyone Can Whistle?*

CARMINES: Uh-huh. And Beckett functioned that way for the theater. You couldn't have a play like *Home* unless *Waiting for Godot* were somewhere in the background.

FORD: Critics sometimes try to make up for a past mistake with a later favorable review. Surely Barnes must have gone to *A Little Night Music* hoping against hope that finally there was going to be a Sondheim-Prince muscial he could rave about.

CARMINES: Don't you suppose Barnes's response to *Night Music* came about because of *Company* and *Follies?* This wasn't the first Sondheim/Prince show he'd ever seen, wasn't he educated to his response?

SWEET: He made specific reference to "conceptual musicals" in his review. He said, "People have been talking about Mr. Prince's conceptual musicals: now I feel I have actually seen one of the actual concepts."

FORD: Something curious happened with Barnes's review of *Shelter*. In the first edition of the *Times*, the final comment was "a pleasant enough evening." In the late edition, the morning paper, it said, "a warmly pleasant evening." I wonder why.

SWEET: The second is the more positive way of saying it. People don't rush off to see things unless they unless they have exclamation marks. For instance, when *Isaac* opened I was delighted that it got all those reviews saying "spectacular," but I didn't think it was spectacular. I thought it was exciting in a kind of quietly intense way.

Do you think the audience has a better time at a musical that has been running a year because they've heard all the songs?

CARMINES: A different *kind* of time, I don't know whether better or not. When you go to see *No, No, Nanette* or *Irene* there is a sense of familiarity, but that is sometimes not as exciting as the sense of strangeness.

SWEET: You have so many responsibilities placed on you when you hear a song for the first time in the musical theater. First of all, you have to figure out what the song means, what it is doing intellectually in terms of how it is building the plot. And at the same time you're taking in the choreography, the lighting, the arrangements and the costumes. It's very easy to miss subtleties amid all that excitement. For instance, I didn't realize that "Side by Side by Side" was a very sad number until I saw *Company* the second time. At the end when he doesn't have anbody to dance with, suddenly it's a sad number. You don't realize this the first time you see it because you are too busy trying to follow the words, and trying to make sense of the musical shape of the piece in your mind. There's so much going on on the stage, so much to listen to and watch the first time you hear a number, I find it something of a miracle that people come out of a show understanding and recognizing as many tunes as they do.

CARMINES: Different composers want different things from an audience, and if you really want total acceptance you do a different kind of thing than if you want something else. The tyranny of an audience over an artist can be just as bad as the tyranny of the producer. Part of what you do as an artist is sometimes alienating, offensive, frightening to an audience, especially anything new. I think you have to know exactly what you want from an audience and be in the position of not being terribly upset if you don't get total acceptance all the time from the crowd. I have a vision of my audience, but I don't think I'd be able to describe it. When you are alone in your room, writing, you have a vision of the audience, of someone hearing what you are doing, that's what pushes you on. But I don't envision the limits of an actual, physcal audience.

How do you deal with your arrangers? Do you just write lead sheets, or do you sit down and write very full piano scores?

CARMINES: Well, with *Promenade* half the arrangements were mine and half were Eddie Sauter's. I took half the songs and simply did them, and the other half I gave to him. I gave him a lead sheet and then sat down with a tape recorder and played and sang each song and talked about it before and afterwards in terms of where it came in the show and the kind of song I thought it should be.

I don't feel that the music is any less mine when I turn it over to an arranger. I doubt if I will ever again do all of the arrangements and orchestrations for a whole show, because it's just too much. It takes time that I should be spending thinking of other things. I should be thinking of the total shape of the show, and here I am back in a room writing a tuba part. You can't afford that amount of time. You have to find someone you trust *absolutely,* someone you feel understands you, to do that work for you.

FORD: The most exciting thing that happens in working with an arranger is hearing the orchestration for the first time and, when it's right, knowing that you have *really* communicated with at least that one other person. When they give you back your work, you feel, "Yes, that's what I meant." That sense of total communication with one person is more exciting than reading a good review.

SWEET: Haven't you ever felt the desire to arrange it all yourself so that every musical sound that comes from the stage is, ego-wise, totally yours?

FORD: The thought has crossed my mind, but it's really impractical. With a Broadway show, there isn't time. When you have nine instruments as we did in *Shelter*, somebody ought to bring a fresh ear to work on the score.

Where do you go to develop new musical material—off off Broadway, a workshop, where?

SWEET: I start with playing my own stuff at the BMI Theater Workshop—the Lehman Engel operation. Most of the composers there know a hell of a lot more than I do about the more technical aspects of musicals, and they are able to suggest a different chord here or there on a song-to-song basis. That's very valuable. For instance, there was a number I had finished, and I was amazed that this guy in the back of the room started telling me the specific notes to change in the ending: "Now, try D in the bass, then in your right hand C sharp, F sharp and B"—and I hadn't even told him the key I was playing in. I find that kind of forum tremendously valuable.

FORD: We first did *Shelter* in Cinicinnati. We hurried to finish it because we wanted the opportunity to try it on an out-of-town audience before coming to New York.

CARMINES: Can I ask you about *Shelter?* Do you mind talking about it?

FORD: No, I don't mind.

CARMINES: I was out of town when it was done. Its reviews were good. I didn't see any bad reviews of the show at all, so it was a great shock to me when it closed. Would you lay that at the critics' feet?

FORD: Not entirely. A couple of the reviews said, "Rush to the boxoffice," but the ones in the New York *Times* didn't. As I said before, Barnes called it "a warmly pleasant evening." Now, I don't think people hurry to the box office for "a warmly pleasant evening." There is a state of fear and state of people's pocketbooks right now that make them choose rather carefully what they go to see. They will go to see the one with the most exclamation points rather than the one that's warmly pleasant.

SWEET: Here we come to audience expectation again. I think that the standard person who came to see *Shelter* didn't expect its kind of subject matter and found it very hard to relate to. I saw it with a person who wasn't getting it at all, I almost felt like slugging him.

How do you feel about tension between composer and librettist? Does it help, or is it destructive?

FORD: Between two partners, there should be strong criticism of each other's work, but it would be better if it could be done without tension. With Gretchen Cryer, we each stay on our own side of the fence, she with the book and lyrics and I with the music. She writes hers and I write mine, and then we do our adjusting. We will make suggestions to one another, but the final decision on the music would rest with me and the final decision on the lyrics, the dialogue, the plot would rest with her.

Gretchen starts the planning of the musical numbers' placement because she writes the play first and then puts in the lyrics as the play goes along. Of course, in the rewrites we talk a lot about the placement of the songs—we would decide that we needed a different song here or there, that the one in place wasn't adding to the dramatic line. But the way I write and the kind of music I write is mainly to help the lyrics set the mood or convey the emotions of the character. It is not independent. With me, the lyrics definitely come first, and I write the music to go with them, to go with the moment. That's the way I determine what kind of music I will write.

CARMINES: Yes, working with a lyricist you generally do need a lyric first, because that's what gets you going as a composer. I'm not sure that tension really helps. The only show I've written with anyone since I started writing my own lyrics was *Wanted* with David Epstein, who wrote the book. We happened to have a very happy collaboration in terms of personalities and artistic ideas. Any tension had to do with the total effect of the show, but there was none between us about what kind of music, lyrics or dialogue should be written.

No matter how talented a person may be, if you are in basic disagreement a lot of the time it's painful. The real problems come in such areas as casting. No matter how well you get along with a collaborator while working, it's when you are casting that you get into basic disagreement because by this time you both have developed a picture of a character, for instance, and you suddenly find out your picture is not his picture. He cries out, "That's just what I had in mind," and you find yourself disagreeing, "That isn't it at all."

SWEET: I once had an unusual collaboration as composer-lyricist with another composer who was also an actor. Sometimes I would set a lyric, and he would say, "That's very nice here, but this part is weak. I think I can do something else with it." He'd work on it, and we arrived at a score that was my music at one point and a chunk of his the next. There were some songs in which the switch was made eight or nine times, sometimes in the middle of a bar. There are people who write songs together, both music and lyrics, but I don't know of any composers who write just the music together, though you sometimes see multiple credits in popular songs. I would have said that music is the completely personal expression of one person, except for this one curious collaboration which I think worked out fine—but of course it wasn't a situation in which two people began by saying, "We will write the music to this song together." The only times we actually went into a piece with the intention of collaborating musically was when we were composing harmony and chorus parts.

FORD: In that sense the composer and orchestrater and vocal arranger all write together.

SWEET: Yes, but there always has to be one person who is the catalyst, the driving force behind the song, just as there is usually a single consciousness which is the driving force behind a musical as a whole. In the case of the Prince-Sondheim musicals, judging from what I see on the stage they understand each other so well now that you can consider them one consciousness. Incidentally, this is one of the few cases I can think of where the director has been so greatly credited for the content and attitude of musical productions. And, of course, there's Jerome Robbins.

FORD: George Abbott is another one.

CARMINES: Yes, but he also writes a lot of them himself.

FORD: I wonder how important music really is in relation to the book. I thought my least good score was the one for my most successful show. I was never happy with the score I did for *Isaac* and yet the show was a success with both the critics and the audience, so it makes me think that the book is the most important element.

SWEET: It was partly the score, because you can tell what is a popular score, with the theater people at least, by what they bring in to an audition. Once I got four songs from *Isaac* in one afternoon.

FORD: That's interesting, none of the songs ever took off commercially.

Who directs the music in a musical—the composer, the director, the musical director, who? Who says how the music is going to sound?

FORD: Do you mean, who teaches the songs? The musical director teaches the songs, but the composer is the ultimate musical supervisor.

CARMINES: They made a big deal with *Promises, Promises* about having separate compartments for the various parts of the orchestra. Some guy back there was mixing the sound the same way you mix a record. I'm sure Burt Bacharach had a great deal to do with that. I suppose if there were an absolute disagreement between the director and the composer, then the producer would arbitrate.

FORD: You must have a producer who will cooperate with you on the sound, because it involves expenditures. We were continually working on the sound in *Shelter,* and I think we got as good a balance as possible between the voices and the orchestra. We had problems and we had to end up with those body mikes—some nights they crackled and popped. Quite frankly, you have to gear the sound to the more expensive seats, and sometimes in the balcony the orchestra covered the voices, because sound rises from the orchestra pit.

SWEET: You couldn't run two different mixes of what was amplified downstairs and upstairs?

FORD: You would need very expensive equipment. We did have four speakers, but they didn't seem to work that way.

SWEET: They all ran through one central system.

FORD: We tried everything to balance the sound, like taking the red curtain off the left side of the orchestra pit and then taking it off the right side. One night I went to the orchestra pit trying to find out *why* we couldn't hear the orchestra in that little theater. I saw that a big board had been placed along the railing, apparently blocking the sound out. One of the stagehands told me the guitarist had asked that it be put up so he could hang his guitars there so the audience wouldn't be kicking them under the railing. I went out and bought a big piece of grating at a hardware store and put it in place of the board. *There's* an example of the composer's function and responsibility.

Why do composers of rock musicals let their music be played so loud?

FORD: Maybe they get used to loud sound in the recording studios. Actually, I thought *Isaac* was *too* loud. Every time I saw the show I'd run up to the sound booth to try to get the volume turned down. Sometimes you can't get anything done about it. I don't know what to do besides throw yourself over the balcony.

SWEET: But that was more of a chamber piece. That was not wild, unrestrained rock, it was very tight.

FORD: When it was loud it was painfully loud. If you don't go to the theater every night you can't keep track of what's happening, and the sound creeps up.

CARMINES: It isn't an artistic decision, you don't say, "I want this played loud for the following artistic reasons." It has to do with young people's consciousness of music, with the whole matrix of living. It has to do with when and how you listen to music, where your roots are in a certain kind of rock, what you think sound *is*. You associate music with a kind of intensity, and if it doesn't have it you feel disappointed.

SWEET: The thing about rock is that it's instantly appreciable music. The fact that it's such an immediate experience may be the reason why it's such a powerful musical theater tool. You aren't supposed to think about it. It just reaches out and grabs you by the shirt. That probably has a lot to do with the volume it's played at. Kids don't so much listen to rock as they *feel it*, feel the room vibrate.

CARMINES: In recent auditions for shows I've had a lot of people who have been in rock musicals, and they sing in a different way than other people. They had microphone voices, not real voices. They couldn't just go to the piano and sing a song, their voices absolutely required amplification in order to be appreciated. Amplified, you could hear whether it was a beautiful voice or an interesting voice or a characteristic voice. But as far as just singing a song is concerned, they didn't know what it meant. I'd ask them to sing "Row, Row, Row, Your Boat" and they'd hum it very softly, because they were used to having this thing jammed against their mouths and not used to singing without it. It has created a different kind of performer.

In terms of musical theater concepts, are there any things you can do now which you might once have been afraid to do?

SWEET: I think there have been several revolutionary developments in recent years. For example, the media as subject matter in *Isaac*. In *Hair*, the abandonment of the traditionally structured book. In *1776*, twenty-five minutes without a musical number, which most people didn't even notice—I can imagine an old-time producer saying, "It's been seven minutes since we have had a song. Give us a song." In *Company*, a very rich subtext.

FORD: I don't think there's any magical formula. You can get away with anything if you happen to hit it right.

SWEET: In the second act of *Isaac* the chorus concept was heresy in terms of traditional musical theater. Ordinarily in chorus numbers you try to pretend that these people are part of the scene, you have a bunch of happy villagers—that's how you justify a choral sound. The lead comes out and starts singing, and happy villagers join in. In *Isaac* it was very specific that these chorus people were an entirely different entity, they were not a part of what was actually happening in the show.

CARMINES: When we talk about concepts, I almost feel as if I'm painting myself into a corner. I suppose any good show has one guiding theme or style. In *Follies*, the lives of these four people are seen through the *Ziegfeld Follies* framework. In *Company* there was a specific framework through which we saw everything, one basic concept of the way things are going to be done, communicated or set.

FORD: As in *A Little Night Music*, with everything in waltz time? Some sort of thing that ties it together? Is that what you mean by concept?

SWEET: You hit it.

FORD: There probably should be that with every theater piece, shouldn't there?

SWEET: It seems that every Sondheim-Prince show begins with a prologue in which the plot isn't entered into, saying to the audience, "These are what your expectations should be for this show. These are our priorities, these are the ideas we're going to be concentrating on." They are conceptual musicals, they get the concept up there in the first number.

FORD: Yes, but all three were different. When we talk about Sondheim-Prince musicals we're leaving out the George Furth, the James Goldman, the Hugh Wheeler elements, which make for very different shows.

SWEET: One major change in recent years has been in the structuring of the songs. At one time in musical comedy they were very simply structured. In Rodgers and Hammerstein songs you always know whether you are in your A or B part, and you know what these parts are supposed to do. But some of the songs of Sondheim and a lot of others often get far away from the traditional AABA structure. Also, there's a difference in melodies. It used to be that you sang a whole melody when you came out of the theater. Nowadays, in many cases it makes no sense just to sing the melody line unless you have the chords.

CARMINES: One of the most thrilling experiences is to hear something musicalized that you thought couldn't be, like the song in *Hair* where they simply repeat all the ways of having a sexual experience. It's fabulous, because you never thought you'd hear a list musicalized with all those words in it. You learn a lot about things by hearing them sung rather than said. I think anything can be musicalized, don't you?

FORD: Certain things lend themselves better than others, but I guess anything can be a musical if you find the right concept.

SWEET: Have you ever been working on a project and then decided it couldn't be musicalized? Have you ever abandoned a project in midstream?

CARMINES: Yes, I just abandoned one, I was all set to write an oratorio on St. Paul, but I found it impossible. Maybe in later years it will be possible. I found that the concept didn't agree with the actual material that was available to me in my mind at that point. There wasn't enough reality to fill in the concept, so it would have been artificial to try to continue with it. I would have had to make things up rather than have it organic. I am not close enough to St. Paul in my mind yet to make it really work.

FORD: Gretchen and I started a couple of projects that we dropped because we felt we just weren't getting off the ground.

SWEET: At Lehman Engel's musical workshop the other day we got onto the subject of anti-heroes, and nobody could think of a successful musical in which the central character was a real stinker, unless he was in some way reformed or made charming. In *The Music Man*, he's reformed. In *110 in the Shade*, he's charming . . .

CARMINES: The Brecht-Weill musicals. I would say *The Threepenny Opera* is a musical with an anti-hero.

SWEET: But he's a charming anti-hero. Our sympathies are with him, he's not really a monster. Do you think sympathy is a crucial part of a musical?

CARMINES: I don't think it has to be.

FORD: I think you have to have an understanding of the main character.

CARMINES: I felt no sympathy for anyone in *Promises, Promises*.

SWEET: You didn't care whether he got together with the girl?

CARMINES: No. And I didn't feel sympathy for anyone in *Company*.

SWEET: Didn't you want the central character to find something to really care about, to want someone to commit himself to? Wasn't there something you wanted to have happen for that character?

CARMINES: No.

While you are writing a theater score, are you considering takeout for the record industry, or do you ignore this possibility?

SWEET: It's crucial that the song be liked, and that the song be the right length and in the right place, but no, I seldom think of takeouts.

CARMINES: My interest in musical theater doesn't have anything to do with the cardboard songs that can be cut out. What I find exciting about musical theater is the connection between talking and singing.

FORD: I write for the moment and the character. I always hope songs can be taken out, but I don't write specifically to that.

CARMINES: Looking over some of the recent Broadway shows, who would guess that in *Fiddler on the Roof* those Jerry Bock songs would be taken out and get so much individual attention? Sherman Edwards's *1776* certainly has one of the least separable scores in musical theater history. Jerry Herman I have to think sometimes does write with the singles market in mind. For instance, in *Mame* "If He Walked Into My Life" is a lovely song which she's singing about a little boy, but the lyrics are phrased so that in a takeout it could sound as though she's singing about a man.

SWEET: Also in Walter Marks's *Golden Rainbow*—there's a score that has some good tunes in it—Eydie Gorme sings "He Needs Me Now," again about a little boy. But it could be taken out and done in a night club act, as could most of the songs in that show, which may have been the score's problem—the lack of specificity in the lyrics.

When you look back now, are you glad that you decided to write music for the theater instead of other forms?

FORD: I am.

CARMINES: The joy of the theater is that after you write a song there are sixty people to teach it to.

SWEET: I have a love for all media and want to write music and scripts for everything.

IV. Settings.....

Those that come to see
Only a show or two, and so agree
The play may pass, if they be still and willing,
I'll undertake may see away their shilling
Richly in two short hours.
                    —HENRY VIII

Our Theater of the 1970s
On and Off Broadway,
Inside and Out

Drawings by Tom Funk

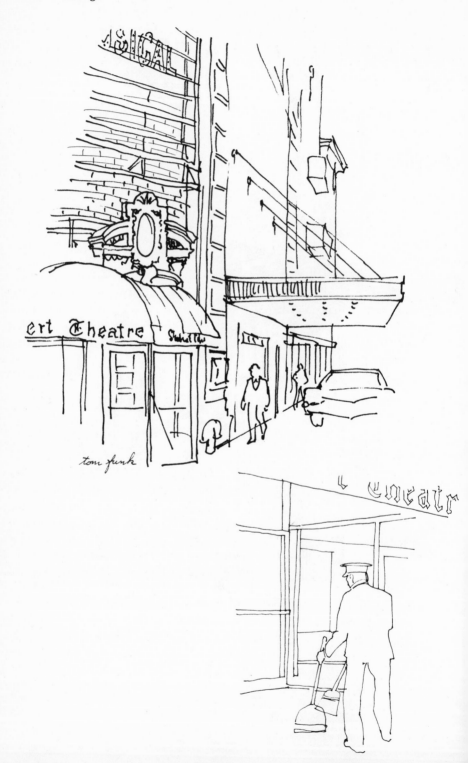

tom funk

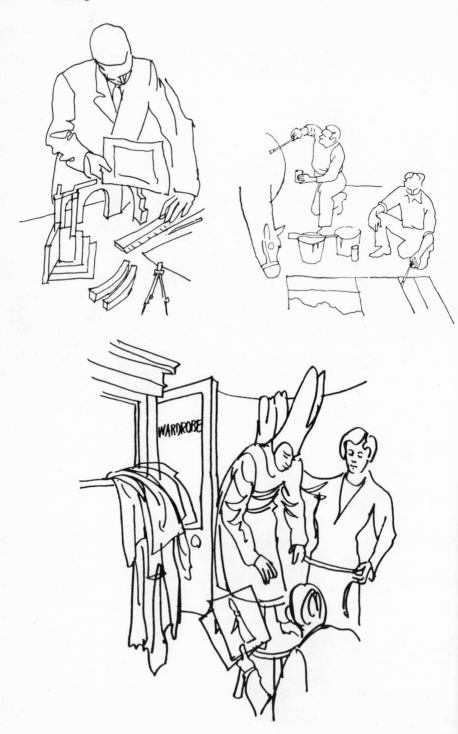

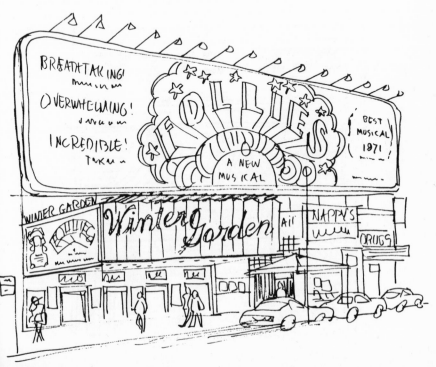

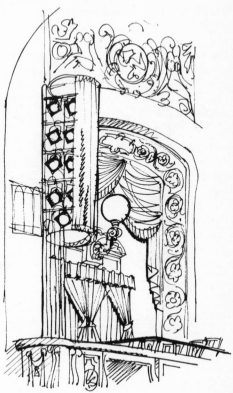

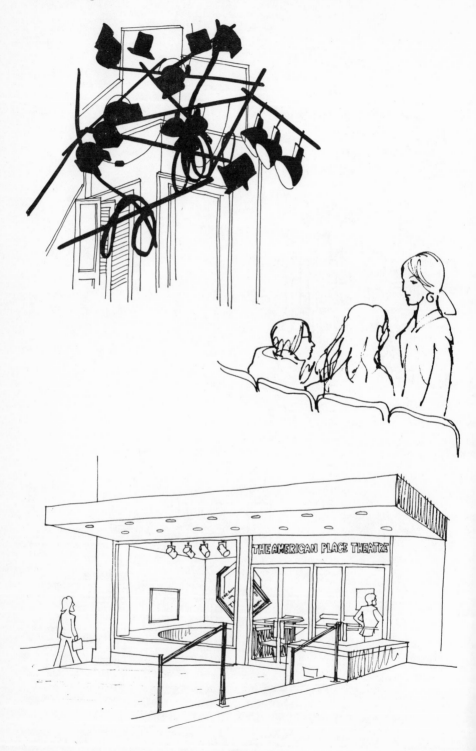

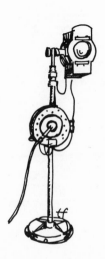

V. Soliloquys.....

. . . I only speak right on.
—Julius Caesar

Censorship begins to exist first and foremost in the mind of the playwright himself when he starts to exercise a form of *self*-censorship upon his own thinking. The writer who has experienced years of continued rejection must eventually come to grips with the ugly unwritten laws of the market place if he is to survive. He will begin to recognize that there are certain taboos in the market place. Since these may assume different guises to suit the fancy of different practitioners, they will create the illusion that they are not there at all; but make no mistake about it, they are there, and if the playwright is skillful enough he can fashion his wares accordingly. This already is a form of censorship. If life in the literary jungle can be treacherous enough to reduce the author of *Moby Dick* to the role of civil servant before he was 40, an age which should mark the beginning and not the end of intellectual maturity, what kind of a chance does the ordinary mortal stand?

—Louis C. Adelman

☆

The only thing that need concern us, I think, is to remember that the playwright is a creative artist and that playwriting is an art form. What should a playwright expect from his art form? Playwriting is an attempt to communicate a sense of one's time, a sense of one's self to other people who are interested in being communicated with. The most important thing for the playwright is to know whether or not he's got somewhere in the world a group of people who care enough about themselves—care enough about

197

their awareness of themselves—to pay serious attention. Without this, no art form can survive. Possibly the greatest dilemma for the serious playwright is that the United States is swinging to a point where it doesn't want to be told any truths about itself, doesn't want to be taken into a further awareness of itself, it merely wants to escape from the reality of itself. If there is a playwright's plight as an artist in the United States it is a simple matter of whether or not he's given the opportunity to communicate with anybody.

The serious artist *must* be able to communicate, for his own self-respect. That doesn't mean that he has to be able to communicate with half the people in the country, but if a society becomes so corrupt that it is totally unwilling to listen, then none of the arts can possibly survive.

—EDWARD ALBEE

☆

My wife and I live in the country, and whenever we are in town we are always asking ourselves, "Do we really want to go to the theater? Is there anything we *really* want to see?" We go to the Long Wharf Theater in New Haven all the time, but we are a different audience in New Haven than we are in New York. We're different in Boston, in Philadelphia—it's very strange. Are we losing our appetite for theater or are we simply losing our appetite for it in New York? Is it the effort of going? Why do we prefer the Long Wharf? Well, their audience is much more fascinating, for one thing, it's a *live* audience. Do you know the French phrase *assister au théâtre?* By and large, the New York audience does not assist in the theater. It goes there and just sits like a lump of lead. I am not saying "you" or "they." I am this way in New York myself. Maybe there's something about the theater being in every street. Young people tell me they don't want theatergoing to become convenient, they want it to be an "event." I once visited Milwaukee while a play of mine was playing on tour there. I was invited to some parties, and people would tell me, "We haven't seen your play," assuring me that they were going to Chicago to see it the next week. When I told them, "That same production is now playing in Milwaukee," they would answer, "We always go to the theater in Chicago."

—ROBERT ANDERSON

☆

Since I am an aging playwright I find prejudice rampant. In these circumstances I am now submitting my work under pseudonyms and finding favorable responses. This has its negative side, however, since 90 per cent of the producers who have responded favorably are nonplused and back away from revelation, probably because they feel ripped off.

—ANONYMOUS

☆

The violence of the mind is the violence of God

Actual killing actual death the hanging the beating the running into fire
the violence of reality is the violence of the unseen the spirit
charging flesh with not being spirit
                                    hacks it open birds and great almighty
Jesus die like live like are like and the similarity
                                    is the complex of all being
We are all in the mind of God in the mind of God
                                    is the mind of God which
is the flexing Olorun driving drifting climbing into Blazing heaven,
forehead touching the earth. We are in the mind of Shaitan,
                                    our whisperer the deadly
white consciousness the other the alternate to Good,
                                    where it lay on the street
nodding in prayer
Till the sky changes
and the sign is to move
and they do, the righteous, the billions of them
blacker than anything but God
do move, and their motion, is the horde drum
in the bush, the wind bathing the mountain,
                                    all the sounds of the universe
and those out beyond, is the motion, the moving,
                                    the stiletto swift doing
                    —Imamu Amiri Baraka (LeRoi Jones)

Howard Lindsay was the most incorrigibly professional man I ever knew. He elevated the professional attitude to the austerity of an art. He was entirely concerned with the craft, the technique, the architecture, the manufacturing of art, the actual writing and performance of the play. The presumption was that drama was an art and anyone affecting to its practise was an artist; and, if you happened to be a poet, then you were a poet, but, if you weren't, the demands of the craft were no less rigorous. To Howard, the practise was the art.

It was all meat and potatoes. His way of saying it might be: "If it's a comedy, your curtains should be laughs. If it's a drama, your curtains should be dramatic." In point of fact, that is no less than Tolstoy's definition of the truth of art or Rimbaud's insistence on the internal integrity of a poem.

Other experiential observations dropped by Howard Lindsay:

"Wherever your biggest laugh is, it ought to be the second act curtain."

"If you're in trouble in the third act, take some dialogue from a secondary character and give it to the lead."

The fact is Howard's workaday reflections are truer to the esthetics of drama than anything I've ever read on the matter.

—PADDY CHAYEFSKY

☆

Numbers

There's warming news from Academe: on the nationwide average, authors earn more than athletes, more than actors, more than funeral directors and embalmers, too, according to a book-length report *Performing Arts—The Economic Dilemma* published by the Twentieth Century Fund. Within this coldly factual listing of average incomes in professional-technical occupations from top-rated physicians and surgeons (too rich to be called merely "doctors") to farm laborers on the bottom, a kindly average glows in the author's favor. The fire on the writer's hearth need not (and does not) burn as merrily as those of veterinarians, college presidents or pharmacists, but indeed he is better off than librarians or football coaches. To pinpoint the economic status of the American author (according to this study), he is in twenty-fifth place—slightly behind accountants and slightly ahead of chiropractors.

Here are some numbers to conjure with. *Slow Dance on the Killing Ground* had:

One author (William Hanley).

Three actors.

Three stagehands.

Six producers (with two Inc.'s and one Enterprises in their credit line).

Mary, Mary proved once again that it's still possible to write a play and make a million dollars. Its Broadway and touring companies grossed over $10,000,000; and although Jean Kerr waived royalities toward the end of the run, the sale of the movie rights brought her share into seven figures. In the face of the belief that comedy doesn't export well, this play was a hit in 20 countries (in Spain there were *two* companies, one for Madrid and one on tour). It was expected to gross about $100,000 its first year in stock royalties; then $50,000 for a few years, finally settling to the $20,000 level.

Asked what was the most vivid part of the whole experience, Mrs. Kerr replied: "That's easy. What I remember are the mixed notices."

We focus our long-run spotlight not on *The Fantasticks* in the American stage's longest run of record, not on *Fiddler on the Roof* in Broadway's longest musical run, but on an even more Methuselated masterpiece: Agatha Christie's *The Mousetrap,* as it goes into its third decade and passes its 8,000th performance on the London stage. *Variety* says this is "believed to be a world legit record." *The Mousetrap* opened a generation ago on Nov. 25, 1952 to mixed-favorable notices. It has grossed (*Variety* estimates) $4,320,000 in its 453-seat house, has employed 137 actors and has made a hollow pun out of a useful saying with a better mousetrap that brought the world into an endless line at its boxoffice.

A confrontation between glamor and substance took place in the Broadway theater when the more than 100 pairs of second-nighters had to choose between attending Marlene Dietrich's one-woman show or John Bowen's fairly well received play *After the Rain.* Alas for the noble art of Shaw and Shakespeare, glamor prevailed. Marlene outdrew the play, attracting slightly more than half the second-nighters with the enticements of her solo act.

The musical opened in late November, 1965 to mostly rave reviews. An exception was Howard Taubman of the *Times,* who qualified his lead paragraph of praise with "a few vulgarities and some triteness" and his later approbation with "Their muse, though it aspires, does not always soar." Its press agent told the *Quarterly's* editor, "We're not selling tickets. I don't see how we can get past next week."

The show, *Man of La Mancha* by Dale Wasserman, Mitch Leigh and Joe Darion, closed a little later than predicted. The raves continued to roll in from the weeklies, word of mouth was tremendous, and the public began to take notice. *Man of La Mancha* caught on and finally closed June 26, 1971 after the fourth longest musical run in Broadway history, 2,328 performances. It has become part of the permanent repertory of the American musical stage, and one of its song hits, "The Impossible Dream," has won a place in the folklore of the 1960s and 1970s.

If one must say goodbye to an old friend, it's some help to do it in a blaze of glory, as was the case with the closing of *Fiddler on the Roof* at the Sunday, July 2, 1973 matinee. This was the great Joseph Stein-Jerry Bock-Sheldon Harnick musical's 3,242d performance, the all-time Broadway long-run record which began with *Fiddler's* opening Sept. 22, 1964 and lasted about two weeks longer than the previous record of 3,224 performances held by the straight play *Life With Father*. These two long-run champs had a lot in common: they were both singularly beloved by theater audiences, they wove themselves into the very texture of New York life during their long stay, and their two indomitable, traditionalistic, unforgettable father figures, Tevye and Clarence Day, have permanently enriched our imaginations.

"Legit's all-time top playwright . . . The most popular writer in modern history . . . The most successful playwright in Broadway history"—these were a few of the superlatives applied by the local press to Neil Simon as his *Last of the Red Hot Lovers* arrived in New York. This "serious comedy" (his own description) was Simon's seventh hit in a row. Joining *Plaza Suite* and *Promises, Promises* in simultaneous Broadway runs, it enhanced Simon's already spectacular feat of playwriting noted in the *Quarterly* in 1967, as follows: "Let it become Broadway legend that one playwright had *four* shows *(Barefoot in the Park, The Odd Couple, Sweet Charity* and *The Star-Spangled Girl)* running *simultaneously* in our problematical commercial theater—and all four of them were hits."

What can we say now that Simon has presented Broadway with *Plaza Suite,* plus a fresh stack of three simultaneous shows *(Promises, Promises, Last of the Red Hot Lovers* and *The Gingerbread Lady),* plus *The Prisoner of Second Avenue, The Sunshine Boys* and *The Good Doctor*—11 straight successes totalling more than 8,000 performances? Mere legend would no longer serve; we must study the techniques of Paul Bunyan yarn-spinning to invent new ways of reporting the career of a playwright who is doing everything right, no matter what else seems to be going wrong. At this point we can only gasp our sincerest congratulations to Neil Simon, our Jean-Baptiste Poquelin of the jet age, and take note of his own words quoted in a New York *Times* interview: "I'll never write a play not basically funny. That's my own point of view."

William Shakespeare finally made the long-run list of shows which have played more than 500 performances in New York's professional theater. *Two Gentlemen of Verona,* with 627 performances, was the first of his plays to make the list under its own title (purists may contend that the original title was

THE *Two Gentlemen of Verona,* but this is merely a quibble). No other of the bard's plays has achieved this distinction except in such radically adapted form as *Kiss Me Kate* (1,070), *Your Own Thing* (933), *West Side Story* (732) or *The Boys From Syracuse* (500). Now William Shakespeare has made it on his own, with maybe a little help from his friends and fellow-dramatists John Guare, Mel Shapiro and Galt MacDermot.

On the occasion of the opening of *Poor Bitos* in 1965, we commented that Jean Anouilh thereby became the most produced Broadway playwright of the mid-20th century. *Poor Bitos* was his 13th new play produced on Broadway; the runner-up, Tennessee Williams, had 12.

Well, things have obviously changed since then. As of now, Broadway's most-produced playwright is—no, not Neil Simon—the abovementioned Tennessee Williams, who has had 15 productions of new plays. In the intervening years since 1965, Anouilh—whose *The Waltz of the Toreadors* was prominently revived on Broadway in 1974, but we're not counting revivals—hasn't sent over a single new script. During the same period, Williams's *Slapstick Tragedy, The Seven Descents of Myrtle* and *Out Cry* were produced in the West Forties. As a formidable extra, there have been two new Williams plays off Broadway—*In the Bar of a Tokyo Hotel* and *Small Craft Warnings.*

Neil Simon? His *The Good Doctor* tied him with Anouilh in the runner-up position, with 13 Broadway productions, apart from his early contributions to revues.

Times and Trib

Like it, dislike it or shrug it off, the New York *Herald Tribune* really *cared* about the theater. It was one of the first local papers to set up coverage of stage performances and events on a regular and important scale. Its Sunday theater section under the editorship of Arthur H. Folwell was an appetizing weekly sample of Broadway excitement, with highly-styled features by Lucius Beebe and others, with its uncompromising criticisms, its drawings of plays and players accenting the glamor and wit of the subject. The *Trib* drama section was no puff sheet, but it wasn't impossible for a struggling play to get a much-needed Sunday break there. The line of descent of *Herald Tribune* drama critics in the modern American theater included Percy Hammond, Richard Watts Jr., Howard Barnes, Otis L. Guernsey Jr., Bert McCord and Walter Kerr. In the 1950s and 1960s the *Trib* didn't receive as much show business circulation and advertising support as did its competitor the *Times,* but it kept on covering the theater completely and expertly—and even at the end its drama department was stronger than the rest of the paper. Like it or not, the *Herald Tribune* was a friend to the theater. It died by surrender on August 15, 1966, in a strike-induced coma, in its

131st year, after a long illness which found no remedy, either of ingenuity or of quackery.

Over on the New York *Times*, Howard Taubman felt "liberated" as he turned his job as drama critic over to his successor, Stanley Kauffmann, at the turn of 1966. Mr Taubman had been attending entertainments on a non-selective basis for 35 years, first as music and then as drama critic, and the burden of going to see everything wasn't getting any lighter through the decades. Looking back upon his tenure of the highly influential post, Mr. Taubman commented, "Some people thought I was too kind. Some thought I was a son of a bitch. Some people even thought I was fair."

Mr. Taubman's valedictory Sunday *Times* essay concluded with the message, "Happy New Year, Stanley Kauffmann." Mr. Kauffmann's salutatory essay began with "No, no more repining" about the theater's commercial health, and it argued that much of the theater's audience has "outdistanced" intellectually the taste of many of its producers. And Mr. Kauffmann moved at once to ease some of the purely journalistic pressure of his post by requesting permission to cover shows at preview performances in order to gain an extra day to write his review, or even to see a play a second time.

The critic situation went critical again in late summer; it began to give off smoke and make funny noises. The New York *Times* thanked Stanley Kauffmann, its drama critic of only half a season's standing, for his services to the paper and named Walter Kerr to the powerful post of *Times* play-reviewer. It had been widely rumored a year ago that the *Times* wanted Kerr as its critic when Howard Taubman was to vacate the post, but Kerr remained loyal to his faltering Old Paint, the *Herald Tribune,* until it folded under him.

Kerr had scarcely written his first *Times* review (of Edward Albee's *A Delicate Balance*) when Clifton Daniel, then the paper's managing editor, admitted in open discussion that the responsibility of this job was "terrible" and that the *Times* was considering a plan to relieve it somewhat by dividing it between two critics—one reviewing in the daily paper and one in the Sunday paper. Kerr himself favors the two-critic plan.

Kauffmann's short run as *Times* drama critic began on Jan. 1, 1966. He stirred up a lot of discussion by adopting a policy of seeing plays at the final preview instead of opening night, to gain more time to write his notice. (Kerr will review at first nights; a *Times* insider remarked, "We're through with all of *that*.") Kauffmann also stirred his readers to comment on his work, pro and con, in a large number of letters published in the paper's Sunday drama section. He was not a crowd-follower in his opinions (as if there were still a crowd of critics to follow). His leanings were away from Broadway, toward areas of regional and other experimentation. His choice of plays in the New

York Drama Critics Circle annual voting named, in one-two-three order, Brecht's *The Caucasian Chalk Circle,* Sartre's *The Condemned of Altona* and Weiss's *Marat/Sade.* His pick for best musical was *Superman.*

As the new 1967-1968 season shows began to appear, the New York *Times* covered them with its fourth play reviewer in four seasons: Clive Barnes, who replaced Walter Kerr in the daily job. How Barnes feels about his new assignment was evident from reading his copious output. He has launched himself into his new milieu with Broadway reviews, off-Broadway reviews; reviews from Montreal; a "think" piece about the season as a whole (he finds it better than last season); even a second viewing of an off-Broadway show. Launched? Barnes has *hurled* himself into the theater. Kerr, after fifteen consecutive seasons as a daily morning-newspaper reviewer with an instant deadline, is now devoting himself to the long-range artillery of a weekly article in the paper's Sunday drama section. He spoke of his feelings in the new situation, thus: "I went to the theater, and after the show I stopped to *talk* to somebody in the *lobby!"*

Theaters: To Be or Not To Be?

The air compressor has replaced subway rumble (which previously re-placed the taxi horn) in the role of Broadway's prime noise nuisance. As demolition and rumors of demolition continue, we keep hearing another sound, too, a certain argument like the refrain "John Brown's body lies a mouldrin' in the grave." It goes like this: our Broadway legit playhouses are in use only a few hours for a limited number of days a year and are therefore wasting valuable midtown Manhattan space that could be put to far more serviceable—and profitable—use as office buildings. These would condes-cend to include theaters and permit them, paternalistically, to go on wasting some but not all of this valuable space.

This is an excellent argument. It is mathematically precise, and morally persuasive (given gross national product as the ultimate good), with Mam-mon remembering to throw Thespis a bone. It is, in fact, exactly this pellucid kind of reasoning which has permitted New York's steady progress into the present era of joyful affluence, of soul-satisfying human relationships, of an ever more comfortable, efficient and reassuring environment. We need bigger buildings and greater densities of people and more dollars-per-square-foot-per-second in order to pursue more and more of this same kind of happiness. By no means let us squander valuable space on a theater or any other building that lets the sky above it go to waste on the eyes of pedes-trians. If you want to know how it's going to be, stand on the corner of 52d Street and Sixth Avenue and feast your soul on the apotheosis of architec-tural efficiency. Notice how this Brobdignagian forest of gray and brown sealed-wall monoliths lifts up your spirits, makes you feel glad just to be alive. Think how enticing for our audiences, how glittering with the sense of occasion, how tingling with life and art, the theater district will be when it finally looks like that.

New York's legitimate theaters are a cultural treasure beyond price or pressure, of permanent value to all the people of the city and nation. No encouraging statistic of new construction should distract our attention; we must be alert for any development which might affect our theaters in the long or short run; there's no telling what imperatives may suddenly and newly be found in the rapidly changing New York circumstances of the 1970s.

The dramatist should be aware, too, that there is evidence that the immediate health of the theater has less influence on the economics of theater ownership and maintenance than outside real estate pressures. London's stage is widely supposed to be in ruddy good health, yet their theater district is threatened in much the same way as our fabulous invalid's. Theater employees voiced their alarm at a British Labor Party conference at "the disappearance of live theater facilities from city centers," as a result of "the machinations of financial and property development interests who pursue profit without regard to community amenities and whose rapacity is highlighted at present in the West End of London."

It mustn't be allowed to happen here. Look west down 44th and 45th Streets some evening and try to see, not the commonplace professional environment familiar to so many Guild members, but a Wonderland dazzling the imagination of the huge plurality of the American and international audiences who have walked those sidewalks on the way to see a Broadway show, or who imagine that some day it will be their turn to do so. We must make sure that when that time comes, whatever else happens, the theaters will be there as well as the pavements.

Read it and weep: the London *Times* reports that an Arts Council study has concluded that "No more London theaters should be allowed to disappear and theaterland, with its restaurants, little shops, barrow boys and other smaller services should be carefully preserved." The report insists that at least 31 of London's 57 theaters are priceless treasures, and that no permission to raze them should henceforth be granted by the planning authorities, for any reason. Here in New York, no Arts Council stepped forward with any strong, let alone effective, recommendation to preserve our equally priceless treasures the Morosco and Helen Hayes Theaters, now assigned to oblivion to make way for some kind of a hotel. Across the ocean in the older and obviously more civilized culture, the Arts Council has received the voluble backing of interested Members of Parliament for its proposals, which include the following: "If the owner of a theater who has been prevented from demolishing it simply leaves it empty, the authority's only recourse is to acquire the building compulsorily and operate it as a theater itself."

Since no such forthright policy statement was issued by any arts agency in connection with the razing of our own Helen Hayes and Morosco (plus the Bijou and Victoria) Theaters, we checked with our New York State Arts Council to find out why not.

The state Arts Council, we learned, is expressly forbidden to enter or impinge on any area of activity involving capital expenditure, and the existence or nonexistence of theaters is in this category. The Council has no power or authority to prevent anyone tearing down buildings, but, a Council spokesman told us, "We know that we all have a stake in the survival of New York City's legitimate theaters, and we *care.*" A member or members of the group have been sitting in on preliminary meetings in which plans for setting up an agency that *does* have power, that *can* protect our theaters from real estate predators, are in the discussion stage and moving forward.

Casting around for other sides to this question, apart from commercial considerations which are not part of our *res gestae*, we found one hyperactive Broadway impresario-type who informed us, "The Helen Hayes had a balcony structure which made it obsolete, and the Morosco was in very bad repair, and those builders *are* going to put a new 1,000-seat theater in their hotel skyscraper." Nevertheless, that word "skyscraper" should give us pause. Theatergoing is above all an enrichment of the human experience. Some of our playhouses have a sort of grandeur, but it is only comfortably larger than life-size; we are not diminished by their conceits, we can comprehend their Italian and Grecian flourishes without feeling dehumanized or belittled by them. But coexistence with the skyscraper that has replaced the Astor hotel is difficult, and it won't be any easier with *another* one right next to it, a block north. The mammoth is too big, physically to be experienced as part of the greater whole, the theater area (it belongs in the elephant graveyard of upper Sixth Avenue), and too sleek to stimulate the imagination. Therefore, forced to pass it on the way to the theater, we try to ignore it—an act of self-dehumanization which tends to defeat the very purpose we have come for. This overwhelming presence works against the theater's primary function of enriching experience and puts us in just that much less receptive a mood as we approach our theatergoing—and makes the dramatist's already heroically difficult job just that much harder.

Forward Through the 1970s

"When everyone is somebody/Then no one's any*body*"—W. S. Gilbert could have told them it was happening here, on Broadway. Billing gimmickry has finally dimmed the high sparkle of stardom. Nowadays, a Broadway "star" is born, not in a burst of talent and popular acclaim, but in the fine print of a contract. A performer may be star-billed above the title not because his name is a magnet but because this form of "stardom" is now for sale across the agent-producer bargaining table, along with other tricks of under-the-title billing such as *"also starring"* so-and-so. These days you can't tell the real stars even *with* a program.

This is not to deny the appeal of a Katharine Hepburn whose name belongs above any stage or screen title in the world without an agent's urging. The reason why we bring this matter up is to strike a note of encouragement (in fairly short supply this season) at a trend heartening for playwrights. As the mystique of the "star" disappears under the mountain of billing tricks, it is just barely possible that the public will begin to understand—even in the case of a Katharine Hepburn—that it is the author, that person whose name appears after the unfudgeable *By*, and not the actor who makes up the words.

"You can say all you want to about the first night audience," a producer was overheard to remark, "but it's the second night audience that puzzles me. They always remind me of a bunch of people who are wearing their shirts for the second day."

The Comédie Française has run into a new—but in our noise-polluted, ear-blasting environment perhaps predictable—problem with its Thursday performances. By tradition, Thursday is the day on which the venerable French theater troupe reduces its prices for young people and attracts packed houses of students and other youthful theatergoers. In a controlled situation (the theater and its Thursday audiences remain the same, the players do not change greatly from year to year nor the plays in some cases from century to century) a new difficulty has arisen. Jean Piat, a leading Comédie Française actor whose roles include Cyrano, told friends that he and his colleagues must play two or three tones louder on Thursdays because otherwise the young audience cannot hear the lines. Stepping up the sound level so exhausts the cast that they wouldn't do it if they weren't sure that the young groups physically can't hear the words at the usual level, perfectly audible to the older audiences at performances on other days of the week.

One of the ideas advanced by Clive Barnes in the course of discussion with playwrights was this: "If the producer *had* to provide running expenses, if it were part of his contract that whatever happened a play would have to run, say, four or six weeks . . . it would give those plays that were put on a much better chance of life."

This stimulated our idle curiosity as to how producers might react to such a suggestion, and we decided to run it up the flagpole and see whether anybody saluted it. First we reached Richard Barr, president of the League of New York Theaters, who called the idea "totally impractical," because the cost would be prohibitive, and "it is hard enough to maintain a decent reserve as it is." Joseph Kipness was more sanguine and suggested that it might be possible to establish a fund from ½ to 1 per cent of the grosses of hit shows, to be administered by a committee named by the League of New York Theaters, Actors Equity, the Dramatists Guild and others to decide which needy, meritorious productions would be helped. Next, we called David Merrick, who declined to comment except through a spokesman who discouraged us from carrying our investigation any further. She told us that anything Mr. Merrick might have to say on this subject would probably be unprintable.

The importance of audience training in the theater's scheme of things became apparent in the Twentieth Century Fund's study of audience reaction to the Mobile Theater production of *A Midsummer Night's Dream* on its tour of the New York City neighborhoods.

According to this research, audience noise was a major problem because many of those who attended had never learned the convention of remaining quiet at a live entertainment. In the words of the report, "pre-existing attitudes requiring quiet during performances" were lacking in their experience. They thought it perfectly all right to chatter away so that the actors could scarcely be heard even with amplifiers. Only "the exercise of social control" (shooshing) by strategically-placed, respected members of the neighborhood finally persuaded the audiences to watch in silence.

As we peer forward into the future, any optimism we can muster is reinforced by recent pronouncements by Joseph Papp and David Merrick. As different in character as giraffe and zebra, Papp and Merrick nevertheless have their genus in common, with its strong legitimate theater strain. Neither had a particularly good year in 1974, but each is planning to persevere, Merrick on Broadway and Papp in his new role as impresario of both the Public and Lincoln Center.

In a *Times* interview, Merrick expressed some worry ("I'm wondering if the number of plays produced each year will continue becoming fewer and fewer") but then he finally came down on the plus side: "Even so, I'm rather optimistic that it will stabilize at the present level." Papp couldn't come out openly with a good word for Broadway—his stripes run the other way—but his inference was clear when he told Mel Gussow of the *Times* that if a playscript proved to be popular at the Vivian Beaumont it would be "summarily moved to higher ground." Higher ground—that's Broadway Papp is referring to, higher not necessarily esthetically but certainly higher in public attention and potential commercial reward, and often higher in aspiration and attainment. In recent seasons Papp has enhanced the higher ground with his transferred shows and vice versa. No doubt it will still stand there boldly and majestically when he and/or David Merrick are ready to make use of it again.

The process of changing the volume number of the *Dramatists Guild Quarterly* (the source of all the material in this anthology) yearly with each

pring issue never fails to induce reflection on the passage of time—now
nore than ever, because with Volume 11 we are starting to reflect on a
lecade instead of single years.

Long ago we decided that the patina of continuity is some compensation
or the aging process—not much, but some. We used to measure ourselves
gainst the runs of *Hello, Dolly!* and *Fiddler on the Roof,* which opened about
he same time we did. Now we must measure our continuity by a different
ardstick, and fortunately there is one ready to hand. We note that in
'olume 1, Number 1 *A Funny Thing Happened on the Way to the Forum* was
isted among the longest-running Broadway musicals, and in the next issue,
Number 2, *Barefoot in the Park* made the list of longest running plays. There
an hardly have been an issue since when a work by Stephen Sondheim or
Neil Simon wasn't a major attraction on the Broadway scene, and often
nore than one by each.

Where are they now, more than ten years later? Why, right here in the
Sroadway theater, of course, and never more conspicuously present with
iits fresh in memory, hits on the boards and certainly more hits on the way.
So the *Quarterly's* first decade has been partly a Sondheim-Simon decade.
Reflecting on our continuity, we rely on that useful old comment *plus ça
hange*—and we have every reason to believe that it is equally appropriate
or looking forward.

—Editorial Comment

☆

Ballad of the Play

Oh, the playgoer now must co-create,
Early and late
Put in Chance and Fate,
Love and Hate,
And all that the play
Omits to state
It's up to him
To co-create.

The playwright smoothes his unfurrowed pate:
Pretty fair gait
And we don't relate,
Communicate
Or consummate.
It's what, plus salacity,
Makes'em debate
And, done with audacity,
Co-create.

What's that you state?
You'd like structure? Plot?
That hoary rot?
That fix you've got?
Gone with the Dodo, out of date!
(They always were a ticklish lot.)

You're saying you'll not?
Not co-create?
Go pro-create!

—HELENE FRAENKEL

☆

A Broadway playwright is a playwright who gets his play performed on
Broadway. An off-Broadway playwright gets *his* off Broadway. By this
definition, I am an off-Broadway playwright and I got mine three times: with
Conerico Was Here To Stay (1965), *Night of the Dunce* (1966)—both presented at
the Cherry Lane Theater and both produced by the Richard Barr, Clinton
Wilder and Edward Albee management—and *Father Uxbridge Wants To
Marry* (1967)—produced by The American Place Theater.

Staples: that's the first thing that comes to mind as I free-associate. *Night
of the Dunce* had opened at the Cherry Lane Theater and I decided I had to

ave a special poster hanging outside the theater, even though *Dunce* had
eceived the Kerr kick in the kishkas and we assumed we would not be long
n the boards.

Still, *Night of the Dunce,* scheduled for a four-week run in a repertory series
f new and old American plays, ran for six weeks, thanks to excellent
eviews from Norman Nadel in the *World Journal Tribune* and Emory Lewis in
ue. And during the run I had this need to have a blowup of the rave reviews
lus a photo of me outside the theater.

The reason for this obsession had to do with a fantasy I developed and
wanted to make reality ever since I saw that great Edward Albee campaign
where Mr. Albee's scowling photo scowled out at you from newspaper ads
nd down on you from ad blowups, daring you to take him lightly. If this
ampaign was part of Mr. Albee's success, I expected it to be part of mine.
What made the expectation feasible was the fact that *Night of the Dunce* was
eing produced, and quite handsonely, by this same Mr. Albee (and Mr.
arr and Mr. Wilder) at the Cherry Lane Theater. The theater itself didn't
elp. It just magnified the obsession because it was filled with poster-sized
lowups of bygone ads of other successful of-Broadway playwrights;
amuel Beckett, William Hanley, LeRoi Jones—scowling, scowling all. Yes,
just had to join that scowling gallery.

Management, however, pointed out that the advertising budget was
imited and the money would be best spent on newspaper advertising. They
lid, after all, have cast photos and other play credits on view in front of the
ouse. A poster of rave reviews and my photo outside, they also pointed out
with some logic, was not likely to attract many customers along Commerce
treet, a street not in any way similar to Shubert Alley.

True.

The only people who just happened by were usually those going to the
Blue Mill restaurant, or, on occasion, a bunch of dropouts who would shout
'ba-fangula" into the theater during the performance.

Still, there are times when a fantasy must be acted out; especially when it's
ill involved with the magic of expectation.

So, I spent $12 and bought my own blowup.

Quite an extravagance. I had already spent $75 on tickets for movie
people, book publishers, etc., most of whom never showed up. An off-
Broadway playwright is a playwright who spends more money trying to
attract the peripheral prospects than he very often makes at the box office;
as, for example, a certain social commentator who would devote some of his
newspaper columns to an occasional theater piece. But his schedule just
could not be arranged for him to make it. Fair enough. And yet his not
coming to *Dunce* was a catastrophe to me at the time. Why?

Down in the mud-layer of fantasy-swamp lay the answer. Edward Albee

was the playwright whose plays this columnist mostly analyzed. His no
taking on my play meant that a link in the sorcery-chain of success wa:
missing.

Singular, you might say, how Edward Albee keeps popping up in thi:
run-on ragout about fantasy-expectation. Not at all. Remember how de
pressed you all got when *Who's Afraid of Virginia Woolf?* happened? Al
right—how depressed I got? I now realize it was owing to that neuroti:
feeling that if another writer "makes it," he takes "it" away from you. And i:
he makes "it" as big as Albee made "it" with *Virginia Woolf* he takes "it" al.
away. (I suspect that Arthur Miller's *Death of a Salesman* and Tennesse
Williams's *A Streetcar Named Desire* had the same effect on the writers of that
period. "That's it. They got it all. Ain't no more room for me.") The irony
here is that Albee and his co-producers pumped part of that *VW* loot back
into the theater by starting the Playwright's Unit, a workshop which later
gave me my start and introduced a great many new voices to American
theater.

By the time of *Night of the Dunce,* I thought I had rid myself of all
Albee-success expectations. Yet there I was wasting energy by expecting to
have some of the superficial ingredients of his success magically rub off on
me via a columnist and a silly poster.

Which brings me back to "staples."

The *Dunce* photo blowup with reviews was made of very thin stat paper.
(A mounted stat on thick board would have cost much more.) The stage
manager kindly offered to mount the poster in the outside showcase. When
I saw it, I was disappointed. I had expected a smoothly pasted-down job.
Too soon the poster began to crack around the staples—and finally there it
was, exposed for all to see; one more ripped expectation.

—FRANK GAGLIANO

☆

For me, as long as things are depicted—in other words, mimed—I can
accept any extreme. I don't care what's said, and I don't care what's acted.
But when you move into the area of the actual act, then suddenly something
in me calls a halt. For instance, I was thinking of *Marat/Sade* and supposing
that the flagellation scene, instead of being done with the girl's hair, was
done with an actual whip. Drew blood, with both actors consenting; all done
for a higher purpose. The audience is certainly there voluntarily. What is my
feeling about it? Well, my feeling is that I would have to cry halt to it, and it
goes beyond a question of the audience. If the actors are doing either
physical or psychic damage, I can't condone it. Then you say, well, how do
you gauge these things? What may be psychic damage in your eyes may not
be in others'. Then you come back to your own personal feelings, your own
personal standards. I remember the play that Peter Brook did, *Us.* I saw it in

London—it never did come here, did it? At one point in the performance, they burn a butterfly. It took a long time for that to sink in. I thought at first it must have been a piece of paper or something. I read subsequently that it was a real butterfly. I don't think I've ever seen anything that infuriated me more. If I had known it was happening I would have had to say something. And of course I can anticipate what the reaction would be: "Well, when they drop napalm on children, how can you holler about a butterfly?" Well, you holler about what you holler about. I would have felt called upon to try to stop it in some way. It violates something in me.

—FRANK D. GILROY

☆

Seen from the point of view of the Broadway composer, the most nonsensical practise is that of casting people in musicals who are unable to sing. No one would cast a dancing part with someone who cannot dance sufficiently to come up to professional standards. The same is true of acting. But when it comes to singing, more often than not it is "Amateur Night in Dixie." Then the hapless composer and lyricist are forced to throw out good material that has been created over a fairly extended length of time and must try to come up with quick solutions to cover for the inadequacies in the singing realm. This makes as little sense as it would to put a gorgeous costume on someone whom it doesn't fit, and then try to keep the actor from looking ridiculous by pinning it with safety pins.

Either musicals should be written for specified performers in the first place, or they should be cast with people who are adequate to its dancing, acting *and singing* demands. Rewriting should be limited to such material as proves disappointing on stage. It should not be abused to relieve performers of the obligation to be up to professional standards in all departments demanded by their roles.

—ERNEST GOLD

☆

Luise M. Sillcox, 1899–1965

Dear Luise,

For the full lifetime of devotion
you have given us—
we thank you:

for the instrument of the Guild
which your intelligence and judgment helped shape
to the benefit of all dramatists
and the Art:
   we thank you:

for the singular selflessness,
largeness of vision,
and boundless energy
with which you took from our shoulders
much of the burden
we should have borne
through three generations—
   we thank you:

for those of us who know
and acknowledge the debt,
for those who know
but choose to forget
for those fledglings amongst us
who owe you so much
and haven't the slightest inkling
of the richness and variety of the debt—
   we thank you!

Alive, you drew us in, one by one,
taught us our responsibility to
each other, fed the sense of continuity
which makes us a piece of history,
and gives us a future
without which
even now
you would not permit either yourself
or us to
   rest in peace.

—Sidney Kingsley

☆

A long time ago when I was a boy, I wrote for the Du Pont "Cavalcade of America" radio programs about the glorious history of this country. It was to make a living, and it wasn't much of a living, but I wrote a script once about Benito Juarez, who was the president of Mexico and led the Mexican revolution against the French. Du Pont supplied the research through an advertising agency. In the research I learned to my surprise that Abraham Lincoln, then President of the United States and busy with some business of his own in this country, had been unable openly to help Juarez because he feared the French government would line up openly against the North in the struggle. But he managed to leave large quantities of arms on the Rio Grande unguarded, and at night the Mexican revolutionaries would cross the river and take those arms to Mexico.

Since I had been told by the Du Pont Company that we were to engender as much Pan American friendship as possible, I thought this was a great thing to use. Well, we had a conference, as they always did, on Tuesday morning. Somebody named Applegate arrived from Delaware with a group of sub-Applegates and went over every line of the script. One line I had was that parrots flew over some territory. Someone said there were no parrots there in Mexico, so I struck that out. The next thing was: "You can't say that the government left arms on the north side of the Rio Grande." And I said, "Why? I thought that was pretty good. It showed how friendly we were to the Latin Americans." "No, you can't do it." "Why can't we do it? I don't understand why. It was a wonderful scene." Well, it turns out that Du Pont owns Remington Rand, and Remington Rand was manufacturing those arms, and they didn't want to be accused of gun-running.

That is a small, but I think indicative, revelation of sensitivity in these areas. And in the times since, of course, it has gotten much worse. As bland as those programs were, they were revolutionary compared to what goes over the air today.

—ARTHUR MILLER

☆

I'm feeling better today! My Italian Catholic Guilt waltzed out the door last night with my Americian Playwright Paranoia. This morning my beagle ate Gainesburgers, and all's somewhat righter with the world. Here's why.

I attended the party for the presentation of the Hull-Warriner Award at Dramatists Guild Headquarters. It was my first one there. I'm a brand new member, you see, and the failure of my first play not long ago nearly persuaded me that I had no right to go. "How in the name of Clive," I thought, "do I dare show my face?" I'll walk in, and all my new-found colleagues will be waiting in a line. They'll point at me with crooked fingers and cluck at me with forked tongues. I'll be anathematized; cast forth to the howling wind beneath a torrent of hors d'oeuvres and half-sucked ice cubes.

But I went anyway, for two reasons. First, I felt the need to celebrate a success; and the presentation of the award to David Rabe provided just that opportunity. I hope my applause was not too loud.

Secondly, I needed to meet people. Playwrights. People who know the Slough of Despond. Who have been there before me. And I met them. And I talked to them. And most beautiful of all, they talked to me. I felt so damned welcome, I wanted to cry. Later on, I did.

I think I'll probably write more plays.

—TED PEZZULO

☆

The Goodman Theater, in conjunction with the Chicago Museum of Science and Industry, received a grant from the National Science Foundation to present four plays dealing with various aspects of science. These plays were to be done in the museum's 1,000-seat theater, were to be played free of charge to junior and senior high school students, and were to be one hour in length. I was asked if I would be interested in cutting *Lamp at Midnight* to one hour to open the series. Indeed I was. I have always been interested in the uses of plays outside of conventional theater structures, and further, the idea of high school students seeing a play about Galileo in an ambiance such as the Museum of Science and Industry appealed to me greatly.

Yes, cutting the play to the required one hour was often traumatic, but I enjoyed solving the technical and esthetic problems involved. The production, which had its run during November, 1972, directed by Kelly Danford and splendidly acted by an all-Equity cast, proved to be most successful. There have already been requests from school systems for performing rights and an offer to publish. But for me, one of the most rewarding moments came from a conversation overheard after one of the performances when the students were moving off to their buses. One youngster, about 10, said to his friend, "Boy, that was a good movie."

—BARRIE STAVIS

☆

Turning the play over to the director is the first act of giving it away, and authors are very possessive about their work. It's been my experience that once an author has turned a play over to a director, he sits in the rehearsal room and later in a theater out of town and then a preview and of course, by that time hopefully has learned from the relationship when to speak and when not to speak and how to speak. One thing that an author has to learn is *how* to contact the director without bugging him, without distracting him, without exasperating him to the point where communication stops. You want to sit there. You want to hover. You want to tap his shoulder, but you know it's not right. You take notes. You never get a chance to deliver them. I know that that is *the* most *difficult* thing for an author once the play is no longer in his hands. I know a great many directors are insensitive to this problem.

—PETER STONE

☆

Theatergoing is something that must be planned way in advance in order to insure getting in. This goes against the grain of young people's habit of spontaneously reaching for entertainment, a habit encouraged by the easy and instant access to television, radio, phonograph records and, to a lesser but still significant extent, films. Planning ahead to see a play doesn't give one any guarantee that when the time comes he'll be up for seeing it. This sort of arrangement just doesn't account for the possibility of being in an unreceptive mood on the day of the performance. When you're talking about the amount of money involved in buying the ticket and the trouble involved in the process of getting it, this seems quite a gamble.

Also, young people make unpleasant associations with the ritual of theatergoing. They don't like to go to the trouble of formal or semiformal attire that they feel is demanded of them. In a generation known for espousing comfort over convention, self-style over established traditions of etiquette and dress, it is too much of a strain to fool around with ties, suits and the like.

And then there is the theater audience surrounding our average student which tends to turn him off. The majority of our audiences are made up of tourists, suburbanites and people from a generally middle-class background, predominantly middle-aged. These are precisely the kinds of people students and young people in general feel disaffected from. They make our average student uncomfortable, and who pays to be uncomfortable?

Consider too that for most kids, exposure to drama has come from either being taught it in school or being dragged to Saturday matinees. The teaching of drama in school, ususlly by English teachers, is pretty dry stuff. A fascinating and exciting play such as *The Little Foxes* or *Death of a Salesman*, to name two of the more frequently-taught dramas, is analyzed, prodded and explained often for as long a period of time as two or three weeks. Usually little or no differentiation is made by the teacher between the written word and the performance, consequently students come away from the experience with the impression of theater as something stodgy, stuffy and preachy. With almost all of the vitality pounded out of a play by classroom symbol-hunts and required ten-page research papers with footnotes on the universality of Willy Loman, is it any wonder that for so many theater seems more a chore than a pleasure? Shakespeare is probably one of the most unpleasant names to students today, what with all of the time they have been forced to spend picking apart *Julius Caesar*.

The chore vs. pleasure concept is reinforced by memories of those few times when the young person *has* gone to the theater. Usually the occasion has been a Saturday matinee tied in with family duty. Surrounded by gray-haired clubwomen (who are not the best audience), forced to get dressed up and stay cooped up inside on a day usually dedicated to freedom after a long week in school, such experiences can only encourage a hatred for the stage in most young people.

All this, of course, is in addition to the reaction the young may have to the quality of the plays they have been taken to see.

—Jeff Sweet

☆

Any playwright who has worked in theater knows how social, cliquish and political it is. Off off Broadway is the same, only worse. Most off-off theaters—with perhaps half a dozen exceptions—are run for and by tight, tiny groups that want very little to do with outsiders. The people who run the theaters prefer to give space to fans, lovers, sycophants and obsequious drones. A writer has to be prepared to put up with banal lectures on the state of the theater, idiotic advice on casting and production, constant laments on the stinginess of foundations, Byzantine intrigues and diversions to keep him ignorant and a swamp of fluctuating loyalties. The performers and directors are better than the owners but many of them suffer from corrosively unfulfilled ambition, and they will take this frustration out on any convenient target. (I must add that writers are by no means exempt from these strictures; hardly.)

As an added fillip, anyone who works off-off must contend with a nearly monolithic homosexuality. A homosexual theater, no matter how well-intentioned, resists the intrusion of heterosexuals in pivotal positions. Playwrights are pivotal in any script-based theater.

This means that a straight writer, especially a male, has to tread very delicately. A sensitive writer, straight or gay, should be able to work with

anybody, but a writer who is uncomfortable with gays, or is not used to collaborating with them, should be careful in choosing his theater and director. Otherwise, he will find himself an outsider looking in at his own work and somtimes not even recognizing it.

If all this sounds discouraging, it is not meant to. . .off off, a diligent playwright can mount two, three, four plays a year. In that one year, if he can get past his vanity and look at his plays coldly, he will learn more than all the agents and producers and producers' readers can teach him in a lifetime. That is a pretty good lesson and at a pretty fair price.

—Tom Topor

☆

Ibsen was considered a radical in his day, and his day was more radically minded than ours. His battle was won only to the extent that an armistice was declared, and his affair ceased to be news. The same people who disliked him then dislike him now. One need only read Ibsen attentively to see how far out e is, and how little he is understood. Ibsen has suffered the common fate of genius. He was practically unintelligible to his contemporaries. Toward the end of his life, he was apotheosized for reasons which had little to do with his greatness. He became a classic while remaining almost completely unknown. Like Euripides, like Shakespeare, he has become a monument which tourists may visit in the company of a guide, but which is not open to unregulated visits by the general public.

It is no simple thing to re-invigorate the theater. After Ibsen, Chekhov attempted a type of drama which evoked a lyric response largely by suppressing the narrative element, thus transforming a story into a poem. But, for a variety of reasons, Chekhov has proved impossible to imitate, and he left no school, save a school of acting, which was perhaps not his own. Attempts were made to find theatrical excitement in the symbolic, the unreal, the fantastic, the absurd, the inane—these were all modes and motives which had been more or less successfully exploited in fields other than the drama—in the plastic and graphic arts, in music, poetry, and the novel. With very few exceptions, the results in the theater have not been impressive. There have also been perennial efforts to lend importance to the drama through the use of important themes—to use the stage, that is, as a means of instruction, criticism, or propaganda. But theme, save insofar as it touches universals, is the most perishable of dramatic commodities. In general, it may be said that the aim of the serious dramatist at the present time remains what it has always been: to tell a good story effectively on the stage. Nothing is more difficult.

—MAURICE VALENCY

☆

One issue, very simply, is: Do we writers approve or disapprove of censorship in any form whatsoever? You either are against censorship indivisibly; or in drawing guidelines, you have to become a censor yourself. The reason we were upset by what they did to *Che* was not because of the content of the play, but because of the way in which they censored it. Nobody went and looked at the play and then said, "We're now going to try to prove that this is obscene or not under the laws of this state," which they would have had to prove in court. At a trial, the producer and the author would have had a chance to defend themselves. The authorities didn't do anything like that at all. It was police-state tactics. They walked into this theater where a public performance was being played, and they arrested the actors and the author and producer as accomplices for performing what they said were acts which under the statutes of the state and the city were illegal. Now, it's possible that they *were* illegal but the authorities were never required to prove it, and yet they closed the play. Now, if they can close that play, I think by extension they can close any play under similar conditions. That we did not see it was deliberate on our part. We talked about it and decided that we did *not* want to see it. We did not want to have an artistic opinion. I'm told that Justice Black, when he issues the Supreme Court decisions, does not read the material on which the cases are being brought. And it seems to me that as writers we must feel the same way. Otherwise, if you start chipping away at the central doctrine, you're really cutting the ground from under your own feet. You'll never know where to stop. It seems to me, no price is too high to pay for a free press, even if the price is allowing something like *Che* to be exhibited to those people who are willing to go to a box office and pay for it. They're the only ones who are going to be damaged. Nobody puts a gun into the small of your back and insists, "Go see that." A general principle as important as this *is* indivisible.

—Jerome Weidman

VI. On Inner Space.....

Poor naked wretches, wheresoe'er you are,
That bide the pelting of this pitiless storm,
How shall your houseless heads and unfed sides
Your loop'd and window'd raggedness, defend you
From seasons such as these?
                                                                KING LEAR

Everything You've Always Wanted to Know About. . .

NEIL SIMON

. . . But Never Had A Chance to Ask

Neil Simon answered the questions of a standing-room-only crowd of his fellow-dramatists at Dramatists Guild headquarters, at a prearranged session which was taped and edited for publication under his supervision.

NEIL SIMON: I haven't prepared anything formal to say, because if I talked about what I would like to talk about it would be mostly tennis and the Knicks. I want to talk about what you would like to hear. All those stories in *Variety* have probably raised some questions in your minds; stories like the one saying I'm retiring from the theater and going into teaching for the next three years. It's untrue. I've received some offers to go and teach and I'd like to do it some day, but things happened in my personal life which dictated that I could not do that now. I hope that doesn't sound wrong, I don't want to seem mysterious or bleak about it. I don't think I'll ever give up writing because if I tried, I couldn't. When I walk past my study it pulls me in like a magnet, and there I am. I wish I didn't *have* to write so much, though I do enjoy it. I'd prefer it to be an enjoyable experience rather than something I am compelled to do, which I am finding out about. I am in analysis now, and it's kind of interesting.

What were the other matters Hobe Morrison took up in *Variety*? He brought up the money I make, I make a lot of money, it's true, but nothing near what he said. He asked somebody on the Coast about my royalties on *The Odd Couple* television show, and they told him, "Not more than $10,000 a week." So he multiplied this by fifty-two, so I get $520,000 a year. The truth is I get nothing, because it was part of an old deal that I made with

Paramount. I'm not unhappy about it, I'm glad the show is a success, but I really get upset about that kind of reporting.

Q: Are you working on something now?

SIMON: Something strange has been happening to me over the last few years. When I first started to write, the first idea I had for a play was the play that I worked on. When I was working on *Barefoot in the Park* I had no other ideas. I just started to work on it, and that was it for the year. We were going into rehearsal with *Barefoot in the Park* when I got the idea for *The Odd Couple*. I started to work on it—and it went along like that for a number of years. Lately I find that either the whole pattern of my existence has changed or I've raised the level of what I'm trying to accomplish in writing, because I keep starting a play and then putting it away, starting another one and putting it away. Last year I wrote eight pages about these two old vaudevillians and left them in the drawer. I came back to it another day and read it and thought, "This is terrible, it's just awful." So I started on something else, and I ended up with six almost complete first acts of plays. I was getting very nervous, I didn't know why I was doing that. I finally went back again to those eight pages, liked them, and in one continuous battle finished the play. The whole thing started again this year, so now I have about six beginnings of plays and am working on one that I like.

Q: About those six beginnings, do you start a play without knowing where you're going?

SIMON: When I've gotten my best ideas the entire thing has presented itself to me—I'm sure many of you have had the same experience. When I got the idea for *Barefoot in the Park* I knew there would be the fight on their wedding night, they would break up and then would get together. To me, that is an idea presented in its entirety, even though it's sketchy. The same thing with *The Odd Couple*—basically, I knew where I was going. By that time I no longer felt the need to write outlines. In the very beginning, when I first started to work on *Come Blow Your Horn*, I didn't know how to write a play. I'd been working in television for years writing sketches, and I read all those books on playwriting that said you *must* make an outline. So I wrote the outline and then I started to write the play, and the play started to go over this way, and I said, "Come back, you have to get back in the outline." The play was getting worse and worse, but it was in the outline. I decided on the next play I'd outline just the first act and then see what happened in the second and third acts. Then I got bored with doing even that. If I have the entire idea in my mind and know basically what it is I want to accomplish I would rather be as surprised as the audience is. I don't want to figure it all out first and then go there. Life isn't that way. We can't say, "In three weeks this is what is going to happen." I don't know what is going to go on an hour from now. And I like to work that way.

Q: In a symposium like this, people are sometimes embarrassed to ask basic simple questions, like "Do you write with a pencil or a pen?" . . .

SIMON: I made one change this year, maybe it's the biggest mistake I've ever made and it may be the end of my career—I bought an electric typewriter. In the twenty-five years I've been working I've never used an electric typewriter before. All of those hours, sitting over the typewriter in the one position, I didn't realize until I went into analysis that there is a lot of tension going on in the mind and body. I always thought I was very relaxed, but there I was—five, six seven hours a day for twenty-five years—getting terrible pains in my neck. I didn't know what to do. I raised the chair. I lowered the typewriter. I got fatter paper. Nothing helped. So I decided maybe I was pressing too hard on the keys and I got an electric typewriter. I plugged it in and I heard "Zum, zum, zum," and I said, "Oh God, shut up please." What I have done now is, I have unplugged the electric typewriter and I have been writing in longhand. That is pretty good, because I save a stage in writing. I save the rewriting stage. I put it down in longhand, and then as I copy it I start to rewrite it. I fix it up as I go along, but I'm still not happy with the electric typewriter. It's that buzzing sound. I haven't been able to find one that's quiet.

Q: How long does it take you to write a play?

SIMON: It depends. *Come Blow Your Horn* took three years and *The Sunshine Boys* took six weeks. I'm a better playwright than I was eleven years ago, because when I am working on something now I know pretty well whether or not it feels good to me. I take less time now, but I'm more apt to give up on something, so it's taking me longer to hit upon an idea I really like.

Q: Did all that television experience hinder you or help you?

SIMON: It influenced me a lot. It both helped and hindered me. It hindered me in that I became very facile after doing six and seven sketches a week for about four years on "Show of Shows." Where it helped me was, it made me unafraid. I said to myself, "What could happen?" It could be bad, but your life wouldn't be over.

Q: There's so much humanity and recognizable current life in your plays, are they portraits?

SIMON: Basically yes, but they become composite portraits. A character may start out as a specific person I know in life, then he or she starts to take on the colors of various other people—myself always included somehow, even in the women, even in the old men. The only play in which I made up characters I never knew in real life was *The Star-Spangled Girl,* and the results were not nearly as good.

Q: Have you ever considered writing a play about an historical character, a real person?

SIMON: I could name you the people, but you wouldn't recognize them in the finished play. I have to be around my characters, I have to hear their speech patterns. That's why I start to write very quickly when I get an idea, to see if I know how they are going to speak, how they react in situations.

Q: I understand you track people around the city, sit next to them on park benches. Is this for somthing you are writing specifically?

SIMON: No.

Q: Or for your "morgue," as it were?

SIMON: Exactly. I don't ever use any of those people, but I guess it's a habit a writer gets into, a penalty he has to pay, finding himself a voyeur. I've always considered myself that person standing in the corner, observing and listening, but never with the intention "This would make good material to write about." I am constantly observing rather than participating because I have the very strange feeling that the other person is doing the same thing to me—and it makes me very self-conscious.

Q: Do you keep notes?

SIMON: No, I've never kept a note nor written down a line except in a play that I am working on. When I'm working on a play and a line comes to me that I might be able to use later on—I don't necessarily mean a comedy line, but any important point—then I'll write it down.

Q: When you get an idea, if you don't make some sort of scenario, how do you discipline yourself to get to the desired end?

SIMON: But I do have it, it's in my head. I just sort of envision it. I imagine it's much as a painter envisions what he is going to do but as he is painting he says to himself, "I need a tree right here." I really do have a vision in my head of where the entire play is going. I had all the *The Sunshine Boys* blocked out in my head without dealing specifically with any one incident—except that I knew I would eventually put the sketch on the stage.

Q: How do you make sure, then, as you approach the end that you don't have extraneous characters?

SIMON: If the character doesn't further the plot, I have no need for him. That's why I don't like to have lots and lots of people on the stage.

Q: Most of your plays seem to be about men. Is that deliberate?

SIMON: I guess it's true that I lean more towards writing about men because I understand them a little bit more, but I think I have touched on women quite a bit.

Q: In your playwriting, are you conscious of the larger social issues?

SIMON: I have thought about them a lot, but I think that when you write a play about social issues you have to write it very quickly, because the issue will change by the time you get through with it. I'd like to write about something lasting, about human behavior in general, in any era. *The Odd Couple,* for example, is still relevant today even though it's not about a very large social issue. There are enough social-issue writers in the theater to take care of that aspect of life. I like to deal in human relations. That's what I like to do in the plays, in confrontations between two people, maybe three, four, five. When you start dealing with masses you don't really get into basics, you get into some political issue that becomes yesterday's news. There've been a lot of brilliant plays about social issues, but I just can't deal with them.

Q: What happens within the framework of the time you work on a play when, as often happens to all of us, you reach the day when the idea stops?

SIMON: Mike Nichols was very helpful to me on that. He used to say, "Stop trying to force it, either the way you want it to go or the way it seems to be going. Just shake it up in your mind and throw it out. Go to the extreme opposite possibility and see what you find there." It's like stepping back and looking at it objectively. I think of something so extreme that the play couldn't possibly do it, and then I ask "Why not? Why was I forcing it to go in that other direction?"

Q: Can you give an example of that?

SIMON: No, not literally. When *The Prisoner of Second Avenue* was in New Haven, we didn't have the snow coming down at the end of the play. They were throwing water down, or something, and Mike said to me, "It's not going to work." So we sat in the hotel lobby and just talked about this for what seemed like hours. Finally I said, "The snow falls down." It was as simple as that. We just kept on talking about things we couldn't possibly do, but I couldn't reenact the whole process of how we got there.

Q: To what extent do you visualize the setting when you stare at a blank page?

SIMON: It's as important to me as knowing the speech patterns of the character. I have to visualize it, I must be prepared to tell the set designer *everything*, even though I don't have to. I have to know where I am and where the actors are going to get on and off.

Q: How do you differ in your approach when you are working on an adaptation in the musicals?

SIMON: I don't like doing it much, it's not much fun. In the beginning I thought I should explore all avenues of writing for the theater, so I did a very free adaptation of *Little Me*—it came out as an original. In *Sweet Charity* there was a book already written by Bob Fosse and I came in to doctor it up, but by the time I finished I had really taken it over. I would have never started this project from the beginning because I never really believed in it— what I believed in were Bob Fosse's and Gwen Verdon's talents, but the story seemed dated to me. With *Promises, Promises* I didn't have an idea for a play, but I wanted to go to work with Burt Bacharach, I thought he should be brought to the theater. We were kicking around some ideas, and a musical stage version of *The Apartment* seemed the logical one. If I were to get an original idea I wouldn't do it as a musical, I'd do it as a play.

Q: Did you have any qualms about doing a show based on a film that had been so well done?

SIMON: I didn't do *Some Like It Hot* because I didn't think I could improve on it—it's a classic comedy, and there's no way you can top it. While I thought *The Apartment* was a marvelous film, I thought the subject could have been dealt with a little differently and made a lot funnier. As I watched the film again I said to myself, "It's very good, but it's a little dreary." I don't mean that in a negative way, but I thought I could add a lot of humor to it, and it seemed to be the right vehicle for Burt Bacharach, a contemporary New York piece. I wasn't sure I was going to do the show, either, until I got into the writing and found the device of the lead character letting the audience into his confidence when he told them he was lying to the girl. If I hadn't found that, at some point I would have withdrawn from the project. But that little thing was enough of a key so I could say to myself, "This can be different from the movie and I can add something to it."

I don't think I become enormously fulfilled writing books for musicals. You write up to the peak moment, and then comes the confrontation—and they sing it. Maybe that creates an ego problem for me. I wish I would write the lyrics like Sheldon Harnick. In the best musicals it sounds as though the lyric writer was the book writer and vice versa, but in the poorer musicals the style suddenly changes when they start to sing.

Q: A lot of us who think in terms of the well-made play with a beginning, a middle and an end have been a little concerned that perhaps we aren't being "with it". Would you care to comment on that?

SIMON: I don't think it's true. I don't think the critics would put down a well-made play just because it fits a pattern that once predominated. I have faith in the theater critics—not all of them, certainly, but I find them fair enough to the plays that have quality, well-made or unwell-made. There was a time about four or five years ago when the whole cult was changing, and they were saying, "We don't want the old-fashioned thing," but my plays have been so-called well-made plays, and the critics haven't objected to them on that ground.

Q: Do you think producers are concerned about it?

SIMON: I don't believe they think in those terms. They just ask, "Is it a good play or is it a bad play?"

Q: In your opinion, is it desirable for a playwright to have a college degree, perhaps a Masters in theater arts?

SIMON: I'm a graduate of DeWitt Clinton, and that's about as far as it went. I went into the army after that, and soon I was deep into writing. When I got out I decided I didn't want to spend four years in college learning something I was already doing, I wanted practical experience. Nobody can deny that a good college education is going to be very beneficial, but there's something unique about writers. There is something that is just *there* which they find sometime in the beginning of their lives.

Comedy and Humor

Q: Do you have a philosophy of comedy, or are you totally concerned with what will make an audience laugh?

SIMON: I write primarily for what will make *me* laugh.

Q: What makes you laugh?

SIMON: It's hard to say, but I know when I'm writing. If I were to say to myself, "Well, they'll laugh but I don't find it amusing," I would just tear it up. I regret not having torn up some things, but basically I like to think that I could go to all of the plays I've written and, if I were able to erase the tape, be able to sit there and enjoy them. I don't mean that the quality of the play is superior, I mean that it's *my* kind of play. I don't write specifically for the audience, but it would be foolish to say that I don't care about the audience. That's what the theater is all about. It's the actors and the playwrights and the audience. Without any one of them you're on twofers.

Q: Did it worry you that there was a change of key in *The Sunshine Boys* when the guy gets a heart attack and suddenly the audience is wrenched from one frame of mind into another, and yet you guided them back into laughter again?

SIMON: I was a little worried because I had two touchy experiences with plays that involved that. One was *The Gingerbread Lady* and the other, where I learned somthing (and I'm not so sure *what* I learned) was *Last of the Red Hot Lovers*. I knew what the first act was going to be, that this Barney Cashman who expresses all his ideas in the first act about not having experienced anything and feeling that life has ignored him, was going to take this one fling. So foolishly he tries it with this lady who is kind of tough and hard-bitten, and their affair is never consummated. That's not what the problem was, the first act worked very well. In the second act Barney meets a girl who is light and funny and silly and goofy, and after about twenty minutes he finds out she's psychotic. I have met people like this, about whom you think, "She's such a funny, goofy girl," and then suddenly you realize, "She's a nut, a complete nut." In real life you may be laughing for the first twenty minutes, but then something else happens that you can't laugh at—and that is what I wanted to do. The Boston critics, who loved the play, pounced on me about this and said, "Don't make her psychotic; it disturbs us." I didn't know what to do. I chickened out by just making her silly and goofy, not really showing her. But the audience wasn't buying this either, so I was really confused by it and still am.

I knew I had that sort of problem coming up in *The Sunshine Boys*. But I wasn't too concerned, because he doesn't die, and the play picked up immediately with the reunion of the uncle and nephew right after that. It's what I felt would happen in real life. A man could conceivably get a heart attack, and why can't you show on the stage what happens in life? I don't believe comedy has to be funny all the way through, that you can't touch on serious matters. It's very delicate, you have to do it with a surgical knife; but when you do it, it's infinitely more rewarding than just being light and funny for the whole evening.

Q: Other than your own, which comedies have you enjoyed enough to be influenced by them?

SIMON: I'm not influenced very much by comedy writers or comedy. I'm much more influenced by serious playwrights. I always like to think that the play I am writing is a serious play so that I can give it a dramatic structure and then twist it through whatever oblique viewpoint I have of life so that it comes out funny. I don't always mean it to come out funny. At the dress rehearsal of *Plaza Suite*, Mike Nichols and I watched it all alone in the empty theater and we were very moved and touched by it, very happy. We went in front of the Boston audience and they laughed all the way through it. This isn't exactly what we wanted to accomplish. There were moments where we wanted laughs, but there were others where it's not funny, so we started taking out laughs. When I took out laughs they would laugh in some other place. I wanted to kill it with a stick.

Q: Why did you identify *The Gingerbread Lady* as "a new play" rather than "a new comedy?"

SIMON: I called it a play because I was aware of my reputation and I didn't want the audience walking in and saying, "Oh boy, this is going to be terrifically funny. We'll start laughing from the moment it goes up." Had another playwright written it, they might have looked at it differently; I'm not saying more favorably, but at least differently. The play that I wrote originally had a much more serious ending. The Maureen Stapleton character's daughter left her all alone, and the delivery boy came in, and she started to play records for him, and you could see that she was about to have an afternoon's affair with him because she had very little to hang on to in life. When we were in New Haven at the dress rehearsal, Saint Subber said to me, "If you change one line of this play I'll never speak to you again." I couldn't really tell from the audience reaction how that ending was going. It's shaky to put much value in what people say when they confront you, because they don't like to come up and say, "That's a piece of trash." But I got the general impression from people coming up to me that they liked the play but were taken aback by it. They said things like, "Gee, this is a new dimension for you." It was the first time that any of the kids from Yale came over to me wanting to talk about my play.

We went to Boston, and you know that opening night audience in Boston, they don't let you in if you are under 90. I always try to forget what happens the first night in Boston and try to go by what the critics say. The audience was just taken aback by the play. They laughed. There was no coughing. I always hear that's a very good sign, but then the reviews came out, and they were pretty bad. They said I was trying to be Tennessee Williams or Edward Albee, and by this time I was so shaken I didn't know where I was and what to do for the play: whether I should leave it or work on it. It was suggested that I close the play, and I was about to agree but then I got very angry at the attitude, there were a lot of *good* things in the play that didn't deserve closing. So I redid the ending, to make it more acceptable to the audience, I guess. But I don't know whether it was the right or the wrong thing to do, because I don't have enough background in solid dramatic structure without relying on laughs. I'm pretty secure when laughs are coming. When laughs are *not* coming, I'm not always certain about what the audience is thinking, so I changed the ending of that play—and I'm sorry I did. I wish I had left it the other way.

Q: How is it published, in the original version?

SIMON: It's published the way it was played, I don't have the patience

Tennessee Williams does to go back and rework a play. To me, the play is over after the opening night. I loved it, but my life is going on. I don't want to prove to the world, "Hey, I did it wrong, I'll do it right this time." I would rather have some fun and do something else.

Q: Talking about this serious element in comedy, you've mentioned anger. Is this social anger, or anger at the human being, or what?

SIMON: It's hard to generalize. Sometimes I have social anger, and sometimes it's very personal what makes me angry. I guess in *The Prisoner of Second Avenue* I was making some kind of comment on social anger about what is happening in the decay of the cities. But I don't have any overriding philosophy about anger and hostility. Some playwrights do. They are constantly angry and writing about the things they hate. The most pleasurable play for me was *Barefoot in the Park,* and it was only about things I love.

Q: Do you ever make use of the large collection of one-line gags available in collections of comedy recordings?

SIMON: I wouldn't know how to find a gag if I needed it. It would take all day to find a gag to fit a given situation.

Q: Not even in motivating or constructing a certain kind of character?

SIMON: No, no, no. The laugh has to come from the character and what is happening to the character at that specific moment. I'm as surprised by the next line as the audience is. I haven't the vaguest idea of what the next line is going to be after the one I have just written, so I never think in terms of gag lines.

Q: Given the *Plaza Suite* situation of a woman discovering that her husband has been having an affair of a number of years' duration, I felt it hard to believe that the wife could be articulate and funny under those circumstances. In other words, I felt gags in there.

SIMON: I didn't think they were gags. She was just using a humorous device to point up her husband's frailties. For example, he was very vain, and he had just come back from having his teeth capped, and he wants to know how they look, do they look white? The wife says, "Oh, beautiful with the blue shirt." That got a big laugh. She wasn't trying to be funny, she was trying to point up to him, "Stop being so vain and be a human being, be real." For me, the theater isn't literally taking life and putting it on the stage, because plays would be fifteen hours long and kind of dull. I try to focus on life like a telescope and heighten the moments. I know I don't do it perfectly, that some of the lines come out as gags, but I don't mean them to. When they come out right they don't sound like gags, they sound like the right thing to be said at that moment.

Q: Haven't you sometimes chafed under the feeling that comedy is considered a lesser art than the serious drama?

SIMON: Yes, but it's a losing battle. I can only do my work, I can't go on platforms and say, "Come on, pay attention." All my younger life what I wanted to be was a very funny playwright. I wanted to be George S. Kaufman, and when they started to say, "This is as funny as George S. Kaufman," I would smile and say to myself, "It's not. It's better. It's funnier."

Q: Do you really believe that certain letters make words funny?

SIMON: Yes, that's not something I made up for *The Sunshine Boys*. It's been handed down by comedy writers, and I remember reading somewhere a statement by Kaufman that "Words with a k in them are funny."

Q: After a laugh line, do you consciously throw away the next two lines?

SIMON: No, I like every line to be important. But I have to be careful, I don't always know where these big laughs are coming. Sometimes they come as big surprises to me. Often I'm standing in the back of the theater with Mike Nichols or Alan Arkin or whoever is directing, and we look at each other and sort of smile and say, "Isn't that terrific. They are laughing there." I know where I'd like them to laugh, but it doesn't always happen. They may laugh on the preceding line because they see what's about to happen. That means there's somthing in the situation that's working.

Colleagues and Other Helpers

Q: Do you test your material out on family and friends as you are writing it?

SIMON: Rarely, but I will give it to my wife sometimes when I finish an act, or perhaps a whole scene. But when I feel that I'm on the right track, that the play is really going to work, then I will wait to surprise her with the entire play.

Q: How much of an influence does a director like Mike Nichols or Alan Arkin have on the actual writing of a play?

SIMON: None on the writing, but on the rewriting. On *The Sunshine Boys* I didn't require much help because the play came out pretty much as it is on the second draft. Alan Arkin and I had a few meetings and he told me which points needed fixing and which weren't quite clear enough, but there was nothing major. With some of the four of my plays directed by Mike Nichols, we required a lot of conversation, but he was as much in the dark as I was. I remember the night before we went into rehearsal with *The Odd Couple*—I had already had a few successes and so had Mike, including *Barefoot in the Park*, so I felt we were pretty professional and knew somewhat what we were doing. And I said, "Mike, tomorrow morning we go into rehearsal, is there anything you want me to change tonight in the play that you're *really* unhappy with and haven't told me about?" And Mike said, "No, I love the play. Why, is something bothering you?" And I said, "No, I'm very happy with it too. How come we're both saying this when we both know that tomorrow after the first reading we're going to be in desperate trouble, and we don't know it? Why don't we know it *now*?"

The next day we read the first act and the actors were falling down laughing. It looked good, and the second act was even better. At the end of the second act, the producer, Saint Subber, got up and said, "You don't need me, I'll see you in Boston," and he went home. We read the third act, and it was disaster. You could tell it wasn't working, you could see little beads of sweat on Walter Matthau's forehead, as though he were saying to himself, "Better call my agent, I gotta get out of this." Mike and I talked it over, wondering "Why didn't we know this yesterday?" You just *don't* know until the actors come into it and it starts to take on some life.

So I went home and rewrote. It took me about six weeks to write the third act originally, but I rewrote it in three and a half days. I stayed at the typwriter night and day and then went back to the theater with a big smile on my face, handed the pages to Mike, and told him, "I'm a genius, I did it in three and a half days, and it's terrific." We sat down and read it, and it was worse than the first time.

Now panic really set in, I didn't know what to do. Mike suggested, "Let's go into rehearsal with this. Let's see what happens." We rehearsed the play and later Mike and I were talking on the train down to Wilmington, two and a half days before the opening. Mike and I kept talking, and suddenly I hit on the idea of a sort of version that now exists in the third act. I said, "That's it," and I started to work on the train. I worked all night in the hotel, and the next morning I brought Mike the draft. He read it and said, "Yes, that works, basically it's right. It needs some work but it's infinitely better than what we have." The actors thought we were crazy when Mike gave them the new third act two days before the opening, but he said, "What's the point of opening up with a third act that doesn't work, and doing it beautifully? It's better to do something less well if at least it's right." There were a lot of tears, but we put it into rehearsal and it worked.

Q: Have you ever given in to a director on a point of staging and then wound up regretting it?

SIMON: Yes, but the great thing about the theater is, you have a chance to prove who's right and who's wrong by looking at it up there on the stage out of town. If you have a battle over something, you just try it, and either it works or it doesn't. It's trial and error.

Q: What do you think of the directors' proposal that they share in the authors' royalties?

SIMON: I will want to share in the directors' royalties so I'll get back what I gave them. I try to write as many directions as I possibly can. I'm not saying the directors aren't very helpful, but they are getting paid for what they do. I don't think they should be getting a portion of the author's royalty.

Q: How does one handle a theater that seems to be becoming a director's theater?

SIMON: Joseph Papp wrote a preface to the published version of *That Championship Season,* in which he talked about all the confrontations he had with A. J. Antoon, the director, and Jason Miller, the author. Miller kept saying "O. K., O. K.," but finally one day he said, "No absolutely no, I think that's wrong." That's the day Miller really became a playwright, Papp commented, and from then on he was on even grounds with the director. I think it's foolish for a playwright to say "No" just for the *sake* of fighting for his rights, but you say "No" if you firmly believe it, and you sink or swim with it.

Q: A lot of people who see the movie *The Heartbreak Kid* wonder where Neil Simon stops and Elaine May begins. Would you comment on that?

SIMON: It's a collaboration, all the words are mine and all the direction is hers. We did the picture just as though we were working in a theater.

Q: All your directors seem to have come out of Second City, do you have a special affinity with them?

SIMON: I do. I never thought about it until recently when I started to work with Alan Arkin, and I looked back and said to myself, "I've had a long experience with these people. I guess we have the same wave frequency."

There's a minimum of discussion with people you're tuned in to. I once worked on a picture called *After the Fox* with De Sica, and we spent three months talking about the title.

Q: Do you ever write with particular actors in mind, and how much do you have to say about casting?

SIMON:I have everything to say about casting because that's the author's privilege, thanks to the Dramatists Guild. Usually I cast together with the director and the producer, we sit there and try to find people that everybody likes. Only a couple of times have I thought of somebody while writing. I was into the first act of *The Odd Couple* when Walter Matthau suddenly came into my mind. I phoned Walter and said, "I'm writing a play for you, please don't do anything for the next year until you see the play," and he said O.K. Sometimes you write musicals for a star. *Little Me* was written specifically for Sid Caesar and *Sweet Charity* for Gwen Verdon.

Q: You expressed interest in tennis and the Knicks. Would you consider writing a play about sports?

SIMON: Yes, I have been spending eight months on and off trying to figure out how to do it, and there's an enormous problem. It's the casting. They didn't have a casting problem in *The Changing Room* because actors playing English football players only have to look kind of rugged. If I want to do a play about basketball, I will have to get six-foot-eight-inch actors.

Q: How much freedom do you allow your actors to change the lines?

SIMON: None. But during rehearsals I will always listen if they have suggestions. Very often the really creative actors have come up with pieces of business or lines that I have put in the play. You'd be foolish not to listen and accept something that is really good.

Q: How do you create a camaraderie between playwright, director and actors?

SIMON: As I said, by being very open, making everybody feel free to come up with anything they want. It's great to watch Mike Nichols direct. Some days he'll come in and say "I have no ideas today" and he'll tell the actors, "Do something." On other days he says, "This is what we will do," really pinning it down. But I think generally you have to be very open.

Q: Don't you think there's a weakness in the chain of command in the theater, when usually it's the secretary who reads the script while the producers are all screaming for new plays?

SIMON: Yes, but that's been going on since there have been plays in New York. It's always been the same story and always will be the same story—you always have to go through somebody. After he saw *Barefoot in the Park*, George Abbott asked me, "Why didn't you ever send me that play?" I told him I did, but it stopped at the desk of his secretary, who read it and didn't like it. This didn't stop me from having a career, but I think producers are the most dangerous people in the theater; not because of the power they have over the young writer, but because of the power they have to choose plays that hurt the theater. The more bad things they see, the more people decide to stay away from the theater.

Q: Do you think the Dramatists Guild should develop a program to offset this influence, some kind of loose producer's educational group?

SIMON: I don't think there's any way of doing it. When I wrote *Come Blow Your Horn* I sent it to a producer who told me, "I like it and I want to produce it." He was the first producer I sent it to so I thought, wow, this is easy. But he wanted me to rewrite the whole play, and I did. After I finished, he didn't like the rewrite and he didn't like the original version, so he said, "Forget it." So I went to another producer, and he liked it, but he also wanted me to work on it. I rewrote twenty different times for twenty different producers and I had twenty different versions until finally I went to Bucks County and tried it out there. I think you just have to stick with it.

Q: When you say something "Doesn't work," do you base that on only one performance, or do you try it with several audiences?

SIMON: Usually you need a couple of performances, but you can be so fooled. That's maybe what's so frightening and so marvelous about this business. Going back to *The Odd Couple,* after I'd finally gotten the third act pretty much right, there was still somthing wrong with it. Mike and I decided we needed another scene in the third act, so I wrote it and gave it to him, and I never heard so much laughing in all my life. I mean, he just couldn't get past the pages. The day we started to rehearse it was one of the funniest days I've ever spent in Boston. We said to ourselves, "They'll be carrying the audience out in ambulances." When we did it on the stage, I never heard such silence. It shows you how incredibly wrong you can be. The reason they didn't laugh is because they didn't *like* what was happening to the characters. They didn't like what the characters were doing; conse-quently, they didn't laugh at anything, and I threw the scene out. On the other hand, I've written scenes where the lines were kind of inferior but the audience liked what was happening so much that they laughed *all* through the scene. That's what you call free laughs, and it's terrific when you fall into that kind of situation.

Q: Do you find yourself writing every day? How do you prevent dry spells?

SIMON: I don't have dry spells, and I don't write every day. One thing that is changing now, because my perspective on life and the theater is changing, is that it's hard to maintain that enthusiasm. But I still feel *compelled* to write and I still do it quite often. I don't seem to have a discipline problem. My problem is not so much "writer's block" or "dry spells" when I can't think of anything. My problem is that I think of too much, and I write it down, and there are these reams of pages, and I am still looking for something that really satisfies me.

Q 1: If you bring those pages that you don't work on, Neil, and just leave them around here . . .

Q 2: Were you ever an actor, did you ever want to be an actor, and when you're working do you ever say the words aloud?

SIMON: Yes, I read it to myself because I want to see if it's going to be garbled, if the actor will be able to say it. I try to cut the spoken words down to a minimum. If I turn those pages and see long speeches I say to myself something is wrong, at least for a comedy. And no, I never wanted to be an actor, never have been, nor do I want to be a director or producer. I just like writing. It's the best fun in the world.

An Adventure in Playwriting: Multiple Contusions But No Regrets

By Richard Dougherty

When I was a little boy in Bolivar, N.Y., I asked little of life except to be rich and good looking when I grew up.

The years passed. It became clear that good looks would elude me. Nor pomades, nor partings of the hair, nor hours in front of mirrors perfecting the elevation of eyebrows could defeat the willful cruelty of an uncharitable Providence.

I settled on fame as a reasonable substitute. Researches revealed so many ugly little guys who had got rich and built empires and wound up in history books.

There were impediments to this. It is hard to win fame from a place like Bolivar, a village of 1,500 souls in the hill country of western New York. It is also hard to get rich there, unless—as was not the case with my family—your father was rich before you.

The obstacles did not end there: I was also lazy.

So it came about that I decided to become a writer.

Writing, as I saw it some 30 years ago, was the one easy way to win the respect of the multitude and make a few dollars to boot; it was the lazy man's avenue to power without responsibility. I have clung to this view through a long and uneven career as a kind of journeyman scribbler, and it is this view which prompts me always to advise the more Angst-ridden of our contemporary writers that he who lives by the pen must be prepared to die by the pen.

This is by way of preface to the tale of how I came a cropper on Broadway and suffered untold losses and humiliations in the process, which I will now describe as requested by the editor of the DGQ.

Some years ago, after I had published one novel and just finished another, an idea came to mind that I thought might make an amusing play. It was pure fluff: a conflict between a resourceful daughter who wants to get married and an equally resourceful father who thinks she's too young. She makes a move; he makes a counter-move; he moves, she counters. Guess who wins in the end.

You can see I was bent on breaking new ground in the theater.

A year or so went by. A summer theater up on Cape Cod picked up a script somehow and decided to put the play on for a week. The play's name by that time was *Fair Game For Lovers;* earlier it had been *Three Cheers For Prudence.* There was an even worse title before that, the memory of which I am now happily spared.

Everything seemed to work all right; the nice people in the audience laughed quite a lot; nobody walked out. The local papers wrote kind reviews, some even going so far as to predict that, with a little work, *Fair Game* might well wind up on Broadway. After I had published a third novel and was at work on another, a would-be Broadway producer appeared. He had read a script; he thought it needed quite a bit of work; but he liked it; he wanted to put it on.

All the business of selecting a director, casting, and the rest, got under way. I won't go into detail because I'm sure my experience only parallels that of every other new writer, new to Broadway at any rate.

Rehearsals began in late November or early December, and in January we flew to Florida for three weeks of tryouts in Miami and Palm Beach. Pretty keen, I thought: who wants New Haven in January? The opening in the Cocounut Grove theater went well; reveiwers for the Miami papers were enthusiastic; so was the stringer for *Variety.* There was one harsh notice in the paper of some smaller city—Fort Lauderdale, I think. But, by and large, the play's reception by both audiences and critics was good. This was repeated in Palm Beach, where we played a week before coming on to New York.

We had four or five previews in New York, and I still cherish the memory of the Saturday night—before Monday's opening—when the theater was absolutely full, the actors at top form, and the laughter easy and quick in coming.

That's the last pleasant memory I have of *Fair Game.* The opening was a nightmare. The curtain rose on the first scene with a couple of key props missing from the stage; the young lovers gabbled a few hysterical lines at each other; the maid came on, looked around, ad libbed something like: "I'll leave you to your own business," and fled. A bit later the young man's bathrobe caught on fire as he lit a cigarette, and he had to beat out the flames with his bare hands.

But even before fire broke out the reviewers had already seen enough to e convinced that they must have stumbled into amateur night at the Grand. hey went back to their offices and wrote accordingly. I don't want to brag, ut I doubt that any playwright living can claim reviews so universally nfavorable and so scalding as those I received for *Fair Game For Lovers.*

Imagine how it feels to be called "witless" by Howard Taubman! For nonths thereafter friends greeted me with downcast eyes: it was as if I had ›een picked up on a morals charge in the men's room of Grand Central.

Occasionally, during the roughly five months of labaor which preceded he disaster, I had often told myself that even if the play failed to be a hit it vould surely stand a chance of being bought by Hollywood. At the very east, I was certain—it being a one-set, six character production—the play ıad a future in summer stock and among amateur groups.

I couldn't have been more wrong. So devastating was the effect of the Broadway reviews that people like the Samuel French company backed off ıs if from something unclean. They wouldn't take *Fair Game* if I gave it to hem.

Regrets?

I really don't have any. I wouldn't want to go through the experience ıgain. But like the old gag about being run out of town on a rail, there is "the ıonor of the thing." I met and worked with a lot of attractive people; I had ;ome fun; I lived in a world I had not known before. At least one of the ıctors—Alan Alda—emerged from the wreckage with reputation enhanced, and I don't think any of the others were grievously hurt.

Criticisms—constructive or otherwise?

Yes: in no special order and against nobody in particular, including the reviewers. Criticism of The System, I suppose.

I see no reason why producers, stars, directors and writers shouldn't be

willing to keep a show out in the hinterlands for a good deal longer than
the general practise. With the exception of the costly big musicals, a ne
play ought to be remunerative for a longer time than the usual three wee
of road tryout and the production itself ought to improve with more tim
Why the big hurry toward that single performance which can kill?

I would also like to see provision made for assessing a new play as a pie
of writing as well as a stage production, for any reviewer who wanted to c
so. Granted that last minute changes occur in a script, it shouldn't be tc
difficult to make certain that a semi-final script is in the hands of reviewers
day or two before opening night.

Reviewers who chose to read the script before seeing the play could the
write their notices with some knowledge of the difference between the pla
as written and the play as staged, directed and acted. This is a knowledg
they do not now have, despite the knowing comments they are all prone 1
make about direction in particular.

I am all for Stanley Kauffmann's scheme for observing a preview as well a
an opening night performance. I speak with the authority of failure, c
course, in lamenting the one-viewing system of critical hit-and-run.

Finally, a few words of advice to those writers who have yet to get 1
Broadway. When lightning strikes at last:

One—Don't allow your friends to invest in the show. You'll never sto
regretting it.

Two—Don't leave blow-ups of out-of-town raves in front of the Broac
way theater on opening night. That annoys New York fellows.

Three—Don't, if you have a small daughter on Long Island, arrange fc
her to call you before school the next morning to ask, "What did th
reviewers say, Daddy?"

Last but not least—Check your props.

Waiting for Godot
Or Dick Whittington?

By Ruth Goodman Goetz

In the summer of 1895, when Shaw had had six months as drama critic of *The Saturday Review*, he wrote a piece called "The Season's Moral." He saw clearly that the public still avoided the "new" theater of Ibsen (and of Shaw himself) with deep bewilderment, not to say distaste, and that the managements which produced their plays committed financial hara-kiri. On the other hand, the "safe" playwrights like Sardou and Pinero whom the public was supposed to like and pay to see—well, that season they had not liked nor had they paid, for the "new" plays they didn't understand had made the plays they did seem old fashioned. The only moral he could find in the London theater was the same as in Ibsen's plays—that there was none.

Seventy years have passed since that mannerly revolution, and now once again a "new" theater uses its knuckles on the old. Of course, Ibsen and Shaw are now the old, along with their playwright descendants, the sons and daughters of social realism. Some of us have been looking in the mirror recently and wondering if our quintessence was showing. The best summing-up I've heard of our state of mind was in the elevator that plies the steep haul to the Dramatists Guild, where one Pulitzer Prize-winner said to another: "The theater I can write bores me. The theater I enjoy, I can't write!" So here we sit, with "Act I" neatly typed at the top of the fresh page, and a peculiar feeling that whether it is the beginning or the end of a story is as irrelevant in today's theater as it was in last night's dream.

I grew up as a playwright hearing the echo of Maugham's words, "In the end, we are all storytellers sitting around the campfire, holding back the darkness by the power of the tale we tell." It must have been a faint echo, for I am not sure I have quoted the old party as accurately as he deserves, but in

247

essence it has seemed to me that that's what the dramatist did—told a story. That was the conscious part of his work. As for the unconscious, I used to say when asked to speak to ladies' matinee clubs on the subject, "The theater is where society acts out the problems of its conscience." And between the campfire and the conscience I seemed to know exactly what I had to do.

I notice the past tense. Do I want to do something different now, and if I do, why do I? I have one devoted young friend in the theater who is enlightened and encouraging when he talks to me about playwriting. "Honestly," he said one night in front of the New Dramatists Workshop, "I don't mind going to see a Broadway play once in a while. That is, if it's not full of phrases like 'Why are you telling me all this?' and situations that are just clean for the sake of being clean." Then, for fear he'd hurt my feelings, "I think your kind of play that's as tight as a syringe has still got something to tell new writers."

"Like what?" I asked, slipping into the dialect.

"Like what it was like during the Ice Age."

"What ice?" I asked.

He looked at me with some compassion. "The ice everybody skated on. The outer skin, the seeming aspects of the world."

"It's the same world!" I said. "You can't say that Chekhov and Ibsen and Shaw didn't know it and show it!" I said. I went on, "Ibsen said it was an onion, with layer under layer, under layer!"

"He did indeed," he said. "They were all pretty fair mediums. They saw some of the future before it happened. But then it happened."

"What?" I asked. "What happened?"

"The world got peeled," he said, "by geniuses and devils, by poets and murderers. There was Freud and Jung, and Joyce and Kafka, and then there was Hitler. They showed us what was underneath—"

"Not all of us can write about what's underneath," I said sadly.

"So leave it for us," he said. "We'll tell it like it is. People like you must tell it like it ought to be."

"Fairy tales?" I said bitterly.

He was very nice, he helped me down off the curb and kicked a broken whisky bottle out of my path, and then he boosted me up the three inches of the opposite sidewalk with a real lift under the elbow, before he answered.

"Some fairy tales have lasted a long time," he said. "When I put my kid to bed at night, I don't start out with 'Once upon a time there were two fellows waiting for Godot.' "

As with all such conversations, my best answers are usually esprit de elevator. Why hadn't I said to him, "If your kids are so eager to show us the fire inside, or the next time, or perhaps the one that's everlasting, why is your work so brief, your plays so short, your attention span so jumpy? Why do you frighten me but not touch me, why do you warn me but not show me? When will you move from horror to horizon, from accusing us to affirming us?" Like all retorts that are made too late, this one carries its answer with it. The "new" theater, for all its seeming license, brassy language and ferocious insight is deeply Puritanical. It presents our unconscious to us in flashes of apocalyptic contempt, and neither the writers of it nor the audiences for it could bear a more sustained vision of what we are and what we know we are. The only question is—Is that all we are? Is that all that's worth saying to humans about humans? Is there no more to show, nothing else to dramatize, nothing further to wait around for?

I went to sleep wondering how I myself would answer those questions, but by the time I woke up the next morning I knew I never could. It worried me, and finally I called my young friend on the telephone. "Friend," I said. "How old is your boy?"

"He'll be seven in March," he said to me. "Why?"

"You didn't say what you *do* tell him when you put him to bed—"

"Is it important?"

"It is to me," I said.

"Well, he's a little scared of the dark, so I leave a night light burning and I sit next to the bed, and hold his hand, and talk about Jack the Giant Killer. That's because I want him not to be scared of the Fee Fie Fum people he's going to have to deal with in his life. Then I tell him about Robert the Bruce—that's so he'll keep working at this new math they're teaching him. And then of course there's Dick Whittington and that damn cat!"

"What's he for?" I asked.

"For him to know that his possibilities are limitless!" he said.

"That's not what you say in your plays," I said to him.

"All that hope? That's not my bit!" he said. "But if I didn't believe it, how could I go on writing?"

There at last we were in agreement.

How could anyone?

Lillian Hellman Reflects
On Her Own Reflection

Here is an edited transcript of a discussion with Lillian Hellman and Dramatists Guild members at Guild Headquarters. At Miss Hellman's request, following Jerome Weidman's introduction, the discussion took the form of a question-and-answer session, edited for publication under Miss Hellman's supervision.

JEROME WEIDMAN: Lillian Hellman and I both had a friend named Margaret Case Harriman who was a brilliant writer for the *New Yorker*. One day I had a date to have a drink with her. She was writing a Profile at the time, and she looked rather glum when we met at the Algonquin. "What happened?" I asked.

"Well, I have made a very bad mistake," she said. "Miss Hellman and I had a lovely lunch and a great afternoon, and then I referred to her as a *woman* playwright. Miss Hellman told me, 'I'm a playwright. I also happen to be a woman, but I am *not* a woman playwright.' "

So, honoring this marvelous distinction and without further ado, let me present to you one of the great writers of English of our time and one of the great ladies of all time—Miss Lillian Hellman.

Q: I was intensely interested in a piece you wrote for the New York *Times* in which you indicated that the Broadway theater has had it. Would you like to go into that for a bit?

MISS HELLMAN: I didn't say the Broadway theater has had it, I said *I've* had it. *I've* been tired of it for a great many years—deeply tired for the last eight or ten years. It's a dangerous, losing game, not worth the candle. The last play I did, *My Mother, Father and Me*, opened during a newspaper strike. I wanted to do it as an off-Broadway production, but, understandably, Ker-

250

it Bloomgarden didn't and I'm not even sure that off-Broadway is the
answer.

Q: What's the alternative?

MISS HELLMAN: I don't know. Maybe if there was an economic change in
this country—and there might well be—there could also be an economic
change in the theater. And if there was an economic change in the theater,
there might be an artistic change. But my interest in the theater was always
in being *alone* with the play. I certainly had great pleasure and rewards from
the theater, but I don't think my nature ever fit too well with it.

Q: How about university theater?

MISS HELLMAN: It's often too slick. It's neither one thing nor the other any
more. None of you should be depressed by my feelings about the theater.
It's an old story for me, a new story for many of you.

Q: Does writing a book satisfy you, as opposed to writing a play?

MISS HELLMAN: I've always had great satisfaction out of *writing* the plays.
I've not always had great satisfaction out of seeing them produced—
although often I've had satisfaction there. When things go well in production, on opening there's no nicer feeling in the world—what could be nicer
than watching an audience respond? You can't get *that* from a book. It's a
fine feeling to walk into the theater and see living people respond to
something you've done.

With a book, there's every chance that it may fail, but you've failed alone,
and that's easier, somehow. I don't think that I'm a collaborator by
nature—nobody else thinks I am either.

Q: Dashiell Hammett once said that you never really enjoyed the theater
except when you were alone in your room with a pad and pencil. Isn't that
what *all* writers feel?

MISS HELLMAN: Perhaps, but I'm not so sure it's what *theater* writers
should feel. It may have been what was always the matter with me as a
playwright.

Q: Let's go back to beginnings. What is the initial passion of playwriting?

MISS HELLMAN: I've learned something about that from teaching, something that is a denial of what I believed most of my life. I was always
convinced that any *good* writer could write a play, given time. I once raised
money from a producer to commission five plays by five well-known writers. I was absolutely convinced that each of them could write a good play,
particularly if I would read the first draft and offer a few suggestions. Well, I
was *totally wrong*. Not one of the plays turned out well.

One finds in students almost the very same thing. I've never taught
playwriting, but I've taught many writing seminars. I pick out a novel or
short story and ask the students to re-work the plot as a short story or piece

of criticism or even a one-act play. Many of them choose to do plays. Some are interesting, except that they are not really *plays*.

So I have finally come to the conclusion that instinct for the theater is not to be defined or taught. I don't know what makes it. Why does one child learn to play the piano at six and another, given the best lessons in the world, never learns? It must be something instinctive, something that can't be taught. The knowledge of poetry, the formation of a poem, for example, is to be learned, but I am not sure the formation of a play can be learned. can't remember what made me write my first play (*The Children's Hour*) What made me write my second play and the others, was that I was a playwright.

Q: Didn't you once say that no serious writer would work in the theater today because it is such a foolish medium?

MISS HELLMAN: No, you're misquoting me. What I said was, the plays of Henry James are bad plays, the one play Hemingway wrote was a bad play, but once upon a time it was normal for good writers to try the theater at least *once*. It's appalling to me that today this is no longer true—that's what I said.

Q: Why has this happened?

MISS HELLMAN: Maybe the writers of today understand that playwriting is something you have to come by instinctively, to be born to. Maybe they feel it's too hard, or not worth it, or a combination of both.

Q: You wrote marvelous plays, you were part of a strong, thrusting theater, you left quite a legacy of literature, and now you want to abandon it?

MISS HELLMAN: Abandon it? No. Do realize that I speak only for myself. I'm tired of listening to the theater's money troubles. When I started I didn't even know about them. And I don't like the idea of success or failure depending on one newspaper.

Q: Why don't more young people turn to the theater?

MISS HELLMAN: Perhaps they can't afford to, and maybe they don't like it very much. Movies are their thing. They know all about movies, even how they get produced. I ended a writing seminar last January by asking how many students had read any of my plays (I picked myself because I was their teacher). Only four out of eleven had read me, but they knew every movie I had done.

Q: Doesn't the theater actually require dramatists rather than writers?

MISS HELLMAN: Yes, and they have always been in short supply. They're probably in shorter supply now than ever before.

Q: The greatest writer in the English language, I suppose, was Shakespeare, and he chose the theater as his medium.

MISS HELLMAN: That's right, and it's perfectly possible to make a case that

the theater was, or might be, the greatest medium of all—even though in our time it has gone steadily downhill. Even musical theater isn't as good as it used to be. Maybe it's just me, but I don't have much fun in the theater any more.

Q: A long time ago I heard a lecture in which you said you intended to turn the Hubbards into a trilogy. You hadn't yet done *Another Part of the Forest*. I'm still waiting for the third play.

MISS HELLMAN: I am, too. I always intended the Hubbards as a trilogy, but I got tired of them. I realized after the revival of *The Little Foxes* at Lincoln Center that certain work belongs with a certain time of your life, and when that is past you are finished with it.

Q: Do you think maybe the theater's audiences have outgrown the theater's producers?

MISS HELLMAN: I think audiences have grown very special. I went to a musical the other night, and there was the most specialized audience I ever saw. It really belonged en masse in a restaurant eating caviar. It had nothing to do with the theater.

Q: Do you think film writing is more exciting?

MISS HELLMAN: Yes, films now are more exciting than plays. I'm sad to say this, because I have certainly changed my point of view. I was one of the few people who liked writing for pictures years ago, but most of my generation made fun of pictures.

Q: The atmosphere, the ambiance of going to the theater used to be thrilling.

MISS HELLMAN: Yes, I remember when *The Children's Hour* opened at the Maxine Elliott Theater at the height of the depression, I was fascinated with the audience and its reactions. I used to stand in front of the theater to see what kind of an audience I was getting. I remember a happy day when four trucks drew up, taking up most of Thirty-ninth Street. Each truck driver got out and conferred with the others. Then one of them came to the box office and bought forty-four tickets. I asked him what he was buying them for, and he said, "We're buying forty-four tickets for our families and friends in Queens." It was a happy minute. I very much doubt that many truck drivers have attended the theater since.

Q: We used to go to the theater with high hearts, all excited.

MISS HELLMAN: I don't see many young people in the theater any more. True, I don't sit in balconies, but you can't sell tickets there any more, nobody sits in balconies. I couldn't guess at the number of students I've taught by now, but it has to be five or six hundred over the years, and while some of them are interested in *writing* for the theater you'd be shocked at how many famous theater names they don't recognize. They will know the name of Arthur Miller or Williams or Albee, but they will not have read their plays, let alone *seen* them.

Q: Young people don't think anything about spending $25 a ticket to hear Joan Sutherland sing or Horowitz play.

MISS HELLMAN: That's not the same thing. They go to *one* concert of Sutherland or *one* concert of Horowitz. A play has to go on every night.

Q: Don't you think there's something to be said in favor of appealing to adults?

MISS HELLMAN: Don't misunderstand me. I'm not using young audiences as a standard. This generation is rather ignorant about literature. They may be respected on social or political grounds, but not on literary grounds.

Q: Then you are in favor of a playwright writing for adults?

MISS HELLMAN: I am for a playwright writing for whomever he wants, adults, children, anybody.

Q: Isn't it the writer's function to concern himself with what works?

MISS HELLMAN: I can never answer a question about what a writer's function is. I don't know what it is, and I hope never to know. As far as I can tell, his function is to do the best he can. That's all, nothing more mysterius, the best that he can do in this world. Whether you are good or not is something else again.

Q: So when you write you aren't thinking of the audience—in other words, of how your play will work?

MISS HELLMAN: Worrying about audiences is a dangerous and losing game. A game that American movies played and lost. Who knows about audiences? They like one thing this year and another thing next year. Good writers will write what pleases them.

Q: Miss Hellman, how many plays have you written?

MISS HELLMAN: Fourteen, including three or four adaptations.

Q: Do you feel a sense of responsibility toward the theater now that it's fallen apart?

MISS HELLMAN: A sense of responsibility? No, I don't think I feel any responsibility. I want to do the best I can do. The writer's only moral obligation is to be as good as he can be. You don't have any *moral* responsibility toward any medium—theater, novel or poetry. The best one can is, perhaps, the greatest moral responsibility.

Q: Miss Hellman, are you writing plays that we are not seeing?

MISS HELLMAN: No, for the last ten or fifteen years I haven't liked the Broadway theater.

Q: If *The Little Foxes* were written today by a playwright who is not well established, what do you think his chances would be for production? Harder now than when it was written?

MISS HELLMAN: I don't think so. The money for *The Little Foxes* was very difficult to raise. I was established in the sense that *The Children's Hour* had been a big hit, but the next play had been a big failure, and at the time of *The Little Foxes* the depression was only just coming to an end.

Q: Was the play's title your own idea?

MISS HELLMAN: No, it was Dorothy Parker's four days after we went into rehearsal. I've always had trouble with titles.

Q: Miss Hellman, you say you're not a good collaborator which means, I think, the problems of compromising with a director in production. Do you think that today's playwright has to do more compromising than when you were writing *The Little Foxes*?

MISS HELLMAN: I don't know. I only know my own experience when I found I was not a good collaborator on *Candide*, the first real collaboration I'd ever done. I went to pieces when something had to be done quickly, because somebody didn't like something, and there was no proper time to think it out, I couldn't go away for a month to decide whether it was right or wrong. Twenty people would be saying, "It has to open Thursday" and I was saying, "It doesn't have to open Thursday." I realized then that I was not fit for collaboration. I had never been through that kind of experience before, and everything I had learned about the theater, all my instinct went out the window. In looking back on *Candide*, I realized that I panicked under conditions I wasn't accustomed to. I wasn't accustomed to five or six people saying such-and-such a scene wouldn't do and had to be fixed, and I was trying terribly hard to be myself and be accommodating, which is not the way collaboration should work. It took me a year or two after *Candide* to understand that it was truly not my nature, that I must never go through it again. During my early days in the theater, good or bad, failures or not, I had sense enough to say to myself, "That's all I can do. That's as good as I can make it now." But during *Candide* I was saying "Yes" when I meant "No" and "No" when I meant "Yes," and all kinds of personal things were coming into it. I would act too disagreeable, and then I would be agreeable because I had been disagreeable . . . I don't think it was a unique experience. It's probably very typical of theater. Anyhow, it never happened to me in the theater before, maybe because I was a very stubborn young woman.

Q: Do you like actors?

MISS HELLMAN: I like some of them, some of them I don't like. They don't like *me* very much. Not because I've been disagreeable to them, but there's a common language in the theater, and I've never learned it.

Q: Do you ever feel that a collaborator makes a contribution . . .

MISS HELLMAN: Oh, certainly, many times, I don't mean that I was right all the time. Many, many times suggestions were made that were better than my own. It isn't a question of whether or not other people come up with excellent ideas, it's whether you can act on them or not, whether you can write them. When *The Children's Hour*, my first play, went into rehearsal I had made up my mind that the play was as good as I could do at that minute of time. It wasn't that I thought other people were wrong. It was that I couldn't do any better than what was already on the page, although by the time *The Children's Hour* had been in rehearsal a few days I knew that the last ten minutes should not be in the play. But I didn't know how to alter it, so we had to ride with what was wrong as well as what was right. For my kind of nature, that was a sensible decision.

Q: Were you able to approach the material with any freshness when they revived the play?

MISS HELLMAN: No, but I tried very hard to change the ending. I went over the play for a year before the revival, but I still couldn't do it. I finally came to the conclusion that you must accept what's bad about your work along with what's good. Maybe they are one and the same. To try to make it perfect is often to muck it up.

Q: In other words, it's better to stick to your guns?

MISS HELLMAN: Unless you're sticking to your guns only because you don't like the blue eyes of the actress or the wife of the director.

Q: But can we hope there will be another play from Lillian Hellman?

MISS HELLMAN: I hope there will be. I don't mean to make a declaration of retirement. I think there will come a time when it might be fun to write another play.

The Playwright's Needs: Renewed Vision and An Invigorated Audience

By Louis Phillips

Playwrights are so various, not to mention perverse, that no man in his right mind would dare speak for them all. Thus the following words speak for me and of my own limitations.

As a playwright, my first desire is to write well, to write with feeling, thoughtful, well-crafted, theatrically exciting plays. By craft I do not mean three-act structure, or five-act structure, or even necessarily "the well-made play." Screw the well-made play. By craft I mean the discovery of the best form, the only form the material can take. Granville-Barker says it well:

> There must, of course, as in every human activity, be a certain order of things involved, there will be certain conditions to be fulfilled, but there will be found—so I mean to suggest to you—not to be laws of playwriting, but only the natural laws of the medium in which plays exist, the laws of the theater, that is to say.

Perhaps the only laws of the theater are not to bore your audience and not to present material in the theater that may be best presented in other media. A play is not dialogue from a novel placed upon the stage and within the mouths of living actors, nor is a play a misplaced movie script looking for a cameraman. Theater has its own province, its own gods, and damned be he who does not worship at the altar with all his heart.

Perhaps it is spiritually comforting to say that playwrights create only for themselves, perhaps comforting for a playwright who is not getting produced—which is most of us most of the time; but unless the playwright's vision stops at closet drama, the playwright is attempting to reach an audience of some sort. Theater is a public and collaborative art, and because this is so, it ranks among the more exasperating of human endeavors. Space for performance is at a premium; producers have turned their moneys into more profitable ventures, though the present state of the economy makes one wonder where these more profitable ventures are; repertory companies and colleges presenting new plays on a regular basis are almost nonexistent. Everywhere business managers cry with alarm, "We can't get people to come see new plays." But the young playwright remains obstinate. They will come to see *my* plays, he insists. He knows they will, and so, knowing audiences cannot accept or reject what they are never offered, he hustles his work. He writes the same letter hundreds, thousands of times, he makes more copies of his scripts, he stuffs manila envelopes and glues on the return postage, always with the same sado-masochistic hope that someone in some theater is going to read his script. He knows that the time spent hustling could be better spent in writing, in thinking, in growing, in studying, in living, but he also knows it is the price one pays for getting one's work produced. After all, no profession is all rewards. There is no dancing unless you are willing pay the piper.

All playwights do not pay the piper in the same way, for some are luckier, healthier, richer than others, but there are still some needs they have in common, needs which if fulfilled would make the theater more vital, more exciting, more attractive for young writers than it is now. How much more "camp" can we stand? How many more "hits" dare we import from other countries? How many more computer-tested, old-hat musicals will the public absorb until American theater wakes up one morning to ask: What did we do to ourselves to make our theatrical works so tame, so obsolete, so irrelevant?

And so our first need is to renew our vision. A playwright must possess a vision of what he wants theater to be, a concept of what theatrical experience he is willing to devote a significant portion of his time to. The vision will change or grow as the playwright changes or grows, but at any given moment a playwright is writing the kinds of plays he himself must see. From the theater of cruelty to the theater of blah, the plays he creates will in no small measure reflect what he believes the theatrical experience should be. It is the existential choice where by choosing for myself, I choose for all men.

If the playwright is lucky, healthy or talented enough, he will create a body of work whose style will be individual and coherent (as opposed to being merely repetitive) and whose theatrical scope will be challenging for director, actor, and audience alike. Sophocles, Aristophanes, Shakespeare, Molière, Chekhov, Shaw, O'Neill, Williams—yes, these are great playwrights, but it is not the goal of the contemporary writer to imitate the works of the past, nor even to imitate the works of the present. The playwright creates, pushes, pulls and thumps his material into being in such a way that he shows clearly and precisely what it means to be one aware human being alive at a particular moment in history. Hopefully, there will be a significant audience to share that vision, an audience to share in the creation of that experience. What Walt Whitman said about poetry is that much true for theater: There are no great plays without great audiences.

We need a vision of what we would become, and the playwright sitting at his typewriter, pounding out pages of material that may never get read, let alone produced, records that vision, that struggle in his work. If necessary, he must recreate his audience. For playwrights that matter, the audience is never simply there, an amalgam of human forms breathlessly awaiting the next theatrical experience. The audience must be shaped, threatened, cajoled into accepting the world anew, just as the audience will shape, threaten, applaud, or refuse the works set before it. The audience is no passive monster waiting to be licked into shape, but it too must play a vigorous part in the collaborative process that is theater. Tyrone Guthrie once observed:

> A live play isn't just made by the actors and received by the audience; the audience influences the actors and vice versa. Live theater is therefore a more creative experience—admittedly a more strenuous one —and since most of us are lazy most of the time, and some of us are lazy all of the time, one obviously settles for the easiest thing—pouring out a bottle of beer, sitting back in a deep chair, and watching the box.

The observation is a true one. In recent years there has been a tendency on Broadway to cater to the laziness of our audiences, to give them warmed-over television programs, TV situation comedies disguised as stage plays. Although this approach may prove satisfying at the box office for a limited time, it will prove disastrous in the long run. If theater is only non-broadcast television, or non-recorded films, soon there will be no reason for audiences to leave home at all. If the last few Broadway and off-Broadway seasons have not been exciting or successful, it is simply the fault of unimaginative producers and untalented playwrights. It is also the fault of the audience. The audience too is afraid to take chances.

Thus, whereas the playwright's relationship to his own vision is straightforward and private, his or her relationship to the audience is paradoxical and not so private. At first, the young playwright would deny the audience any rights at all. What matter to me all the praise or blame in the world unless I am doing good work? Then, slowly, the playwright, seeing his work changed in live performances, grants a grudging collaboration. Still, his first aim is not to please, for audiences seem all too easily pleased. It takes no great research to see how large numbers of spectators are nourished by sugar tits, by works utterly devoid of quality or of lasting value. Today's "unforgettable and memorable" evenings are soon forgotten, and we all sit back and wait for the latest trend. Will we perform *Macbeth* clothed or unclothed this season? No, the playwright needs, nay demands, vigorous and sensitive audiences who will forsake the boob-tube and who will challenge him to challenge them, and through collaboration, baptism in fire, the playwright and audience will sense the anguish, absurdity and holiness of human experience.

If the lack of an active and aware audience is a playwright's heartache, so too is the lack of a vigorous critical forum. Plays get reviewed in the local papers, but rarely examined in depth; and the review, usually hastily written and hastily read, determines the fate of the playwright's work. Few playwrights in the commercial theater are fortunate enough to have contracts which will guarantee their plays a minimum run, and thus few plays ever get the opportunity to build their own audiences by word of mouth. This is not the fault of the critics alone, for it is the audience, it is we who have relinquished our own abilities to enjoy, judge, and perceive. In New York, God help the play that does not receive a good review from the *Times*. A book may receive a bad review and still find its readers; a film may be damned with or without faint praise and still be shown; but a play, a modern play, must be a rave, a no-holds-barred hit or it is nothing.

This demand for instant success has had a debilitating effect on the careers of many fine playwrights, for no sooner does a young playwright mount one honest, decent play than immediately articles pour forth comparing him to Eugene O'Neill or Tennessee Williams. This is not fair to the prospective audience, for it arrives at the theater with expectations that cannot possibly be fulfilled, nor is it fair to the young playwright who must live up to his instant reputation. Mass communication makes and breaks careers in an instant. We no longer have the time or the concern to develop a talented playwright slowly, which is another way of saying that we do not allow enough opportunity for failure. The careers of our major American playwrights, with the possible exception of O'Neill, have been downhill careers. Early giddy triumph is followed by insistent demands that the playwright repeat himself like a machine turning out tailor-made goods.

But real playwrights are not tailors; they are artists and craftsmen who need access to the best criticism that the age has to offer. The young playwright must not confuse reviewing with criticism, and he must have enough theatrical experience, must be allowed to see enough productions of his own plays so that when he enters the market place, he can enter it on his own terms. In our age of instant production, instant analysis, and the constant turnover of products, we forget that good work takes time, time buttressed by vision, by faith, by kindly encouragement.

The playwright needs many more small theaters to function in. He needs a producer who will stick by him through thin and thin because of unyielding belief in the thickening of his talent. How many repertory companies will take on a playwright and nurture him by producing a number of his works in succession? What college or university will do it? Certainly Joseph Papp and Ellen Stewart must be applauded for sticking by their playwrights, and certainly off-off-Broadway theaters such as the Workshop of the Players Art and the New York Theater Ensemble and the Playwrights' Horizons deserve full support, but even so these are not enough. We need street theaters, we need lab theaters, we need store-front theaters where people can enter free of charge or for a minimum fee. On Broadway we need more 199-seat theaters, theaters governed by special union regulations that would encourage constant work for writers, actors, designers, directors, etc.

Not only do we need more theaters, we need to see that the productions at these theaters receive adequate critical coverage. We need publications that will promote more dialogue in the theatrical community, publications that will help educate new audiences and which will begin to focus on theatrical activity as a whole. We need publications which will publish new plays and which will give regional theaters access to the best writing by young playwrights.

We need colleges and universities to realize that it is a valuable experience for their students to work with living playwrights; for not all the playwrights are dead ones, not yet anyway.

There are many good playwrights in this country, many talented playwrights in New York City alone, but the careers of our best young playwrights, no matter where they are, no matter if they be men, women, black, white, Indian, Eskimo, or whatever, are being unnecessarily thwarted by lack of courage in the theatrical community as a whole. A theater without risk will ultimately prove to be more devastating than no theater at all, for gutless theater is the theater of lies. A society cannot be sustained by worn-out forms and worn-out visions. A loss of faith in theater, in the power of the honest imagination, is symptomatic of the loss of faith in ourselves.

An Ad Lib for
Four Playwrights

The scene is Dramatists Guild headquarters. The cast—Paddy Chayefsky, Israel Horovitz, Arthur Laurents and Leonard Melfi—is small in number but large in the sum of their playwriting experience in all areas from the pinnacles of Broadway to the lower floors of the Cafe La Mama. They are seated before a slowly-revolving tape recorder. Their free-wheeling discussion of the esthetics, motivations, status, techniques, etc., of their art begins to roll when someone asks, "What satisfaction do you get out of writing a play?"

ARTHUR LAURENTS: I just enjoy writing, I put my fantasies down on paper.

ISRAEL HOROVITZ*: Being very objective, I consider myself artsy-craftsy, sophomoric. I don't worry about my greatest fantasy: that I'm going to change the world by writing a play. . .

LAURENTS: That is a fantasy.

HOROVITZ: . . . that what I write is going to endure, be studied and analyzed for 300 years. I really have terrific fantasies, then I sit down and write plays. I'm embarrassed to admit that I draft probably six or seven plays a year. I know I've got to write like a sonofabitch to get a good play.

LEONARD MELFI: Terrence McNally who was on *Morning, Noon and Night* with us, Terrence said to me, my God, do you realize Israel just wrote a full-length play during the time we were in production? How'd he do it? And that's the thing—how you did it, Israel.

LAURENTS: When do you make love?

HOROVITZ: All I do is write and make love. I eat only when I have spare time.

*My instinct, after re-reading this conversation of several years ago, was to burn the text and forbid the editor to reprint my comments in this anthology. On reflection, such action seemed unfair to Messrs. Chayefsky, Laurents and Melfi, whose comments were, unlike my own, quite intelligent and useful. While I've always known I must apologize for what I will become, I didn't think I'd have to apologize so soon for what I was. I do—Israel Horovitz, 1974.

LAURENTS: I mean literally, physically, the amount of time. . . .

PADDY CHAYEFSKY: Lately I seem mostly to be eating.

LAURENTS: Well, I like to ski.

MELFI: When I'm writing I always think of the play being done, the whole thing, the characters together and what they're saying. To me, that seems the best thing. I try and try to write a novel or short stories, but it's murder. But I sit down and . . . there's something about when you put people together and things come out of their mouths one after another, and action happens. And the fact that you think of it coming to life, and there's an audience. This makes me want to write more and more, and the more plays I write the more I dig it. So I can't stop.

CHAYEFSKY: I write because it's the simplest, perhaps purest, satisfaction I get out of life.

MELFI: I still tell myself, well, the greatest of all writers is the playwright. Everyone knows who he is. It's kinda nice. Like my father said to me last week, "You're a playwright and Shakespeare was a playwright." That's kind of good company.

HOROVITZ: Don't you agree that when you have written a play that really excites you, it started with something that was bothering you so much that you had to write about it?

LAURENTS: It's also a matter of pleasure. When you're writing a play you think life is marvellous. Between plays, you get bugged by the conditions of living. When you're working, you think: I don't know why people are bitching so, I can cope with life very well.

CHAYEFSKY: I think you have to be in love, that helps.

HOROVITZ: That helps a hell of a lot, yes.

CHAYEFSKY: I don't think writing alone gives you the substance. Being in love gives you the illusion that life is worthwhile. Writing, you know that life is not, that it is miserable and wretched, but you can face that fact.

LAURENTS: Yes, but as you're writing that it's oh, so miserable and wretched, you're having a ball writing it.

MELFI: Paddy, what if you love writing? can't writing be your first love? I'm not married now. And I'm not thinking about getting married, but I always think that I would like to be married, you know I really would. But if I get married I know for a fact that my wife is gonna have to understand that I *love writing plays.* Before I love my wife, if I had a wife.

CHAYEFSKY: I put the living world ahead of my writing once, and it was a serious mistake, that is, for my writing. I got a lot of writing done that way, but it was a bit fraudulent. The living world demands some fraud, you see.

HOROVITZ: I come back to my sophomoric point of view that it's all that giant fantasy that you're going to change the world. Something's burning in your life, and you really want to make a statement. You can't paint, you can't build a sofa, so you write *plays*. Something's bothering you, and you want to be effective, so you write a play about it. And chances are if it starts from that at least there'll be excitement in the play.

LAURENTS: Honesty is not nearly enough. You may care very deeply about something and put it on the stage, and the audience says, "We've known that for a hundred years," even though it's coming out of the playwright's guts. The Living Theater went around telling everyone, "You can't live without money." Big news! That's a metaphor for horseshit. At the performance of the Living Theater that I attended, when they started to strip, the audience yelled down from the balcony, "Taking your clothes off is not where it's at, baby!"

CHAYEFSKY: I think what I have against this new kind of theater is the youthful hypocrisy of enthusiasm that goes into it, you know? The play-wright has to go off by himself and think up what he's going to write; it is not a spontaneous happening. No happening is, for that matter. The writing alone is real to the writer.

HOROVITZ: Yes, but there are two levels of reality. One is writing the play, and one is getting the play produced and accepted. . . .

CHAYEFSKY: If you're not by yourself writing it out of yourself, you're not writing. Once you get into rehearsal and once you get into dealing with improvisational actors and directors, it *is* less lonely, but it is no longer a part of the playwright's artistic impulse. It is simply community, friendship, yak-a doodles, and somebody else's contribution comes in. Now, when I say "The youthful hypocrisy of enthusiasm" . . . Is that what I said?

HOROVITZ: Yes. Precisely. That's what you said.

CHAYEFSKY: Not a bad phrase at all. It describes the total experience of youth now, around the country—a great enthusiasm to get in and do something, somehow, out of humanitarian impulse. In drama, I call it the Theater of the Disenfranchised, the theater of the junkie, the very young, the homosexual, the underprivileged. There's no longer a broad oppressed class over which youth can generate a great compassion, so they generate their compassion over more and more precious classes of people who are oppressed and disenfranchised, and what comes out of it is a more precious and thinner kind of art. When I say hypocrisy, I mean the hypocrisy of saying, this is a great truth and merits great compassion and is worthwhile writing about. But in fact, the new theater is a miniature in painting, not a mural. Only the writer's enthusiasm is the hypocrisy.

HOROVITZ: But there's a flaw. You can't apply the word hypocrisy to honest enthusiasm.

CHAYEFSKY: Stay with me a moment. The hypocrisy comes from the studious youthful shock at what *they* consider social hypocrisy. Or to get a little glib, I would say that there's nothing more hypocritical than being shocked by hypocrisy. That's what I find tiresome among young writers, nineteen, twenty-year-olds. The sudden concept that the reason to write is the hypocrisy of *other people*. Personally, I can't generate that kind of anger at other people's hypocrisies.

HOROVITZ: Paddy, you said your reason for writing is the satisfaction. Where do you find hypocrisy in a nineteen-year-old who also says the only real satisfaction he gets out of life is from writing?

CHAYEFSKY: I don't believe him.

HOROVITZ: Why?

CHAYEFSKY: Because nineteen-year-old writers want more out of their writing than mere satisfaction. They want approbation, acceptance, to change the world and many other things. Besides, at nineteen he does't know his ass from his elbow. I think we can look back and say honestly that the one thing we know about youth is, it is always wrong.

HOROVITZ: What makes you so sure?

CHAYEFSKY: I *was* nineteen, you know, I can read what I wrote at nineteen, and *I* was a very bright nineteen.

HOROVITZ: I know what I felt when I was nineteen, and I know that I have sustained most of that feeling thus far. It's hard for me to think of myself as a young playwright, because I've been writing plays for twelve years. . . .

MELFI: I don't know any young playwrights.

LAURENTS: A young playwright is somebody who has a success. At any age, and not necessarily your first. Any kind of fulfillment makes you young.

HOROVITZ: It's a gigantic pain in the ass to be a young playwright.

CHAYEFSKY: Or a promising one.

HOROVITZ: A promising playwright is one cut below a young playwright.

MELFI: I think we should talk about off-off-Broadway, to me it's the most important thing. I think the Cafe La Mama is one of the best things that's happening because, in a sense, of what is happening on Broadway and off Broadway. It saved a lot of scripts from being. . . . There were a lot of plays done, and a lot of crap, but out of the crap came things that were worthwhile, a little playwright here, a little playwright there. . . .

CHAYEFSKY: No argument.

MELFI: And they are really *playwrights,* they believe in the script. You can read their plays and you can love them. Sam Shepard, Lanford Wilson, Rochelle Owens. I think she's a poet. People disagree because of *Futz*—the production, not the script—but you read the book of plays she wrote. The production is somewhere else because of Tom O'Horgan and the group, but I tell her all the time that play's a poem but you made the choice and the audience doesn't see it that way. But the point is, out of all this come playwrights who are really *playwrights*, who believe in the text.

HOROVITZ: It has to start with the art of it. We *are* working in an art form. Then come the pressures, the two realities: writing plays and getting plays on. And the thing I call getting plays on encompasses all kinds of success patterns and ego things. It really has very little to do with what happens between you and the typewriter. It was after ten years of real frustration as a playwright, of not knowing what my role was—that I just said, "To hell with it. I'm going to yell about everything. I'm going to talk to the actors, I'm going to be all over the set." It was around that time that I learned there is really no such thing as acting. Actors have a life style, and if you match their life style to the life style of the people in your play, you get a good cast. If you mismatch, you get a bad cast. I started to question the conventional playwright-to-production relationship, and I really started to jump around the set, and do everything and say everything that I wanted to about what I had written and what I intended to communicate. I talked about results with the actors, I did all the things you're not supposed to do. And I got my first good production.

LAURENTS: When you write a play and see fifty per cent of it on the stage I think you're lucky, because you're dealing with human beings. You can't match the actor's life style *exactly* to the character you had in mind. Then there are times when you're *stupidly* grateful. An actor does something with a line you hadn't thought of and you say God, that's brilliant. Two weeks after the play opened you think Jesus, he screwed me with that reading, he distorted what I meant. Clifford Odets wrote a rather lovely play called *The Flowering Peach*. In the climax, Noah is so disillusioned with the people on the Ark, he calls them all monsters. They say there is no God, and Noah says there's a God who's going to strike them dead. And Noah turns and hides his head. Then the actor who played the part in the Broadway production turns around and looks at them and says "Still alive?" on a rising comic inflection. Yock. Point of the play out the window. Because this man should have been absolutely destroyed that they were still alive. God didn't come through. You never got it. And the play went. In two words.

HOROVITZ: Look, there *is* no such thing as acting. It's the whole thing of life style. Do you people write for actors? I know Leonard does.

MELFI: I never . . . those kids *say* that I write for them!

HOROVITZ: Don't you have an actor in mind, ever?

CHAYEFSKY: I always have Olivier in mind. That's the grief.

LAURENTS: I think you can use an actor's quality in your work. For *Gypsy* I used Ethel Merman's innocence. She could do the most hideous things in the world, and you would think she didn't know what she was doing. So you could have a monster that the audience would go along with.

HOROVITZ: You start out, you're creating a character, a person. If you go one step further and think of a specific actor, there's even more reality in the character—so even if you don't get that actor to play the role, you've *still* got more reality.

LAURENTS: You sound like an old-fashioned playwright, talking about writing characters. I thought they were out.

MELFI: They're not!

CHAYEFSKY: They are out. People are out, why not characters?

MELFI: They're not!

LAURENTS: The idea of this kind of mime theater with occasional lines of dialogue—fine. If you like that kind of theater to work in or see, fine, but don't try to convince me that everything else is old hat or boring. The Open Theater did a lot of improvisation and choreographed movement. . . .

MELFI: It's collaborative.

HOROVITZ: It's "collaborative" when the playwright is considered equal to the actor. And the director.

LAURENTS: And anybody who has gone to acting classes is stunned by their talent? Usually you question, why did they charge admission?

CHAYEFSKY: I assume the word for them is "enthusiastic."

LAURENTS: We're getting more and more into a theater of metaphor, and I guess the playwrights who are most suited to it, the most contemporary playwrights, are Pinter and Chekhov. The trouble with Pinter, I think, is that his form is his content. His style is mainly his matter. And he can sustain it for only one act.

MELFI: I saw Chekhov's *The Sea Gull* on TV and the thing was, that playwright, Constantine, he reminded me of right now. Yeah, the same thing. He was trying out new theater forms. He had all those fumes coming out, and sulphur.

LAURENTS: Another thing, these days they're always talking about it being a directors's theater. I think it always has been—because the directors select what they do. If they get anywhere, they can select those scripts which improve their name rather than the playwright's. The director interprets the play and it becomes his production. Kazan, for example, has a certain style. Maybe it distorted Tennessee and maybe it didn't, but at least he used Tennessee's words. Nowadays, though, they don't have *any* words. The directors have really taken over.

CHAYEFSKY: Peter Brook has a production in which there's no script at all.

MELFI: But you have to fight Peter Brook.

LAURENTS: Or you have to fight what's-his-name, Tom O'Horgan. Now, I don't have any clue as to whether the author of *Tom Paine* can write, because I only heard one line where a girl says to another actor, "I didn't quite hear your ad lib." That was the only line that came clear from all those mumblings and jazzings around on the stage.

HOROVITZ: Paul Foster wrote *Tom Paine,* and I believe, without putting any value judgment on his work, that the play was absolutely designed for the direction it got, that the direction was not superimposed on that play, that Paul wrote that play to have that kind of movement, that kind of activity.

CHAYEFSKY: Doesn't that suggest that the playwrights are writing for the directors? I detest production.

MELFI: I want to write the play and then go away and then come back and see it. I don't want to be involved with production at all. I hate directors too. I think my job is at that desk with the orginal idea, and I'm the master. Arthur, what you said, you know, about the words. I'll name a couple of playwrights, I'm not putting them down at all, but I disagree with them so much, you know. They sort of have established their reputations, they have become representative of quote "new" unquote theater, whatever it is. They're from off off Broadway, and then they got to off Broadway. *America Hurrah* and *Viet Rock* are good examples. Now, those two playwrights made choices that I would never make in a million years. They sat down and they gave the actors improvisations. To me, it has nothing to do with playwriting any more.

LAURENTS: *America Hurrah* really impressed me, not for the writing but for the group. And the metaphor of those dolls was marvelous. But I didn't hear a word.

MELFI: That's why, you see, they're an anti-playwright theater. I don't want to be part of that.

LAURENT: They're belligerent about what they can't do, even turn it into an asset. They don't bother to write characters or words, really, so they say one shouldn't. But what really bothers me is the tininess of the idea.

CHAYEFSKY: I don't think many people would write in today and say that the most revolutionary figure in the theater is Arthur Laurents, but it just struck me that the last real revolution was *Gypsy.* To close a show on a recitative monologue was absolutely revolutionary. There's been nothing in the theater since that compared. I have a small theory that the only real revolutionaries are middle-aged masters. The last marvel in the theater is Tyrone Guthrie, who dates back into the twenties. Tyrone Guthrie simply couldn't do *anything* the way it was done before. He did two plays of mine, and he treated them exactly as if they were dusty old classics that needed a whole new way of doing.

HOROVITZ: At my age, I'm learning how to be a revolutionary.

CHAYEFSKY: The real rebels are the people who keep the faith till they finish polishing the tools of their craft. The old pros have used up all the tools, they want something new.

LAURENTS: That's so true, because the years go on, and if you keep at it till you've really polished your craft, you reach the point at which you don't care what anybody thinks, you're going to do it your way and it's not going to be the old way. You have to work, and you have to think it through. There is no instant playwriting.

HOROVITZ: What I feel is this: if a play has a pristine concept—if *you* have a clear concept of what the hell you're writing about *before* you sit down to write, you have a chance of writing a good play. But if you sit down at a typewriter because you want to be a playwright when you grow up, you'll probably warm up with two acts and maybe try to pull it all together in the third act, and you'll probably be in trouble. I think this is symptomatic of a lot of the plays we see, especially those in the so-called "new" theater. There's a tremendous sense of the playwright warming up, a tremendous permissiveness. The Cafe La Mama burns up media. A playwright can go to Ellen Stewart and ask, "May I have a slot in March?" and Ellen will say, "O.K., you take March 15 to March 30." The playwright may have already written a great play, a good play, an honest play. Or he may, on March 1, say "Holy Christ, I've gotta have a play!" He sits down and he writes. You see it, and what you really feel is a playwright warming up. There was no real or proper vision for the play.

MELFI: All the time working off off Broadway I had the vision of coming to Broadway. Some of the playwrights will not admit it, but they'd give anything to be on Broadway. I've always wanted to be on Broadway.

LAURENTS: You wanted to get to the place where your profession is really tested.

CHAYEFSKY: Part of my current alienation from the Broadway theater is that I came from a generation that thought of Broadway as the place you took your noblest work. Whether it was a light farce or whatever, it was something you had written the best you know how. I don't believe anyone thinks of doing *noble* work on Broadway any more.

LAURENTS: I don't agree with you, Paddy. I'm finishing a play that I hope will be done on Broadway.

CHAYEFSKY: I took a play to the regional theater and had a disastrous experience. But I did have a good production in London, although I myself don't think it's worth writing plays to have them done only by the Aldwych

Theater, wonderful as that company was. So the only reason I write plays at all now is for myself.

HOROVITZ: I'm committed to social activism as a playwright.

CHAYEFSKY: Your basic impulse is propagandistic?

HOROVITZ: I think it is, yes.

LAURENTS: People are too affluent today to listen to a call to action. Every real revolution was made for economic reasons. They're not about to revolt today.

CHAYEFSKY: There's no real revolution to make, that's the trouble. Now the whole effort is to get *back* to where we were, to where we had some control over our individual lives, to get rid of this massive, monolithic, incorporated way of life. What they're saying now is, if we could only be poor. It's revolution against affluence.

HOROVITZ: Or, if we could all be rich?

CHAYEFSKY: That's really what the blacks are saying. They want to be rich and despairing like the rest of us. They can have it! I find it rather distateful being a successful white American. Very unsatisfying.

LAURENTS: When we were running around and having passports taken away, being blacklisted and all that, it was oddly easier.

CHAYEFSKY: Society had a purpose in our depression generation, ingenuous as it was, to create some kind of social security.

LAURENTS: Now the poor liberal's getting it in the neck.

CHAYEFSKY: Listen, the liberal's the only sensible fellow around, because he really tries to make a go of day-to-day life.

LAURENTS: Black liberals, white liberals, they're all trying. I grew up as a liberal, and I refuse to be put down.

MELFI: Like, I live down in the East Village, and I'm really beginning to hate it. I've been down there eight years in the heart of all that shit. I used to love it down there, and I really sort of hate it down there now.

CHAYEFSKY: What the hell has the hippie business been but a dropping-out of the corporate thing? On the other hand, you don't have to drop out entirely.

HOROVITZ: That's a gross generalization!

CHAYEFSKY: We're living on generalizations now, we're talking about a mass state of affairs.

MELFI: The thing was, there used to be a reason for their new ways of revolting—the kids have to have a reason for doing something. They think of things, and they do them, and that's where the hypocrisy comes in. Because all those kids now, like, they've screwed it for all the bums, the real authentic bums, the hoboes. The hippies all congregate like two or three minutes away from the bums in the same neighborhood. The bums can no longer get a dime from anybody. The hippies come from the suburbs, and the girls have mink coats on when they ask for money. The bums don't have a chance any more.

CHAYEFSKY: The hippies are the only distasteful group of all the action groups, perhaps because they are not activist.

HOROVITZ: Didn't I meet you in the Bohemian movement in Paris in 1949?

CHAYEFSKY: No, you met me in the Bohemian movement on Barrow Street.

MELFI: We were beatniks.

HOROVITZ: The hippies represent what you represented as a Bohemian and what Leonard and I represented as beatniks.

CHAYEFSKY: I was a beat, too. I worked among beats for a year.

HOROVITZ: Are you telling me in the wisdom of your years that you wasted that time? You came back to writing. Do you in any way presume that today's twenty-year-old hippies will be forty-year-old hippies twenty years from now?

CHAYEFSKY: But I was a writer before. No, no it wasn't wasted, what I learned from that time was total despair. But it's usable for getting me back to the typewriter.

HOROVITZ: It suddenly occurs to me that the writers who are going to endure must live out what their work stands for, in a curious way. They have to have an image in life as people, beyond their plays.

CHAYEFSKY: I think that's true. Let's take Israel for example—by his own definition he's a social activist playwright. That is, he thinks of everything he writes in terms of a social commitment to affect an audience. Right? As such, then, he has to live out his life in person. Including going on television, articles, interviews. . . .

LAURENTS: Does he have to do that as a writer, or as a human being?

CHAYEFSKY: I think what he's saying is, there's no difference anymore.

HOROVITZ: That it is in fact part of the *writing*. I will publicly commit myself to this statement now, that if I came across a great play by an unknown playwright, part of my advice to that writer would be to get a press agent.

MELFI: Oh, no, no. . .

CHAYEFSKY: I wouldn't.

LAURENTS: A playwright's job is to write his *plays*. I don't give a damn about my image, and playwrights who do are more concerned with becoming public figures than good writers.

HOROVITZ: The whole problem of *being* a playwright has changed.

MELFI: I've found it's much better to stay home and write my plays than to wander around with the image of being a playwright.

HOROVITZ: Leonard, you have to put that to the test. Will you not go on a Johnny Carson show? Will you not use television or radio or newspapers as another way to reach people?

MELFI: Yes, to sell my play, to get an audience for it, yes I would. I would do anything to sell a play, but never do it for the image of being a playwright.

CHAYEFSKY: It doesn't sell plays. For an hour I went on the Johnny Carson show. Exhausted, because I couldn't understand what I was doing there. I went in a state of funk, I couldn't sleep for a week, and I said never again—and the producer asked me one more time. And I did it, and we didn't sell another ticket.

HOROVITZ: I honestly believe that to be able to sell your plays in *this* generation, which is an electronic-media-oriented generation, you must be known as a person as well. It's very, very difficult to separate yourself as a personality, as a celebrity—I'll be that ugly—from your work.

CHAYEFSKY: I know that when I was first rising, I went after publicity like a bitch. It's very hard to separate the desire for public acknowledgement and the picture in *Life* and all of that—very hard to separate that from wanting to be identified with what's going on. In the old days that we came in on the tag end of, Arthur, the theater was really an avenue of social communication. What went from Broadway outward really mattered. Lines were quoted and used for editorial purposes. The playwright was an important figure with an important social function. Well, what the hell does the theater provide today for the serious artist, for the social activist writer, for Odets if he were writing today? The theater now is an adjunct to a sales campaign. When a buyer comes to town, the businessman gets him tickets to a hot show. The theater also serves the function of raising money for charity. Where the hell does it serve an esthetic function? I say the poor playwright no longer has what Arthur and I came in on the rag-tag end of. We were still considered leaders of the people. T.S. Eliot said when the moral fiber of a community disappears, the poets have to stand up. When the priests and rabbis and all the great moralists fade, it's the writer who has to establish some kind of moral contact. Well, the playwright has fallen into disrepute along with the priest.

LAURENTS: They stood up then, they stand up now, but it never meant anything in terms of social action. A play means something only to the man who wrote it.

CHAYEFSKY: I don't think a playwright could generate any enthusiastic social activism now, about anything. Therefore if he *is* a social activist playwright, Israel may be right, the playwright has to give some of his attention to becoming a public figure.

LAURENTS: You want to become an important public figure as a playwright, write a good play.

MELFI: That's it! Tennessee Williams never had a press agent in his life.

CHAYEFSKY: Tennessee Williams is not a social activist playwright, and he is not our generation. He was already a great playwright when I was just starting.

MELFI: But he didn't need a press agent.

LAURENTS: If a playwright has something interesting or important to say, he should say it in a play. The reason the playwright's position is demeaned is because you demean yourself by becoming this jazzy public character.

CHAYEFSKY: Perhaps in the end, a writer is what he writes. But as we look over literature there are a lot of lousy writers who persist because of their social function. Tom Paine is not a good writer compared to the esthetes of his day. In our generation, Malraux represented the writer who lived out his revolutionary and literary life.

HOROVITZ: Obviously, we're in an age of television. If we can accept the fact that the last five years were strongly influenced by television, why is it so difficult to accept the role of the playwright as a personality? The playwright is an artist who transcends his writing, really, or joins his writing actively, as a personality.

MELFI: You almost contradict yourself, Israel. Which really bugs me, you know? Because you're almost like apologizing for your talent. A lot of guys go around with the image of being a playwright, but they're not really playwrights unless they're writing a play.

HOROVITZ: Of course, Leonard, I agree completely. But I assume we're only talking about the serious playwright who has committed his life to writing plays. All my talk about press agentry doesn't even vaguely relate to self-promotion as an end in itself. What I mean is this: the theater reaches only a limited number of people in a very special way. Most people are now conditioned to respond differently from the way they responded twenty years ago. I do not feel personally, that hiding behind a play is enough. I think that I must go further and use whatever media are available to me. No, I really don't recommend this life style to every writer. That would be presumptuous. This is a choice I've made for myself. If writing plays puts me in a position to speak through newspapers and television, then I am committed to use those forms for social activism, to repeat what I say in my plays. I'm committed to reaching as many people as I can, as often as I can. I think we must fight. I am not at all content with our country and our world. I love humanity and loathe human beings. I am driven. But the basic drive to write goes beyond one's lifetime. The ultimate fantasy is that our plays will live after us. Certainly history will record only what we wrote, not what we said. But I'm not living in history. History is fantasy, Now is reality. Yes, I want my plays to last. But I can't control that. I can control what I say and how I live today and tomorrow. And though it's complex, I can't see a way to separate my plays from my life style. My plays fight, I fight. It's that complex and that simple, both at the same time.

LAURENTS: There are good writers and bad writers who have lasted. I happen to consider myself a social playwright, I always was, that's what I care about. I care about man's relation to life.

CHAYEFSKY: I belong to the generation of playwrights which believes in the end you must make your own security as a writer. We all aspire to some form of posterity. The most modest of us would like to think that in fifty years—if the continents are still here—people will look at our work and say "Oooooh!" To become the rage in fifty years is more important than now to a writer. But I believe that in the end when they ask who is Arthur Laurents and Leonard Melfi and Israel Horovitz and Paddy Chayefsky, in the end it will be, what the hell has he written?

VII. On the Theater.....

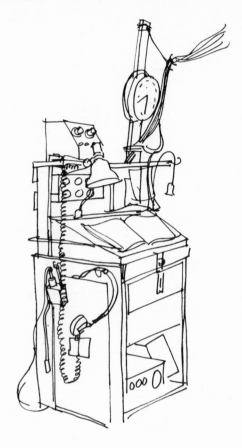

. . . melancholy is the nurse of frenzy:
Therefore they thought it good you hear a play
And frame your mind to mirth and merriment,
Which bars a thousand harms and lengthens life.
—THE TAMING OF THE SHREW

Don't Want To See
The Uncut Version
of *Anything*

By Jean Kerr

Recently I was heard to murmur against the endless frustrations connected with getting a play produced. I mean I was exploding in all directions
and pounding on the table with the handle of a broom. My husband finally
quieted me by saying, "How can you complain so much—do you know that
Euripides was *exiled*?" Actually, I didn't. But now that I know, it makes all
the difference. In the future when shadows gather and vexations mount I
shall take solace from the fact that, in any event, I was never exiled.

But I am not here to talk about playwriting. My experience as a plyawright
is so limited that I think it would be hasty for me to theorize about it. On the
other hand, because of my husband's sorry occupation, my experience as a
member of the audience is enormous. It occurs to me that I have become the
most experienced audience in America.

We are agreed that a critic is not, and never will be, a member of the
audience. Not only is he paid to attend, he is paid to listen; and this sobering
circumstance colors his whole attitude toward the material on the stage. The
critic says: this is an extremely bad play—why is that? The audience says:
this is an extremely bad play—why was I born? There is a real difference
here.

Anyway, on these melancholy occasions when (one sees) the jig is up and
the closing notice will be, I make little notes to myself. I list some of them
here in the wistful hope that somewhere there is a beginning playwright

Don't Want to See the Uncut Version of Anything from *Penny Candy* by Jean Kerr. Copyright ©
1966, 1967, 1968, 1969, 1970 by Collin Productions, Inc. Used by permission of the author and
Doubleday & Company, Inc.

who will believe that my prejudices are shared by some other people. I think
they are. I think I am pretty close to being the square root of the *ordinary*
audience. I notice that I perk up when other people perk up. I slump when
they slump. And I most certainly do not keep my head when all about me are
losing theirs. I think paradise will be regained on 44th Street when young
playwrights understand that they must try not to write plays that will cause
nice, ordinary people from Riverdale to wish they were dead.

Little Notes to Myself:
 I believe that plays that are successful are usually more entertaining then
plays that fail. This will come as a revolutionary idea only to those who allow
themselves to be intimidated by small critics who have spent their lives
avoiding beautiful girls, because they are rumored to be dumb.
 I think that if there are only three characters in a play one of them ought to
be a girl.
 I do not wish to see musical comedies performed entirely on bleachers in
which the leading man wears clown-white makeup. The only man in the
world who can put on clown-white makeup and be Marcel Marceau is
Marcel Marceau.
 I do not like to hear the most explicit four-letter words spoken from the
stage because I number among my acquaintances persons of such candor
and quick temper that, for me, the thrill is gone.
 It is perfectly all right with me when a character in an avant-garde play
points to a realistic iron bed and says "That is a piano." It is still all right with
me when another character sits down in front of the bed and plays the Blue
Danube Waltz on the mattress. But thereafter I expect that nobody will lie
down on the piano.
 It strikes me as less than hilarious when an actor, impersonating a
foreigner, is required to struggle with our quaint American colloquialism.
("How ees eet you put it—I shovel you? Ah, no. I dig you.")
 I have noticed that in plays where the characters on stage laugh a great
deal the people out front laugh very little. (This is notoriously true of
Shakespeare's comedies. "Well, sirrah," says one buffoon, "he did go
heigh-ho upon a birdbolt." This gem is followed by such guffaws and
general merriment as would leave Olsen and Johnson wondering how they
failed).
 I don't know why this is true but nevertheless I have noticed that plays
announced in advance to be "full of compassion" are generally full of
something quite else.
 It may have been bearable the first time it was done but it is no longer
bearable to see a comedy in which the ingenue yap yap yaps the whole first
act long about the burdens of her virginity.
 Also—speaking of the same kind of play—the heroine does look cute as

ll get-out when, for reasons of the plot, she has to wear the hero's bathrobe. On the other hand (and this is happening more and more) when the hero is required to wear her brunch-coat, he looks just plain terrible.

I have noticed that an entertainment which opens or closes with the setting-up or dismantling of a circus tent always gets good notices. I don't know what to make of this.

I have seen plays performed on steps in front of a cyclorama that I enjoyed, but not many.

I am wary of plays in which God or the devil appear as characters. We will waive any discussion of theology and I don't mean to be irreverent when I say that, for all practical purposes in the theater, God is a lousy part. (A play I really loved, *The Tenth Man*, had to do with a girl who was being exorcised of the devil but it may be relevant to note that we never saw the devil).

I don't want to see any entertainment that runs four-and-one-half hours. In a recent production of *King Lear*, the first act ran for two and one-half hours. By that time I considered that I had given up smoking, and I spent the entire intermission wondering if I should begin again. And I was once more made aware—during that interminable first act—that the most serious materials eventually seem comic if they are allowed to go on too long. For instance, during the protracted scene in which Lear (now mad) is talking to poor, blinded Gloucester, all I could think was: first they put his eyes out, now they're going to talk his ears off.

I don't want to see the uncut version of *anything*.

The Theater Is Such
An Impossible Place, Maybe
It's Meant Only for Miracles

By Robert Anderson

The English plays of the 16th century were called Miracle plays. I think
that every American play in the 20th century is also, in a way, a Miracle play
It is a miracle that it is produced. This goes for new playwrights and for
playwrights who have "arrived". They find that they have "arrived" a
nothing but the uncertainty of the production of their next play.

This is probably a terrible way to run a theater, but it seems almos
inevitable, and in this period when we are "hot for certainties" and looking
for final solutions to all problems, it is well to remember that talent is a very
personal thing. Its development is even more personal, depending or
changes in life experiences, and probably no amount of arranging of "the
proper conditions" will help much.

Some years ago I was in London (before Osborne, Pinter, Bolt and Shaffer) and I was exclaiming about all the stock and repertory companies. How
wonderful for developing the playwright! My London friends pointed out
that these theaters were all very busy doing mostly American plays nurtured
under our "unfortunate" Broadway system.

When I was an undergraduate at Harvard we were clamoring for a brand
new theater. "It would make all the difference in the world if the creative
writing talents were exposed to a theater. They would come out playwrights
and not poets and novelists as they do now," we argued.

Well, Harvard has had a fine new theater now for a while, and it doesn't
seem to make much difference in the number of playwrights coming down
from Cambridge.

At this point I should say that this is the eighth draft of this piece I have
written. In the first seven I came off looking so grumpy that I couldn't stand

myself. So I have rewritten myself into a mood of affirmative resignation . . . acceptance of things as they are and probably always have been and always will be.

One minute the chancy aspects of the theater have me depressed, the next moment I wonder if they are not part of the extraordinary nature of the theater. In most every other mid-20th century endeavor, a given set of circumstances will lead to a more or less predictable conclusion. But in the theater, A+B+C=? There is something maddening and yet marvelous about this. You can package a play expensively, set it aglitter with stars, surround it with endorsements and still have it add up to nothing. I hope it always remains this way.

Playwrights like myself without a play on the boards at the moment are likely to be querulous and mean-spirited. We are likely to look back on the golden age when things were different. Anyone who has read the Gelb-'O'Neill knows the agonies he went through with casting and production problems. I sat in on the last years of the Playwrights Company and saw the great men—Robert Sherwood, Elmer Rice and Maxwell Anderson —tremulous as neophytes as they waited the word from some actor or actress which would activate their plays. I saw then, though obviously didn't learn the lesson or I would have either stopped writing or stopped grumbling, that you can climb the steps to the top of Parnassus, but as far as theatrical production goes you remain low man on the totem pole.

Every playwright, young or old, has seen his producer's face get longer and longer as director after director, star after star, turns down his play. We all know it's ridiculous. We all know the often highly personal and some-times absurd reasons for a star or director doing a play. We have all seen the play turned down by everyone suddenly become the hit of the season when done in desperation with unknowns. My mother had not read *Tea and Sympathy* before it was produced, and when she heard that Deborah Kerr was going to star in the play, she said, "It must be better than I had supposed." My mother is gone, God bless her, but her attitude lingers on, even though we know that in the theater, as I said, A+B+C may equal zero. (Incidentally, in this case I was the one who wanted Deborah; my director, who had never met her, did not want her, and Deborah turned down the play three times! You want problems?)

Each time that I have hoped to set my house in order, to insure some certainty, to guarantee a less maddening, less catch-as-catch-can future, I have been brought up short with the futility of it. A famous movie director and I, after we had made a picture we were proud of, threw our arms around each other and vowed to work together and only together forevermore. A few months later he sent me a story he wanted to do. I read it and found I could bring nothing to it but a kind of professional skill. We were sad, but he took another writer. My next original screenplay he admired, but he felt he couldn't relate creatively to it. And we parted again. And so, I'm afraic it goes.

We seek in each creative venture the miracle of just the right perso relating creatively in every department. Just doing a job, a piece of work, i not enough . . . turning it out, manufacturing product. So each play is kind of shaky invitation to form a new relationship, to create new whole greater-than-their-parts.

The situation in our theater is, of course, deplorable. But I doubt if we ca legislate talent or impose culture or really in any way lure the privat demons of genius from their hiding places. We are a diligent, practica people. And we hate to think that anything is beyond our control. So we ar building theaters throughout the country. This is tangible. This is possible Now all you playwrights, actors and directors, come out of hiding and fil these theaters with magnificence. It's wonderful, and yet rather naive an pathetic. We get angry when human beings don't instantly live up to th buildings. But we have raised the millions, built the theaters, shown ou good will. They told us that's what we needed, and we did it!

I hope it works. I hate to see people of good will disappointed. But talent i a hit-or-miss affair. It ebbs and flows, thus enraging those who expec continuity of excellence in repayment for their buildings. You may build palace for talent, and yet it may perversely choose to perform in a loft.

So, in this eighth draft, I have become philosophical and have come t understand slightly what I have always found frustrating as a practicing playwright. I applaud and support any effort to make things different . . . t speed the progress from page to stage, to make theater have some continuity for a playwright, to let him see his bad plays as well as his good ones, to le him make a living in the theater and not just a killing. (If I go on, I shall write a ninth draft with an entirely different tone!) But if none of these thing happens, I think I am more ready to accept the idea that perhaps they are against the essential nature of the theater, which is a place for miracles.

Can or Will We Support Repertory? Let's Get the Facts

By Arthur Miller

In 1971 the New York City Center proposed to take over the Vivian Beaumont and Forum Theaters from the chronically financially ailing Repertory Theater of Lincoln Center. It was planned to break up the Forum and eliminate the large storage space especially designed for repertory needs, replacing them with a three-theater movie center. This provoked an immediate reaction from stage folk, including many dramatists. They formed the Ad Hoc Committee to Save Theater at Lincoln Center, whose name describes its purpose. The committee was successful after a struggle—obviously, since the two Lincoln Center theaters still exist and house plays. The theaters were saved but not the repertory operation, which has been discontinued.

Arthur Miller was a playwright-member of the Ad Hoc Committee. This article, prepared under Mr. Miller's supervision from his comments at a symposium at the time of the controversy, is not only a piece of theater history; it is also a still-relevant summary of the ideals as well as the very great difficulties of any effort to mount permanent repertory in New York City.

It seems to me that it is logical to ask first how this egg ever got scrambled. What was the origin of this disaster which has been threatening the existence of repertory at the Vivian Beaumont and Forum Theaters?

I'll say something I've never said before: the Lincoln Center board *never* intended to have a repertory theater, and they don't intend to now because they cannot and will not supply the money for repertory. When they originally consulted Robert Whitehead about the plans for a theater he explained that it would have to have a vast area for the storage of scenery and everything else that goes with a repertory theater. His one aim was a repertory theater, but he told them there was no rule which said they had to build a repertory theater and suggested that maybe they should just build a place to put on plays, which would cost much less than a repertory installation. They told Whitehead no, don't bother your head about costs, just build the nicest theater you can imagine. But when the point arrived at which the operational budget began to come up, it turned out that they had never established a budget on how much money would be allotted to the building, and how much was to be reserved for paying salaries for actors, and so forth. It was as simple as that. They were building a twelve-million-dollar monument, period. It's like building a new department store with practically no merchandise or employees.

The smallest repertory company I know of in Europe has about 75 people in its company. Lincoln Center originally eked about 23 out of its budget. The city of Munich pays $750,000 a year for the salaries and scenery and costumes of one repertory company out of four in that city. When the time came for the Lincoln Center board to bring repertory into being, they had no budget anywhere near to sufficient for it (by the way, the Robert Whitehead-Elia Kazan operation of the ANTA Theater downtown cost some $200,000 *less* than anticipated). The Vivian Beaumont Theater was ready to open three months earlier than expected, but instead of giving Whitehead and Kazan the extra rehearsal time, the board began secretly dealing with Alexander H. Cohen to bring in Rex Harrison to open this theater in a revival of some British comedy instead of opening it with a repertory production. This charade went on for months, mind you; they were on the verge of signing a contract with Cohen. In other words, they wanted a show in there at which you could really *dress.*

The Lincoln Center board's persistent, adamantine refusal to admit the facts continues to the present moment. These great giants of industry, banking and commerce can't get it through their heads that the more successful a repertory theater is, the more it must cost. It contradicts all business principles.

The only explanation of their behavior I've ever come up with that made any sense was that they see credit to themselves in building monuments but not in paying actors. In their favor it can be said that they would like to have had a repertory theater, but once having seen what it would cost they should not have assumed the responsibility and then refused to make good on it, while at the same time pretending that they were indeed subsidizing such a theater. Lincoln Center has not operated as a repertory theater for one week.*

*Editor's note: Mr. Miller is correct. King Lear *and* A Cry of Players *alternated for a few weeks during the 1968–69 season, but two plays don't make a repertory theater.*

It may be as stupid as this: donors like to have their names on the back of a seat. When you pay an actor's salary your name doesn't get engraved on the back of his head. Who will ever know that Mr. Rockefeller helped develop some great actor? Donors not only want to do good, they want their good to be seen being done.

What was their idea of a solution in the present Lincoln Center Repertory situation? Moving concrete. That makes some sense to them. They will raise money to break down an existing thing as long as they can see an object being moved from one place to another. But they cannot conceive that the man who acts on the stage has got to get paid, *especially* if some weeks he's not working. Now you have finally run into the ultimate absurdity where they planned to tear down the Forum, the best theater in the mess over there, and eliminate it.

At first the board was great with Kazan and Whitehead, because Whitehead had a reputation as a tasteful and successful producer, and Kazan—well, Kazan was Kazan. Then the New York City drama critics began to slam these men, and the board decided to get rid of them. When they canned Whitehead there were fourteen of the best American actors about to sign with Lincoln Center. I don't want to use names now, but in a season or two you would have had a marvelous company which no Broadway show could afford to hire, and they were going possibly to act for salaries close to minimum. As it was, the core of the company was in being. Faye Dunaway, John Phillip Law, Joseph Wiseman, Zohra Lampert, Hal Holbrook, David Wayne, Barbara Loden, Michael Strong and Jason Robards are all first-class talents, and something alive could have begun with them.

I don't know Jules Irving at all, I only met him once, I have no opinion about him one way or another as an administrator. But why did they reach all the way to California for Irving and Herbert Blau to run a New York theater? At the time I thought it was because of the onslaught by your so-called intellectual critics, and these two fellows were more or less on the academic side. They had run a small provincial repertory company which had gotten good reviews in the local press, and everybody loved them out there. I figured the board looked around and said, "Who is loved?" and found Irving and Blau, poor fellows.

But the answer is simpler, I think now. They'd be *cheaper* than Whitehead, who was not trying to build a San Francisco repertory company but something in America that would vie with the great companies of the world.

When Whitehead was fired I challenged the board, and I lost. I was the only one to make a statement in the New York *Times*. Nobody else would, and nobody picked mine up. The critics went right on yelling at the actors. If the critics would criticize *them*—the members of the Lincoln Center board—for a change, they might start to get very nervous, and when they get nervous they start to listen to *everybody*. You can't imagine how insecure these guys are. They're afraid of publicity, they want people to at least not notice. As you start to home in on them, I believe something would happen.

The critic has a duty here, because this is a public business. It's not entirely the board's business how they run Lincoln Center, because public money is involved and it's New York City's land, our property, that they're sitting on. It doesn't belong to them. You will *never* have a repertory company so long as that board is in control, and that is where the critics should make their attack, carefully and coolly. The critics must stop regarding Lincoln Center as just another Broadway operation where you hit the producer or director. You can't reach them by criticizing Jules Irving, or the actors, or the scenery design—this just creates a diversion and allows them to sit back and explain, "Well, you see, we didn't get a good set this time."

Remarkably enough, in this age of anti-establishment feeling, this is one establishment which has never been attacked, and they are at the root of the entire Lincoln Center disaster. Look at them up there, you've got the heads of some of the biggest banks and other institutions in this country . . . nobody takes a critical shot at them. The critics will beat up the actors, the author, the director, that's easy. But it never occures to any critic to go after those board fellows. Why not? Because the surrounding sociology of repertory is unknown to us. All of us are always complaining about the death of the theater, now here's an instance where we can conceivably exercise an influence because we're dealing with a public institution. Now is the time for all of us including the press to say to them, "Anything doesn't go. You can't have it this way."

Most critics and other Americans don't understand what a repertory theater is, anyway. What does it take to run a repertory theater? Is it possible within the budgets the Lincoln Center board has envisaged? Let's investigate. These aren't mysteries on the moon. There are hundreds of repertory theaters all over the world. A study could be made, we could then lay out some kind of schematic idea of what it really takes to run a repertory theater. Start with that, and leave artistic matters aside for the moment. Tell them: all right, gentlemen, this is what is required to run a repertory theater, according to every piece of evidence. Can you supply it? If not, get out and let people in who can and will.*

We have to face the economic issue, or else let's stop fooling around and rent the damned building out for whatever it will bring. The present situation is merely perpetuating a demoralizing feeling, as if to say, "Look, repertory doesn't work." We've never *had* anything like real repertory, so the alternative to the commercial Broadway theater has never come to be. The board is only pretending that it can come to be, and is thus preventing it from happening. When we first started at the ANTA Theater downtown, Laurence Olivier asked me, "What are the critics screaming about? We were in Chichester for seven years before we ever came in to London. Our company was weeded out from hundreds of actors before we ever faced the London critics." He was bowled over by the fact that nobody here understood the rudiments of what goes into making a repertory company. It's an extraordinarily difficult thing to do, but it is worthwhile and so we must be clear about what the difficulties are, what the aims are, what it really takes to do this job, instead of going on saying, "When are we going to have a good show at Lincoln Center?" That is not the way to do it.

Let's look at budgets of repertory companies anywhere. If indeed the public or the donors will *not* give the money it takes to run a repertory theater, then let's stop pretending we have anything called the Lincoln Center Repertory Company and get rid of it. Maybe our culture will not support a repertory theater, or maybe some day when we are all dead there will be a repertory theater, when they make up their minds to have it. If you go to German theaters, you see facilities that are much larger than ours. Some of them, as in Frankfurt, have two stages, one to rehearse on behind the one they play on, with a moveable wall between. So we should't imagine that the Vivian Beaumont is outstandingly elaborate. It's simply an impossibility to run this kind of an operation anywhere by selling tickets, even though the response of the audience with their subscriptions and admissions at Lincoln Center has been immense, tremendous. Let's clear the air. There could be no Kabuki, No, Ballet Theater, opera, hospitals or libraries without an act of will. No marketplace ever has or can support such things.

Our cultural life seems to be drying up, we're becoming a utilitarian society in the crudest sense, namely, that which is not bought cannot be art. Whole sections of the New York Public Library, one of the greatest libraries

*Editor's note: All the members of this board departed when Joseph Papp's New York Shakespeare Festival took over the Lincoln Center legitimate theaters in the spring of 1973.

in the world, are closed. Museums have short hours. Even the hospitals have to curtail their services and are threatened with closing because they have no money. We are becoming a second-class cultural power and in theater we are neck and neck with the Congo. But the Lincoln Center situation may be amenable to improvement, theoretically, because it is not a part of the government. These guys are not elected officials, and they do not have the defense of the elected official, "How many votes do actors have?" The constituency of the Lincoln Center board is public opinion in general, and therefore something might come of our efforts.

All of which presumes that a repertory theater is really wanted here. Objectively speaking, though, maybe we'd do more good trying to raise money for libraries and hospitals, but let that lie for the moment. Maybe it isn't wanted as yet because it isn't understood. The first thing we have to do is declare our ignorance, and I include the lot of us. I would also like to mention a mystery, however. Before there was a single production at the ANTA Theater downtown, before an actor had walked onto that stage, the mere announcement of the project set off an incomprehensible eruption of ridicule, cynicism and outright hostility in many theater people and the press. I still am unable to understand why. Maybe something in our culture rejects the idea as some kind of foreign body. We can't seem to connect prestige with repertory as we do with Broadway, God save the mark, while at the same time we are on our knees before the Royal Shakespeare and British National Theaters.

Repertory is certainly no panacea. It often breeds bureaucracy, time-serving, lethargy. It always stands or falls on far-seeing, talented and selflessly ambitious artists at its helm, and these are scarce anywhere. But these problems can wait. Right now we don't even have a problem, because we have nothing. So the first order of business now is to get clear in our own minds what such a theater is, what it can do, and what is financially needed to do it. Then if we are convinced of its value, a considered, serious attempt must be made to transform Lincoln Center into such a theater.

I think it is time the Lincoln Center board is called to account, just as playwrights, directors and actors are. What is their policy? Surely they have a defense; what is it? They must no longer be allowed to fob off their failure on the artists working for them.

I repeat that a real repertory company may be impossible in the social system of New York today. Or it might be possible. We don't have the facts to make a judgment. The first thing to do, I believe, is to go in and challenge those men, to face the realities together, and decide what is to become of a potentially great theater that belongs to all of us.

On the Theater of No Meaning

By Maurice Valency

In the theater, as elsewhere, I suppose, every age outgrows itself. This we call progress, and it is evident that our time is characterized by a passion for progress. Our avidity for the new doubtless reflects our dissatisfaction with the things that we have; the teenager is at the helm of state, and nothing lasts long enough to acquire, or even to require a foundation. In an earlier phase of our cultural development, a poet could boast, "not marble nor the gilded monuments of princes can outlive this powerful rhyme." I think nobody can talk like that in our time without being suspected of paranoia. The one thing an artist can be certain of in our day is the provisional nature of his work.

It is no longer enough that a work of art be beautiful. It must be interesting. And, as a rule, in order to be interesting, it must be "contemporary." What this word implies, at bottom, is not very clear to me; but, obviously, it suggests an alarming acceleration of obsolescence. Of course, the rate of aging varies with the subject matter. We make, as I intimated, the tacit assumption that certain works have universality, even though they tend in time to become a little moth-eaten and scholarly unless they are brought smartly up to date. The implication is that if we play Hamlet in a sweatshirt and Ophelia in tennis shorts, their problems become interestingly modern. The hem-line of many an old masterpiece has been raised and lowered a dozen times in the course of the century, but no pop artist has thought of bringing the Venus de Milo up to date in this fashion. To become interesting, she must first be reduced to first principles. She must become a cylinder, surmounted by a cube, and adorned with spheres, before and behind.

291

What is happening in present-day drama is obviously not at all an isolated phenomenon. I think it is not related with any special closeness to the dwindling of the medieval world-picture, or to the metaphysical confusions of our time. These things undoubtedly have something to do with the case; but, in fact, the history of modern drama is simply another aspect of the history of modern art. If one wishes to understand what is happening on the contemporary stage, one must go and look at an exhibition of contemporary painting. It may not help much, but at least it will define the area of confusion.

To be precise, the avant-garde drama results from a somewhat tardy application of the techniques of post-impression. Since these techniques have already had a very full development in painting and sculpture and music, we may expect in the coming years to see on the stage some elaboration of all the post-impressionist styles, all the way from the Nabis to Jackson Pollock, from abstraction to "Dribblekunst."

There is, doubtless, a certain difference between *The Bald Soprano* and an arrangement by Jackson Pollock, but to me the difference does not seem essential. Both forms are outside the traditionally intellectual structure of art. In both, the principle of design is below and beyond the level of logic, and the accidental factor in each case is an essential element of the composition. In the play, as in the painting, nothing is planned, or plannable in advance, so that the result is in doubt since the design has no terminal principle. This method of artistic creation has, of course, a charming spontaneity; it involves also a serious protest against the system of carefully regulated art which we inherit from the 19th century—the art, let's say, of Delacroix or Berlioz or Ibsen. Dumas advised the new playwright to write the end of his play first so that he would have the outcome completely in mind at the outset. This is the sort of planning we associate with the *pièce bien faite;* few people write, and fewer still have the ability to write, this way in our time. Even a technician like Shaw in his later years confessed that when he began a play he had no idea of how it was going to end. To some extent, I suppose, this neglect of form depends upon our idea of the nature of the universe. An orderly drama reflects an orderly universe—in a disorderly universe a logically constructed play seems artficial and obtrusive.

Nineteenth century art, in the main, was mimetic. Its goal was a representation of nature in its more noteworthy aspects. Since the time of the cubists, the goal of art has been, not the representation of selected natural forms, but the creation of a totally new reality based upon the artist's fantasy. Imagination, not observation, not definintion, thus becomes the essential artistic activity. This attitude has, I think, interesting consequences from the side of what Freud called the "reality principle." In the absence of a controlling reality of external character, socially established, I suppose, by majority vote, all experience has equal validity. The reality of the theater then becomes indistinguishable from any other reality, and experience tends to be stabilized on a single level, the level of dreams. This idea, is, doubtless, at the bottom of plays like *Six Characters in Search of an Author*, and the Pirandellian drama in turn furnishes a basis for plays like *Marat/Sade*.

The nucleus of the whole "modern" movement in art is, I think, to be found in Baudelaire. He is often thought of as a symbolist. In *The Salon of 1859* he wrote: "All the visible universe is merely a store of images and signs to which imagination gives a place and a relative value." The thought comes more or less directly from Swedenborg. It means that the outer world has only a symbolic reality; it has no intrinsic configuration, save that which it derives from the insight of the artist. The artist's fantasy has, supposedly, something divine in it—it is the source, and perhaps the sole source, of creation. The consequence of this do-it-yourself attitude with regard to the outer world is that this Nature, which art has been at such pains to imitate since Aristotle told us that it is the function of art to imitate it, becomes a convention which the imaginative man is at liberty to manipulate to suit himself. *"L'imaginatif dit,"* Baudelaire wrote, *"je veux illuminer les choses avec mon esprit, et en projeter le reflet sur les autres esprits."* This idea, as much as any, is the basis of expressionism.

For the expressionist, the outer world, the visible universe, is in the main a projection of the inner spirit of the artist. It has no other reality. Nature is a work of art. At this point, naturally, the subject, as such, dwindles; the inner and the outer worlds merge; and Nature ceases to be a controlling factor in the artistic process. It becomes simply the canvas on which the artist's fantasy of nature is projected. The human form, to take a banal example, becomes what you make of it. You may contemplate the consequences in any art gallery or fashion magazine, and in the New York subway you may feel them quite directly in all their ambiguity. None of this, of course, is very new. The avant garde of today belongs, not to the electric age, as McLuhan suggests, but to the gaslight era. In the theater, the earliest landmark of contemporary existentialism is, no doubt, *Peer Gynt*: Ibsen wrote it in 1867. Dramatic expressionism begins with Strindberg. *To Damascus I* was written in 1898. The so-called "Theater of the Absurd," together with other dramatic manifestations of Dada, began with Alfred Jarry's *Ubu Roi*, and this was written in 1897. It is true, however, that it is only quite recently that we have begun to comprehend these attitudes, and even more recently that the symbolism of Baudelaire has become of interest to the commercial playwright.

Renaissance drama, as an interpretation of life, was nothing if not symbolist. Shakespeare was not so much interested in reproducing the detail of external nature on his rudimentary stage as in revealing to the mind through a dramatic action the inner aspects of the cosmic plan, in laying bare in the theater, that is to say, the moral structure of the universe, something which in the hurly-burly of experience we do not normally see. This was generally held to be the function of the theater in Shakespeare's time, and in great measure this is true also of Renaissance art. In those piping times, the artist was involved primarily with the Idea, the archetype, the essence of things. It is perfectly true, nevertheless, that in time the Renaissance artist became deeply absorbed in observing the external forms, developed a keen eye for detail and elaborated techniques for coping with it which in time became

ends in themselves. The dramatist too, before long, became a representational artist and was suitably rewarded with membership in an academy. He became part of the Establishment, and represented in the theater a reality which was also part of the Establishment—indeed, it was the Establishment.

But in thus holding the mirror up to the Nature of the Establishment, the academic artist unhappily forgot that it was his high function, traditionally, to select out of the chaos of experience what was meaningful and permanent in it—the significant pattern, the essential line, in short, the Idea. Michelangelo had seen the significant form as already resident in the unhewn block. In his view, it was the function of the artist simply to clear away what was irrelevant, the obscuring rubbish. Late in the 19th century, we find Rodin doing much the same thing, and from a similar standpoint. His sculpture demonstrates the significant form, the meaningful outline, torn out of chaos, often with shreds of chaos still clinging to it. The Renaissance artists, and their 19th-century legatees, thought of themselves primarily as explicators of nature; they were mediators between nature and man, and explained the one to the other. Thus it was their function to experience nature deeply and to make their special experience available to those who were not able to experience it as deeply as they.

Accordingly, for the Renaissance and for the following centuries, art had a

completely practical aim—it served to reveal the truth of things, and truth was experienced as beauty and power. The principal difference between life and art was in the degree of realization. Experience was amorphous. Art had form. It was a distillation of life, its quintessence. The whole matter concerned primarily the intellect. In life we do not understand what is going on. In the theater we do—or should. The dramatist abstracts, defines, and explicates the forms of experience, and represents an action which is not life, but more real than life, an action which is both beautiful and intelligible, and therefore true. Such was the Renaissance viewpoint. Throughout the long period of Renaissance classicism, the essence of art was meaning. And since what is intelligible can be put into words, all art, at bottom, tended to be literary. A cathedral was not only a house of worship; it was also a book of instruction, a stone Bible with colored-glass illustrations. A madrigal was an example of musical eloquence; a fugue was an exercise in rhetoric. In these circumstances, the development of eloquence and rhetoric was spectacular. The 12th-century frescos are taciturn; but the aisles of St. Peter's are loquacious beyond words, and as insistent in their hubbub as a market in Naples. This baroque atmosphere pretty well defines the climate of dramatic art up to the time of Ibsen. It is declamatory, hortatory, edifying, moral; above all, it is intelligible.

The reaction against the intellectual basis of Renaissance art was already perceptible in the Renaissance itself. It is indicated by the rise of sensibility as a principle of art. For centuries it had been assumed that the intellect was the essentially human faculty, the ultimate goal of the artist's effort. A great deal of the drama of the period between Shakespeare and Steele turned upon the conflict of the heart and the mind, the struggle of desire and reason. The classic solution, of course, was invariably the triumph of reason. This left the tragic hero unhappy, but it left him glorious. Corneille's Cid, for example, or his other heroes—Horace, Polyeucte, Titus—are completely self-mastered, self-conscious men, who are, above all, rational in their choices, difficult as these may be, and the difficulty of the choice measures the intensity of their drama. Shakespeare's heroes are of another stripe. They are all a bit mad—Hamlet, Lear, Othello, Romeo, even Shylock. They are all magnificently articulate creatures, magnificently irrational. Mostly, they don't dig this world at all; they don't belong in it, and they protest its ways. They look to an ideal world for happiness, and their tragedy lies in the disparity between expectation and possibility.

It was this type of hero that captured the imagination of later times; not the hero of Corneille. In the days of *Tristram Shandy,* in the 18th century, it was conceded that the man of heart is somehow more interesting than the man of mind, truer, and infinitely more valid as a human being. The assumption was that the heart may reach what the mind cannot fathom, and that therefore the heart has its reasons which the mind does not know. The rise of the sentimental drama of the 18th century illustrated the shift of emphasis from a rational to an irrational basis of art, and the artist now gradually relinquished his post on the frontiers of reason. From the esthetic standpoint, the contrast, of course, was shocking. In the 13th century nearly everything was comprehensible and demonstrable. Thomas Aquinas knew everthing. Dante not only knew everything, but explained everything in a single, magnificent, vast conceit. But by the time of Kant it had become obvious that logic leads everywhere, in other words, nowhere, and that reason is perhaps not the shortest way to God. At this point, Nature became the subject of lyricism. Art ceased to be demonstrative. After Coleridge and Wordsworth, poets tried to evoke understanding through incantation. They stopped interpreting and began to sing. And as poetry became increasingly musical, it became less and less comprehensible. It ceased to address itself to the intellect; it spoke to the heart; and eventually somewhere below the heart it found its way into the Unconscious. This is where its progress ended.

In our day we don't try to explicate poetry, any more than we try to explain painting. Art is not supposed to make sense; and insofar as it does, is not held to be valid. The function of the artist is not to open the mind, but to touch a nerve. This shift in emphasis from what Freud called the secondary, to the primary faculty—from logic to fantasy—has had very far-reaching consequences for the art of our time. At present, the ruling assumption is that whatever is intelligible is not worth knowing, and therefore cannot be the basis of an esthetic experience. The faculty that knows has no need to comprehend. The art that addresses itself to the primary faculty, the deepest self, has no need of syntax. Art in our day does not syllogize. It juxtaposes figures in more or less free association, and it uses words in non-verbal ways, instrumentally.

From this standpoint, language becomes at the most a source of sounds with which one may evoke, by a kind of magic, an emotional experience. Language is then no longer a means of rational communication; it becomes a musical instrument, a drum, a flute, a hurdy-gurdy. A play modeled upon such ideas is likely to be no more than a pattern of suggestions, a montage of images and sounds. Eliot's *The Waste Land* is an example of this technique in poetry. Within the frame of the overarching conceit, this type of art does not imply a conclusion, nor does it prove a point. It evokes acquiescence through participation in a psychic experience. In the theater, such an experience, obviously, may not be the same for each spectator. The contemporary dramatist is quite prepared for this. He has been taught what to say. If you ask him, "What does your play mean?" he answers at once, "You tell me."

The drama is, however, traditionally a dialogue directed to the intelligence. Generally, plays are meant to be understood. Some of the newer dramatists evidently aspire to be considered puzzling, but few good plays are really incomprehensible. What seems eccentric in the new drama is, as a rule, merely its technique. A play like Brecht's *The Caucasian Chalk Circle* has an avant-garde look to it; it is in fact a *pièce à thèse*, a demonstration. The same may be said of Ionesco's *The Chairs*. *The Caucasian Chalk Circle* is a parable. It attempts to demonstrate that property belongs to the people who create it; in this case the analogue happens to be a child. *The Chairs* is a little more complex; it is a *reductio ad absurdum* of the very process of demonstration. In *The Chairs* we have a parody of a public meeting. There are elaborate preparations; but, in fact, there is nothing; the orator who comes to deliver his world-shaking message cannot speak; moreover, he has nothing to say and there is no one to listen. What the play says, however, is perfectly clear. Like *The Caucasian Chalk Circle*, *The Chairs* is a dramatic conceit, a metaphor. These are examples of Renaissance "wit," essentially meaningful; even embarrassingly meaningful. The same may be said of *The Bald Soprano*, a montage of cliches, a parody of the nonsense that passes for conversation. In none of these plays is there an attempt to arrive at a deeper reality than traditional drama can evoke. Nor do these plays express truths or feelings that conventional dramatists cannot express. But they do attempt to create a dream-like atmosphere that is not naturalistic, and thus they arrive at a caricature of reality reminiscent of the paintings of Grosz or Kokoschka.

In the same way, Genet's *The Balcony* is based on a conceit; so are *Endgame* and *Waiting for Godot*. Such plays are acted metaphors. Weiss's *Marat/Sade*, on the other hand, is an example of surrealism, and involves the deliberate juxtaposition of carefully detailed, but normally disparate elements on a single canvas, with an effect of spontaneity that passes for accident. The result is an effect of nightmare, which is justified realistically in terms of the artificial frame which encloses the action, the madhouse. None of this, however, seems very far out as art. Both in painting and in music we are accustomed to deviations from convention which are incomparably more daring than anything yet attempted in the theater. But let's hold our hats: there is every reason to expect that the stage will soon catch up with Bartok and Chagall.

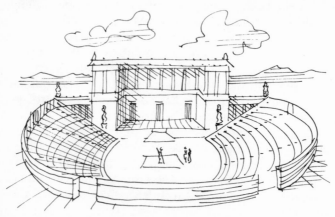

The contemporary theater, it must be granted, steps beyoud realism only with the greatest reluctance and great timidity. The history of drama is, at bottom, the history of realism. This history, of course, involves a changing concept of what is real, a revaluation of validity. Tragedy and comedy were not at all realistic. They conveyed a sense of reality only through suggestion. By the time of Scribe, the cosmic picture had changed a good deal from what it had been in the time of Sophocles or Shakespeare. It was now pretty well agreed that the universe was shaped, not along moral, but along physical lines, so that in a world that no longer absorbed God's undivided attention, a man would have to work out his destiny without much help from the Creator. In this new world, since everything was visible, everything was predictable. The type of drama which reflected these attitudes was actually a mechanical contraption, arranged along rigorously logical lines, solid, and neat. In this drama every event is forseeable; at least it is clearly visible to the hindsight; and events follow one another in an unbreakable chain of cause and consequence, so that the hero, if he is sufficiently bright, can calculate the train of events from the start and await the inevitable surprise with some confidence. Such a play tends to fall, of course, into a fairly rigid formal pattern, the phases of which are invariable: preparation, complication, climax, reversal, denouement. For a long time, it was assumed that this system was the only possible way to tell a story acceptably on the stage.

The essence of Scribe's drama was conflict. Since, after Darwin, the cosmic process itself was mainly seen as a struggle, the Scribean idea of drama was said to be "realistic." The play of character and action, however, became progressively more and more realistic through the years after Scribe, until eventually the stage-anecdote and the events of real life were brought quite close together. This process of debunking the theater found its culmination in the naturalism of the school of Zola. By this time, the idealistic basis of drama had been pretty well relinquished, together with the moral structure of the universe, and the system of stage-artifice which Scribe had developed was considered no longer appropriate to a realistic presentation of experience. Theater was not supposed to represent "life as it is."

"Life as it is" has no stories. It makes no points. It has no special pattern, and is not particularly amusing. Neither was the naturalistic drama. This drama attempted to represent nature without the intervention of art. It professed to tell the observable truth in the manner of the laboratory. It did not, of course, succeed; and it was soon realized that the candid-camera approach to playwriting had no future.

Luckily, the symbolists came to the rescue about this point. The dramatist began now to comment on the outer world in much the same manner as the post-impressionist painter, and also at about the same time. He began to use dramatic techniques of distortion, exaggeration, reduction, grimace. Before long, the dream-like effects of expressionism began to be seen on the stage. The first experiments in this genre were made about 1890. They involved the suppression of the time factor, the negation of causality, and a deliberate effort to make an effect of the unreal. What was held to be essential in this style, which was, in its earliest stages associated with the symbolism of Villiers de l'Isle-Adam and Maeterlinck, was to portray not an outer reality, but the landscape of the soul, the inner life, of which one is normally conscious only when the outer world does not intrude upon it. This inner life could not be directly communicated or represented. It must be evoked—mainly through the association of images, through sign and symbol, analogy, or suggestion. A play of this sort would approximate a reverie, a daydream. It might not lead to a sudden mystical revelation of truth, a *satori*, as we say nowadays—though this possibility was not excluded. It would, in all likelihood, be equivocal—but it would be, at the least, a true experience. This experience, of course, would not be the same for each spectator in the audience; for the playwright could not hope to retain complete control of a medium which suggested, rather than depicted, its essential action. At this point, plays began to be called incomprehensible, and playwrights mad. The contemporary era had begun.

In 1898, Strindberg, in fact, was mad, and as a result he created *To Damascus*, which must be considered a new art form. *To Damascus* takes place in what we may call an infra-reality, a world that has its roots in the commonplace, but its branches in another world. Such a play has no counterpart in external reality and presents nothing that the candid camera can photograph. The realism of such plays is completely a matter of the inner life. But in giving up the external subject, the dramatist gave up completely the possibility of control. His effect depends almost completely on the enthusiasm of the spectator. His plays give the impression of meaning, without actually meaning anything whatever that can be defined with confidence. This brings us to the logical conclusion of the process: every spectator his own playwright. Such at present is the state of the art.

If we look back over this perspective, we become aware that we have arrived at the opposite pole from the classic conception of drama. Our realism mirrors no longer a perfectly ordered universe, but a nightmare which only madness can render intelligible. Perhaps such plays more truly represent the human condition than the well-ordered plays of Scribe and Dumas. At any rate, we must concede that the artist in the theater has never been so sincere and so vigorous in his effort to reach reality. It is also true that he has never been quite so inept. The achievement of an acceptable signal-to-noise ratio in drama conceived along these lines is incredibly difficult. For a long time, the world seemed stable: it stood still. We are now aware that the world is spinning. Our art very probably is the manifestation of our vertigo. It is not an especially comfortable symptom, but it has at least one reassuring aspect—it does not falsify the facts.

The loss of meaning in art is perhaps the major casualty of our time; but the old meanings no longer satisfy us, and until we discover new meanings in life, there is not much we can do but temporize. Meanwhile, we shall grin, if we can, and we shall bear it, until that genius comes who will be able to transform our universe once again in terms of a more enduring beauty, a beauty more tolerable than the beauty of despair.

Ours Is a Theater of And by Man; And Now We Need a Theater of Woman

By Mildred Janz

Until this time theater has been written by and about Man, so we have learned that he suffers nobly his love, hate, war, disillusion and his age, as no one else can suffer them. And because of this suffering, theater has known all degrees of greatness and pettiness.

Except for a few good "female" parts on the stage, Woman is still the vast unexplored territory of the theater; for though there have been a few female writers, their themes have had to be suited to the taste and business of theater, for these things, too, are mostly *male*.

Just as Shakespeare, Shaw, Strindberg, Ibsen, Miller and Beckett represent a composite Theater of Man, let us consider a Theater of Woman. In it, audiences would see in each play a microcosm of Woman, and Woman could see herself as she never could before. Her suffering could be the counterpart of the male nobility, but specifically it is, and always will be, her own. Woman could learn about herself and her place in the world, and she could then become more comfortable as a woman; not a self-conscious female man, or an old, oversized young girl who refuses to don the cloak of knowledge that only full-blooded women appreciate.

Our 20th century is being shaped by Man. Literate, civilized Woman must accept this, as always, without question. But her job now is a formidable one, for she must learn to love, and learn to teach love, as she always has, in the face of all achievement; and some achievements of the century are hideous indeed. The world has grown up and become a monster for the lack of love it knew in its childhood.

Every woman is a woman for some time in her life; sometimes for a limited time, sometimes for the whole time. The amount of woman-time to a woman is an intellectually emotional involvement that begins with her sex and revolves around it. A baby girl is born (in our present Western society) and in time she becomes an adolescent, a wife-to-be, a bride, then a mother. It is in these years between adolesence and motherhood that Woman develops. It is in these years that her intuition is highest, her intelligence greatest, and her curiousity most overwhelming. If she turns outside and puts her intuition, educational training, and natural intelligence to work, she becomes an unbeatable competitor in commerce, the professions and marriage. In the professions and in business her real value has not yet been assessed, but these activities probably could not continue at their present pace without her presence. When Woman turns inside, she learns how much of a woman she is and what her obligations are. The deeper she probes, the more she learns that in every life and in every age Woman is essentially strong and very different from Man . . . and only the smallest bit different from Eve.

The seas, the mountains and deserts and the moon have been explored, but 20th-century woman is still uncharted. She is the last unexplored territory of the theater.

From the beginning until not too long ago, women on stage were portrayed by young boys. Audiences accepted it, women accepted it. The words were written by men about the worlds of men, and all were entertained.

For instance, a woman would never have written the words of Shakespeare's *Hamlet*:

"To be, or not to be; that is the question:
Whether 'tis nobler in the mind to suffer
The slings and arrows of outrageous fortune . . . "

If Hamlet (Shakespeare) were a woman, the words would have been more: Should I expose my mother, uncle and their deeds?—every act I do from now on will pivot on my decision. But if Shakespeare were a woman, he would not have given Hamlet this choice, for the answer in his mind would have been predetermined. A woman does not decide to have a baby once she is pregnant.

Queen Gertrude asks:

"Alas, how is't with you,
That you do bend your eye on vacancy
And with the incorporal air do hold discourse?"

This was written by a man who did not know that the inside woman questions constantly. Gertrude should have accepted Hamlet's stare as a simple daydream. Inside women believe in daydreams, and respect the daydreams of others.

In Strindberg's *Miss Julie*, Julie says: ". . . Everyone knows my secrets. . . . I had to wear boys' clothes, was taught to handle horses. All the men on the estate were given women's jobs, and the women men's, until the whole place went to rack and ruin. . . ."

Here Strindberg is describing Julie's problem in outside terms, or his very own viewpoint of Julie. Strindberg could not have written it differently. A woman knows that the mere superficialities of work and clothing are exactly that —superficial, outside things.

There are times when a woman confuses the outside with the inside—and it is during these times that she, herself, and those surrounding her, are most troubled. In Lillian Hellman's play *The Little Foxes* Regina tells us about herself at the very beginning: ". . . Chicago may be the . . . noisiest, dirtiest city in the world, but I should still prefer it to the sound of our horses and the smell of our azaleas. I should like the crowds of people and theaters and lovely women . . ."

From this point on Regina's strength grows, and in this growth her viewpoint could very well be that of a business man going about his business. In essence, this is exactly what the play is about. Marshall says it very well: " . . . You live better than the rest of us, you eat better, you drink better. I wonder you find time, or want to find time, to do business."

Regina is an outside woman, written by a playwright with an outside viewpoint. This is not a play of the heart. This is a play of action. The characters in it are deeply involved in the intricacies of business. They develop slowly and steadily from their creation at the beginning, to their very last breath at the end. They do not change, they merely grow, become larger and greedier, more vicious than they were at the beginning of the play.

At the end, Regina says to the disappointed, bewildered daughter who has seen her exposed: ". . . It will be good for you to get away from here. Good for me, too. Time heals most wounds, Alexandra. You're young, you shall have all the things I wanted. I'll make the world for you the way I wanted it to be for me . . ."

And so it is obvious that Regina has become the hunter, the builder of worlds—the woman with the fully expanded viewpoint, turned completely outside and away from herself. Except for the flesh and the clothes she wears, Regina could be anything.

"Alexandra, I've come to the end of my rope. Somewhere there has to be what I want, too. Life goes too fast . . ." Regina has passed the point of no return in her life. She cannot go back to any point in her womanhood. The husband to whom she has hardly been a wife has died, her daughter has grown up and away from her, and she chooses to surround herself with staunch men of greed that she knows and has learned to recognize. This group will be her society now and forever.

At the very beginning of the play, Regina still has charm, though she is quite past being a woman. At the end, she is hard and bitter, past everything in her sex, and can never return.

Only once, not too long ago, did a modern play about a modern woman make sense to—and about—herself. It proved that a woman's problem is uniquely hers, and can be met intelligently, without sentiment, and with a soft and gentle humor. The light, bright comedy was *Mary, Mary* by Jean Kerr. It circumvented the seriousness of almost every problem it touched; but actually, this was to its credit, because it was the very first honest attempt at making a modern woman's problem acceptable.

In the newer plays which are being written by women, the problems of the playwrights and the context of the play are being confused with theatrical revolution. If the writers would pause for a moment in their lives to make contact with themselves as human beings, they would find that there is no revolution except the one that is smoldering within them.

Shrewd, sharp women today find that they suddenly have a need to say something of their own, and what they say is usually shrewd and sharp. They are forcing themselves to use their imaginations to unearth uncanny situations in order to find recognition. Most of the new plays must be explained by gesture, prologue and epilogue, for the material is too repulsive to accept at face value, or just too vague for audiences to grasp.

Rochelle Owens has taken the oldest, most abhorrent sexual example known, and she has used it as a focal point in her play *Futz*. Man cohabiting with a pig is symbolic of the personal outrage she feels with the society that surrounds her. Her own personal problem of identity is so intricately woven into the play that they have become one cloth. And so it is with modern woman—if she probes, her inside viewpoint will be that of Everywoman. If she looks outside herself, her viewpoint becomes very far out.

Modern woman would prefer her own place in society—but she has been condemned as an excuse, a receptacle for every ill and every madness in the world. Man, society and the theater have not given her the way to be a woman. They merely blame her for their own inadequacies. Just as art imitates life, life imitates art. And so it is that Woman, Herself, must show the way to woman, herself.

Every society and every age has made different demands upon Woman, and yet she has managed to adjust to the demands, and in many instances, she has become stronger because of them. But there is a terrible confusion now, for Man is not able to explain some of his achievements even to himself, and all that is left for Woman is to keep playing her "part" and wait until Man is able to understand himself and take his proper place in the world again.

Theater has a long way to go in many areas, but more than anything else, it must encourage the inside woman to grope further, and bring forth from herself a Theater of Woman.

Playwright-less Theater, Street Crime, Other Adventures Of the Theatrical 1970s

By Robert Schroeder

"In the beginning was the Word," saith the Good Book. Aristophanes, Shakespeare, Racine, Goethe, Chekhov, and O'Neill, and the theater people around them, seem to have agreed. It is only now that the theater's self-proclaimed prophets have decided that the word enlighteneth not our darkness, for today's darkness (they say) comprehendeth it not.

On one level, modern-day theatrical enlightenment seems to derive from such non-verbal resorts as advanced onstage nudity, audience-participation copulation and their *quid pro quos*, marauding audience-raids, "total" environmental theater, and ritualistic incantations of gibberish.

On another level, that of such apostles of the "new" theater as the Royal Shakespeare Company's Peter Brook, the Open Theater's Joe Chaikin, the Polish Laboratory Theater's Jerzy Grotowski and the Performance Group's Richard Schechner, the enactment of playscripts is to be replaced with a rediscovery of tribal ritual—a modern evocation of whatever ineffable but "recognized" Jungian commonality defines our time and our experience.

The word-weaver, we are told, must give way to one or another level of witch doctor, and then all will be restored to right in the theater world.

What, then, of the playwright? Is he to dig a new gig? Is the playwright obsolete, about to go the way of the alchemist, the medieval scriptoria copier, the crafter of coats of mail?

According to Richard Schechner, director of New York's Performance Group, an "international movement" of scope and vitality is "upon us." It is "a movement not generated by playwrights and protected by critics," he says, "but one sponsored by directors and performers. A movement not yet sealed in books but revealed in many productions and bringing together in a

305

new synthesis such diverse influences as yoga and the Kathakali of southern India, the visionary outcries of Antonin Artaud, the rituals of many non-literate peoples, the passion for systemization of Stanislavski, and the peculiar anxieties of today's Western world."

Jerzy Grotowski, patron saint of the "new" theater, explains: "The plays in (our) . . . repertory are more a springboard than anything else. We take plays that act as a stimulus for us, that demand a certain response, that make

us create our own work and not just illustrate the play. They function for us on a certain level of association. They are alive but they are also archaic. Removed from us. Classical pieces. *The Constant Prince,* by Calderon, is one. *Akropolis,* by Wyspianski, is another."

Mark Shivas, writing of Grotowski's Polish Laboratory Theater production of *Akropolis* as played in London, amplifies: "*Akropolis* was written by Wyspianski in 1904. Its time is the eve of Resurrection Day, and its setting is Krakow, where the figures on the cathedral's tapestries are miraculously animated and step down to enact passages from Homer and the Bible. The drama ends with the resurrection of Christ-Apollo, triumphant symbol of European culture. Grotowski has changed the setting from Krakow to Auschwitz, and the performers are the dazed and ghostly inmates of the concentration camp. He's tried to restore the relevance that Wyspianski's symbols may once have possessed."

What of Wyspianski's dialogue? Grotowski believes that he has succeeded in defining what is distinctively theater, as opposed to what is something else. "I contrast the Rich Theater with the Poor Theater," he says. "The Rich Theater is rich in flaws. It depends on artistic kleptomania, drawing from other disciplines, multiplying elements to escape the impasse presented by movies and television. It's all nonsense, and it's technically inferior to films and television. Consequently, I propose poverty in the theater."

Grotowski's "poverty" excludes a stage, stage lighting, sound effects, scenery, make-up and the poetry of language as such. What it does not exclude is the actor-spectator relationship. To Grotowski, that is the only determinant—the existence or non-existence of that relationship defines the existence or non-existence of theater. The audience must be there, in a Polish Laboratory Theater performance, for the same reason that a Priest must be present in the Catholic confessional ritual, so that the actors may make their "creative confessional."

George Wellwarth, a professor at Pennsylvania State University, and a frequent commentator on drama topics, sums it up this way: "Mr. Schechner is setting up straw men for himself to knock down when he states that the current theatrical quarrel is between verbal and non-verbal communication. It is nothing of the sort. It is a quarrel between the traditional concept of theater as an objective imposition of ideas on the audience, and theater as an emotional efflorescence enveloping the audience and stimulating it into a mindless and ecstatic feeling of participation. What Mr. Schechner is essentially doing in (the Performance Group's) *Dionysus in '69* is mass psychodrama."

Jerzy Grotowski, in telling interviewers about his production of Marlowe's *Dr. Faustus,* explained that his spectators sat around a long table with the actor playing Faustus and engaged in an unrehearsed and unscripted simulated patient-doctor dialogue with "Faustus." Grotowski told also of an earlier (pre-*Marat/Sade*) production of *Kordian,* in which the Polish Laboratory Theater's space was transformed "into an insane asylum. The entire room became a hospital with beds and so on. The actors were on the beds along with the spectators. The actors were either doctors or patients, the most interesting cases. The doctors treated the spectators as also sick. Those spectators who were treated as patients were furious—the others were very proud because they had been judged 'sane'."

Obviously, to Grotowski, the playwright is either a dead "classic" who is "brought back to life" in free translation—the translation being supplied by the director; or the playwright is the actor conversing ad lib with the spectator, who in that process becomes also, gratuituously and willy-nilly, the playwright.

It is Schechner's view that "The writer is either there or he is not there . . . Words are part of the scenic action and must be thought of as no more and no less than that. All elements of the theater are improved by rehearsal; words, performers, space, audience. And once you begin exploring space and audience you are into audience participation." You are into Grotowski's *Dr. Faustus. Akropolis,* etc.; the Open Theater's *The Serpent;* the

Living Theater's *Mysteries* and *Paradise Now;* Peter Brook's *Marat/Sade, Us, Oedipus,* and *The Tempest,* and the Performance Group's *Dionysus in '69.* In Schechner's words, "All attempt new spatial uses of the theater, new audience-performer relationships, new outlooks on what the theatrical function is. Each has sought to define 'ritual' for our time and find uses for ritual in the theater."

When the Becks' Living Theater was playing *Paradise Now* in Brooklyn, and when the cast began ritualistically to remove its clothes as it chanted "we are not allowed to take our clothes off," playwright George Birimisa (an individual having no relationship with the Living Theater) rose and began also to take off his clothes. After having stripped completely, he ran from the audience to the stage, stood facing the audience and said, loud and clear, "Hooray! I've got my clothes off and now I'm free!" Then a smile slowly crossed his face, and he shared the thought that prompted it with the audience, "But what do I do now?" He left the stage, and resumed his seat, where he sat nude for the remaining three hours of the performance, exposing considerably more than himself.

The "new" theater seeks to resurrect that truth—that holy and evanescent truth—that current theatrical insipidities obscure. But so did naturalistic theater when it sought to counteract the excesses of "classic" declamation and of Victorian melodrama; and so did Molière and Goldoni when they sought to counteract the excesses of the commedia dell'arte's unscripted inanities; and so did Euripides when he sought to counteract the excesses of Aeschylus's and Sophocles's supra-rational grandiloquences.

When the proponents of the newest "new" theater call for "a rediscovery of tribal ritual" or for "audience-as-humanity's-representative receiving the actors' creative confessional," and when Birimisa sits in naked judgment of one of today's manifestations of "new audience-performer relationships," what is wanted, and found wanting, is truth—the audience's truth.

In the light of this truth all of the dichotomies of the current "new" versus "traditional" theater's advocates are dispelled. George Wellwarth's either/or of "mindless audience-ecstasy" versus "objective imposition of ideas " disintegrates. Grotowski's either/or of "rich" versus "poor" theater loses cogency. Schechner's either/or of the writer's being "there or not there" is revealed as not germane. For the truth an audience discovers or rediscovers in a true theater experience—think now of *your* favorite—is both ecstatic *and* ideational; both artifactically-evoked *and* artlessly received; both written *and* nonverbally apprehended.

The question is not, then, whether the word-weaver is to be dismissed in favor of the witch doctor, or whether the witch doctor "continues," as has been imagined by some, to have been superseded by the word-weaver. Nor has this ever been the question. Aeschylus's word-weaving counteracted Bacchic witchery; but the commedia's witchery counteracted Aeschylus's

)rds; but Molière's and Shakespeare's words counteracted the
mmedia's witchery; but Reinhardt's and Piscator's and Belasco's
echanized witchery counteracted Shakespeare's words; but Brook's and
rotowski's rejection of mechanical witchery for psychological wizardry is a
rther counteraction; and so ad infinitum; amen.

The word-weaver who does not understand the stage's witchcraft had
·tter stay with his essays and novels; and the theatrical witch doctor who
)es not comprehend or know how to invoke the magic of words—the
)etry of words—had better stay a stage-manager.

In the performance of his Polish Laboratory Theater that I experienced,
rotowski achieved a mystical, an inexplicably archetypical, evocation of
e human condition. He accomplished this—I can only say demoniacally
·through intricately choreographed passages of sound and amazingly
)ntrolled and orchestrated body movements. Grotowski is the composer,
e choreographer, the poet, the artist. He is, of course, and what else, the
aywright.

The playwright is not obsolete, nor will he be. But sometimes, especially
troubled times, he functions under other, temporary labels.

{elodrama in the Streets

When New York City provided gerrymandered sanctuaries of secure
·fluence, it was the theater capital of America, and, perhaps with London,
f the world. No offering could achieve trans-regional prominence without
well-received New York production. And it was in the central city that
eater was most magic.

Can this city remain pivotal to the theater, now that every neighborhood
-even the Great White Way—is the potential site of inconveniences rang-
g from power and telephone outages to mugging, murder, or mayhem?
)r will the city's cancerous blight not only wither its centrality to theater, but
ap the fiber of theater itself?

Certain rituals are best entered into in a state of anxiety and tension, such
s making war, riding the subway, or shopping during the noon hour at
loomingdale's. But the ritual of theater is not in this category. The
ficionado prepares for the theater the way he would prepare for the Mass.
he nuances of Olivier's *Othello*, Hepburn's *Coco*, or Bacall's *Applause* were
est apprehended from the vantage of an assuaged appetite, effortlessly-
ompleted phone calls or appointments, less-than-lethal air for breath, and
mode of approaching the theater that is the opposite of running the
antlet.

These amenities can no longer be taken for granted even in the Broadway
rea. The rising theater district crime rate is the primary reason for the
nove to adopt a 7:30 curtain time, although other reasons are given publicly.
he muggings have tended to occur after the main crowds have left the

streets—straggler patrons or actors or stagehands leaving after finishin make-up removal or chores have been the prime victims. The belief is that those who leave the theater district after the post-curtain surge could leav an hour earlier, there would be more non-theatrical foot and auto traffi more taxis available, and a consequently lower incidence of muggings.

Crime rates in most off-Broadway theater locations exceed those of th Broadway theater district. As Broadway production costs have soared, an virtually every incoming property of less than extravaganza proportions ha been forced into an off-Broadway situation, the theatergoer is appalled the environs he is expected to survive in order to experience theater. What i happening off Broadway parallels what has been happening in the Broad way area—the theaters offering the greatest probability of incident-fre access are preferred. Many of the new off-Broadway theaters announced a being "under construction" have failed to open, and the talk of "middl theater" construction or conversions has subsided. A survey of the location of the announced theaters that were not completed supports the conclusio that increasing crime in their neighborhoods was a factor in the projects suspension.

Plans for new theaters in the Broadway area have been affected. Fo example, City Center Plaza, which was to include four new theaters in tower on the site of the former Madison Square Garden, is dead. While suc factors as tight money, business recession, inadequacy of utility capacity etc., are referred to, conversations with mid-towners continue to dwel upon a general malaise—a growing feeling that getting oneself out of the city that Jules Feiffer predicted so accurately in *Little Murders* was mor realistic than participation in remedial action.

In the mid-1960s the Repertory Theater of Lincoln Center conducted survey which showed a linear relationship between theater attendance and distance between place of residence and the theater district. It was foun that when a family moves from, say, the West Village or the East Seventie to Westchester County, that family's theater attendance drops precipi tously. If the family moves to Fairfield County in Connecticut, it is for al practical purposes lost to the Broadway theater forever. If New York Cit fails to remedy its pollution, utility service and public safety problem: substantially and at once, it will find a growing majority of its formerl regular theatergoers living out of town, and find itself a remnant city of *Dail News* readers, rooster fight fans and OTBniks.

Audience Participation

Proponents of non-scripted, audience-participation theater had a crack a a meeting of Drama Desk, the organization of New York theater editors and reporters, at convincing the assembled scribes that an active audience is happy audience. Spokesmen for some ten troupes represented on the pane ave some ten versions of the virtues of non-scripted theater. Stephen orst, one of the Performance Group actors, proclaimed that he is a staunch roponent of participation; but he admitted that the first time a pectator interrupted his performance, "I almost punched him in the nouth." Alec Rubin, director of the Theater of Encounter, said, "The goal of heater is to be together in the world with others, and yourself. Maybe a undred years from now people will come together and have orgiastic xperiences. Unfortunately, we're not at that point now." David Shepherd, ounder-director of a relatively new troupe known as the Responsive Scene, aid that the best drama occurs when audiences "make their own enterainment."

When some audience participation developed in the meeting, however, he "experts" quickly moved to squelch anyone voicing dissent, dubbing uch objectionable persons "square," "uninformed" and "too uptight to omprehend the new theater." Dissention rose particularly from the noncripters' claim to exclusivity in providing "genuine" theater. Especially ffensive to the panelists was one scribe's observation that he found the Performance Group, the Liquid Theater, et al, to be "Madison Avenue." He xplained that if an impersonal caress, a groupie kiss, a professionallyproffered touch, was passed off as "genuine" human contact, then this theater was as "genuine" as the posed love or lover in the deodorant ads.

Several reviewers pleaded with the panelists to let them know ahead of time what they were in for so that they could dress or undress for the occasion. One critic said that he had purchased two new wash-and-wear suits for participatory theater reviewing, but needed notice as to when he should wear them. His dry-cleaning bills had been exceeding his salary in recent months, he claimed.

The Woman as Playwright, or Something

"It is hell to be a woman and a writer," June Havoc told a Dramatists Guild symposium on The Woman Playwright. Her co-panelist, Joan Rivers, wasn't so sure. "Sometimes, it's great to be a woman," she said, "You can fight'em on their own level, and when everything else fails, start to cry. Or if you're pregnant, that's a wonderful time to go to a business negotiation."

Chaired by Howard Teichmann, the Symposium dealt with a wide spectrum of problems and attitudes specific to women in the theater. "The woman writer is comparatively well treated in the theater," Miss Rivers said. "TV shuts its doors to women writers. Carson won't have a woman on his writing staff. Women write lines that go over a man's head. Gabe Dell told me he loves matinees, because women—the audience is mostly women then—pick up more nuances."

"As an actor I can corroborate that," Miss Havoc responded, "I used to look forward to matinees. Particularly if it was a comedy. Not with a drama so much. Because the ladies—they like to cry, if it's a safe cry. But they don't

like to have that first layer of skin disturbed. They prefer to laugh. And
they'll love anything that has to do with man-women, child-parent
parent-child, lover-mistress—they love all of this. It's quite marvelous. But
don't, don't go any deeper. In a matinee. They—the ladies—are not a good
audience for anything important."

After a Pinter pause, Teichmann: "What's more important . . . than what
you have just listed?" Havoc: "You're treating me like a cutie!" "No! No, I'm
asking what's more important." "Well, there are many issues more important than the human relationships on the marriage level. Or the parent-child
level. There are world issues." Joan Rivers, interposing: "Oh, I think that
comes up here . . . I mean . . . you've got to get your one to one straightened
out—before you worry about . . ." Teichmann: "I think they pay their
money at the box office to see plays that appeal to them emotionally rather
than intellectually on that world level." Havoc: "I agree. That's what I just
got through saying. Only you said it much better."

But that has to do with women as audience. What about women as actors,
directors, technicians, playwrights? It was now that Havoc voiced her "it is
hell to be a woman and a writer." Teichmann: "What about a man?" Havoc:
"I don't know. I've never been a man. First of all, many rules don't apply to
me . . . I have had to live under the shadow of preconceiveditis . . . Years
ago, I had to have a birth certificate to get a passport. I tried to
remember—where could I have been born? I didn't know—could remember nothing. What were the possibilities? There were three or four.
Vancouver, some others. My agent mailed out four inquiries—requests.
Back come *four* birth certificates. One from each of the towns. It is a fact. All
were signed by my mother, using all her umlauts (Hovick was only one
Anglicization). All averred, 'other children by this mother: none.' We since
thought of two more possible birth sites and received two more birth
certificates, similar in content. All in my mother's handwriting and all the
same name but all different dates.

"So first, I was never born. I can prove it. When I came to New York after
the marathons, and stopped the show—*Forbidden Melody*—mother came to
see me. She invited me to see the family—my beloved sister, she's gone
now—to see them for the first time, in all those years. 'We never expected to
see you again,' my mother explained, 'so you must understand why you
have no identity. Your past has become your sister's past—you must understand.' So I had no past—no identity. Mother said, 'You'll have to dream
one up for yourself.' I never did a number with my sister. We never worked
together, not once. That is all fable. She didn't join us until after I was on the
circuit. In fact, I didn't know her at all in my childhood—in my babyhood. I
never saw her but once, and I was vowed to secrecy by mother. My sister
arrived on the scene first, so it was, of course, first come, first served. And
there was only one identity apparently considered worth using. After it got

sed there was very little left. But in spite of that it seems to have worked out ll right. I'm only pointing out—you talk about being a woman, being a ian, being whatever we are. It's all so much less important than being alive, t least. You see, I wasn't even alive." Teichmann: "You were exploited!" No! Not even exploited! Ignored!" "By two other women." "Men haven't een much help!"

Teichmann (reflectively): "I do have a decided advantage over the wo- ien. I had a play on the road. Before New York. We opened in Princeton. I ad been in the theater for 33 years. I had never heard professional actors efore an audience that paid money—the audience said 'Louder!' . . . I'd iever heard this. The day after the opening the producer, associate pro- lucer, everybody gathered around. We sent for the director, who wouldn't ome because he was relighting a scene. Eventually he came, and I said, Listen—did you hear the people saying Louder?' He answered, 'It was errible, wasn't it?' I said, 'Yes.' He said, 'Yes.' I didn't realize it then—but ie meant the audience. 'What would you rather have,' he asked rhetorical- y, 'actors who felt, understood, appreciated what you've written, or robots vho made themselves heard to the audience?' I said, 'Robots!'

"He was horrified. I said, 'Listen to me . . . understand what I am saying o you—or else?' 'Or else what?' Now you look at me. Do I look like I could . ." (He doesn't. Teichmann, soaking, even dripping wet, must weigh all of 137 pounds). " 'Or else,' I said, 'I will pop you right in the nose!' I hadn't iit anybody since I was eight years old. So he stood up and he said, 'Strike ne! I call upon all in this room to see me struck!' I broke up. I laughed. I oared. I thought it was funny. And then about 45 minutes later, I went after iim. I really went after him. I chased him down the hall of the Princeton Inn ind I caught him in the corridor and I grabbed him with my left hand and I hrew him against the wall and I crossed with my right and honest to God he vent down! I haven't hit anyone since. Great tears welled up in his eyes and ie said, 'You hit me!' 'I hit you', I replied. It was a wonderful feeling. Did :hose actors speak louder the next performance? You know they spoke louder!"

Where Has All the Power Gone?

The fact that playwrights can no longer get a jury trial, but must submit their work to a single judge, has materially reduced the availability of playscripts to the professional theater, Frank D. Gilroy told Drama Desk. Gilroy turned to such critics as George Oppenheimer of *Newsday,* Henry Hewes of *Saturday Review World,* Edith Oliver of *The New Yorker* and Marilyn Stasio of *Cue* and said, "You have no influence. Your opinion is of interest after the fact, but the only power in today's New York theater scene is exercised by the man who writes the daily *Times* review.

"The professional playwright is understandably reluctant to risk three

years' labor on the whim of one man one night," Gilroy continued, "s
many just stop writing plays altogether, others turn from the stage to movie
or TV. Some write their plays, then simply file them away." He told o
correspondence with the New York Times, in the course of which Gilro
pressed that something—anything—be tried in a last-ditch effort to brea
out of the existing impasse. There is no present evidence, Gilroy concluded
that anything is actually going to be done at the Times.

Richard Shepard, then editor of the cultural section of the daily Times, wa
asked to respond. After reviewing some of the suggestions that have bee
made from time to time over the years in an effort to curb the apparen
life-and-death power of the Times's daily critic—such suggestions as th
addition of a second daily critic, publication alongside the Times review of a
guest review by members of the New York Drama Critics Circle, moving th
box score of other critics' opinions from the Sunday to the daily Times
changing the nature of opening night coverage from criticism to reportage
etc.—Shepard said that he himself did not have the authority to undertak
these or any other remedies, and that he would be hard put to say who, i
anyone, on the Times did.

Jerome Lawrence told the meeting that the one sure way to beat the powe
of the Times's daily critic was to submit new work to the regional and college
theaters outside New York City. He went on to chide the Times personne
present for not reporting on the increasing viability of such organizations a
the American Playwrights Theater, and on regional theater generally.

Merle Debuskey, president of the New York theatrical press agents
association, expressed his growing dissatisfaction with the New York theater scene by pointing out that all New York editors, producers, and theatergoers seem to want any more is a "Successful Thing," that everyone will
then have to see, and have to cover, and have to glorify. "It is too bad," he
said, "that these 'Successful Things' have been confused in most peoples'
minds with theater."

Nudity Is Easier to 'Do' Onstage Than to Accept As Part of an Illusion

By Jeff Sweet

Scuba Duba took me by surprise. A virginal NYU freshman, recently arrived from a town which then prohibited the sale of liquor within its limits and which, for several years, refused the high school permission to stage *Inherit the Wind* because of objections from the religious community, I was not prepared for the sight of a bare-breasted lady bouncing around Harold Wonder's chateau. I wrote to a friend about this amazing occurrence, and he replied, albeit inaccurately, "Well, now you've seen everything!"

That was just a few seasons ago. In the meantime, nudity has lost its status as an innovation and become assimilated as a common theatrical device. And how quickly it was assimilated! One moment Robert Anderson's *You Know I Can't Hear You When the Water's Running* had us laughing at the ridiculous possibility of an actor auditioning in the buff for a part requiring frontal nudity, and the next, Equity was issuing guidelines on just what would be allowed in nude auditions. Overnight, Anderson's playlet had become an anachronism, and the titles *Geese, Sweet Eros* and *Che* took their places in the off-Broadway listings.

This doesn't imply that nudity was or is limited to off-Broadway and experimental efforts. In the past few seasons we have seen a number of establishment-based productions, such as *The Prime of Miss Jean Brodie, Abelard and Heloise* and *The Mother Lover,* in which the costume designers' talents were not always in evidence, and Lincoln Center acknowledged the trend with Susan Tyrell's unsuccessful attempts to remain completely clothed in *Camino Real.* Many took it as a sign of the times when *The Best Plays of 1968–1969* ran a layout of photos from *Oh! Calcutta!* which was, then, stronger stuff than *Playboy.*

315

With it nudity has brought a bumper crop of questions, jokes and opin ions. The most immediate questions are about those who actually "do nudity—the actors. So over beers and hamburgers I asked a marvelously talented young actress named Boni Enten about her thoughts on the subjec The conversation was centered mainly around her experiences as a membe of the original cast of *Oh! Calcutta!*:

"Auditioning for the show, I had to read and sing and dance, and I had t do this nude improvisation. There were fifty people who'd been called back and they drew names out of a hat to see what order we would be seen in, an I was first. I had never taken my clothes off in public before. But I did the and I wasn't nervous at all. Actually, I *was* nervous, but the thing I wa nervous about was doing the improvisation because I'd never done on before. And after it was all over, and I'd put my clothes back on, Jacque Levy, the director, asked me, 'Well, how do you feel?' I was beaming and said, 'Fantastic! I feel fantastic!' I gave him a big hug and a kiss and I thanke him. There was something so fantastic about—not about exhibiting m body—but being *able* to. It was a very free feeling. I came out of the auditio room and all the others were out there being very nervous, and I said, 'It' fantastic, you'll love it!' They thought I was crazy. I came back that afternoo for dance auditions, and everybody felt the same way. I think maybe ther was one girl who wouldn't take her underpants off. She didn't get into th show.

"Jacques was incredible. You know, he's a shrink, too. And the first day o rehearsal he read to us from *The Naked Ape* and Freud. Then he said, 'OK now, go and get changed into your robes,' and as we were changing , the girls were asking each other, 'Do you think we should keep our underpants on?' We decided, no, if you're going to do it, you do it all the way. We came back, and everybody was sitting there with their robes very tight around them. Then we went on stage to dance and do warm-up exercises. The robes would come open and everybody would look, and that's how we were sort of eased into this thing of accepting each other's body and how funny it looks when you're naked and jumping around. We worked like that for a month to sort of free us so that we would be able to be nude onstage without thinking about it. I didn't think about the fact I was naked any of the time I was in the show except for one time during previews. We were experiment- ing with different endings, and one night we wound up taking nude curtain calls, which was just about the most embarrassing thing that's happened to me in my life. And we all felt that way. We were all just sort of standing there, you know, with our legs together. We took quick bows and just ran off. The way the show's ending was finally set, we were all in a line doing a dance thing. It wasn't like a curtain call where I, Boni Enten, take my bow to the public for acceptance or whatever without anything on."

The question: How is it possible to be naked onstage and not get aroused?

"Like I said," Boni answered, "you're thinking of other things. In the opening number, for instance, we'd come on dressed in the back, take our clothes off and put these white robes on. Then everybody would expose a part of himself, but to a count. I counted for three whole months in that show. I couldn't think about being naked. Now in the opening of the second act, everybody comes out nude and moves and dances together, and there were times when a guy would get an erection and he'd whisper to the cast, 'Listen, I've got an erection,' but it was kind of dark, and he would sort of hide it."

Tom Eyen, the playwright-director of *The Dirtiest Show in Town,* reported a similar attitude pervaded his cast. Commenting on the rehearsals, he said, "There were no real hangups regarding the nude scenes. When we started working on the orgy scene, one of the girls asked if she should take her clothes off then. I said no, it wasn't necessary. All that is just a matter of how quickly they can be removed, but beyond that we didn't have to be too concerned with it in rehearsal. Actually the orgy scene may be the dullest scene in the show. Its only real tension came from the nudity. I suppose *The Dirtiest Show in Town* lived up to its title because we did get very heavy at points. But I don't think there was anything embarrassing going on onstage. The orgy scene is very stylized and it was done very frankly. There wasn't any tease.

"A number of people condemned the show without having even seen it. Elliot Norton, for instance, wrote a big piece attacking 'dirty shows' without having seen us. I remember I was having difficulty casting the second company because there really aren't that many people who are beautiful and can act. So I called a leading agent and said, 'Hello, I'm Tom Eyen and I was wondering if you have any people who might fit into my show.' She immediately snapped that she didn't send any of her people to calls for nude shows. And I said, 'Why don't you come down and see us before making up your mind?'"

It would seem, then, that nudity is not too much of a hassle on the creative end, but other considerations come into play when the doors are opened to the public.

Theater is the creation of an illusion and making that illusion a reality in the minds of those watching. One tries to make the audience think of the people onstage not as actors repeating lines, but as real people involved in real situations (which is not to imply that actors are not real people). But as soon as the clothes come off, the audience automatically starts asking itself the same questions Boni discussed above, and, bam!, there goes the illusion. Watching *Abelard and Heloise,* when the nude scene was played I wasn't thinking, "There are Abelard and Heloise making love," I was thinking, "There are Keith Michell and Diana Rigg naked onstage." Which is understandable because Miss Rigg, aside from being an immensely gifted actress, is also one of the most beautiful women around. Of course, while I was thinking of this, I'd stopped concentrating on the play itself. The reality had been broken, and it took several valuable minutes before I could again believe in what was happening.

Regarding nudity's erotic potential, I'm afraid this is another instance in which films can do it better. It is natural that one should feel a stronger physical attraction to a beautiful naked lady blown up to gigantic proportions on a screen than a beautiful naked lady standing yards away. This is a case in which what we learned in college physics about the gravitational attraction between two masses or bodies seems to have a very apt esthetic application.

I don't believe that the appeal of theater as a medium is based on physical involvement. Of course, the actuality of live performers is a characteristic that helps make the theater something special, but the interaction between the live performer and his audience is not a physical but a spiritual interaction. Stage presence means the communication of a personality, but this communication is based on emotional rather than physical projection. In fact, when, in the course of experimentation, actors have broken through the fourth wall to make direct contact with the audience, the audience reaction is usually one of self-consciousness and embarrassment, a reaction which is to my mind a more impenetrable barrier than the thickest of fourth walls. I do not mean to say that these experiments have no purpose, but I think that physical contact with an actor and belief in the part that the actor is playing are mutually exclusive. This may be useful in presentations reflecting a Pirandellian quality, but in terms of maintaining the illusion of reality which, as a rule, we as playwrights (whether traditional or experimental in orientation) try to project, it can prove destructive.

In recent seasons, I have seen a number of other productions employing

nudity which have tended to bear out my conclusions. In the Chelsea
Theater production of *Total Eclipse,* the Christopher Hampton play about
Verlaine and Rimbaud, one of the key scenes was a lengthy and quite
graphic nude homosexual love scene by the two leads. I doubt that during
his scene the audience was thinking much about Verlaine and Rimbaud. I,
for one, was wondering, "Jesus, how can these two guys perform this scene
in front of a nightly audience of strangers sitting a few yards away?"

In Ira Levin's *Veronica's Room,* Regina Baff was handed a double problem
in trying to maintain the illusion of reality. Towards the end of the play her
character was murdered and then her body was stripped. It's difficult
enough to persuade an audience that a character being played by a live actor
is dead, but the addition of nudity was too much. The audience inevitably
thought, "That actress is nude," which immediately reminded it of the fact
that that was an actress up there giving a performance, which immediately
negated beliving that the character was dead.

The only truly effective use of nudity I have seen was in David Storey's
The Changing Room. True, there was an initial jarring of the illusion when the
men began disrobing, but, partially because there was no sexual activity
involved and partially because the cast was made up of actors the public had
not known outside of the play, it was relatively easy to accept the reality
being offered. Of course, the fact that the play was brilliantly written, acted
and directed helped.

The future of nudity in the theater? Tom Eyen believes that we have only
begun to experiment, adding that he thinks nudity could be used very
effectively in a production of *A Streetcar Named Desire.* I have my reservations
about this last proposition, but it seems that as long as playmakers believe in
its box office advantages, esthetics or no esthetics, epidermis will continue
to be displayed.

How to Survive an Off-Off-Broadway Triumph And Confessions Of a Born Loser

By Gloria Gonzalez

You can stop any person on the street and ask them the turning point of their life. And they'll tell you! Right down to the day and hour they 1. "quit that deadend job"; 2. "took the mail-order correspondence course"; 3. "divorced the stiff"; 4. "joined the Jehovah Witnessess" or 5. "moved to Florida."

There are enough happy endings walking around town to make one hope there may still be a few potential sunrises for the seekers.

I had a "turning point" once—and if you're looking for a happy end . . . you won't find it here. (Go out and get your own.)

It happened, one evening, somewhere in the late 1950s, when I went to see my first theatrical play, *Compulsion*. Since the play dealt with murder, kidnapping, depravity, the class struggle, politics, homosexuality, capital punishment, courtroom drama, attempted rape, the "Superman" theory —and for a change of pace, bird watching—it seems, in retrospect, that it was an accidental wise choice on my part. My cram course on the theater saved me years in attending individual plays on those subjects.

Compulsion also sparked my own insanity in that I, too, could write plays. I managed to live with my affliction for nearly ten years before it manifested itself in physical, discernible symptoms when I wrote my first one-act play. I was obviously no longer in control. I had been had.

In the process of having my first one-act play produced off off Broadway, I lost: weight, sleep, appetite, friends, money, a gall bladder, relatives, two directors, four actresses, one theater, a stage manager, my car (towed away), sense of humor and all innocence.

Okay. It was my first play. A complete novice. But I had some things going for me. Namely, ten years' experience as a daily newspaper reporter with a strong, hard-earned background in murders, airplane hijackings, suicide, political indictments, night court, sewer ordinances and the PTA combat zone.

Clearly, I was not to be toyed with.

My demise began one summer day when I answered an ad in *Show Business* placed by a production company that was seeking one-act plays. I bundled up my seven-character play, enclosed a self-addressed-stamped-envelope and jogged to the post office.

A month later the producers called me in. No sleep the night before. I'm thinking ahead to the movie sale and whether Steve McQueen is available for the lead. After much agony, I relent and will accept Joe Namath as a substitute.

My first crash from the heights is the Eighth Avenue office of the producers: on the second floor of a candy store. (What the hell, maybe Prince started this way!)

Once inside, one of the three partners of the company informs me that he loves the script but can't put it on because of the cost involved when dealing with seven characters. (It would be a year later that I learn that a 50-character play and a two-character play cost the same to produce off off Broadway: nothing! No one gets paid—actor, playwright, director, stage manager.)

Then the second partner inquires if I have any "less character" plays. I tell him about the one I just finished, *Let's Hear It for Miss America!*, which involves only the beauty contestant and her mother. He replies something like: "Whydon'tyousenditintousrightawayandletushavealookatitto seeifithasanysocialrelevanceorsomething." (He's a method actor.) I send the play and five months later—now the dead of winter—partner three calls to say, "We're putting on your play."

I drop the phone on my foot, gag on my cigarette smoke, bang my head on the table while leaning down to retrieve the phone and the thing flies up and hits me in the mouth. I laugh. I'm produceable, baby!

Next month a contract arrives. It takes seven pages to tell me I will not be paid a cent, no one else can read the play for 18 months, and if the play—by some quirk—ever makes money, most of it goes to the producers. I can't wait to sign! A "civilian" friend—a toll taker at the Lincoln Tunnel—cautions me against signing. I drive to New York and tell the three partners I can't sign without legal advice.

For two and a half hours (while my car is being towed to the West Side waterfront against its will) the trio informs me (but at least free of charge) how uncommonly dumb, ungrateful, insensitive, brazen and UNPROFES-SIONAL I am. I agree with them . . . begin hating my own dumbness (which till then I thought I had concealed pretty well) and crawl out into the street where I inform a policeman that my car has been stolen. He makes a call and tells me it was towed away. Now four people think I'm dumb.

I can't even drive through the Lincoln Tunnel to seek comfort with my friend. Clearly, I have blown my entire future . . . in the very least, my life.

I send the contract to the Dramatists Guild and they tell me, in polite language, I'm a damn fool if I sign. I call the producers. They say sign or go back to newspapers. I'm not that dumb. I sign. Right on the spot. We are now into February . . . a Friday . . . the 13th, to be exact.

Okay. We move on to St. Mary's Hospital in Hoboken, it's March, I left my gall bladder somewhere in surgery on the seventh floor and the producers call to announce a production meeting in preparation for meeting the rest of the company. (Mine is one of three plays on the bill.)

I pull out the intravenous and announce to my doctor I've never felt better. He sticks it back in and says "you're nuts." A week later I bust out—with medical permission.

I arrive at the first production meeting and am immediately overwhelmed by the assembly of arty, theatrical, heavy, philosophical, professional peo-ple I am now associated with. If the victory isn't sweet enough, I'm intro-duced to a director of La Mama fame, who has consented to nurture my little *Miss America*. I fight the impulse to break out into Irving Berlin's song.

Two weeks later—in an ugly, grime-coated loft—we hold auditions and 50 actresses arrive to read for a part in my play. The director likes none of them and settles instead for an actress we meet in the elevator who's come to meet her boy friend. (Talk about creative casting!) Two nights later she gets a paying job—doing a commercial for Bounty Paper Towels—and we resume casting.

This time we're in an actual theater, the Courtyard Playhouse on West 45th Street where our performances (all six of them) will be held. There's no stopping my parade now! That is, until the next day, when the director, my Miss America and her mother—the second one—walk out.

We're now 15 days from opening night and the other two plays have been rehearsing regularly. Regularly, that is, since they obtained their second director and cast.

But when all looks darkest, the producers produce a beautiful, tall, lanky redhead with sleepy green eyes. My new director! She reads my play and spends three hours explaining it to me. She "uncovers" at least 50 hidden "values." I'm stunned! I didn't remember writing one.

We audition again and search the city for a mother and a beauty contestant. (My sense of humor posts its provisional closing notice.) We find a mother—actress Evelyn Ward—who has lately gained fame as the real-life mother of David Cassidy of the Partridge Family . . . and we lose the theater. We're now in a third-floor walkup loft on West 14th Street. It is almost August, and 11 days from opening night. I convince myself that if they rehearse 20 hours a day—with four hours for sleeping and eating—we'll make it!

My optimism has a short run. The director and lead actress walk out after three days. (The director borrows five dollars cab fare from me. She must have been planning a long journey.)

With what seems like only hours before opening night, we gain the services of a new director, the veteran actress and performer, Sue Lawless. Someone notices we don't have an actress to play the lead.

"No problem," says the producer. He lends us his secretary, who, besides typing letters and going out for coffee, is an actress.

Now we're flying! Six days before opening we assemble our entire cast (two bodies) and begin rehearsals. The first thing that has to go—I'm told by the director—is pages of dialogue. The actresses can't possibly learn so many lines in such a short time. I try to explain that you can't cut random lines out of a comedy because they set up punch lines in later scenes. The director nods as she cuts away. (At this point, my sense of humor carries out its threat. It pulls a walkout and with it some of the best comedy dialogue from the play—they stride off, giggle in giggle.)

Two faulty suicide attempts later, my play opens to an SRO crowd which consists mainly of people who were formerly associated with the production. Head producer, who is now directing one of the plays after the director disappeared, sits broodingly in one of the 50 wooden chairs waiting for the lights to dim. They not only dim, but one explodes over an actor's head. A spark from the electrical wiring lands on his lip as he attempts to probe love. Very effective!

The audience, which didn't pay a cent to get in, rushes out of the theater after the third play. But they trail far behind the playwrights and actors who race into the streets for safety.

The second night, a summer thunderstorm blackens the city and many people appear seeking shelter. Few notice that a play of great "hidden values" is in progress.

Next night, the August temperature soars into the top 90s and the audience drowns in its own perspiration. The only applause comes when Miss America's mother drinks water from a cup. This is class material!

Okay. Even the gods can't be against me forever. Even they must have summer vacations.

A relative attends, imagines herself slandered by certain dialogue, and stalks out—flicking her sweat on the audience.

The following evening, Dr. Russell Barber, a handsome, blonde CBS executive shows up with a friend from Columbia Pictures. The actresses blow their lines and the play dies a prolonged death. Harold Callen, my instructor of playwriting at The New School, offers a hesitant handshake and departs with an air of bereavement. I wonder if he holds himself partly to blame.

At last (who says there are no happy endings) . . . closing night! I can't bear to watch the show for what seems the hundredth time, so Sue Lawless and I sit on the floor behind a row of seats (unable to see the performance) listening to the dialogue, each with our private thoughts of where in the hell we went wrong in our formative years.

Suddenly, at a point in the play which never even drew a snicker before, the audience howls! The howling gains momentum and people are stamping their feet to help release this great wave of laughter that has captured them. Sue and I are stunned. We look at each other blankly. She leaps up to see what is happening on stage and drops back to the floor, convulsed in laughter. The audience roars. Sue holds her stomach and can't speak. I'm numb. I'm delirious! I'm a hit!

I jump to my feet—ready to accept my acclaim—and stand in shock. Miss America's left nipple is hanging out of her sarong—unknown to her. The audience goes wild. The actress, who assumes it is her performance that has ignited the house, begins hamming it up for more laughs. She parades around the floor, her bare arms over her head, her legs wide apart, singing: "You can take Salem out of the country . . . But!"

I'm ecstatic! I tell Sue it's great! We keep the nipple in from now on. Rather, out! Sue agrees but says it could use some makeup and proper lighting.

The audience gives the cast a standing ovation.

During intermission, someone runs in with a copy of *Show Business*. I'm told my play is reviewed. I grab for it! I tear through the pages, my eyes darting over the black print, and there on the top of the page, the reviewer proclaims to all the subscribers, that *Miss America*—the demon which consumed me for an entire year—is "a piece of froth."

Confessions of a Born Loser

There are failures—and there are failures! We know them well. . . . the underachievers, also-rans, underdogs and your run of the gin-mill loser. We comfort them, love them, suffer with them and more often than not marry them.

They are the weeds in Mother Nature's landscape and society thrives on their misfortunes. Without them. . . . who would inspire our Pulitzer Prize plays, novels and films? They have their rightful place in the sun—however unearned—and if they weren't such total zeros, they would realize their collective power and organize their calamities. Whole networks of "Losers' Leagues" could spring up overnight, only to go out of business the following day—thereby, even in defeat living up to their letterhead.

But enough about them. Let's talk about me—a loser of the first order.

Unlike my fellow washouts, my affliction was not thrust upon me by society, environment or the system. No, mine was perpetrated by my parents at birth. What they perpetrated on me, a comedy writer—(I can't in all fairness hit them with that rap, too)—is one of life's least amusing incidents: namely, my birth date.

My devious parents, in concert, conspired to make certain that their child would miss the "Golden Age" of silent movies, talkies, radio and television.

That they were able to conceal this nefarious plot from me for so long is ample evidence of their cunning design and meticulous planning. In fact, it was only three months ago that the ugly truth was revealed to me.

Until then—like all naive, unsuspecting writers—I innocently assumed that my lack of success had to do with the commonly-known fact that producers and editors have no taste. I was happily prepared to wait out their annual replacement by younger, more sensitive minds. I would still be humming to my mailbox each day had not my fantasy been permanently shattered by—of all evils—my agent.

It was he, three months ago, who spoke my doom: "Sorry, kid, you missed it!"

"What? What?" I trembled. Had I forgotten to include a stamped, self-addressed envelope? Had I misplaced the first act of my three-act comedy? Was my obligatory scene less than obligatory?

"What did I do wrong?" I wept.

"Simple," he said, taking my manuscripts from his file and flinging them in my general direction, "you were born too late."

"I couldn't help it! Honest!" I pleaded.

He smiled. There was even a hint of unused tenderness, a fleeting glimpse—even to my untrained eye—that maybe before he became an agent he had been a human being. "Look, kid, it's this way," he said, patting 10 per cent of my hand. "You're a comedy writer, right?"

I choked. Was it an indictable offense?

"That stuff you write is terrific—knocks me out. You would have made a fortune at Mack Sennett's studio. Or even the early Depression two-reelers—people would've lined up for blocks. Or back in the days of radio—I could've gotten you to Fred Allen, Jack Benny, Amos 'n' Andy. You name it!"

He started for the door, careful not to sidestep my manuscripts.

"Then!" he glowed, "then there was the Golden Age of Television! You could've commuted between Sid Caesar, Milton Berle, *I Love Lucy, Our Miss Brooks*! You could've called your own shots!"

As he reached for the doorknob, I flung myself at his bell-bottomless cuffs.

"I won't even tell you about the Golden Age of Broadway when 200 plays opened every season and there was an audience for all of them. Producers actually used to read scripts and talk to playwrights! Anybody who could write 'At Rise' and 'Final Curtain' and throw in some middle dialogue could get a production!"

I clawed the carpet.

"Sorry, kid," he edged me away with his high-heeled canvas clog.

I pleaded unashamedly: "Is there no hope? No chance? Nothing?"

He shook his hand-dried, layered hair style and looked down at me. "If you'd been around forty, thirty, even twenty years ago—then!"

Ugly word, "then." Never knew that before. Ugly.

I begged. Was I to be cast off—permanently entombed on my pile of color-coordinated leatherette script covers? Was I doomed to be an eternal victim of my parents' nocturnal conspiracy? Was there no statute of limitations on this conjugal crime that had been committed thirty-three years ago?

My tears and gasping protestations must have telegraphed my grief, for he paused at the door, drew in an air-conditioned breath and offered me the comfort and wisdom of his transplanted heart.

"Cheer up, kid," he smiled, gently removing my hold on his leg. "There's still the Golden Age of cassettes!"

The Theater of the 1970s Surveyed by Its Authors

The playwrights, lyricists and composers of the modern theater are generally distressed by the problematical state of its art and disarray of its economics—but their dedication is still showing. A goodly number are determined to persevere.

According to replies to a survey circulated among dramatists now or recently active in the New York theater, straight-play authors are equally divided on the question of whether or not the modern theater is able to provide them with an audience for their work; musical authors are in the afflrmative by two to one. Many dramatists decline to estimate the percentage of today's audience actually *attainable* by their work, but among those who do the consensus of optimists and pessimists is 15 per cent.

Questioned as to which element of the *available* audience (presumably that 15 per cent) is most empathic to their work, dramatists give "younger audiences" a plurality of citations. Almost every conceivable element of the audience is cited at least once as favoring the work of a particular musical or straight-play author, however, including "older audiences," "literate, intelligent playlovers," "TV-type audiences," "upper middle class," etc.

A majority of both musical and straight-play dramatists feels that elements are missing from the available audience which, if attainable, might be particularly empathic to their work. In a seeming contradiction, "young people" also receive a plurality of citations in this "missing" category, in which "middle income, age, class" and "less affluent audiences" are also cited prominently.

Dramatists' opinions as to how to bring these missing audiences into the theater give "lower ticket prices" a plurality but name lower production

327

costs only once. In descending order of frequency, they also call for better and/or different kinds of plays, improvement in producers' judgment, publicity and audience education, more perceptive critics and more subsidy.

Musical and straight-play dramatists agree that esthetically the theater of the 1970s is about 36 per cent a dramatists' theater. By a margin of three to one they believe it is in a process of change, but they are in disagreement as to the direction of that change. Many sense a strong drift away from collaborative theater toward increasing reliance on the playwright; as many feel that the director is steadily taking over. Certainly the director receives the largest number of citations as an influence on the interior esthetics of the dramatists' work when they address their attention to the subject of their colleagues—director, producer, performers, agent and others. The result of this influence, in the combined view of musical and straight-play authors, is mixed or uncharacterizable in the large majority of cases; but where judgement on the directors' influence is definitely made, "good" far outnumbers "bad."

A very large proportion of those playwrights, lyricists and composers who were working in the theater a quarter century or a decade ago would have held different views on these matters in the past than the ones they express now, providing still more evidence, if it were needed, that the dramatist's art form has been changing in the second half of the 20th century.

The above are some of the conclusions and compilations to be derived from the survey answers of 63 straight-play and musical authors, representing a sampling of about 10 per cent of all active Dramatists Guild members produced on or off Broadway (which is to say, the very large majority of American and many European dramatists).

Most of the replies were signed (though signature was optional), and many signed comments on the status and function of the contemporary dramatist appear at the end of this report. The questionnaire was color-keyed three ways to identify unsigned straight-play authors, lyricist-librettists and composers as to category. The replies were a sampling of the full breadth of the theater's authorship as well as its depth, in every discipline and in every career stage from the just beginning to the most distinguished. The prominent citation of "younger audiences" as both a "most empathic" and a "missing" element of contemporary audiences makes it obvious that the sampling includes numbers of new authors as well as numbers of traditionalists whose work illuminated the stages of the 1940s and 1950s.

Every reply is taken into account in the following report; but since some ignored certain questions and others gave multiple answers, the result numbers never exactly equal the number of replies.

The Audience

Question #1 asked: *Is the theater of the 1970s providing you with an audience for your work? Can you express your yes or no answer in terms of the percentage of the attainable audience you are actually reaching?* On balance, the dramatists feel that there is an audience for their work in today's theater, but the majority are unwilling to estimate its size. In the opinion of those who did venture an estimate, the audience they are reaching is only 15 per cent of the attainable audience, the elusive ghost audience that makes its presence felt once in a while but is not regularly drawn to the theater in present circumstances.

Of the dramatists who chose to give an estimate, not one was willing to guess that he or she was reaching more than 50 per cent of those attainable, not even one of the musical authors. One musical author obviously felt he *should* be reaching a large number of people, because he voted "no" to the first part of the question even though he estimated that he is indeed reaching 50 per cent now. The figures in the compilation of replies to this question pretty much speak for themselves (see the statistical summary of Question #1 accompanying this report). Even though the majority believes there is an audience for their work, an uncomfortably large minority of dramatists believes there is *not*, and those who do are either unsure or pessimistic about its size.

Marginal comments accompanying the answers to Question #1 repeatedly emphasized the decentralization of the present-day stage audience: "Everywhere except on Broadway," or "Modest audience in N. Y., large audience across the U.S., or the broader vision "Off Broadway a

☆

Q. Is the theater of the 1970s providing you with an audience for your work? Can you express your yes or no answer in terms of the percentage of the attainable audience you are actually reaching?

	50%	25%	10%+	9%–0	No % Given
ALL DRAMATISTS					
Yes (29)	2	3	2	3	19
No (24)	1	3	2	10	8
PLAYWRIGHTS					
Yes (18)	1	3	2	1	11
No (18)	0	2	2	8	6
MUSICAL AUTHORS					
Yes (11)	1	0	0	2	8
No (6)	1	1	0	2	2

few thousands, on Broadway many thousands, on film millions, on TV millions."

A musical author noted tersely: "Not being produced, not reaching any." One playwright commented, "I'd put it the other way round—I can't provide work for todays' audience," and another stated "Wrong question. The real question is, am I providing the theater with the kind of plays its audiences like?"

The few who chose to mention the size of audiences in Europe in their replies to this question also cited very small percentages. One European playwright added the consoling remark, "But the theater is *not* meant to be a mass medium." Another reported from France that "The audience is half what it was two years ago."

Question #2 asked: *Which element of this available audience seems particularly empathic to your work?* Here the dramatists were invited to name the most favorable element of the small but still *available* audience for the theater. A significant plurality of 18 named "younger audiences" as most empathic to their work. Two dramatists claimed both the young and the old. One feels that 75 per cent of the whole available vertical audience is in his corner; another that only 40 per cent digs him. Only one answered that nobody but nobody, is out there waiting: "I have the pervasive sense that there would be *no* audience for the kind of theater I write and enjoy writing." There were six don't-knows, about a dozen no-repliers, and somewhat surprisingly there wasn't much difference in the response of musical and non-musical authors, whose replies were spread over a wide area in both classifications.

Here are the audience elements cited as "particularly empathic," with the number of citations in parentheses:

Younger audiences, including "under 40," "high school" and "University" (18).

Literate, intelligent playlovers (4).

Regional theater and stock (4).

Upper middle and middle class (3).

Off-Broadway audiences (2).

Blacks (2).

Broadway audiences, apolitical adults, socially aware, middle aged, parents of grown children, off-off-Broadway audiences, almost everyone except effetes, over-30s, artists, TV-type audiences, serious theater people, urbanites (1 each).

One lyricist answered the question rather plaintively: "Those that enjoy it, I guess." One long-established playwright supported his claim on younger audiences: "The Generation Gap is getting narrower in the 1970s (the young are getting older)." Here are some other characterizations:

"Intelligent people open to mystery and power theater and self-knowledge or crisis of spirit, not blind opinionated smug frightened non-growing sleepy dreamy fertilizer."

"Uncynical audiences and non-destructive critics in communities where theatergoing is a joy, not a duty or necessitating cashing in an entire bank account for one evening in the theater."

"TV killed Broadway and night clubs, and it is making simpletons of possible audiences."

"I'm a diehard Broadway playwright (as opposed to off Broadway) and that is the audience I aim for and hope to reach. The problem of course is not the audience—which will come if the show is a hit—but in locating the producer willing to produce the untried, new, serious play. Alas, such a creature no longer exists (for proof, look at the newspaper listings)."

Question #3 asked: *Is any element missing from this available audience which you feel would be particularly empathic to your work? If so, which? How might it be attracted?* More than half the replies of both musical and straight-play dramatists agreed that there are elements missing in the available audience. Here again, "young people" are cited in a plurality of the replies, indicating that if there is a significantly large group of dramatists who feel that they are reaching young people (as per the replies to Question #2), there is also a significantly large group of dramatists who feel they are *not* reaching them and would wish to. A very small group of 8 dramatists are of the opinion that there is no major element missing from their audience; they tend to be the same ones who feel they are reaching both young and old (as per the Question #2 answers) or are content with the audience they are reaching outside New York City. One "no"-answering playwright commented: "The New York Broadway audience is the greatest in the world—but it's also the most demanding and refuses to accept second best. The record shows that the real masterpeices of the theater receive critical acclaim and appreciative audiences. Occasionally a play like *Moonchildren* fails to capture the audience, but it was the fault of the producer—not the critics or cast—that it failed in its publicity campaign. There was not sufficient advance publicity to build up big sales prior to the opening nor enough money in the till to insure running for more than a week. It's not enough to invent the best mouse trap. The path to the door won't be beaten without creative advertising."

A "no"-answering composer commented: "I can't think of audiences as 'elements.' They are people bound together by a simultaneous experience. I believe all people have a craving for this experience if the work itself is good. But this is seldom so, and the audience is commonly cheated."

More than 20 of the responding dramatists were unable or unwilling to answer this question. One don't-know commented: "Generally, it might be an idea if newspaper advertisements included a synopsis of the plot to each play. Let the audience choose what it wants to see." Another stated: "I happen to like plays that affirm the worth of an ideal—without being Polyanna about it—but this is not the life style or the art style today. The theater, like life, moves in little cliques, and there are few cliques for believers these days. And I wouldn't like them if there were. I don't think the theater should be approached like a political campaign." Another dismissed us: "These questions are simply too complicated to answer here."

The majority who *did* answer Question #3 in the affirmative were generous and wide-ranging in their suggestions as to how the missing audience elements might be brought into the theatergoing fold. We report these "yes" replies and their accompanying suggestions in as much detail as we can in the summary below. Each cited element of the audience in the listing received one mention unless otherwise specified by a number in parentheses. Individual dramatists' suggestions of ways to attract each specific element appear beneath each heading in the list, either in a direct quote or in a general identifying phrase, again with a number in parentheses in the case of multiple citations.

Young people (14), including "students," "young marrieds," "teen agers," "under 35," "the TV generation":
"Better dissemination via works and productions in community-

oriented theaters with ongoing developing interest in real theater paralleled by better education and preparation of/for its meaning."

"*Théâtre complet*, as they call it."

Lower ticket prices (6).

More courageous producers (2).

Imaginative publicity.

"Younger audiences must be trained to the theatergoing habit, particularly in the New York area. In the Soviet Union, theatergoing is part of the school program, from the very youngest ages. We must cultivate and build a whole new generation of dedicated theater-lovers."

"Critics more empathic to the entertainment interests of the audience."

"If my plays were just done. If producers and artistic directors were not such dull-heads."

"By bringing theater up to the level of movies and the recording industry in terms of innovation, creativity and relevance."

"Free tickets and school junkets, combined with after-show discussions onstage."

"The TV generation is becoming more and more alienated from traditional theater. Pragmatically, it *is* attracted by TV names; but this is depressingly non-theater. Long-range turnaround is complicated."

Middle-aged, middle income, middle class (7):

"Fire every existing critic who has been a critic over four years. Their present reference point is 1940. Critics should be appointed by editorial staffs every four years least they become jaded, backward-looking ancestor-worshippers. We are a theater community. No community appoints a mayor for life."

Lower ticket prices (2).

"By making the New York theater district safe for evening theatergoing."

More courageous producers.

Imaginative publicity.

Lower production costs.

All classes and ages (3):

"By generally improving the health of the theater; more intelligent and venturesome producers, and subsidized theater."

"By allowing a show to stay open long enough for word of mouth reviews to get around (critics ignore any taste but their own). The economics forbid this to happen. Unless you have a hit it's useless to try, so it's better just to forget it."

Lower ticket prices.

Intelligent, passionate, artistically-oriented (3):
    "A boot up everyone's arse."
    "Intellectuals have all but given up on the theater. Good plays would bring them back, but good plays are seldom produced."

The non-affluent (3), including "those unable to pay the high cost of tickets, even off Broadway:"
    Subsidized theater.
    Lower ticket prices (2).

Real people (2), including "the common man":
    "As has probably been said for centuries, we are losing the common man. He comes to New York, goes to a Broadway show (because that is what legend dictates), is not especially titillated by what he sees and doesn't come back again. We can't go on like this forever. I think the 'social' theater (and that includes black, war, sexual, etc.) is of special interest to New Yorkers—and they are around us, they are our friends —but I think we are just entertaining ourselves. We are not talking to the world."
    "Lower prices and have more plays that genuinely entertain—so that audiences want to come *back* to the theater again and again."

Blacks (2), including "certain hardcore black ghetto residents:"
    "Probably by television."
    "By presenting (and in the first instance writing) plays and musicals with which blacks of all ages and classes can identify. I am not referring just to sociological themes. This audience wants light entertainment too, but one black face in the chorus will hardly get this audience flocking to the box office! To judge by many of our 'white liberal' authors, America is lily white from top to bottom."

The foreign film audience (2):
    "By an intelligent producer—and a creative one too (that might be asking too much.)"
    "Expert, imaginative promotion."

Blue-collar audiences (2):
    "One wishes to be heard by all, especially by those who make things."
    "Less expensive tickets, available theaters in other neighborhoods."

Older people (2):
    Lower ticket prices (2).

Drop-ins:
    "More radio advertising, more Ticketron, better street conditions."

Serious theater fans:

"Those interested in serious plays with humanistic themes relevant to our times, and not current obscurism."

Money itself:

"Rave reviews."

Many suggestions in the foregoing replies are related to each other in groups. The summary of the theater's needs cited by the dramatists comes out as follows, with the number of citations in parentheses: lower ticket prices (15), better and/or different plays (10), abler producers (7), improved publicity and advertising (6), audience education (4), abler critics (3), subsidy (3), decentralization (2), TV promotion (2), safer theater district (2), lower production costs (1).

Colleagues

The first three questions concerned the size and character of the contemporary theater audience. The next three attempted to probe the dramatist's relation to his theater and those who work in it with him.

Question #4 asked: *Esthetically, to what extent is the theater of the 1970s a dramatists' theater, expressed in percentage? Is this changing? If so, in what direction?* Almost two-thirds of the responding dramatists consented to express an opinion of their position in the theater in terms of actual or approximate (i.e., "strong," "small," etc.) percentages—see the statistical summary of Question #4 accompanying this report.

On the average, the dramatists see their part as amounting to about 36 per cent of the action, with straight-play and musical replies averaging out to within one percentage point of each other. But in this case as in so many others an average is only a part of the story. Eleven of 28 responding playwrights and five of 12 responding musical authors view our modern stage as 50 per cent or better a dramatists' theater. According to these

☆

Q. Esthetically, to what extent is the theater of the 1970s a dramatists' theater, expressed in percentage?

	ALL	PLAYWRIGHTS	MUSICAL AUTHORS
75+%	8	7	1
50+%	8	4	4
25+%	9	6	3
10+%	10	6	4
9%−0	5	5	0
Average	36.3%	36.6%	35.7%

figures, then, 40 per cent of the dramatists feel that they are the major force in the modern theater, 60 per cent that they are not.

An overwhelming majority of 3 to 1 believe that this position of the dramatist in the modern theater is changing—frequently but not always for the worse, with a noticeable drift toward the director as a rising force. The few who believe the dramatist's position is *not* changing also tend to evaluate his present importance much lower—an average of only 20 per cent, with only one, a playwright, in the 50 per cent-plus bracket. Two of these no-change repliers believe the playwright is entrenched: "They still need us, though they'd rather not, in spite of the pious noises they make," and "The theater, I think, is always the dramatists' and I take no heed of the complaints about directors or stars having too great an influence. I simply don't believe it."

Others suggested in one way or another that the lack of change might be owing to esthetic stagnation: "Except for a tiny minority there is nothing but useless 'stuff' being shown as 'theater' " and "Critics have stuck the theater's head into the sand and so it explodes in variety shows in a desperate effort to bring life into it. The dramatic function is served by classics" and, in a sort of shorthand, "Status quo—Orwell—Follow the Leader."

The large majority of repliers who believe the dramatists' position in the theater *is* changing hold different views about that change's character and direction. Here is a summary of their answers and comments for the latter part of Question #4, with the number of citations appearing in parentheses.

Changing generally for the worse (8):
"With the possible exception of Neil Simon, there is no playwright whose name alone insures an advance sale. In Paris any play by Andre Roussin will automatically have an audience, regardless of who is in the company or who is the producer. But on Broadway even plays by Arthur Miller, Tennessee Williams and Edward Albee close the week they open unless they're cast with stars, receive critical raves and are launched with a big publicity build-up."

"The 1960s were a time for playmakers. This is less so now, alas."

"Toward a smaller percentage of contemporary dramas and a larger percentage of classic authors revived."

Changing generally for the better (6):
"I believe the 'razzle-dazzle' of the 1960s will be replaced by a move towards simplicity of form—and more emphasis on 'perfected' work by writer, director and actor."

"Becoming more a dramatists' theater, thanks to regional theater."

"Upward, I believe."

Changing toward director-dominated and/or collaborative working relationships (6):

"The dramatist is subject more and more to the star system both as to actors and directors."

"It seems evident that actors, directors, producers, etc., getting extremely restless from this protracted period of not having any scripts to actually perform and yet wanting to keep busy, have championed a new sort of theater (which must be called a movement) generally based on what actors and directors can do when they don't have much of a script; i.e. body movements, studio exercises, improvisations, tableaux and spectaculars . . . and revivals. There is more of this (because there are more actors, directors and producers than there are writers) so it becomes the dominant movement. I don't think this is out of desire, purpose or even choice, but just necessity."

"The overestimated importance of the director, as in films, is coming to the fore in the theater."

"Becoming more and more like Hollywood: a collaborative compromise, except in some rare cases."

"Toward directorial flamboyance."

"In some cases, directors are becoming auteurs."

Changing in character and esthetics of the dramatists' work (5):

"More musicals—fewer dramas."

"Toward 'traditional' theater."

"The only visible change is in black theater, which is being ethnically rather than commercially supported; this accounts for its vitality and (sadly) narrowness of purpose."

"If so, it is changing more toward shock value than well-written literature."

Changing away from director-dominated and/or collaborative working relationships (3):

"I think the theater of the director or the improvisational theater (where actors conduct jam sessions) has sunk into the west. A strong theater has *always* been a dramatists' theater—in the past, now, and in the future."

"Soon the playwright will dominate the theater completely. The age of the director-oriented and actor-oriented theater seems to be over for the moment."

Changing under economic pressures (2):

"I feel that the esthetic or intelligent audience is not being adequately considered by realtors."

Question #5 asked: *Please rate the following colleagues on a scale of 0 to 10 on the amount of influence exerted on the interior esthetics of your work between its leaving the typewriter (or piano) and opening night. Please indicate whether any such influence brought about good, bad, mixed or no results.* Having arrived at a consensus via Question #4 that the dramatist is about 36 per cent of the action today, the questionnaire then proceeded in Question #5 to try to form a collective opinion on how the action is distributed over the remaining 64 per cent in the group experience of play production. One reply questioned the phrase "interior esthetics;" by it, we meant esthetics as opposed to economics (not whether the agent was able to sell the play, for example, but whether he brought influence to bear to alter it in order to make it more saleable). By *interior* esthetics (a serviceable if not a felicitous phrase) we meant the esthetics of the script or score itself, not the sound level of the singing or the size of the proscenium opening or other largely *exterior* values of physical production (though we are ready to admit that often they are inseparable).

The produced dramatists who received this questionnaire were asked to reduce the degree and kind of esthetic influence to numbers for the purposes of Question #5—not because of an obsession with numerical values, but in an effort to express an extremely complex and interlocking situation in both comprehensive and comprehendable terms. The result is the elaborate statistical summary accompanying this section of the report. The director commands the most attention from the dramatist, with the most citations and a relatively high factor of influence on esthetics, particularly in his influence for good. The producer is next in the number of citations, but not nearly so strong an influence in either direction. The star, we see, can be a powerful influence for good.

For the most part in the answers to Question #5 the numbers speak for themselves (see the accompanying summary). No additional comment was asked for here, but some was forthcoming, as follows:

"Theater is intensely collaborative."

"I choose performers carefully" (a playwright).

"A producer must be devoted to the theater *per se*."

"Producers' relatives and office help—bad."

"You can't run things like this through a computer, at least I can't. But then I have been lucky—especially in Europe. Directors, stars, producers took the script as written. So did some here—the blessed few who believed the writer knew what he was about. Agents? Very important for the first contact with the right producer."

"I am influenced by good performers very much" (a composer).

"It would seem from my limited New York experience that most dramatists do not have enough knowledge of all the elements that go into a successful production and are therefore unable to make sound judgments in staging. My musical was in the hands of clowns. Old bull shit, to be sure, and my fault; but you asked."

☆

Q. Please rate the following colleagues on a scale of 0 to 10 on the amount of influence exerted on the interior esthetics of your work between its leaving the typewriter (or piano) and opening night. Please indicate whether any such influence brought about good, bad, mixed or no results.

(*Numbers in parentheses give number of citations in the replies. Numbers with decimal points give average cited degree of influence on a scale of 0 to 10*).

Agent

	Good		Mixed		Bad		No
ALL (41)	(8)	4.5	(10)	2.2	(1)	5.0	(22)
PLAYWRIGHTS (26)	(4)	5.5	(9)	2.3	(0)		(13)
COMPOSERS (7)	(3)	4.3	(1)	2.0	(0)		(3)
LIBRETTISTS/LYRICISTS (8)	(1)	1.0	(0)		(1)	5.0	(6)

Director

	Good		Mixed		Bad		No
ALL (52)	(10)	7.8	(33)	6.3	(6)	6.6	(3)
PLAYWRIGHTS (36)	(7)	7.8	(22)	4.9	(6)	6.6	(1)
COMPOSERS (8)	(2)	6.5	(4)	7.6	(0)		(2)
LIBRETTISTS/LYRICISTS (8)	(1)	10.0	(7)	6.6	(0)		(0)

Producer

	Good		Mixed		Bad		No
ALL (47)	(8)	4.6	(28)	5.0	(4)	8.0	(7)
PLAYWRIGHTS (33)	(5)	5.2	(19)	4.7	(4)	8.0	(5)
COMPOSERS (6)	(1)	5.0	(3)	5.0	(0)		(2)
LIBRETTISTS/LYRICISTS (8)	(2)	3.0	(6)	4.4	(0)		(0)

Star

	Good		Mixed		Bad		No
ALL (43)	(9)	7.1	(21)	4.0	(3)	5.0	(10)
PLAYWRIGHTS (29)	(6)	6.9	(16)	3.8	(3)	5.0	(4)
COMPOSERS (7)	(1)	8.0	(1)	10.0	(0)		(5)
LIBRETTISTS/LYRICISTS (7)	(2)	7.5	(4)	3.8	(0)		(1)

Other Performers

	Good		Mixed		Bad		No
ALL (40)	(9)	6.0	(21)	4.5	(1)	5.0	(9)
PLAYWRIGHTS (26)	(5)	6.4	(15)	4.4	(0)		(6)
COMPOSERS (7)	(3)	4.7	(2)	6.5	(0)		(2)
LIBRETTISTS/LYRICISTS (7)	(1)	8.0	(4)	4.3	(1)	5.0	(1)

The following were cited as influences under "Others": costume designer (3 good), set designer (3 good), lighting designer (2 good); audience, co-author, wife, record company, lawyer, conductor (1 good each); author's children, friends, backers, choreographer (1 mixed each); producers' assistants (1 bad).

The Changing Scene

Question #6 addressed itself to the produced dramatist as a member of a changing, developing (and in some ways attenuating) theater: *If your career as a produced dramatist is of about 10 years or longer duration, are there any important ways in which you might have answered these questions differently a decade ago? A quarter century ago?* A keynote answer among the replies was this playwright's simile: "Like an innocent duckling taking a walk in hot sand." Classifying and adding up the replies, we find that 26 dramatists are of the opinion that, yes, their theater did change in important ways over the last decade, usually not for the better.

Eleven dramatists answered no, they would *not* have answered these questions differently a decade ago; and among the quarter-century veterans the reply was also in the affirmative as regards change, by a margin of 10 citations to 3. Three repliers were uncertain as to their answer, and 16 declined to address this particular question. Thus it can be concluded that the sense of change within the art form is very strongly felt by its authors, by the large majority of 36 to 14.

One 25-year veteran maintained that things are as they always were —now as ever, "The theater needs *writing* above all else." Another remarked cheerfully, "I suspect things are looking up a bit, or maybe I'm just more with it." For the most part, though, the comments in this section were gloomily tinted as well as strongly felt, and they bear reporting in

ome detail. One 25-year playwright states that he once would have ans-
vered these questions "enthusiastically," ten years ago he would have done
o "hopefully," but now he regards the dramatist as "the undertaker to a
lying art." Another cites a steady decline in optimism; another that there
vas a different (and presumably better) audience 25 years ago; that ticket
rices were lower; that "there was some hope for a living U.S. theater. Other
omments by 25-year playwrights were:

"The advent of off Broadway has had a great impact on young writers,
who, realizing that there is little hope of their work being accepted by
Broadway producers, turn to that outlet. But the established writers,
when rejected by Broadway, seldom turn to the off-Broadway form of
theater, which with rare exception offers so little financial return. Therefore they give up writing for the theater entirely."

"The New York audience would have seemed most empathic to my
work. Critics were generally of a higher quality—had more literary style
and a higher level of esthetic sensibility. Broadway was safe for straight
drama. The musical was not the absolute monarch it is now."

"TV critics were more responsible—their sneering and sarcasm is appalling. Records were played for months over the air before a musical came
in—audiences wanted to hear the score and see the show. It brought
them in."

"Things were more tightly organized then—fewer producers, stricter
managerial structures and no 'off' media."

The comments on how the dramatists might have answered this questionnaire differently a decade ago expressed some of the same thoughts and
emotions: "With more hope and joy in the theater," "Ten years ago it was
Broadway or nothing," "Most theater, more writers, more interest," "More
diversity of work, better standards, better economics" and "Yes—I would
have had something to say." Here are some of the more detailed ten-year
comments:

"I would not have answered the questionnaire at all. I had assumed the
only important thing was to write the very best I could. I did not realize
you had to fight for your point of view."

"Prices and costs were lower—so the play itself was more important
than the people associated with it."

"It never occurred to me that there would come a time in the New York
theater when a serious play would require so enormous an investment of
capital that it would be folly to produce it."

"There was less emphasis on the director and the 'package.' Producers
took a personal, esthetic interest in plays and playwrights, not merely a
commercial one."

"There was an urban and urbane audience to speak to."

"TV has changed it all. Porno has changed it all."

"Ten years ago I had hopes—dreams—now it's where it is at—ba‹ —and surrounded by whores, pimps and a frightened theater audience."

"I was more optimistic a decade ago—and all my hopes were aimed a‹ New York."

Finally there were these ten-year comments by two of the theater's distin‹ guished modern authors, the first a playwright and the second a composer

"I would have been more idealistic. I would have believed the worl‹ discovers genius in its midst by its own desire to learn truth."

"Ten years ago we were going into the period of 'razzle-dazzle'—o‹ improvisation and quick cuts and nudity and rock and strobe lights an‹ over-amplification. Now we are coming out of it. I look to somethin‹ simpler and better."

Status and Responsibility

The final Question #7 was an invitation to the produced dramatists t‹ comment on their situation today: *Please comment in a word, a sentence, ‹ paragraph or longer on your idea of the dramatist's position and function ir present-day society.* Most repliers chose to make a comment, and most o‹ those signed their statements. Unsigned and signed comments alik‹ tended to bear group resemblances to each other: one group considerin‹ the philosophical implications of playwriting, another its esthetic func‹ tion, another the general condition of the environment, others suc‹ matters as decentralization, opportunity, pressure, publicity, politica‹ influences, etc.

Here are the signed comments on the contemporary dramatist's posi‹ tion and function, in alphabetical order.

The dramatist's position today is lousy. But the gauchist repertory "no‹ fathers, only sons" is losing its supremacy.

—Marcel Achard

The dramatist's function is (1) to earn a living for his family and himself and (2) to try to entertain people for a few hours. His "position," with the possible exception of a half-dozen playwrights, is sitting wistfully in a quiet corner of The Theat-uh, which has become a minor backwater of the arts in this Age of Electronics.

—Lee Adams

The position should be one of adding to the dialogue at the present day on any subject affecting our society. We should take part in the continuing

iscussion of the fears and foibles of our lifetime. Our comments may be
ɔmical, serious or anything in between. Hopefully, in some small way our
ʹork may help change something. At any rate, it should not be merely
ʹaste material. Unfortunately in today's theater—small as it is—we are on
ɪe fringe just as the theater itself is on the fringe. The French have an
xpression, "A fish is rotten from the head down." That's our theater.

—Irv Bauer

I spend most of my time these days in Maine, and out on the Upper
Iississippi where dramatists have no position or function. In my legal
esidence, Connecticut, where I spend three or four months a year,
lramatists are in great demand and serve an important function by being
ʹitty at cocktail parties. The ones who are not witty are invited anyway and
.sked to pass the onion dip.

—Richard Bissell

I feel I owe it to the world to share my ignorance and uncertainty with my
ellow men. I try to reveal my personal vision of life within a contemporary,
ɪntertaining framework. Each dramatist is a soloist, battening on others'
ʹfforts and creations. I expect my co-dramatists to provide me with ideas,
echniques and stimulations which will increase my own skills. Any
lramatist who increases me is my friend. Any who diminishes me by
ʹasting my time, by serving me gilded trays filled with gall and ashes, wins
ny derision. If he makes me smile at truth, weep at beauty and cheer for
evelations of verisimilitude, I envy him—I follow him. And when I have
ʹomething to say onstage, I want to use every theater technique ever
levised to shake *my* audience as my peers have shaken me. I will use the
:heater of the grotesque, the chemical theater, the physiological theater, the
:heater of the absurd; the suburban platitude, the cosmopolitan supercili-
ɔusness, the comic riposte or the tragic shriek *de profundis* . . . anything to
frame my art, anything to move my audience. I don't ask them to agree with
me or march to my composition, but I want them to know my vision, my
perspective, and assess it. And if, for one almost imperceptible moment
they are struck by a possibility of truth, I am satisfied. I am in all my work. A
dramatist who writes for someone else's perceptions has my sympathy, but
not my imprimatur.

—Oscar Brand

To entertain the public! Not just a song and a dance and a joke necessarily
. . . to enthrall, to emotionally involve, to entertain in the broadest sense of
the word. If in the course of entertaining the writer can make the audience
more socially aware, awaken it to new ideas, project a political
viewpoint—all to the good. But when this becomes the prime objective to

the exclusion of "theater," then the writer should seek other forms such a
politics. Should this be misinterpreted as a reactionary statement, I shoul
hasten to add that I very much feel the writer *should* be socially aware and
is incumbent on the *American* writer to create a truer picture of our multi
racial society.

—JOHNNY BRANDON

Open.

—ED BULLINS

I don't think these questions have much relevance to the theater today
What we need, as always, are better plays—but the reasons we're no
getting them are so many, it would take many, many questionnaires to
answer them. Some economic forums on the state of the theater might begin
to approach the problem.

—JEROME CHODOROV

This is extremely difficult for me to answer. So far, I've had two plays
done on Broadway—both extremely commercial plays, both failures. One
Norman, Is That You?, went on to become a huge international hit as well as
mainstay of stock and amateur production in this country. The second one
No Hard Feelings, is set for three countries in Europe so far. I don't think
could write either of these plays any more, however. I would very much like
to write something much more meaningful—even if the chance of success is
slim. I'll simply have to earn my living in other fields such as television and
motion pictures. I now feel that plays cannot merely entertain. They should
also move the playgoer in one way or another.

—RON CLARK

As a lyricist there is more open freedom of expression but less quality
standards. The wit and depth of Cole Porter, Oscar Hammerstein, Larry
Hart seem to have disappeared, and there has been a general decline in
popular music. Many musicals today tend to the opera form, and there are
marvelous counterpoints, involvements and dramatics which, when done
well—as in the case of Sondheim—are a new plateau in the art. The "in
one" comedy personality song of past decades seems to have disappeared.
There is too much emphasis on "mod," "with it" and tunelessness.

—RAY EVANS

The dramatist's position in society is a fairly honorable one. But the
dramatist's position in the theater is that of an undesirable, an outcast, a
moron, an ignoramus, an outsider, an intruder; one that is better out than
in, and best dead, since it is said that the best playwright is a dead play-

wright. When he or she is treated kindly, then, he is an orphan who is offered something because someone is good, not because he has earned it.

—Maria Irene Fornes

We work, I assume, to converse with that very, very small part of any population that has that extra little gene in them which makes them want and need and appreciate beauty and meaning around them.

—Paul Foster

Same function now as always: to provide an emotional experience for his audience; to evoke emotional response; to make people laugh or cry, more or less. This is the pure art of the theater. Any other "function" is a perversion.

—William Francis

For 28 years I have loved theater seven days a week—as an actor, director and playwright. A little while ago I sat down and I cried. My love died. I don't love the theater any more—it's too expensive! Children eat—a playwright has to be dedicated to insanity. I can't be crazy any more. Money—as in movies—film cries out for material. Theater is—cold. The only theater I still love is workshop theater where work matters and money is the least of it.

—Michael V. Gazzo

To write plays.

—Clark Gesner

The dramatist's position and function have changed. At one time, actors director, producer et al. were there to serve the play. The TV influence has now permeated the people of the theater. Actors and directors feel they are free to write, rewrite, and as one actor in a recent tryout of my play *The New Mt. Olive Motel* said, "improvise." My answer was that he was free to use any method suitable, including improvisation, to explore the character, but the final words would be those on the page as written by the playwright. Basically, the theater has lost its discipline. A return is essential to the survival of the playwright and his play.

—Steven Gethers

With the vast shrinkage in the middle class audience in this country, I see very little function for him, or her. I always thought that the theater was the place where society acted out the problems of its conscience. But now, in America, it acts it out in different places—in the streets, the press, the courtrooms. The more sophisticated the means of communication has become, the more susceptible it is to manipulation of all kind. So the distance between the dramatist and his public becomes ever greater, except to the comic artist or the satirist. Our humorists are the only ones who can save us. I would say to new dramatists, "Learn how to be funny. It's the only way you'll get through to them!"

—Ruth Goodman Goetz

The place of the dramatist in present day or any society is to tell good stories, stories on the stage about people whose actions, intents, strains and decisions have importance to the author himself and likewise to the audience—in other words, stories that entertain and do it with some significance. (I hear a critic snickering over the word "significance.") It is obvious that the calibre of a play is that of the personality out of which it is discharged. A cheap writer means a cheap play.

—Paul Green

The dramatist had better lie low today, writing books, movies, TV, because there simply isn't a market for plays these days—except at the college, community theater and amateur level. Some day a theatergoing audience will re-congeal, but not at the moment.

—A. R. Gurney Jr.

The regional theater is the answer—and the only real answer—for all of us. Plays get done. All kinds. New *and* with the stigma of New York flop stamped on them. And the best actors and actresses now seem willing to participate in regional theater. And the best directors—or at least *among* the best (certainly George Keathley of Chicago's Ivanhoe springs to mind)—are ow working "out there." Robert Anderson said it first, but it rings in my ear daily: "I wouldn't go to the typewriter if there weren't a regional theater for which to write."

—OLIVER HAILEY

To write of whatever facets of life interest the dramatist in such a way as to interest the public.

—NANCY HAMILTON

I feel the dramatist's position in present-day American society has diminished along with and owing to the diminishment of theater in New York City. It's true that with the coming of dinner theaters and a pretty active regular stock theater scene in many ways more Americans are going to and enjoying live theater than, say, ten years ago. The diminishing opportunity for dramatists to get new plays produced is sapping the vigor of the theater in New York, and eventually elsewhere because the source of plays to do elsewhere is drying up. An undeniable manifestation of this is the fact that such top dramatists as Frank Gilroy and Robert Anderson are working in other media. And so, I have found, are scores of others not so prominent on the theatrical scene. I feel the decay of New York as a city, and therefore as cultural area, is dragging down with it theater, dramatists and others involved with new productions. Where this will bottom out is something I shudder to contemplate.

—CHARLES HORINE

Futile! I begin to write plays with budgets, unions, set costs, prop costs, etc. in mind simply because I realize your show seems to have a better chance of being produced somewhere if there's only one set involved, not many characters, not many costumes, etc.

—JIM JACOBS

As always: to reveal us to ourselves. To help us to perceive the "poetry" (that is to say, the "form") beneath the prose and minutiae of our lives. To make us exalt. To make us feel. Quite simply, if I could go to the theater and have an "experience"—if I could laugh a lot and/or cry—if I could feel excitement and/or terror and/or lust, then I would go to the theater more often. If, in addition, I could feel enlightened and cleansed (by both the terror and the laughter) then I would go always. So would everyone else. It is too small. Too easy. Too scared. Nobody tries much, and when they do they are punished (by critics and the "fashionables") for daring to attempt. But the audiences are willing. There is a great hunger.

—TOM JONES

I believe his or her function is to tell a story in dramatic terms involving characters with whose emotions and motivations an audience can identify because they reflect some aspect of universal experience. The other approach to dramatic writing, perhaps more in vogue today, is a more subjec tive one which we term avant garde. Both are legitimate expressions but the first, I believe, appeals to a wider audience and would bring more people back to the theater.

—Howard Koch

I believe all elements of the theater world must realize that the theater of America and indeed the world of the 1970s is no longer confined to a few blocks of real estate on Manhattan Island. Everyone, including the Dramatists Guild, the best-play selectors, the Pulitzer Prize jury, even some outlying theaters (still wedded to the notion that a play is only a success, artistically and financially, if it's "made it" on Broadway) must expand their horizons and take in a Broadway which runs the length and breadth of America.

—Jerome Lawrence

As Walter Kerr wrote, many of us would finish the damn play, given a theater and a deadline. We are a lazy lot (exceptions prove the rule), and we need more impetus (not necessarily money) to get to it, instead of resting on old laurels, or the ad copy biz, or not wanting to "bother" our good producer friends with stuff that doesn't seem (to us) to be up to our own snuff.

—Mark Lawrence

To me, the stage is an altar, a soap box, a nut house, whatever, but it's my religion. When I stop believing, my work will be dead.

—Robert J. Lowery

I believe it is the responsibility of the playwright to entertain the theater ticket buying public—not just the critics—and at the same time comment on, and perhaps point out, what is wrong with today's society and say what, if anything, can be done to rectify things. But I don't believe the latter should be done at the expense of the former. It has been my experience that audiences prefer to be entertained rather than preached to. I also don't believe they only want the pap they can see on television. There has to be the right proportion of entertainment and so-called "meaningful" material. But unfortunately there is a large gap between what the audience wants or believes meaningful and what the critics will accept. A critic sees a play every night, or as often as one comes to New York. The average theatergoer goes maybe once a year; his or her standards are quite a bit different.

—Arthur Marx

Don't think he has much unless he (a) fawns on the audience, (b) flatters the ego of critics, (c) doesn't alienate groups, particularly the far left and right, (d) dies, preferably so that they can categorize you for good and even be nice for a while.

—JOHN OSBORNE

To improve the well-being of the human psyche by revealing the multitudinous levels of human experience. To get rid of the false, dangerous and sanctimonious images the society inevitably is fixated on. To inspire and generate the possibility of an authentic awareness of the sacred obligation of being alive.

—ROCHELLE OWENS

New York has nearly ceased to provide any audience for any playwright, whereas there is a tremendous and eager audience awaiting him almost anywhere else across the country. It's very sad that the playwright must still make his name and reputation in New York where theater is defeated, if not dead. And one of the problems I (and other playwrights) have been wrestling with is how the playwright can establish himself securely and *bypass* New York. Critics are difficult and stupid and imperceptive everywhere, but in New York they have the power of life and death. It ain't so out of town. My play *The Last of Mrs. Lincoln* got fairly mixed reviews in Washington, but audiences flocked to the Opera House to the tune of $90,000 a week. (And a major factor here is that places like the Kennedy Center have made theatergoing fashionable and safe—you drive right into the building, have dinner, see the show, get back into your car and never have to chance a nocturnal street—whereas you know what happens to you when you venture into Times Square at night. I don't mean that they must be fed the pap of the dinner theater, which turns theater into a floor show. They come to see Beckett, too.) So I would say that the theater outside New York provides me with all kinds of wonderful audiences; New York provides none.

As to the percentage of the attainable audience, well, here we might turn to television. My play *Lemonade* was produced *in toto*, without a word altered, on Hollywood Televison Theater, and 9,000,000 people saw it. Everywhere I go, people talk to me about it. So television could be a terrific boon to the playwright. He can reach *everybody* through it.

Things have gotten much rougher for the new playwright in the last ten years. When I started out, New York was crawling with experimental workshops. I happened to be taken up by the Playwrights Unit of Barr-Albee-Wilder, but there were any number of places a playwright could go to be produced. And audiences used to fight to get in. I can remember long lines waiting outside the Theater South, composed of theater people—producers, directors, agents—and just plain people who loved the theater. That's all gone. Now a twice-produced Broadway playwright, I recently had a fine production of a new play at Clark Center, and nobody came. Nobody cares about the experimental workshop any more. And where is the new playwright going to get produced? I'd be terrified to go into playwriting today. I was lucky. And today, once produced, the playwright has those appalling financial restrictions that limit his work so: his plays should be limited to six characters, not period, one set, etc. It's scary and very damaging to any artistic endeavor. (We won't even go into censorship.) I can't think why anyone would go into playwriting now, and fewer and fewer do. And yet, I love it (once in) and continue to write for the theater. Nothing else satisfies so much. And it has been very good to me, financially. And—thank God!—there is nowhere else that the writer can enjoy so much prestige.

—JAMES PRIDEAUX

Present-day American society can live very well without the legitimate theater and does not care to support the dramatist any longer. It is sad to note that he has been replaced by the television writer. The few producers who are still functioning are looking for musicals or comedies (rather than for serious plays) to please the shrinking audience. The theater in London or Moscow is a necessity, in New York it is a luxury. Today's dramatist can be compared to the blacksmith: there are no longer enough horses around, and he had better get used to a starvation diet. I can see no future for him, but luckily he is a fool and will not listen to reason.

—RICHARD REICH

In spite of all the negative things that can be said against present-day theater—Broadway, off Broadway or wherever—the dramatist is still the leading literary figure of our time, and the playwright who can somehow achieve success in the theater (and he hasn't really made it until he's made it on Broadway) has a sounding board for his viewpoint on the human condition that carries greater weight and can have tremendous effect upon his society. *Sticks and Bones* had more impact on those in a position to mold public opinion than any statement from President Nixon, and David Rabe can take as much credit for ending the war in Vietnam as any other one individual. Our modern theater—thanks to a large extent to the Dramatists Guild—gives the power to the playwright to mold his work from its conception through to performance. His contract gives him control unheard-of in either motion pictures or television. For this reason alone, the theatrical writer of integrity can write only for the New York theater if he insists that his work be truly his own. Unfortunately, the odds are stacked against the fact that his play will ever be produced, which makes his achievement all the more marvelous and self-satisfying when it does come to pass. I believe it is uttlerly impossible for a playwright to have success when his impetus is to please the public. He must be concerned only with pleasing himself and hope that his taste will reflect that of the audience. That is the genius of Neil Simon, who is blessed with a creative imagination that mirrors the common denominator of the American theatergoing public.

—HOWARD RICHARDSON

This must be judged in the economic context. Production cost of plays is prohibitive; cost of playgoing to the individual theatergoer is exorbitant. With real estate controlling the situation and "free" entertainment available on TV, the basic nature of theater is being revolutionized. We never had a healthy cultural tradition of theater priced to reach people without corporate expense accounts, and now we tend more and more toward a theater based on a few smash hits. It is becoming economically, if not culturally, elite; and the dramatist's function is to survive if he can.

—FRED SAIDY

The dramatist's function in present-day "society" is to entertain an expense account audience and an English dance critic. His position is accordingly low, with the exception of those few dramatists who have become millionaires and who are very empathic indeed to their audiences on that account.

—JOSEPH SCHRANK

We must reflect our age, of course, with our own view. Unfortunately, Broadway has become the repository of the best of regional theater. It is unfortunate, however, only because it is inconvenient to the dramatist to work away from home. But until Eighth Avenue is made walkable again I'm very grateful to Buffalo, Atlanta, Washington and all points east and west who welcome our new works.

—RICHARD SEFF

Because the public is now privy to Instant Replay, the dramatist's comments re society are passe almost at the time he makes them. This is why more and more dramatists are seeking protection in the past entirely. At least the past doesn't change as instantly as today's events do. And with the unleashing of porn, the stage has been robbed of drama that sex once connoted for the theatergoer. I suspect that religion is just about used up, too. Future shock and panicky producers are Broadway bedfellows.

—BEN STARR

Every society, so far, is based on a set of lies, commonly referred to as civilization. The function of art is to "name" these mendacities and evasions; to tell how it is, not the way it appears to be. This is a matter of hygiene: "Beauty is health, health is beauty." Art is as therapeutic as medicine. Man, alone or in society, is by nature pathological; the cause of every sickness is some sort of untruth. If we are telling a measure of truth, we cannot help helping people—whether, as Brecht, we want to change the world, or, as Beckett, we do not. The particular glory and terror that makes the theater endure is the fact of its uniqueness; of all the art forms it is the only non-reproducible. It is for tonight only, for the first and last time; it will survive the horrors of quantity.

—GEORGE TABORI

The secret of success in the American Theater (what little there is of it) is to write a happy play with a sad ending—or better yet, a sad play with a happy ending.

Unfortunately, the honest dramatist, like most other honest artists in our society, has been replaced by the con-artist. We now sadly live in a country in which publicity has truimphed over culture.

—YALE M. UDOFF

Writers today are so busy trying to be "different" or "now" or "original." Instead of trying to be different, they should just try to be good—because today, that's being different. A little more heart and a little less brain might help too.

—MICHAEL VALENTI

All of us laboring on plays know our position and function is ludicrously marginal. Why do we persist? We're addicted. We're writing for that stubborn, enduring corporal's guard of playgoers for whom good theater is a rare and heady charge, like nothing else in this land of commodities. We don't write many good plays, but somehow we're convinced it's worth trying.

—LESLIE WEINER

The playwright must be at once his personal catharsis and that of the audience—he must enjoy his work and make as many others enjoy it as reasonably possible. He must constantly exercise all respectable means of "holding the house."

—TENNESSEE WILLIAMS

A playwright is considered a prophet by the academic community and a fossil by the movie industry and most youth. He is closer to a working member of an artistic community. I don't think we can do better than to try to create an entertainment of a few hours' duration out of the society which we see, and for them, using as many of the possiblities of theater as our imagination can muster. For myself, I try to write roles for actors which will use their abilities and hopefully stretch those abilities further than they have allowed themselves to go previously. I am almost never satisfied with whatever microcosm I've settled on, and always pledge to include more possibilities (both social and theatrical) in the next project. Our position in society is something we have no business considering. Our function is to work—always taxing our imagination within whatever limits of order we consider necessary to produce a cohesive work for the stage.

—LANFORD WILSON

My last play was written and produced in 1957. When I was working in the theater, the New York audience for any plays but commercial smash hits was rapidly dwindling; and so the artistic target was narrowing rather onerously. The playwright, like the novelist, can—at his best—be the poet or the social historian of his time, perceiving and showing the essences under the journalistic swirl. But in the fiction art we don't have to produce smash hits or perish. There is room for a book simply worth reading. Possibly the expansion of the theater outside New York—which appears to be a trend—will create such room for plays simply worth seeing. Playwrights need such room, for livelihood and for growth.

—HERMAN WOUK

Of waning strength.

—EUGENE YANNI

VIII. On Critics.....

Most dear actors, eat no onions nor garlic, for we are to utter sweet breath; and I do not doubt but to hear them say, it is a sweet comedy.
—A MIDSUMMER NIGHT'S DREAM

Critics: Consider A Play's Reach as Well As Its Grasp

By Edward Albee

I heartily subscribe to the opinion—one I hold dear, in fact—that if an author's work can not speak clearly for itself, then no length of clarification by the author as to his intention will make the work of art in question (if, indeed, it is a work of art to begin with) any less opaque.

But it is equally true that no two works of art are of the same density; one play, for example, will make its points much more immediately than another, but this in no way suggests that the true worth of a work is to be determined by its simplicity, by the ease with which its content can be weighed. A book that you read only once, a play that leaves you as quickly as you leave it, may have value as diversion and may, as well, be very skillfully done—had better be, in fact—but works of that sort tend to reap greater immediate rewards for their creators than they do lasting ones for their audiences.

Now, at the same time, I'm certainly not trying to suggest that a work that is difficult, or confusing, or elusive, is automatically better than a simpler one. But the truth is that art isn't easy; it isn't easy for its perpetrators, and it demands of its audience the willingness to bring to it some of the intensity and perception its creator put into it. The more complex the work, the less passive may be the audience. Unless. Unless, of course, the audience does not desire participation. We hear so often of the responsibility of the artist to his audience, but far too little is ever said about the responsibility of an audience—of a society, if you will—to the people who fashion its entertainments. But, more of that later.

When it was first suggested to me that it might not be a bad idea to discuss *Tiny Alice*, her complexities and obscurities, I was more than a little leery. I reasoned that if *Tiny Alice* wasn't getting across to audiences, I couldn't explain it into clarity. Perhaps I'd better just let it run its course and go on to the next play. A shrug is, after all, always a great deal better than a whine, and I could always console myself with my own private estimate of the play—sharing, as I do, the view of about half the critics.

But then I got to thinking a little more, began rereading some of the hundreds of letters people have been kind enough to write me about their reactions to the play, read over the reviews the play got which, naturally enough, ranged from glowing to provocative to antagonistic and which ranged, as well, from perceptive to idiotic. I began, simultaneously, to sniff at the smells of success emanating from Broadway in recent seasons. And I have come to one or two gloomy conclusions.

I have come to the conclusion—and it will not be a popular one with many, but what the hell—that plays like *Tiny Alice*, plays of a somewhat greater density than their more immediately apprehendable counterparts, run into trouble when they attempt the commercial theater because of a roundabout of misunderstanding between the critic and the audience. It may be unconscious, but it renders the circle no less vicious. The critic, far too often, believes it to be his responsibility, his function, to reflect what he considers to be the taste of his readers: And the reader—the audience—has come to the no less lamentable conclusion that a play review he reads does, indeed, reflect his taste. It would be a laughable game of blind man's buff if the implications were not so melancholy, if the damage done to the theater as an art form as well as an entertainment medium were not so cruel.

If the critic, in our theater setup, were not so powerful a force, it would matter less how he approached his job. But since the audience tends to take the critic on face value, the critic might do well to face up to the responsibilities of his awesome power. It is the responsibility of the critic not only to inform the public what has occurred by its present standards, but, as well, to inform the public taste. It is not enough for a critic to tell his audience how well a play succeeds in its intention; he must also judge that intention by the absolute standards of the theater as an art form.

The point is easily made. The Broadway theaters that are full each night are full at entertainments that succeed entirely in their intentions, even though these intentions are relatively low on any absolute scale. It is far easier for a play that attempts the point of twenty on a graph of one hundred to achieve the point of nineteen than for a play that attempts eighty to reach even forty. But we all know that forty is higher than nineteen. Yet, at the end of each season, the critics, in their summary pieces, lament the lack of serious and ambitious plays on the boards. The odd thing is that these same critics have spent the season urging their readers to rush to the nineteen-point plays. The audience is led to believe that these are better plays. Well, perhaps they are better plays *to* their audience, but they are not better plays *for* the audience. And since the critic fashions the audience taste, whether he intends to or not, he succeeds, each season, in merely lowering it.

Walter Kerr has, among his many alarming opinions, the theory that the excellence of a play is determined by its immediate mass appeal. To bolster this theory—a sad one if it is true—Mr. Kerr cites the Greek theater, where 18,000 people a night would crowd in to see *Oedipus Rex,* let us say. Mr. Kerr neglects to mention, among many qualifiers, that the Greeks had nothing worse to do. And if we carry Mr. Kerr's idea to its logical and dank end, then *The Grand Canyon Suite* is a better piece of music than Beethoven's last quartet, say; Norman Rockwell is a better painter than Soutine; *Forever Amber* a finer book than *Remembrance of Things Past.*

But the contrary is true, as Mr. Kerr knows, as we all know. The final determination of the value of a work of art is the opinion of an informed and educated people over a long period of time. It may well be true that a tree which falls in a forest with no one to hear it makes no sound; but the crucial point is that it can matter only to people who have been taught the difference between a sapling and a weed.

Now, what has all this to do with *Tiny Alice?* Well, a great deal, but as much about plays like *Tiny Alice* as herself, serious plays of some complexity in the commercial arena. And I'm more concerned about whether, in the years to come, serious plays of intellectual complexity, formal experimentation and out-of-the-way idea will be allowed to coexist with (not take over from, but merely *coexist* with) the musicals and the comedies which are making the theater owners, the producers and, presumably, the critics and the audience so happy.

Now, *Tiny Alice* has been called everything from a hoax to a masterpiece. In my opinion, it is neither. It has been called, by many critics, my best play. And that, at best, is a very relative judgment. It has also been called obscure, confused, confusing, opaque, and difficult. It has been suggested that the audience had best watch out, for they will not understand it. And here we get to the point which makes me fight.

It is indecent to fault a work for being difficult. Are we to assume that audiences can grasp nothing more complex than simple addition or subtraction? And I might add that it is the height of immodesty for a critic to assume that what he finds confusing will necessarily puzzle an audience. *Tiny Alice* is a fairly simple play, and not at all unclear, once you approach it on its own terms. The story is simply this:

A lay brother, a man who would have become a priest except that he could not reconcile his idea of God with the God which men create in their own image, is sent by his superior to tie up loose ends of a business matter between the church and a wealthy woman. The lay brother becomes enmeshed in an environment which, at its core and shifting surface, contains all the elements which have confused and bothered him throughout his life; the relationship between sexual hysteria and religious ecstasy; the conflict between the selflessness of service and the conspicuous splendor of martyrdom. The lay brother is brought to the point, finally, of having to accept what he had insisted he wanted: union with the abstraction, rather than the man-made image of it, its substitution. He is left with pure abstraction —whatever it be called: God, or Alice—and in the end, according to your faith, one of two things happens. Either the abstraction personifies itself, is proved real, or the dying man, in the last necessary effort of self-delusion creates and believes in what he knows does not exist.

It is, you see, a perfectly straightforward story, dealt with in the terms of reality and illusion, symbol and actuality. It is the very simplicity of the play, I think, that has confused so many. It is, of course, neither a straight psychological study nor a philosophical tract, but something of a metaphysical dream play which must be entered into and experienced without preconception, without predetermination of how a play is supposed to go. One must let the play happen to one; one must let the mind loose to respond as it will, to receive impressions without immediately categorizing them, to sense rather than know, to gather rather than immediately understand. The play is full of symbols and allusions, naturally, but they are to be taken as echoes in a cave, things overheard, not fully understood at first. If the play is approached this way, the experience of it will be quite simple. If, on the other hand, one is instructed to follow the allegory as it moves, to count and relate the symbols, then, of course, the result is confusion, opacity, difficulty.

I couldn't bring any of this up if I didn't feel that the audience has been led astray. I spoke before of the hundreds of letters I have received from people who have seen *Tiny Alice*. With the exception of two letters, which have accused me of being the devil, and one signed "H. L. Mencken," the general tone has been this: We went to see *Tiny Alice* with much misgiving, because we had read we wouldn't understand it, that it was difficult and confusing; well, we don't pretend to understand every subtlety, but the experience of the play, once we let it happen to us on its own terms was . . . and then follow words like thrilling, satisfying, overwhelming, strange and wonderful, and so forth.

It may be, of course, that these several hundred people are the only ones out of the tens of thousands who have seen it who have responded this way—but I doubt it.

I'm not suggesting that the play is without fault; all of my plays are imperfect, I'm rather happy to say—it leaves me something to do. And there may be flaws in the production as well, but I suspect—and I am not paranoid yet, because I haven't been in the playwriting business very long—I suspect that there are many, many people who have been intimidated into either not understanding *Tiny Alice* or not taking the trouble to see for themselves if they *would* understand it for no better reason than that they have been told they would not.

Directly after the play opened, much was made of the fact that I was enjoying the confusion and keeping mum on purpose. Nothing could be further from the truth. It was simply that I couldn't, for the life of me, understand how anything so simple need be explained. And my instruction to anyone who wanted to see the play would be this: sit back, let it happen to you, and take it in rather as you would a piece of music or a dream.

Of course it's always disturbing not to have your intention understood, and it sends you back to the theater to look at your play to see whether or not indeed you have been as clear as you thought you might. It's always disturbing not to be understood especially if you're trying to be understood. There are some artists who intentionally try to confuse; I am not one of them. I am more concerned with why people don't understand than I am with the fact that they don't understand. I am more concerned with the fact that I don't think enough people approach not only the theater, but music, painting, and anything else with an open mind, without preconception and without prejudging the work.

I don't think there's necessarily any virtue per se in a work of art that can be apprehended completely in only one viewing, one listening, one reading. I'm perfectly delighted if a member of the audience finds that, from his point of view, he delves very deeply into *Tiny Alice*. Some people found a great deal more in the play—at least a great deal more of coherence in the play—than I consciously intended, but in cases like this I fall back on that wonderful thing (as all writers can), the collective unconscious, and say, "Of course I meant that." My only objection is that so many people feel that experiencing a work of art shouldn't be any work, shouldn't be an experience of participation on the part of the audience.

I suppose my ideal audience would be one that had seen a lot of plays, one that knew the history of the drama from Sophocles on up; an audience that was willing to go to the theater with a completely open mind; an audience that didn't necessarily take its cue always from the critics; an audience that didn't want always to be taken out of itself only but perhaps wanted to be put into itself; an audience that didn't necessarily want the theater to be an escape but perhaps for it to be an arena of engagement; an audience willing to accept a work of art on its own terms and not ask that it be on the terms that the audience thinks it wants.

Of the critic I suppose I would ask—in an ideal situation which we'll never get, perhaps fortunately—I would ask that the critic know as much about the theater as the most educated member of the audience; and that the critic concern himself more with the health of the theater as an art form. I'm not suggesting that the theater should be an unpleasant place to go to, that we must see only difficult plays, depressing plays, plays that are good for us. I'm merely asking for coexistence between serious theater and a somewhat more popular theater.

And I suppose I would say one further thing to the audience. I would ask the audience if it really wants as little from the theater as those critics who believe they reflect its taste would have it believe.

In the Case of Musicals, A Proposal

By Richard Lewine

It is one of the sturdier cliches of television that the rating system is accurate when you're on top and ought to be investigated by Congress when you're not. Playwrights, lyricists and composers, recovering from a set of bad notices, have their own set of rationales; it was ahead of its time, the cast was nervous, the critics were stoned and, cliche of cliches, well, the *audience* liked it.

No new method for television rating or dramatic criticism seems to present itself and none follows here. What does follow is a suggestion which, at least in the case of musicals, might make both reviewer and composer feel that the fight was a fair one.

At the opening of a new musical—a night that resembles the opening of the season at a Roman arena—the critic elbows his way among the flashbulbs, the ermine and the rubbernecking. Finally the house lights go down and there is an overture, the first official hearing of the score—some of the score, that is, since according to the rules an overture must be colorful, snappy and, above all, brief. Four minutes is considered about right. Actually, all an overture accomplishes at one of these galas is to cut the audience hubbub by about half. Nobody reviews overtures, anyhow.

Then comes the hearing of the songs themselves through the evening. There are perhaps twelve, fifteen, eighteen of them, running two or three minutes each. A dance development may extend the time allotted to a song to four or five minutes. Add to this a reprise or two, and you have the first-night critic's whole experience with the music. Yet from this he must make a judgment that is printed the next day to be read by a lot of people:

customers, recording companies, publishers, television, radio, all of considerable importance to a composer.

Somehow or other, in spite of the Roman circus atmosphere, reviewers seem able to make judgments about the words, spoken or sung; about the performances, the direction, the costumes, the scenery. But how they can make basic decisions about a score after this short brush with it is a puzzlement. What about the new song forms that turn up more and more these days and need some getting used to? What about unusual harmonic structures that seem dissonant and strange at first? What about the deceptively simple strain that doesn't seem like much until you find yourself humming it two days later? *After* the notices are out.

To appreciate fully a new score in a single opening-night performance must be an impossible assignment, even for the most musically oriented critic. Undoubtedly its extreme difficulty accounts for some of the hundreds of examples of bizarre reviewing of scores over the years. A critic for a New York daily liked *Oklahoma* but found the score "lacking in variety." And there was the New York *Times* reviewer's description of Harold Arlen's superb *House of Flowers* score: commonplace, uninteresting, it was called. No one expects the drama critics to pick hits—the publishers have enough trouble doing that—but something is wrong and should be fixed when a review of *West Side Story* describes the score as "noisy;" not good or bad, or interesting or unusual—just noisy.

Well, it's the hazards of the trade, you might say, but a show's score is a very different commodity from the book, the acting and the production. It can have a life of its own quite separate and away from the show. There may be as many as a thousand standard songs in our popular music, and more than half of them are theater songs. And some of them received some frightening blasts from the critics in their day.

It is obvious that a score of any real importance needs more hearing than the opening night rat race permits. So here is a proposal: that a recording of four or five of the principal songs from a show be sent to the critics a week or two before the opening. It should be nothing fancy, not a cast album, no plot or comedy songs. It should include only those songs which most need some familiarization. The record can be sent, as they say, in a plain wrapper.

To be useful, the plan should be tried for an entire season and should involve *all* the musicals and *all* the critics. There would be risks, of course. A reviewer could now pinpoint a middle strain or chord change he particularly loathed, something which might have otherwise escaped his attention. But there's also the chance that with a little more listening the good could be more easily recognized and appreciated. It might eliminate some of those old words that keep cropping up in reviews of scores, the best and the worst of them: brassy, derivative, undistinguished, adequate.

U. S. Critics and Others
On the London Scene

By Frank Marcus

During a recent London theater season there was an unfamiliar and somewhat interesting sight on the other side of the footlights, as the ranks of theater critics were augmented by two visitors from America: John Lahr and Robert Brustein. Already there had been talk that this should be taken as a massive retaliation on an almost Israeli scale for having sent you our Clive Barnes. Unfortunately, however, the two gentlemen were honored but only temporary guests. Mr. Lahr was in London in order to work on his biography of Joe Orton and deputized on *The New Statesman* for only a few weeks; Mr. Brustein was on sabbatical leave from Yale and, therefore, his stint on *The Observer* was strictly limited. Interestingly in one of their first reviews, their reactions differed considerably. As the issue involved principles of crucial importance, it may be worth recounting.

I should be inclined to forgive any American who witnesses our present troubles in Northern Ireland with a small degree of *schadenfreude*. Our smug condemnations of American action in Vietnam from a safe distance must have grated considerably. Even the perverse concern shown six years ago by Peter Brook in his notorious revue entitled *Us*—at the climax of which Glenda Jackson, in a chic St. Joan haircut, pleaded shrilly for bombs to fall in our well-kept back-gardens, so that we'd know what it was like—must have seemed crass and naive.

Now her pleas have been answered, and the back-garden of Ulster has become a battlefield. How are our dramatists reacting? First in the field was an unknown young man who showed the divisions by the well-tried device of presenting a family split by conflicting allegiances. His piece was performed at the Theater Upstairs (an adjunct of the Royal Court Theater). Next

365

to enter the fray were John Arden and his formidable wife, Margaretta D'Arcy. It is their play, *The Ballygombeen Bequest*, which caused the dissension among the critics.

After lengthy peregrinations, which took them as far as India, the Arden family are currently inhabiting an island off the coast of Galway. For some years past they have concerned themselves with community drama: writing, acting, and organizing on a local, amateur basis. This time, they struck

gold (from the point of view of their conscience, not their pockets). On the mainland, a family of tenant farmers were about to be evicted by their absentee English landlord. They had occupied their cottage for 150 years and, according to Irish law, the property would have reverted to them if they had not signed a contract a year before the date of accession, agreeing to act as "caretakers" and thus giving the Englishman a further legal hold on the property. The case caused much local resentment, especially when the landlord—a former Commander and estate agent from Sussex—had his claim upheld in the Irish courts of law.

The Ardens dramatized the conflict in terms of melodrama in the Victorian manner, with interspersed ballads, and the villain in a green spotlight. The program gave details of the facts of the case, including the Commander's private and business address and telephone number (the exchange was "West Wittering"), and at the end the audience was asked to append their names to a petition—or, rather, a demand—addressed to the landlord, pointing out his moral, as opposed to legal, responsibility. Although the passion of the performance did not incite a lynch-mob to march to West Wittering, it was hardly surprising that the Commander took out a writ against the producers. As a result, my notice of the play was deleted from the pages ot *The Sunday Telegraph*; other, more courageous newspapers risked publication.

There was, however, a further complication, which seemed to me of greater importance. In order to prove their contention that capitalism lies at the root of the Irish problem, the Ardens invented a son of the unfortunate family. He goes North to sell three ponies, is stopped at the border on his way back by British soldiers, tortured by them (this was shown graphically in vile detail), killed, and his corpse left tarred and feathered on the roadside, so that blame could be attached to the Provisional I.R.A. for propaganda purposes.

So, how were we, the audience, meant to take the play? As polemical, agit-prop, Marxist interpretation of history or, in view of the program note and the petition, as documentary realism simplified or elevated by art? In particular, were we supposed to extend poetic license to the Ardens to include their outrageous allegations against the conduct of "our boys"? I am not so unsophisticated as to imagine that the soldiers in Northern Ireland wear velvet gloves in their treatment of suspects—indeed, a Commission of Inquiry concluded that the methods of interrogation used in the internment camps were too severe—but so far no one has found a tarred and feathered *corpse*. The victims were live, and their tormentors were the fanatical extremists of the I.R.A. Should a dramatist be allowed, in the name of a political dogma to which he subscribes, to distort verifiable facts? In my opinion, that depends on the moral purpose of the play. There is no such thing as absolute truth, and theater is make-believe. But, proceeding from the premise that it is the function of the theater to humanize—and it is uniquely suited by its nature to flesh actuality—are we not entitled to judge it by its effect rather than by its intention? Surely it is deeply disturbing that an author of the calibre of Arden should seek to incite hatred, approve of violence, and spit on the idea of reconciliation? I'm sure that he and his wife are deeply sincere in wanting to kill the dragon of capitalism. It may sometimes be necessary to be cruel only to be kind: witness the kind of protest drama which bubbled to the surface off off Broadway in the latter half of the 1960s. The Ardens borrow Brendan Behan's device of having the corpse sit up and sing, but we do not feel that this springs from a greathearted, death-defying humanity. Sean O'Casey's genius could accommodate compassion as well as Communist principles; among the living, Brian Friel, Hugh Leonard and Conor Cruise O'Brien have not yet spoken on this subject through the medium of theater. I fervently hope they will.

So, how did our newly-arrived American visitors react to the experience? John Lahr enthusiastically endorsed the play *as art*: he felt that the Ardens had successfully reanimated the defunct conventions of melodrama. As another onetime English export to the States, Eric Bentley, once remarked, the term "avant garde" often denotes a return to ancient forms. What Mr. Lahr failed to recognize was that the flattening of characters to the two dimensions of heroes or villains, especially when used to purvey an "ennobling" social message, suited not only the taste of the masses a century ago, but also helped their masters in keeping a firm, paternalistic hold on them. Mr. Brustein trod more warily, giving equivocal praise and expressing considerable reservations.

To my mind, the issue is clear. The Ardens have used the real pain and misery of their new neighbors and reduced them to the most simplistic form of theatrical expression. Acting undoubtedly from the most impeccable ideological motives, they have committed the artist's unpardonable crime: they have dehumanized life.

Criticism Not Wanted

At one time the administrative offices of the National Theater were situated in an army hut on a bombed site in the backstreet slums adjacent to the southern end of Waterloo Bridge. Here, the London theater critics were summoned to a press conference. Chairs were placed against the walls of the little room, and a table covered with an immaculate white cloth bore the requisite supply of glasses, bottles and miniature triangular sandwiches. Clearly, the critics were about to be corrupted by hospitality.

They certainly looked corruptible. The older ones, with their sober dark suits made shiny-seated from years of sedentary labor, might have been taken for conscientious but seedy solicitors; the younger ones, in sweaters and hopefully-fashionable longish hair styles, affected an air of impecunious student gaiety. In contrast, the staff of the National Theater looked discreetly and expensively elegant and, in one case, flamboyant (Kenneth Tynan's second name is Peacock).

What favors did they hope to buy? The critics' silence. An experimental three-week season was to be launched at the small Jeannetta Cochrane Theater, and reviews following the first performances of the three programs in question would be irrelevant to the purpose of the enterprise. They would be workshop productions, changing and evolving in the course of the run, and anyway all the performances were sold out in advance. Laurence Olivier recalled that he and his distinguished contemporaries (Gielgud, Redgrave, Richardson) were able to essay the great Shakespearean roles at the Old Vic under Lilian Baylis while still in their 20s. Audiences accepted them although, inevitably, the interpretations were often brash and immature. Above all, they gave the actors stamina: "If we hadn't had these chances," declared Olivier, "we couldn't have become leading players." "Do come and see the plays towards the end of the run," added Joan Plowright, cheerfully, "and then tell us what you think of them." Thoughtfully, the critics walked away into the misty winter night.

What it amounted to was this: in the early years of its life, the National Theater had established itself as an institution. The policy of adventurous eclecticism had brought the expected dividends. Whether all-male Shakespeare, Artaudian Seneca, poetic Chekhov, or balletic Feydeau, the public (and critics) were demanding perfection. Anything less than this was castigated with brutality. The strain of occupying the pinnacle, fettered by memories of achievement, had begun to erode enjoyment. The workshop season was to provide opportunities for recklessness, relaxation, experimental non-type casting, and the presentation of untried material.

In the circumstances, the results were rather tame. Three of the four short plays commissioned from women novelists were clumsy and/or self-conscious, written with the kind of self-awareness that confirms the schoolboy view that femininity is something that is confined to below the waist. A similar attitude but a greater degree of invention distinguished Maureen Duffy's *Rites*: a gruesome fantasy derived from *The Bacchae*. Robert Stephens hid himself in an extravagant beard as a drunk old Scottish painter (doubling with the ghost of Karl Marx) in a play by John Spurling about the myth of Che Guevara. Cerebral and stimulating in a Pirandellian sort of way, this was a Cubist rather than Cuban investigation of the famous face on the poster. The third entertainment, a classroom exercise in mime called *Scrabble*, made one grateful for memories of Marceau.

As promised, there was an inquest. Again they met, this time in an exhibition hall of an Arts School. The critics began tentatively to say what they *would* have written—and immediately there was disagreement. The meeting accomplished something. It created a precedent in forcing the critics to face their victims, which was psychologically revealing, and it proved that critical reactions will in most cases cancel each other out. Both discoveries are comforting to artists.

It also eliminated doubts, if doubts there were, that it is wholly desirable for permanent subsidized ensembles to present more risky work as a complementary activity, so that the actors can flex their muscles and stretch their talents. And why indeed shouldn't the younger members of the company have a go at the great heroic parts? On the literary side, Tynan foreshadowed productions of first acts of plays in the process of being written, to help the authors to carry on. It is an intriguing idea.

Critics Vote on the "Bests"

Is the theater a form of competitive sport? This is not a frivolous question: it is prompted by the ever-increasing obsession with awarding prizes, medals, place marks, and (in England) titles and other honors to artists working in the theater.

What can be said in favor of them? They publicize the theater; they invest it with a spurious glamor; they please the recipients—the ephemeral nature of theater leaves behind only memories and yellowing press-cuttings; and they flatter the image of the donors. Many people regard them as a harmless form of self-indulgence or as positively benefical. Apart from awards, it is felt, the only other tangible evidence of success and achievement lies in financial reward. The duration of a play's run and the extent of the box office takings appear as less glittering emblems.

Have they any meaning beyond this? Are awards expressions of serious value judgments? I think not. In fact, I want to go further and assert that they can do real damage. The kind of performance that wins a medal or is dubbed the best of the year is almost invariably showy and superficial, and the play that is honored is frequently pretentious or obscure, bestowing the aura of an apparently superior intellectual discernment on the judges. Meanwhile, work of integrity, originality and unselfish devotion lies mouldering and forgotten.

The London theater is subjected to three different assessments every year. The annual London critics' poll published each summer in *Variety* is the most comprehensive. We are asked to select our favorites in some 18 different categories, including such obscure slots as "best supporting femme in a musical." This is quite simply a useful index to the taste of London's theater critics. It has little publicity value, although an ailing show might avail itself of a winner's tag in the advertisements.

A similar poll is conducted at the end of the year by the magazine *Plays & Players*. Here, 16 critics vote in eight categories; additionally, they sum up their impressions of the year in a couple of brief paragraphs. This is of some interest to theater workers, because it indicates the differences of opinion among the critics. The more diverse they are, the more hope they engender among the artists. Thank heaven, nobody in England feels tempted to tailor a play to the known requirements of a specific powerful critic.

The most highly publicized awards of the year are the *Evening Standard* awards for the best play, best musical, best actor and actress and most promising playwright. Bronze statuettes are presented at a gala showbiz luncheon, speeches are made, and a page or two of photographs appear in the newspaper in question. The fun is augmented by a "Win a lunch with the stars" competition for the readers.

There are five judges. In the season under discussion, they included three theater critics, a playwright (John Osborne), a society hostess and authoress, and a television personality. The best actor and actress chosen were Nicol Williamson (for *Hamlet*) and Rosemary Harris (for *Plaza Suite*).

This result was surprising, not because Mr. Williamson and Miss Harris gave bad performances but because neither of them had received a single vote from the 16 critics whose selections had been published in *Plays & Players*. The latter's choice for best actor, by a commanding margin, was Leonard Rossiter (for *Arturo Ui*), with Ian McKellen as runner-up, and for best actress Dame Peggy Ashcroft, with Geraldine McEwan and Eileen Atkins close on her heels. In other words, the *Evening Standard* awards were the results of compromise, arrived at haphazardly by five judges, two of whom were only indirectly involved in the theater. Other English newspapers have acted as regular sponsors of events like the annual Students' Drama Festival, the National Youth Theater, and the excellent World Theater Season, held at the Aldwych Theater. To my way of thinking, they are of far greater value.

One more example of critical vagaries: Harold Hobson, writing in the *Sunday Times*, tore an amusing and intelligent comedy to shreds. It was an extraordinarily violent review, disproportionate in its anger and vindictiveness, culminating in a plea to the management to take the play off at once. Several days later, Mr. Hobson and the author met over lunch and, as a result of this, Mr. Hobson paid a return visit to the play. The following Sunday he recanted and praised the play to the skies. Apart from the regrettable evidence of lack of balance, I could see nothing wrong in this *volte-face*: all honor to Mr. Hobson for admitting his mistake. There are no absolute values in criticism; they are intensely personal reactions.

A little later, however, Mr. Hobson was reminded of this curious lapse. It was a television confrontation, this time with Peter Shaffer and Peter Hall complaining of injustice. To my amazement, Mr. Hobson claimed that he enjoyed his second visit to the play because it had been altered as a result of his original criticism. This would have created an alarming precedent; to my surprise, the claim remained unchallenged. Now, however, the author has assured me that only very minor changes were made and that they were decidedly not inspired by Mr. Hobson or any other specific criticism. It was the *audience* Mr. Hobson preferred on his second visit. He had been antagonized by his neighbors on the first night. No comment.

Enter Clive Barnes

Once again, we have had the perennial jousting between playwrights and critics—and it was all started inadvertently by your very own Mr. Clive Barnes. This genial and well-meaning gentleman is currently fulfilling the therapeutic function of one of those carved figures outside entrances in Mexico, which are viciously cursed and derided by all who enter, who feel consequently purged and relieved.

It all began when he suggested in a review printed in the London *Times* that the music of *The Firebird* was written as a kind of incidental accompaniment at the bidding and to the requirements of Fokine. Mr. Barnes must have thought that the late Igor Stravinsky was then too old to care. He was wrong. The letter published in the *Times* from Stravinsky was the most devastating demolition of a critic by an artist that I have read.

Now John Osborne gleefully entered the fray, but *his* letter to the *Times* was not published. He did, however, make the contents available to other newspapers. Osborne wrote: "I know of no spectacle more pleasing than that of an elephant of achievement and distinction like Igor Stravinsky merely shifting weight to tread a critical insect out of sight." He writes of "the established fact of the power of the New York *Times*, the cowardice of Broadway producers and the patent idiocy of its audiences."

But the London critics did not get off scot free. Arnold Wesker, bruised by the critical mauling of his play *The Friends*, wrote a lengthy indictment for *The Theater Quarterly*. His sub-headings gave some idea of the range and nature of his accusations: "Criticizing on the basis of misquotation, The critics' need for fresh sensations, The playwright as victim of private hates, Disarming through self-abasement, The sad withdrawal of blessings, Truth sacrificed to feeble humor, Opinions offered with no substantiation, Failure to link up facts, Confident use of vague information, Just not listening, and They can—I cannot."

Many of his comments were pertinent, but unfortunately most of his major complaints are not amenable to rectification. There is some evidence that his very understandable resentment has festered into an obsession. Wanton destructiveness is not a characteristic of any of the critics that I know, and his charge of disloyalty—because several critics admired his earlier plays but did not approve of his later ones—is preposterous. Wesker's ideal critic would be a kind of mentor-guide who had studied the text of the play and preferably attended rehearsals of it: a role not unlike that of the learned Rabbi of yore who interpreted the Talmud. It is a forlorn hope.

Still, there is no reason whatever why the critics should be themselves beyond criticism. Controversy is healthy and sometimes destructive. With a foot in both camps, my reaction to the dispute is predictably schizoid. I am pro-Stravinsky but anti-Wesker. I happen to like Stravinsky's music and detested *The Friends*. Also, no single London critic possesses the power of Mr. Barnes.

In London, certain shows are critic-proof. A few very popular stars can survive in the most ramshackle vehicles, and the exposure of flesh can attract enough voyeurs to ensure a profitable run. Apart from that, there is no magic formula for success. A new play receives some dozen notices of roughly equal importance and influence; the verdict is rarely unanimous; the decision lies with the public. By and large, a London critic feels that he may alter slightly the course of a play's progress but he will not be able to sink it without assistance from a majority of his colleagues—this was true even of Kenneth Tynan at the peak of his influence. On the other hand, a really loud cheer from one critic out on a limb can sometimes give a play a short lease of life; he will certainly earn himself the undying gratitude of the author and the cast.

When I last visited New York I saw two Broadway hits, both ecstatically recommended by Mr. Barnes. I thought they were terrible and said so in an article for my paper. I am delighted to report that one of them opened in London and was an enormous success. I am delighted because I do not conceive it my duty to act as censor for the public; I have no wish to exercise paternalistic control over what they are to see. I watch a play, evaluate it according to certain standards of taste peculiar to myself (and known after a time to my more discerning readers), and approve it or reject it. A wasted evening is not a major tragedy, but to kill the joy of creation in an artist can be. Some are resilient, some not. I know from personal experience the precise effects of posititive and negative criticism.

You may say "so what"? Mr. Barnes happens to wield influence and I don't. He may say that he never solicited this power; the *Times* may protest that it has no wish for it. But Mr. Barnes *has* this power, and if he really believes that his knowledge does not in any way influence his judgment as a

critic, then he is deluding himself and his readers. All right, what is he to do
Abdicate? Alternate with another critic who is his exact opposite—a thin ol
American who hates dancing?

No, the crux is the New York theatergoing public. Seat prices are high
and they appear to sit back and say, as Diaghilev said to Cocteau
"Etonne-moi!" They expect polish, glamour, volume, spectacle and an ir
sidious kind of emotional pandering to their prejudices and self-esteen
They want to leave the theater feeling better than when they entered it. T
an Englishman, they appear hide-bound, arrogant and self-satisfied, poss
bly because they lack the typical English audience's indulgence c
amateurism.

Is Mr. Barnes trying to educate them, or does he want them to remain a
they are? And are they, in turn, satisfied with Mr. Barnes and content t
abide by his decisions? How wonderful it would be if there were a revolt c
the slaves, if banner-carrying militants laid siege to the offices of Broadwa
producers. demanding to see shows that Mr. Barnes didn't like.

Criticism is by its very nature subjective: there are no objective criteria i
art. But respect for the creative act *as such* is an essential qualification fo
criticism. Quite probably, my benevolence springs partly from persona
knowledge of the critics. They are not at all like monsters. My presen
attitude towards them is additionally suspect because on the occasion of a
revival of my play *The Formation Dancers* the critical reaction was almos
unanimously enthusiastic; there were even a couple of generous recanta
tions. I am certain that Mr. Wesker will find some sinister conspiratoria
motive in this: a case of professional solidarity, an assertion of *esprit de corps*.

I can promise him, though, that on the next occasion that they demolish a
play of mine—and I regard this prospect as inevitable—I shall be up there
on the barricades with him, firing and sniping at the evil creatures. Inconsis-
tency, sensitivity to criticism, and hurt pride are human failings to which
both playwrights and critics are susceptible by nature of their occupation. It
is as well to recognize this sad fact.

Ronald Bryden: A Critic Appreciated

Good news for critics: not all of them are hated and despised. When
Ronald Bryden relinquished his job as theater critic of the Sunday *Observer*
after a five-year stint, young artists who felt that their careers had benefited
crucially from his criticism threw a party in his honor as a spontaneous
gesture of appreciation. Tom Stoppard and Peter Nichols were there—and
who knows what course they would have steered if Mr. Bryden had not
discovered *Rosencrantz and Guildenstern Are Dead* and *Joe Egg* on the fringe of
the Edinburgh Festival, lauded them to the skies, and thus aroused curiousity among producers? But perhaps the special affection and esteem felt for
him among artists (and theatergoers, too) sprang from his knack of explor-

ing the hidden qualities in plays and performances which everyone else disliked and dismissed. He radiated warmth towards those lame ducks, and the effects of his encouragement must be incalculable. I firmly believe that some of our best writers might have forsaken the theater, but for his faith in their ability.

The actors turned out in force, too, and contributed generously to a handsome present. Alec McCowen, Geraldine McEwan, Eileen Atkins, and such gorgeously pretty and talented girls as Julia Foster, Anna Calder-Marshall, Gemma Jones and a wonderfully nutty up-and-coming actress called Rosemary McHale, who told me that as an audition piece for *Oh! Calcutta!* she had sung a Schumann Lied—in German, and fully clothed! She didn't get the part; she will go far. (Note for the theater historian: Miss McHale found a place at the Royal Court Theater, having an autopsy performed on her in Edward Bond's stark and searing new play *Lear.*)

Ronald Bryden, incidentally, has joined the Royal Shakespeare Company in a newly-created positon called "Play Adviser." Nobody—including, I suspect, Mr. Bryden—knows for certain what this entails, but making contact with living writers, as well as studying and rediscovering defunct ones, would appear to come within its scope.

High Noon on 44th Street: Walter Kerr

What really happens when a highly perceptive, articulate and powerful critic is confronted in free-for-all discussion by the creative artists whose work he dissects and whose careers he influences, sometimes profoundly?

The answer is right here, in detail, in two such encounters—one with Walter Kerr and the other with Clive Barnes—taped and edited for publication. Both took place in private (in the sense that there was no public audience, no observers other than the scores of playwrights, lyricists and composers who packed the large reception room at Dramatists Guild headquarters on both occasions, which took place in the 1970s about a year apart).

Questioners are not individually identified in the transcripts; they are spokesmen for a collective curiosity, a group calling-to-account. Questions and answers were fired at random, from the hip. Though a minimum of conversational order was preserved at the meetings and of syntactical order in the subsequent texts, there was no inhibition placed on total confrontation either during the discussion or in the editing.

The dramatists' "guest of honor" at the first session was Walter Kerr, former drama critic of the New York Herald Tribune *and* Times *and now Sunday drama critic of the* Times. *Following his introduction by Jerome Weidman on behalf of the Dramatists Guild's symposium committee, Mr. Kerr set the ball rolling with an evaluation of the work of Jerzy Grotowski, the Polish impresario, leading into the comment:"You could say that a little silence around a word may make us hear the word a little more clearly. It's like what Sacha Guitry said about Mozart: 'When you listen to a piece of music by Mozart the silence that follows it is also by Mozart.'"*

Q: Pinter uses silences, doesn't he?

WALTER KERR: That's right, he does. That's why his plays don't read very well. Pinter's interesting to me on another score, too. He calls himself a conventional playwright. At first that seems like a joke. But as a matter of fact, compared to his source he *is* a conventional playwright—because his prime source is Samuel Beckett. Beckett really means to write anti-theater, anti-drama. We've always considered drama an action of some kind or another; a change. Beckett denies that—he wants to push that to the wall, so he writes a play in which absolutely nothing happens, and nothing *can* happen. Stasis, total stasis. Pinter was very much influenced by Beckett, he began writing having seen a Beckett play, but the first thing he did was to restore action. Something always happens in a Pinter play. You may not know what it is, he may keep it secret from you, but take any one of the Pinter plays—somebody is killed, somebody has been transformed.

Q: Jerzy Grotowski's work seems to me to be very close to dance. And we already have dance, very brilliant dance. I, for one, miss the word, I feel more of a stimulus than ever to go back to the pure word.

KERR: One of our problems is that we've been very careless about the word. We have not paid enough attention to the fact that the word has been the principal tool of the theater. We ought to make it count for absolutely everything that can be done with it. Instead, for a long time we have agreed to write our dialogue at the level, say, of film dialogue. There's no great difference between most play dialogue and most film dialogue at the present time. And yet, in a film, dialogue is *not* very important. The picture is going to carry the prime burden. And still we write our words only at the same level without having all that visual stuff to keep us going. Why do we do that? Why do we betray or misuse the tool that is so important to us? I think we've been very, very foolish in that regard.

Q: Many film directors like Rene Clair consider words to be the defeat of the director. They try to conceive their films wordless. Clair says that every time he has to revert to a word he considers it a defeat of some kind. So would you agree that film creators aren't crazy about words either?

KERR: Yes, Clair started in silent films where the ideal was the title-less film—no words whatever, achieved, I think, only once, in *The Last Laugh*, an Emil Jannings film. If you look at Chaplin you'll find very, very few titles, the absolute minimum. More and more today in the better films you're finding exclusively visual effects, and not only do they not pay much attention to the words, they don't pay much attention to the sound track. Half the films I see today I can't hear half of. I don't mean that as a criticism, I think they want it that way. They like the throwaway. I don't mind that the word is underplayed when I go to see an Ingmar Bergman film, I'm really looking at the images, depending on getting the meaning of the film from the images, but when I go to the theater I've *got* to get it from the words.

Q: At the time Elia Kazan directed *Death of a Salesman,* a great mystique arose that it was Kazan's rewrite of Arthur Miller's play that made it such a success. I'm sure it isn't true at all, but I've heard it for years. Now, this is what it has produced: every director says to himself first thing, not "What will I direct in this script?" but "What will I rewrite in this script?" This has built up until the first question at the first meeting is "Well, what rewriting are you going to do?" This has even spread to the producer. Everybody involved becomes a rewrite man for the play.

KERR: I'm sure you run into the problem everywhere, from the time you go into rehearsal to the time you come in from out of town. I don't know that the mystique of the director has increased in our theater, though. Nobody would be more furious at what you've just said than Kazan himself. Kazan, even if he wanted you to rewrite, wouldn't want to do it himself, wouldn't take over the word power of the play. Some of the time, as you know, requests for rewrite are entirely legitimate. The difficulty is that you're dealing with ten people, each of whom sees the play in a different way and wants a different rewrite. And then you've got to stand and fight for yourself and hope to God you're right and not being stupid on the particular issue.

Our problem of words did not really begin because of the power of a Kazan. Our problem began when films came in. We made the mistake of assuming that this new medium had to be met on its own terms. The theater tried to become more visual, with turntables and treadmills and fragmenting scenery flying apart before your eyes while another piece comes in behind it, ıntil finally it became really quite fast considering how clumsy it was; but ven so it could never be as fast as film. It was a mistake to try. All that time ve were neglecting the word, which is our only chance. We ought to have tood still and delivered the word, which is our identity, but that we did not lo. We did not insist on who we were as distinct from this other medium, we very foolishly tried to compete with it directly.

Q: A while ago you wrote a column entitled "Where Have All the Playwrights Gone?" I wish you'd comment on it, I know it raised some questions ın my mind.

KERR: Surprisingly, I got more mail on that piece than on anything I've lone in years—but most of it came from people who've never been produced, and I wasn't talking about them at all. The burden of the piece was: vhat about the people who have been produced *successfully* and are not vriting?

I did suggest that maybe part of our problem was intimidation; that too many writers who could do conventional plays were afraid of the New Wave, afraid that they were going to seem old fashioned and not with it, maybe became timid or even paralyzed. All I've got to say is, some playwrights worried during the reign of the Theater of the Absurd—and where, pray, is the Theater of the Absurd now? It's gone, but *Butterflies Are Free* is still running. I think it is a terrible mistake to be intimidated, *if* that is what is happening. I may have called this form of theater "filler," and that may seem a derogatory word, but it's what keeps the theaters open and going and keeps actors acting and being paid, and audiences coming in, so that everything will be there when we write something better.

Q: Isn't that a curious reason to write, just to keep theaters open?

KERR: You may eventually want to write something for the theater, right?

Q: I write for my own satisfaction.

KERR: We can't expect you to be conducting a charitable operation. But surely you want to keep the institution available for the moment when you turn up with the work that satisfies you. What if there's nothing and nobody there to do it? You're doing it for *you*. If you have a playful idea, and it's the best you've got at the moment, why not write it? I think there's a virtue in keeping in trim. If each of you was aligned, as Shakespeare and Molière were, with a permanent company in which you had a stake, if you had to deliver a manuscript every year or the company would fold, you would meet the deadline.

Q: Aren't you talking about comedy only?

KERR: No, no, serious plays too . . . Remember that Shakespeare and Molière worked that way, under *that* kind of pressure.

Q: The nice little comedy idea with one set and six characters used to be one of several choices for the playwright. Now it's the only kind of play that's required.

KERR: Wait a minute, you're saying that you can't get a serious play, or a distinguished play, on.

Q: I can get it on, but there's no audience for it.

KERR: There was an audience for *A Man for All Seasons*, there was even an audience for *Rosencrantz* and *Guildenstern Are Dead*. That audience may have disappeared at intermission, but there *was* an audience for it.

Q: I think we should address ourselves to the ghost that's not in the room tonight. I mean the New York *Times* daily drama criticism and its power to destroy.

KERR: Destructive power is always greater than affirmative power, and partly that is in the way our theater is regarded—and not necessarily beloved—in our time. The audience is quicker to respond to a negative than to a positive notice. When they pick up the paper in the morning, they're really asking themselves, "What can I miss this time?" Not "What can I go to?" but "What don't I *have* to go to?" They have been disaffected for a long time. Perhaps they have been bored too often.

Q: The problem of the so-called "serious" play is not a new phenomenon. The Burns Mantle theater yearbook is now listing about 160 plays that have run 500 performances or more, and you will find the list includes only 16 serious plays, and there's a tremendous absence of Pulitzer Prize and Critics Award plays. The audience has *always* been a little indifferent to the serious play.

KERR: Yes, comedy does outrun serious drama every time. It probably did for Shakespeare, too, excepting *Hamlet* maybe. But if you concentrate on the 500-performance jobs, you're eliminating, say, the 379-performance jobs which were the good serious plays. 379 is enough, though, and I don't think we should then say that the theater or the audience is somehow inadequate to our purposes.

As for the *Times's* power, I do think it is overestimated and can be fought and beaten. Such power as the *Times* reviews do have is handed to them in some part by press agents. No matter who you are, two days after you go on the *Times* you're a national figure. All producers immediately quote you in block capitals. They make the assumption that anybody who goes onto the *Times* has this power, and then they hand it to you by promoting you so tremendously. There is power of course, but I don't think it is that great.

Q: Is there an example over the past few years of a serious play that was panned by the daily *Times* but went on to be a success?

KERR: I don't know whether you will consider the *Times* notice of *The Price* a pan or not. It was ambivalent. But *The Price* went on more or less untroubled.

Q1: I wouldn't consider that a pan.

Q2: If *you'd* gotten the notice you'd have thought it was a pan.

KERR: I would not call it a money notice.

Q1: How about an example of a non-serious play running that was killed by the New York *Times: Fiddler on the Roof.*

KERR: No, no, that got a *good* notice.

Q2: You murdered it.

KERR: But I wasn't on the *Times* then, I was on the *Tribune.* And by the way, I did *not* "murder" it, I regretted that it had not lived up to its promises. But mine was an unfavorable notice, you're right about that.

Q: Without going into personalities, anybody who has that chair at the *Times* does have a great deal of power. That power is not going to stop anybody from writing a play. You're going to write what you have to write. But it does give you a very queasy feeling to know that a man, *any* man regardless of who he is, would have a power of life and death over your work. I mean, we all have our prejudices. I wouldn't feel qualified myself to pass judgment on certain works that are perfectly valid but to which I know that for personal reasons I don't respond. If you could envision a better situation, what would you look for? How could the situation be changed? I know there has been some kind of discussion with the *Times* about doing two reviews, or maybe even three. The *Times does* have the power of death over most of our careers, and we ask you. . . .

KERR: That of course is why we made this effort, such as it was, to split the Sunday and daily reviewing. It doesn't really work in terms of splitting the vote—no. My review comes out too late, for one thing. But think what it would be like to have *two* pans side by side in the *Times* on the same day.

Q: It couldn't be any worse than this. . . .

KERR: Oh yes it could, much worse. Or, if you split them what would happen? I'd be as interested as you to find out, because I'm on the other side of this problem. I've been watching my own notices for eighteen years on one paper or another, watching how little influence I really have. My wife says I was influential in the theater exactly once. That's when I pointed out that Kim Stanley wearing a certain wig looked exactly like Benjamin Franklin—and the next night the wig was gone.

Ideally, I wish we could get back to a policy of not quoting critics, which existed in this theater of ours fifty years ago. During the period of George M. Cohan and William Gillette they didn't quote critics' reviews. Cohan was attacked—and savagely—in almost every musical that he opened, each of which made a million dollars. The reviews didn't make any difference. The audience knew Cohan, they didn't care what somebody said in the papers. William Gillette forbade the quotation of criticism in his ads, and used to say, "I'm sorry, I don't need reviews. I have my following." Over the years we have gradually *taught* the theatergoer to lean on the combined quotes. They still know what they want—there are a lot of shows with good combined quotes they wouldn't be caught dead at. Their attitude is, "Oh yeah, he liked it, not me." I think we have invited the theatergoer to lean on the papers and therefore multiplied such power as they do have. Would you be willing, now, to forego quotes? Most critics would be happy if you did.

Q: But the theater's changed since the days of William Gillette. Everything now is so very expensive. Speaking as a theatergoer rather than as a writer, I find myself—despite my knowledge of the difference between my own taste and that of critics—I find myself leaning on critics. I don't lean on critics for the movies because I don't have to spend as much to go to the movies.

KERR: Think how recently films didn't bother with quotes or didn't need them. You see, if you have a loyal audience as Cohan and Gillette had, or as *films* had until very recently, you can say to hell with any group of critics—if the audience is enamored of this form at this time. We've got to face the fact that a large part of the audience is not enamored of the theater at the present time. We don't have a loyal audience of people who can't breathe until they see their next play. That is out of the theater, and the biggest job of all is to find out how to bring it back.

Q: I have a seventeen-year-old son who goes to ballet and laughs out loud when he reads Aristophanes. He is willing to pay three dollars for a good film. I think it's the *word* that has failed the young. My son and his group go to ballet and movies and are far more sophisticated than my generation was, far more *aware* of the word and respectful of word and movement and very much involved—probably as a fad—in mysticism of a kind, with body movement, with things that they can read into rather than read into them. You made the point that some of the playwrights of the past knew their audience, that Molière wrote for his audience. Are we aware of *our* audience? Do we really know what our audience is?

KERR: I doubt if there is any homogenized, characteristic, specific audience for theater at the present time. I think we have an audience that goes by what is chic, what will work into the next cocktail party conversation—theater party audience, out-of-town business men, there are enormous numbers of them once you get the momentum going. But I don't think we have an audience that is specifically interested in the theater as such, who can't live without it. I'm all for the word, as you know. I believe your son is looking for the word used in a new, more powerful way. He searches for it mystically in some sense because he's been turned off by the old linear, rational structuring of the word. He didn't have to read McLuhan, he grew up in front of a television set on which the channel was twitching, twitching, twitching, twitching every six seconds. And he never got his information by going from A to B to C to D; he got it by going from A to Z to W, Q, N, L . . . and he got it, that's the astonishing thing. I used to worry about my children on that score. They never see the end of anything, they never see the second stage of anything, they wander in and out, they turn the channel selector, they see six programs in an hour, fragments of six programs—how do they understand anything? What pleasure do they get? I've now discovered that they got it all, they filled in the gaps, they supplied any pieces that were missing after they tuned out to something else. They work by radar. They assimilate in all directions simultaneously. We must learn how to cope with this—I think poetry is the best, because poetry works in something of that way, too. It's non-linear, non-logical.

Q: In regard to the filling-in of gaps, could it be agreed once and for all that the playwright does not merely write dialogue, but three different kinds of words: he writes dialogue, he writes stage directions (which sometimes create the play to some extent) and thirdly he writes between the lines?

KERR: Of course he does, or it's not a play.

Q: And there are two kinds of writing in between the lines. There's the kind that Pinter does in which he sometimes knows what he means by his pauses and sometimes only pretends that he knows what he means; and the kind in which the writer uses the in-between-the-lines words to write his play.

KERR: Pinter really does represent a kind of phenomenon of our time. He says he doesn't work logically. He doesn't go from cause to effect; he goes to effect right away. You look for the causes yourself. This is a result, I think, of his temperamental existentialism. He really believes that we live, as the existentialists tell us we do, without prior knowledge of what will happen if we take the next step; that we have no guidelines; that we're in a void, each of us, and we're finding ourselves gradually by what happens to us as we move about in the void bumping into other people moving about in the same void. That's why in Pinter you always get a contest over possession of territory—two people working over the same glass or table or little tiny patch of ground. You don't know why they're fighting, but they're both trying to get in there. Pinter believes that this is the way life *is*, that it's only by contending with the other person in the void that we arrive at some kind of identity, and that is mostly what his plays are about. I think he's damned good, but I like his shorter plays better than his longer plays. His effect sustains very well from forty-five minutes to an hour and fifteen minutes, but not beyond.

Q: I have known many instances where something that the critic has mentioned as a magic moment in the theater in terms of the directorial touch was written into the playwright's original script. Should the critic read the script of a play before he goes to see it?

KERR: I know that some reviewers have read manuscripts in advance when they could get them. It is practised more often in England than it is here. I don't like it and I've never done it. In fact, I'd absolutely refuse to do it, simply because when I read a manuscript I visualize the play in my head. Then I go to the theater and find that somebody had the nerve to do it differently. But even if you had just read the script of a new play, I don't think you could remember all of the little details written into the playwright's stage directions. All a reviewer can do in a case such as you described is to try to recognize the *style* of the director. If you've seen the director do something similar before, take a chance on crediting him. You still will make a mistake once in a while.

Q: As a group of playwrights, we seem to be concerning ourselves more with the show than with the play. You as a critic must be concerned with show. In this day and age, from your point of view the production is the play. But we create plays, not shows. Other people step forward and turn our plays into shows. It's an encompassing point about the threat of Grotowski, and form, and 500 or 379 performances, and all that. But as a group of dramatists we are refusing to talk about our vision for plays and why we write plays. We must as writers be concerned with what is wrong with this world and use the theater as an instrument, almost a political instrument. There isn't a form first that encompasses the subject; the form will simply emerge from the subject you're dealing with. And I can feel just as proud of a four-performance flop as any 500-performance hit, even in critical terms. I think we must reinspect our basic values as writers—if in Mr. Kerr's presence, fine. I'm concerned with Mr. Kerr's concern with show. . . .

KERR: I do want to disagree with you on this. I realize we have been speaking mostly of externals and not about what was inside the play. It is not irrelevant, however, to talk of performances, because if your play which you worked so hard on and hoped so much for only has four performances, it has not served well as an instrument. You're talking about the theater as an instrument—that is to say, of activating society, of making it go to work on this, that or the other thing, of relevant concerns. But if nobody has seen your play I don't think you've achieved your goal, and therefore I think number of performances has some bearing on the number of people you may have influenced. I don't think this is an irrelevant consideration, though we might well give consideration to other matters.

Q: Four performances against 379 performances becomes almost negligible when Johnny Carson can go on television and reach forty million people. If it's quantity you're after, the theater is the wrong business. I see the theater as an instrument to get things *started*. My play doesn't end when the actors take their curtain calls. Hopefully, my play has been socially active enough to get people to stand up and say O.K., I'll do something.

KERR: Naturally, in political theater you expect a carryover from the final curtain. But you've still got to have people see it in order to be affected by it. This thing worries me, the privacy of "make my statement" as though that were the be-all and end-all: "I've had *my* say, I've done *my* work and put it up there and nobody came—well and good, it's still complete," I don't dig, I'm not with it. Peter Brook has said about Grotowski that audiences are not meant to be moved or involved or very much influenced, but rather they come as neutral witnesses to the act. In other words, the actors come on the stage and give their performance, which is theirs and is private, their own working-out. When they are through they go away. They have not really addressed themselves to you, they don't come back for curtain calls, anything like that. Peter Brook said that when the audience is permitted in—which is only occasionally and in limited numbers—it is a witness to the act of the actor in the same way that people were witnesses to that murder of a woman several years ago, when not one of the many people who saw it called the police. Brook used that as a favorable example of the audience relationship to this performance. The actor's statement was totally outside their concern. They only looked, they only witnessed, they only saw and went their separate ways.

My own belief is that we should try to reach the maximum number of people and involve them all at once. I think we get a richer and more complex theater that way, because the more diverse the group you can pull in from various walks of life and differing interests and I.Q.s and weld them into a unit, the more total has your social act been. If you have made a bond between strangely divergent people for two hours, if you can bring it off, it's almost a miracle. I'm in favor of pursuing that miracle rather than settling for the more limited audience.

Q1: You cannot merchandize something as big business that's meant as an intellectual exercise. The theater is organized as business.

Q2: Then we should burn Broadway.

KERR: There's no point in burning Broadway unless you should also have burned Shakespeare's Globe Theater. You must not wipe any theater out merely because its material has to be sold in some way to an audience. Everybody who ever worked for the theater has had to do that, including the Greeks, who were state-subsidized but were in competition with other playwrights. They fought hard for prizes, and when they didn't get one they were very angry indeed. Aristophanes kept telling you how sore he was in play after play, as he rewrote to go back and persuade those judges to give him the prize next time.

Q: But our society's values are lower, more shoddy. Therefore, the play which appeals to that society, the play which wins *that* competition, is going to be a shoddy, corrupt, superficial, soft-palated kind of play. . . .

KERR: I grant you that the cultural and intellectual level of our society is a great deal lower than that of Pericles's Greece. On the other hand, if you start to think about prize plays of our own time, you're going to think of *Death of a Salesman, A Streetcar Named Desire, A Man for All Seasons* and so forth. I submit that these are not cheap or pandering.

Q: We have not been talking about the theater as it is now. We have been talking about the theater in a pre-industrial and industrial age, not in a post-industrial, now well into a technological, age, in which the sensibilities of the mass of people in the United States must be appealed to in some way other than has been tried before. It does seem that our theater is going to have to follow the other humanities into some kind of activist work. I don't mean simply agit-prop, I mean it is going to have to go into the streets. In your experience, how many among college youth are interested in going to their college plays, and find some social value in going to see them?

KERR: Not too many, But I think you would have more going to see something like *The Serpent* than to a conventional play. What the kids are doing, not only the kids but everybody at the present day—if I see it correctly—is asking, "Is it so?" One by one, across the board, they have pushed to see what was real and what fell over. They are questioning all authority, not in a negative or hostile way; I think they will accept an authority if they can find one, but what they're trying to do is find it. If it falls over, obviously it was rotten and should have gone away. If it was finally left standing they say, "All right, I'll buy that." They must apply this action to the theater as they do to everything else—politics, religion, education. The question they're asking is, "What is this stupid thing you're calling theater and does it even exist any more?"

Q: In other words, is there an audience and is there a theater that I couldn't participate in?

KERR: There's a very strange one that I have difficulty with very often. It doesn't follow any of the esthetic norms that I know anything about. You can't get inside it—it's like the Living Theater, they tell you when you go in that you can't judge it or know what it's about unless you join in. You must go up on the stage, sit down in the big circle with Julian Beck and pause for twenty minutes. Then listen to Julian Beck say "Umbrella." Then pause for twenty minutes. Then he says "Dishrag." Then pause for twenty minutes, then he says something else. Finally something is supposed to happen among you that binds you all together, but unless you've gone up and done it you can't tell what it is. And if it doesn't happen, you can't prove to everybody else that it didn't happen. That makes criticism kind of difficult. The Living Theater I personally detest, but the students fought to get into it at Yale, and the company did very well in all their other campus bookings.

I went to one college where there was a banner up on the wall quoting Teilhard de Chardin to the effect that mankind has just taken one unforeseen and enormous step forward in the evolutionary process, the point of this being that today, suddenly, we have evolved to a degree that we are more conscious of more things than we ever were before. Therefore we have to reckon with them, and they tend to shatter all the previous boundaries. Suddenly we see more—or we see that we *have* to see more and that there is more to be *seen*. De Chardin proposed a genuine evolutionary breakthrough into the space of knowledge, the space of fact, the space of what is. I believe him, by the way, and I believe that this new generation is in part a product of the breakthrough.

Q: I wonder, what really did come first? Did the word actually come first? I know that in songs the troubadour came first, and then came the song. In the theater, did the playwright come first, and was the director a later technological innovation?

KERR: The playwright probably did not come first—I think the actor came first. You had this chorus singing and dancing in praise of Dionysus or whatever other god. They talk about his deeds and exploits saying he did so-and-so. One day somebody, maybe Thespis, suddenly turns around and says, "I am Dionysus, I did so-and-so." And everybody accuses him of blasphemy. Solon of Athens gets after him because it is terrible what he is doing—lying in public like this. And Thespis answers, "Yes, it's a lie, but it's all in sport." Which means the theater really began as a cross between a lie and a sport and has been so ever since. First the actor did that, and then he needed somebody to write him better lines because he couldn't keep going, and so he got a playwright; and after *that* he needed somebody to keep everybody else in line, so he got a director. That's my guess.

High Noon on 44th Street:
Clive Barnes

Clive Barnes, the daily drama critic of the New York **Times,** *graciously accepted the dramatists' invitation to answer questions in a subsequent meeting. Mr. Barnes is the only major participant in the articles, comments and conversations in this volume who is not a dramatist (his colleague Mr. Kerr is co-author of five Broadway productions). We make this one exception of inclusion in our dramatists' anthology because, by virtue of his position on the* **Times,** *Mr. Barnes is a mirror to which Broadway and off-Broadway dramatists must hold up their works to be told how beautiful they are, as inexorably if perhaps not as irrevocably as in the case of Snow White's wicked stepmother.*

After an official introduction to the roomful of dramatists by Jerome Weidman on behalf of the Dramatists Guild's symposium committee, Mr. Barnes opened the discussion with a few remarks.

CLIVE BARNES: When I accepted your kind invitation, I said that I was both honored and stupid—but not entirely stupid. I have taken precautions. First, I am armed. Second, I have left a message with my wife that if I am not out of here in time to meet her at the theater at 7:30 she is to call the police; and third, I have left a letter with my secretary, addressed to the publisher, bequeathing my job to John Simon.

A lot of you imagine that I am to criticism what Erich von Stroheim was to chauffeurs, and I think you have some misconceptions about me. I am kind of a running joke in that magazine, you know, your *Quarterly*. And one of your members once wrote a book about me—at least I got the impression that it was about me—and he actually never spoke with me. I suppose some of you do have some things to say to me, and I am not fragile. I'd like to talk things over with you.

Q: As I understand it, Walter Kerr gave up his job as daily critic on the *Times* because he felt he had too much power. How do you feel about having this power?

BARNES: You must remember that it is not *I* who have this power, it is the drama critic of the New York *Times*. It is fairly humbling to remember that if I closed the case on my typewriter I would be forgotten in two weeks flat. It is the power of position, not the power of person. I agree the power is shocking. When I took the job over I said I wanted to cut down on that power. I have tried to make the reviews rather more personal, tried to remove the sense of judgment in them. I said once, and I believe it, if the drama critic of the *Times* must stand on his head in public to stop people from taking him so seriously, that's a valuable duty for him to do. Critics don't want power, they want influence, and there is a big difference. But it is really the producers who give the critics power.

Q: How is that?

BARNES: The producers are continually making the public aware of the critics' judgment in advertisements and other public statements. As soon as you have full-page advertisements shouting about "unanimous raves," you immediately put yourself into a vulnerable position when you have unanimous pans. Remember, the real box office power is word of mouth. When a play opens on Monday and the reviews come out on Tuesday, at that moment the word of mouth is almost entirely the critics, and the *Times* is the most important. But after two or three weeks that power has already eroded, and what people are saying becomes most important. It's curious how sometimes you take more notice of what a complete stranger at a cocktail party thinks of a play or movie than of a critic you've been reading for years. And I very often know what Vincent Canby thinks of a movie but I will ring him to hear him *say* it in his own words before going to see it, such is the power of word of mouth. If the producers were ready to nurse certain shows, if they showed more faith in their product, I think they could often do a lot better. Very often they use the critics as an excuse to go to their backers and say, "Look, we had this very nice show and it would have run for years if only those idiot critics had liked it."

Q: The producers wouldn't quote you or any other critic unless they were aware that the audience takes what you say as fact rather than opinion. Can the critic educate the audience to think for itself, to take what you say as opinion rather than fact?

BARNES: A critic can say "in my opinion," and I often do. I often put in such parenthetical clauses, though the paper doesn't like it. I also use the first person, which critics at one time didn't do. I started to do this as a dance critic. One night, being fed up with "in this reporter's opinion" and all of that, I wrote: "We said last night that the floor cloth in Jerome Robbins's *Fancy Free* was salmon pink, our wife informs us that we should have said fuchsia," and they printed this without changing it. The next day I started to use "I" and nothing was ever said—I don't know whether they ever noticed.

You can try to explain that your review is only one person's opinion, but it would be very difficult to report on the audience reaction. On first nights the audience reaction is very often completely atypical, which is why I like to see a play at a preview. It's also why I often like to read a play before going to see it, though I'm not a good visualizer and find it very difficult to tell just from reading the script whether a play is likely to be good or bad.

Q: Has the *Times* ever discussed with you personally any of the proposals made recently by the Dramatists Guild?

BARNES: Yes, on two or three occasions. I'd love to see a much healthier critical situation than we have at the moment, but I don't think your proposals were realistic. The idea of having a second critic is extremely problematical for a number of reasons, the first being the problem of space. We have only eight columns for the arts each day, and I don't think one could justify taking up space for two drama criticisms within those columns, any more than you could for two music or film criticisms.

I know you made the point about the theater being a very special part of New York life, and remember it's a very special part of *my* life as well as yours. I am part of the theater, and when I talk to the *Times* I am in a very curious position with one foot in each camp, the theater and the newspaper. But I think it would be extraordinarily difficult to have two critics in the way you envisage. What would be the result? If they agree, you get two good notices—perhaps two good notices would have more box office punch than one good notice, perhaps not. If you get two bad notices, you're out. I think a split vote would be the equivalent of a bad notice, so in actual fact you probably would lose more by having two *Times* criticisms than you would gain.

One technical difficulty is, any two reviews of the same play would have quite a large amount of similar material. You have to tell the story, you know. If you were going out on a job with Charlie Brown who is going to be the other critic, you would have to say, "Well Charlie, I told the story last night, you tell the story tonight." Otherwise the reader would be plagued by duplication, right?

Q: As I remember it, the proposal wasn't for just one other critic, but several, who would not be required to do the obvious chore of telling the story or giving facts about the production. It was simply to have them write something like, "I am a professor recognized in my own field, and this is what I felt about the play I saw last night."

BARNES: You mean, just give votes? "I liked it, I didn't like it?"

Q: Why not?

BARNES: That would be ridiculous. For one thing, I doubt you could get any respectable person to do it.

Q: You just spoke about listening to other people in terms of word of mouth. . . .

BARNES: In word of mouth people don't say just "I liked it." When I mentioned word of mouth I think I meant something more sophisticated than what you are talking about. It would be demeaning to the theater, and I can't imagine anyone of quality lending himself to such a project. Walter Kerr once remarked that if you consider the critics crazy for power, just give them a yes-or-no ballot to drop in a box as they leave after the first night. You would save them a lot of trouble.

Q: The *World-Telegram* once published a box score. On opening night, several responsible members of the paper's staff would talk to various people—a psychiatrist, a dentist, a grocer. What is your objection to having other opinions?

BARNES: I want criticisms, I don't want opinions.

Q: If someone didn't want to have a play reviewed, would you stay away from the opening?

BARNES: That wouldn't be a decision for me to make, it would be a decision for the *Times* managing editor, Abe Rosenthal, to make. The *Times* doesn't exist for the theater, it exists for its readers. I couldn't make such a decision, but I would be perfectly prepared not to go.

Q: If the producer didn't want you to cover the opening, would Mr. Rosenthal make you go?

BARNES: I don't know. I can't answer that question, I can't answer for Mr. Rosenthal.

Q1: I'd be inclined to think the producer would insist that he come, because my general feeling is that nobody comes to the theater unless the New York *Times* tells them to come, unless it's a very popular attraction. I think we need the *Times* and we need more people who want to see a play.

Q2: Mr. Barnes was kind enough to say about the last play I had done on Broadway: "If you care anything about the serious theater in New York City, you've got to see this play." It killed us, naturally.

BARNES: There you are, the power of the New York *Times*. But there are some grounds on which I certainly would decide *not* to go to a play. For example, I had seen *The Flip Side* in London and hadn't liked it, so I didn't review it here. I sent Dan Sullivan, who was then my number two. In the *Dramatists Guild Quarterly* it was once mentioned that the producers had asked me not to go to see it. In actual fact, the producers objected strenuously until I told them why. I also bowed out of covering Thornton Wilder's *Our Town* in a production I'd seen and hadn't liked too much. I can't see any reason for going to the theater if you know you aren't going to like it and someone else might. As it happened in the case of *The Flip Side*, no American critics liked it.

Q: But Mr. Barnes, when you decide *not* to go and see a play, isn't that itself a form of criticism?

BARNES: Some people say when my wife decides not to go and see a play it is a form of criticism. I suppose that when a second critic is sent it obviously is, unless there is some other reason like a conflict of Broadway openings. Yes, I would say that does represent some kind of prior judgment.

Q: Then your service to the theater in that particular instance would be to go and say something nice.

BARNES: A critic who would say something nice every time he went to the theater would have no value to the theater at all.

Q: Could one make a choice between you and Mr. Kerr on opening nights?

BARNES: Certainly not, no, because Mr. Kerr at his own request is Sunday critic, and why should he do a chore for me?

Q: Mr. Barnes, before you write a review of a show, do you decide "I'm for it" or "I'm against it"? Is there a strong line between the two? Usually, reviewers take one stand or another—a play may get mixed reviews, but each individual review will be 90 per cent for it or 90 per cent against it. Do you feel it is your duty to take a definite yes or no position, rather than "Well, this was very good and that wasn't," leaving it up to the reader himself to make up his mind whether he should see the play or not?

BARNES: That is quite a difficult question to answer. The critics as a group never do take a stand, one doesn't know what the other critics are going to say. As for the individual, what was it Dr. Johnson said?—"The prospect of imminent execution clears the mind." I don't know that anyone knows or can explain how they write a notice when they get to that typewriter.

Q: Could you condense your opinions in your reviews?

BARNES: I don't know, but I *do* know that I write shorter than any New

York *Times* drama critic in living memory. I write markedly shorter than Walter used to, I even write shorter than Brooks Atkinson.

Q: Mr. Barnes, I'd like to hear what solutions to the power problem you think there might be, because I think we need you as much as you need us.

BARNES: There are three things that occur to me. First, I think that if there is going to be another critic, it would be far too difficult for the New York *Times* to provide that critic. What could be done, the League of New York Theaters could hire a critic and spend a large amount of money advertising his views. Even then, I don't see how it would have the effect you want, I don't think the idea of double criticism would be a good one for reasons I've already outlined.

Second, we have some very good weekly critics including Mr. Kerr, whose reviews might tend to minimize the effect of the *Times* daily notice if it would be possible, as in films, to have their reviews come out more or less at the same time, after having attended a very advanced preview. I think it would make a big difference to read Kerr on the Sunday after a play was reviewed. This is something the producers could very well consider.

Third, if a producer *had* to provide running expenses, if it were part of his contract that whatever happened a play would have to run, say, four or six weeks, it would a) stop the futile producer who does bad plays and b) it would give those plays that were put on a much better chance of life.

And the solution to our problems is partly a matter of education of persuading people to read criticism in a more sensible fashion than they do at the moment.

Q: Reviewing Julius Epstein's *But Seriously* you found it necessary to say in the course of your review that he wrote *Casablanca* which proves that movies are not written. It's like death to put into your theater program biography that you wrote a motion picture.

BARNES: Can I say that one of the difficulties of the first night, and I think this is true of any critic, is that sometimes we write things we regret the next morning. That was possibly one of them. I intended it as a light-hearted joke. Perhaps the author didn't take it that way. I'm sorry, it wasn't meant to be. . . .

Q: By the time you finish your light-hearted joke, the play was dead.

BARNES: But look, it would not have lasted, even with a rave notice from the *Times*.

Q: In your review of *Lovely Ladies, Kind Gentlemen* you saw fit to mention that John Patrick wrote such epics as *Suzie Wong*. He also wrote one of the best American plays ever written, the brilliant *The Hasty Heart*, and one wonders why you didn't say, "It's a shame that John Patrick who wrote *The Hasty Heart* is mixed up in this." One wonders, what kind of a cynical attitude, what lack of knowledge am I up against?

BARNES: I don't mind being criticized. . . .

Q: Oh, yes you do.

BARNES: I don't. Really, I don't. But I don't think you should take jokes to indicate a lack of knowledge.

Q: We've been addressing questions rather critically. I think we have something to learn from you about the general problems of the theater as a critic sees them. Have you any thoughts for us as playwrights? We know we are in desperate straits. You write reviews of individual plays, but you never write what you think about the American theater. What is your attitude towards it?

BARNES: Well, one of the difficulties, it seems to me, is that so many of the old plays are the kind that should be done for television, and people are not going to pay good money to see a play when they can see much the same thing done on television. And I think the theater perhaps has not been as agile and resourceful as it could have been in fighting off the movies. Movies cost a lot less, they are more casual, you don't have to book in advance, you don't have to stand for three hours in the rain waiting to buy tickets.

Perhaps what we are also seeing is the difficulty of an unsubsidized theater. I get very tired of hearing how much better the theater is in England, because I don't think it is, fundamentally. People come back from England saying, "I went to the theater every night and saw absolutely marvelous plays," and when you question them a bit you find they have been almost entirely to the subsidized theater, *highly* subsidized theater doing not just classic revivals but modern plays. I don't think *Home* would have been done on Broadway if it hadn't been done first by the subsidized Royal Court. I don't think *Rosencrantz and Guildenstern, Joe Egg* and a lot of other plays would ever have been done on Broadway except that the producers and backers were able to see them before money was gotten together to do them here. And the British playwright, being subsidized, has much greater free-dom to develop, to write about the twentieth century than a lot of American playwrights who are trying to get a commercial success and are really writing about the nineteenth century, it sometimes seems.

Q: This bothers me, because I think I know most of the playwrights in the business, and I don't think they write for any given audience. I think they write the best plays they know how to write, and they may end up on Broadway or they may end up in Timbuctoo. I'm asked this question very often: given the commercial conditions in today's theater, why don't you sit down and write a commercial success? But I don't.

BARNES: I think what you say is true, I didn't mean to give the wrong impression. No one tries to write a bad play, or even a purely commercial play. Someone once raised the question that I didn't like "formal" plays —well, this is just gibberish. If I have any quality at all as a critic, it is that I don't know what I am looking for. I have no set rules. I don't sit down and think, "This isn't a play." I am perfectly prepared to love a funny bedroom farce or a Grand Guignol melodrama or anything else as long as I can see . . . as long as I can be entertained. I am looking for entertainment, and enter-tainment can be a great number of different things.

Q: What is your policy on re-reviewing a play?

BARNES: It's a kind of reader's service more than anything else. When I took over the drama job nearly four years ago, I was going around catching up on some shows I hadn't seen. I was seeing casts that sometimes were not the original ones, giving, some of them, terribly sloppy performances. It occurred to me that if the producers and others know the play is going to be re-reviewed, it gives them an incentive to try to brush it up for the public. The policy is a very arbitrary one—some things I haven't re-reviewed, some things I have. I'll be perfectly honest with you—sometimes a press agent will tell me that a play I like is in trouble, and I will go to try to help it out if I can.

Q: I hate the whole subject of reviewing. Why do I, after spending two years writing a play, have to submit myself to a critic whose credentials I don't know, except that Abe Rosenthal hired him? What makes a newspaperman like Abe Rosenthal say that *you* are our drama reviewer? Why do we have to sit and wait for *you* to tell us whether our work is good or bad? What gives a man the courage and the confidence to sit in judgment? What are your qualifications, Mr. Barnes?

BARNES: What are your qualifications as a playwright? Chiefly you do the job . . .

Q: Not at all . . .

BARNES: Well, I suppose the critic has just about the same qualifications. I am not a failed playwright. I am not a failed actor. I am not a failed director. I have no creative talent at all, and it doesn't worry me a bit, because I doubt whether a creative talent is the best kind of critic. A *failed* creative talent can make a critic very bitter, he can be jealous of success. It has been my experience that people who are failed playwrights haven't always been the best of critics.

Probably my own qualifications are modest. I love the theater. I go to the theater an enormous amount, more than any of you, I suspect—playwrights very often don't. I have a kind of virgin-like response to the theater. I am able to retain my receptivity, I wouldn't do the job otherwise. It's something I've always wanted to do. At 14, when most boys want to be engine drivers, I wanted to be a critic.

That doesn't mean that I believe that the individual critic is a very important person. It's the *theater* that is news. People want to talk about the theater, and they want to read about it. In general, America overrates its critics in every field.

Q: If you review a play unfavorably in London, chances are that play won't get produced in New York. You can go to California and not like one, and the chances are it won't get to New York. Now, that's considerable power or influence, whatever you want to call it.

BARNES: I don't mean people overrate the critics' *power*, I mean they overrate the critics' *importance*, and as I said I think this is a matter of education. About this question of California and London, people have wondered whether I have a policy. Yes, I do have a policy about plays in London, right, and I think every producer knows it. If a London play is going to be done in New York, the producer can say, "I don't want you to see this play," and I won't. If he says, "I want you to see the play if you like, but please don't write about it," that is what I will do. Or he can say, "Go see the play and write about it if you want to." I can't see why this is not legitimate. There is a very large audience of *Times* readers in London, and a lot of readers go to London. London is a big theater center, and what goes on there is a matter of public interest and public concern.

Q: But why do you give that right to the producer and not the author?

BARNES: Because it is the producer who can guarantee that a play is going to be produced.

Q: Mr. Barnes, you function in the New York arena. Why doesn't the *Times* allow its man in London to cover that play? You are the man who is going to review that play here in New York when it arrives, and if you have already announced that the play is bad and that you don't like it, the playwright doesn't have a chance, does he?

BARNES: Look at it this way, I am doing nothing that every other New York critic hasn't traditionally done.

Q: If you review a London play and later if that same play comes to New York, you will *not* review it. Is that true?

BARNES: No, it is not true. I would only *not* review it if I had given it a bad review. If I had given it a bad review and it came to New York, I think I would not review it.

Q: There was a play in London called *Forty Years On*. In the case of that play, were you asked by the producer to see it or not to see it?

BARNES: I was not asked by the producer to see it or not to see it because the play was not scheduled for a New York opening. There was an option taken on it, but there are options taken on every play.

Q: When an option is taken, then, do you consider that a play is fair game for you?

BARNES: I don't regard any play . . .

Q: I don't mean "fair game" in that sense.

BARNES: I feel that I have a duty to the readers to cover the European scene. I only feel that if a producer has a definite opening, if he has a cast set, then I think it is fair.

Q: I was told, maybe erroneously, that *Forty Years On*—which is a play that I happened to like and you didn't, and I have no personal interest in it whatsoever—was scheduled for production, and that upon reading your negative review in the New York *Times* the producers decided against producing the show in New York. Had you heard anything like that?

BARNES: I know that it was optioned. I know also that Alex Cohen had an option on *The Secretary Bird*, but no definite commitment.

Q: Did he ask you to see it?

BARNES: No, he didn't. I think I made this policy, I got this kind of policy very properly going last year.

Q: Why would you review in London and not in Philadelphia when a play is on the road?

BARNES: There is an enormous difference. When a play is on the road in Philadelphia, it is being shaped up for a New York showing. A play in London is not being shaped up for New York, it is a London production. If any author of a play being produced in America outside New York would ask me not to review his play, I think I probably would not. I would let the author decide nowadays, out of town.

Q: Why as the reviewer for the New York *Times* do you feel that it is necessary to go to London and cover plays that are being done there and warn people off from seeing them in New York?

BARNES: Sometimes I may warn people off, as you put it, but sometimes I encourage people to go.

Q: Some years ago when Brooks Atkinson was the *Times* drama critic, a group of playwrights and producers met with him to discuss the problems of reviewing. The suggestion was made that in the case of plays about which he had mixed feelings he put his reservations in the middle of the review and the positive things at the beginning and end, if possible. He agreed and did do that. How do you feel about it?

BARNES: I don't know. I think that sometimes I try to do that myself. It's sometimes a matter of concentrating on an actor rather than the play itself when you have reservations about the play but none about the performance. Normally, though, I think I write more about plays than about acting.

Q: How about publishing a sort of consensus, a box score of all the critics including the TV reviewers?

BARNES: The *Times* runs one on Sunday.

Q: It's too late on Sunday. The ship has already sailed. I mean in the daily paper.

BARNES: This was put up to Mr. Rosenthal, and he didn't like the idea. For the daily paper, a box score would consist only of the *News*, the *Post* and the TV reviewers—who, by the way, are becoming more powerful. And there would be the technical difficulty of getting the information for the box score that night. Remember, the last copy has to go at 11:30 p.m. I don't know. I wonder. You would have only those few opinions. I don't know if it would really make a great deal of difference.

Q: It would mitigate the thunderbolt you wield there. . .

BARNES: I have nothing to do with the decision on the box score.

Q: Richard Watts of the *Post* had a column of Random Notes on Fridays, looking back on a show, writing something to help it. Would you consider a column like that?

BARNES: It's been discussed, but the feeling is that it might add to the power of the daily critic, which no one really wants to do. That is against it, as well as the space problem.

Q: Ideally, what do you think the function of a critic ought to be?

BARNES: He is a link between the artist and the audience. Obviously, part of the job involves an act of judgment, but I think those who consider the judgment the most important element of his function are wrong. We really are all talking here about money rather than art, aren't we? Well, I know that on some occasions I have helped a play along. On a number of occasions I have written a notice about a play or musical that I personally didn't like very much but thought other people would—as far as one can tell for other people—a notice in which my own feelings were very clear, but written to get people to the box office. I think that can be done occasionally. I have learned quite a lot since I was thrown into this job almost four years ago, and I think I can now see quality in things that do not appeal to me personally.

Q 1: Mr. Barnes, why don't you ask the playwrights what *they* think the function of a critic should be? It sounds like all we want is good reviews.

Q 2: A London critic once told me years ago, "I am writing for amusement so in a way I am a reporter, but I am not asked to give my personal opinion. What I do is try to give my impression of what has been seen on the stage, and let people make their own judgment." You believe that over and above your impressions of an evening's entertainment, it is your job to give your own personal feelings?

BARNES: I'll answer that as well as I can. You see, there was a school of thought both in American and England that believed, or tried to kid people, that criticism could be *objective*. I don't think that criticism can be objective. I think you can do an objective view of a fire, but only God can do an objective view of a play. You must be absolutely honest, you must have your own opinions. When you are describing a play it's possible to say, "There is a fantastically awful scene of fornication in the third act," which may in fact get some people along to see it. But I think that those who pretend that they are being objective are really kidding themselves and giving themselves the airs and graces of a judge. They are perhaps more dangerous, potentially, than the critic who tries to be absolutely honest in writing from what is very obviously a personal viewpoint, so that people who read him will eventually get to know his prejudices. We all have prejudices, and there is nothing more secret than hidden prejudices, if you see what I mean. Very often, so-called "objectivity" veils that kind of hidden prejudice.

Let's get away from plays for a moment and imagine a concert review. What would you say? "Mr. Stern came onto the platform last night and there he was, still wearing that white tie and black suit of his, still carrying his fiddle. He played Beethoven's violin concerto." Now, apart from that, what are you going to say that is objective? Do you know that music critics disagree even as to whether a man is in tune or not? So do orchestras, so objectivity is very much a snare and a delusion, and also something of a put-on to the audience.

q: Mr. Barnes, would it console you to know that Brooks Atkinson once reviewed a Maxwell Anderson play, and the next day Anderson announced that he would no longer write plays?

BARNES: Can I speak to this? I think it is an interesting point. I once asked David Merrick on television—because I thought that was the best place to ask him—whether he could recall a *good* play that had been killed by the critics. He said he couldn't. I think they can be bruised, I think they can be damaged. *Little Murders*, for example, got bad reviews on Broadway (incidentally, I didn't see it) but was later revived and became quite successful.

Harold Pinter's *The Birthday Party* was absolutely clobbered the first time out, and came back. Good plays are much more indestructible than people think. The danger is that you might bruise or hurt someone's hopes, but I also doubt that a playwright can be easily discouraged by a critic he despises.

William Goldman's *The Season* had about eleven pages of vituperation about me. I nearly gave up there and then. There were areas of truth in what he said about me—and areas of arrant nonsense. I very nearly gave up, but eventually I girded my loins, or whatever one does, and said, "Oh, shit," if you forgive the expression—most of you have used it in your plays. I said, "To hell with the guy." And then for about three or four weeks I would write him two or three vituperative letters a week, which I never posted of course, and I felt a lot better.

Q: A playwright who attempts a serious play may be contributing some-thing ultimately more valuable to the historical continuity of the theater than one who attempts something less. I suggested to Walter Kerr a number of years ago that it is his responsibility to review not only the success of a play in its intention, but also the historical value of the play to the theater. He disagreed with me totally. Do you feel you have the responsibility to educate the audience about the value of the play to the theater, to educate the audience to make criticism ultimately unecessary? Do you feel you should encourage the play that tried something more difficult and obviously suc-ceeded less than the play which succeeded more in a lesser intention?

BARNES: The answer to that question is yes.

Q: Do you feel that you compensate enough? It's a terrible way to put it, but do you feel that you overcompensate enough for that kind of play?

BARNES: I honestly don't know. It's very difficult to look at one's self subjectively, let alone objectively, and I honestly don't know. All I can say is that I do my best under the circumstances, and that's all I think anyone can say. Education is a very solemn word, but as a critic I want to help provide a fruitful atmosphere in which the theater can develop. And I do have an awareness of the aspiration of a play as well as its success.

Q: But isn't your thing more the off-beat play or musical—for example *Hair* or *The Last Sweet Days of Isaac*—than the formal play?

BARNES: I don't think so. I certainly am not the only critic that praised *Hair*—most critics praised it. Most critics praised *The Last Sweet Days of Isaac*. Audiences liked both shows—remember, critics can get people into the theater for a certain time, but they can't keep them coming. I happened to like *Zorbá*, as did most critics. But *Zorbá* had a very surprisingly short run, so perhaps the critics were wrong. Who can tell? *Promenade* is a musical I liked very much, but audiences didn't. I could tell from my mail bag. I always have a very strong temperature of reaction from my mail bag when I am out of "think" with the readership. I'm not against the formal play—many of the plays I've praised, like *Child's Play*, are formal plays. People who write formal plays think I am all in favor of the avant garde and people who consider themselves in the avant garde think I am a fuddy duddy, but the truth is I am open to any theatrical experience and have no preconceptions.

Q: Do you have any general conclusions or opinions in your years of theatergoing that would be useful for us to hear?

BARNES: At the moment, I wonder whether we organize theater in a very sensible fashion. I'm not sure that this horse race concept we've inherited is a very good one. There's a lot of money spent on Broadway, but only a few make it. We need financial support to encourage experiment on Broadway, because on Broadway the playwright is not given a fair chance to fail. Take an example I've already cited—*Joe Egg*. If you were telling backers, "I have this killingly funny play about a spastic child," you just would not get the money for a Broadway production. We have very little fresh playwriting on Broadway, and I don't blame the playwright, I blame the producer, although the producer himself is in a very tough situation here. So we must somehow persuade people to give us more support.

Q: What do you mean by "fresh playwriting?"

BARNES: There is the kind of play that is a development of an existing form and maybe absolutely superb of its kind—a superbly funny comedy. For example, look how well *The Front Page* has held up. I doubt very much that anyone could write *The Front Page* today, but if someone did it would be a perfectly acceptable kind of play. But there is another kind of play that puts you off into a new thing, by a different kind of playwright, maybe eventually the better kind of playwright. Not all playwrights are equal, just as all critics are not, and the really adventurous kind of playwright is the difficult one for the critic to spot because the critic is essentially a man who is looking backward rather than forward. This is why, for example, a lot of reputable critics were absolutely wrong about Pinter's *The Birthday Party*. They were able to eat their words later, but I think it is very difficult for that kind of fresh, adventurous playwright to get a chance at the moment.

Q: Have you been made to feel that your function as a critic is to sell tickets?

BARNES: A lot of *you* think that is my function. I refuse to accept it, although it would be utterly unrealistic of me to adopt the completely pure attitude—this is one of the things Goldman made me realize. It is not the function of a critic to sell tickets, but it would be unrealistic of him not to recognize that he *does* sell tickets—he's often responsible for a line at the box office, or for a line not being there.

Q: What you are saying is, it's a less than ideal situation?

BARNES: Of course. The ideal situation is that of a dance critic. I can say anything I like about a ballet without killing it—that ballet will go into the repertory. Every dance critic is living with ballet he's slaughtered thirty years ago. It's a continuing situation which we don't have in the theater, though I think of the American Place Theater as an ideal situation in some respects, because the playwright can either have his play reviewed or not. The play is sold out anyway, and he's got an eight-week run. The critic can't even sell tickets, because it's a club theater. I think that is a very good idea, because the critic can then become the helper and assistant of the theater, which I think he should be.

JEROME WEIDMAN: Speaking for myself and as chairman of this committee, I have been most pleasantly surprised. I expected an ogre, but instead of that we got a very human man. I want to thank you, Mr. Barnes.

Criticizing the Critics

From time to time during the past decade the Dramatists Guild Quarterly polled recently-produced dramatists on the subject of the critics, asking the authors which critic wrote the most perceptive, the most understanding, the most readable, etc. review of their current work.

To many dramatists, the New York drama critics—particularly the next-day newspaper reviewers—seem like the many-tentacled giant squid at the end of Dr. No's deadly obstacle course. The critics are the final ordeal arranged to destroy any hero hardy enough to survive the nerve-wracking, flesh-flaying, bone-cracking hazards leading to the eve of a New York production. The intention of the Quarterly's polls on this subject was to let off a little steam, maybe, to sauce the gander, to vote on their work for a change; to exchange views on this perplexing final obstacle.

The recently-produced and therefore freshly-criticized dramatists were asked to comment on any aspect of the subject. Here are some of the critic-criticisms received over the years, in alphabetical order of the responding dramatists.

Each individual critic is a fallible being subject to his prejudices and his sense of well-being at the time he is in the theater. But collectively, they are almost always right.

—GEORGE ABBOTT

My critics are myself, my wife, my collaborator, and in turn our collaborators, my publisher, my peers, some friends, a relative or two, the first trumpet player, a stage manager, an out-of-town hotel clerk, my son, the room service waiter, a few agents, my lawyer, my daughter and the audience. This motley crew are my true critics. They help me, level me, inspire me, berate me, comfort and cajole me. I've come to regard the professional

pening-night critic of any media as an anticlimax to this motley crew, an
ftermath, a provocative post mortem, a curiosity piece, a necessary fetish of
he opening night festival, but surely not the ultimate reward of my writing.
That reward, those rewards have come long before, and will come long
fter. To insist that they come from a few men in one night is to make the bet
with the devil.

I believe the power of the critics is derived, not from their personal
mbitions, but from our willingness to appoint that power to them. We seem
almost anxious to pay blind obeisance to the critical deity. But what is the
price of that payment? At what cost? Why can't they be one of many, one of
ur persuasions, our references, our influences, one of many in our artistic
nvironment? Why do we celebrate them as the only one? Why do we make
uch an enormous investment in their judgment of our worth? It is, in effect,
elling out. And whether they put us in a state of euphoria or in the inferno
hat morning after, either state is corrosive for the artist. And the final irony
s, they haven't put us there at all. We have.

Recently I saw the matinee of a play in preview. I spoke to the author, who
was four days away from opening night. He trembled at the prefabricated
onslaught of one critic. That was his overwhelming concern. It sounded like
he was making his career that concern. He seemed willing to make that bet.
Almost hypnotically. I know the feeling. I'm sure we all do.

And I think it's about time somebody snapped his fingers.

—JERRY BOCK

Much has been said about the power of the critics (who, when this point is
raised in their presence, carefully point to a few well-known exceptions) but
it seems at least in some cases that a tremendous gap exists between what
the critics like or don't like, and what an audience likes or doesn't like. Too
often, the last word is the critics'. The economy of the theater being what it
is, once a show is condemned there is seldom a chance for a reprieve. What
would happen if instead of critics, word-of-mouth was the determining
factor? What would happen if the critics—and with only three left in New
York now—were to preview a show out of town, as *Variety* does? In that
case, might not there be a chance for revisions, rewrites, or whatever, that
would offer better chance of success in New York? To preserve Broadway
theater, to make it flourish, naturally it's the responsibility of playwrights,
directors, actors and producers to do the best they can. I sometimes wonder
with the power of the critics whether they don't have a responsibility that
goes deeper than the witty knife-thrusts of cleverly-carved pans.

—WILLIAM F. BROWN

It's my opinion that the critics don't really know—and actually *can't*
know—what the contributions of the director and actors are (or are *not*) to a
play, particularly a musical. Only one who has been through the rehearsals,

the preparations, the struggle from start to finish can judge that. The mos
they can do is judge the quality of the writing—and how can you separate
that from all the rest?

Criticism is admirable when they like you—hateful when they don't
Most critics are all too human—and sometimes they admit it. It's not the
critics' fault they have their unnatural power. Prices of theater tickets are so
outrageous. I can't blame the public for wanting some guarantee before they
buy. But they're missing a lot!

—JEROME CHODOROV

Despite the controversy over Stanley Kauffmann's attendance at fina
previews instead of opening nights, I am of the opinion that his point was
valid. It would encourage critics to be more perceptive and thorough in their
reviews if they hadn't the pressure of meeting deadlines—turning in their
reviews an hour and a half after seeing the performance.

—HOWARD DA SILVA

I did not know any of the gentlemen who reviewed my play, but the
average reader, or indeed, my immediate family, might have gathered from
their reviews that I knew them all intimately and must have done something, at some point in my life, to deeply offend them. The level of their
attack was so personal and vituperative that I am hard put, even six months
later, to contemplate, much less attempt, another play.

With the exception of Norman Nadel, who pointed out a structural weakness within the play and offered constructive criticism, and Douglas Watt,
who acknowledged the presence of wit and fresh humor in my writing, all of
the critics engaged in a personal free-for-all, one even going so far as to
review my baby, to whom I had given birth two days before the opening.

The sadness is that it was a comedy: at best a happy evening's diversion,
at worst—because of a combination of circumstances—not funny enough
for the gentlemen.

But the real sadness, especially in view of the critical cry for new writers, is
that this play might not have been the best, or all that I had to contribute, and
because of the level of the criticism I don't know that we'll ever find out.
(Actually, I suppose I am overstating it a little; not all the reviews attacked
me personally: one of them destroyed my husband for daring to co-produce
the play.)

So I return to the less perilous, destructive world of my fourth novel.
Maybe one day, if I feel a deep surge of masochism coming on, and long
once again for public flagellation, I can think about writing another play. But
not now, gentlemen. Not right now.

—GWEN DAVIS

At the first Eugene O'Neill Memorial Foundation Playwrights' Conference in Waterford, Conn., Elliot Norton, in defining the role of the newspaper critic, said: " . . . our primary obligation is to tell the reader of
newspapers what the play is all about and then what we think of it. I think
this is basic. *We're not primarily concerned with telling the playwright what we
think of his play* (italics mine). We're primarily concerned in our kind of work
with telling the reader what kind of play it is."

Mr. Norton then went on to outline the reviewer's secondary obligation
which *is* to the writer. Among other things, the reviewer should try to
determine what the writer's intention is; whether he achieved it. If so—how
so? If not—why not? A third obligation, he said, was to educate the audience; an area in which he felt most reviewers had failed.

Of course, if reviewers did get past Mr. Norton's primary obligation and
got to his second and third, any writer would be more than satisfied. But
most reviewers rarely have the time, space and, perhaps, the ability to
illuminate so thoroughly the complete theatrical experience. So all they
do—can do (I now understand this)—is to tell the reader "what kind of play
it is." Period.

—FRANK GAGLIANO

Since the New York *Times* remains the one and only morning paper and
most influential, the oligarchic power which it holds over a show is a
monster that every author must be prepared to face. In the case of *Darling of
the Day*, which was produced by top echelon authors and producers at a cost
of $600,000, the drama department of the *Times* had the audacity to let its
first-string critic review a ballet opening in preference to our show. The
second- or third-string critic with strong psychic hostility toward what he
called "Charm for the older generation" came to review us. To compound
this injustice, we were given second billing on the drama page the next
morning, and an off-Broadway revival of *House of Flowers* received the
headline notice, whereas we came in for the secondary notice. The young
man's review was so obviously a subjective one and so venal that he
misquoted lines of lyrics which later the *Times* had to correct.

Mr. Walter Kerr, who had also seen the show on opening night, wrote a
favorable Sunday review which is better evidence than anything I can say.
But by the time this review appeared two weeks later in the Sunday *Times*, so
much money had been lost on the show that the producers did not have the
funds to counteract the damage done by the second stringer. In their
desperation to rectify some of their injustice, the *Times* drama department
finally sent Mr. Barnes to see the show. His review was short of excellent,
but they failed to publish it. He managed during a Sunday piece to slip in
one line saying "effortlessly the season's best musical."

—E. Y. HARBURG

By and large, we have no critics in New York. We have newsmen who view a work and give their opinions of it based on their own personal likes and dislikes. They do not reflect the community taste or their readers' taste they indicate merely their own taste, which is a personal matter. These, then are *reviewers*, not *critics*. (Critic: "One who expresses a reasoned opinion on any matter, involving a judgment of its beauty or technique"—Webster's Dictionary) Please note the words "reasoned opinion" and "technique". No critic of the New York newspapers is adequately equipped to give a "reasoned opinion", nor do any of them have the background to provide a sufficient criticism of theatrical technique.

—Jeff Steve Harris

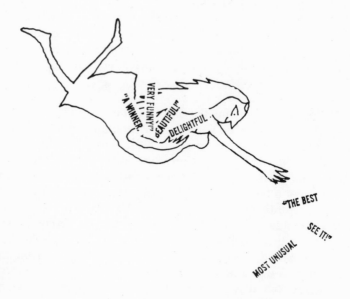

I had four plays open and get reviewed last season (1967–68), in the space of five months. (That's a lot for a little kid; probably too much.) Of course, I loved and approved of all that love and approval, but I must pull back from my berserk good fortune and register a small complaint about our critics and all of us too, I guess. I never met a playwright who was an enemy of the theater. Nobody ever sits down to write a bad play. Everybody—every one of us—puts a play he loves into a world-theater he loves. The critics, and other playwrights too, seem to forget this all too often. Couldn't we arrange for somebody famous to say that, so it would become a famous quote?

—Israel Horovitz

Something must be done to remove the pressure of opening night, at which plays are often distorted. Many openings, because of the adrenalin and hyperthyroid performance of that moment of time, make plays better than they are. By the same token, fear and panic can turn a good play into a distortion of itself. The critic must recognize both. We worked for ten years on a play of major importance. The critics never saw the play we wrote.

—JEROME LAWRENCE

A critic has a responsibility to report more than merely what he sees on a first night. His experience should lead him to see a *play*, not just a single production or a single performance. A play can be lost to literature because of the critics' shallow perception. I believe every major critic is an honorable man and a dedicated journalist. But honor is not knowledge and dedication is not perception.

—ROBERT E. LEE

Norman Nadel was most constructive in pointing out that the play's theme was big enough not to have been directed at a special audience. His was the only positive evaluation of how we could have avoided our biggest mistake. The others just threw rocks and imputed crass motives to us. Watts was lovable as always.

—FELIX LEON

When you tell drama critics they have power they get mad and yell at you. They will point out the plays the critics have rallied around but could not keep afloat. They will cite instances of plays surviving doubtful notices to become successful. But if you told the critics they were without influence I feel they might burst into tears. And well they should. Over the play doomed to failure and the undeniable hit, they have no power. Over the play that falls between these two extremes their influence is considerable.

Certainly we have never had a critic who wrote about the theater better than Walter Kerr. This persuades people he is also our best critic, and he well may be. He has amazing gifts of perception, sensitivity, observation and wit. Forgiving him his touch of the essayist, he writes like an angel.

Critics are an integral part of our theater and must share responsibility for it. It is in their special pieces more than in their first-night reviews that they temper the climate, shape public attitudes, cultivate and educate the public mind. Their influence is pervasive and effectual. For the most part their influence has been wholesome. I feel, and this will seem an odd statement, they have failed us not so much in their lack of appreciation as in their enthusiasms.

In our past, for example, the serious play was celebrated because it "convinced the taste and consoled the spirit." Then, starting some few years ago, came a succession of dramatic plays that, in the opinion of many

theatergoers, offended the taste and depressed the spirit. Yet these play
were given high critical acclaim and enthusiastically recommended. Th
public dutifully gave these plays their support for a considerable length c
time. Now a sizable proportion of the audience is in revolt. Resentful o
nights in the theater when the experience has been distasteful and depres
sing; they are shying away from all serious plays. It is not only the tire
businessman who has withdrawn his custom from the drama and turne
wholly to comedies and musicals, but genuine theater-lovers as well. Thi
defection is being felt at the box office. Backers are frightened and producer
are hesitating. The whole structure of our theater has been shaken and w
cannot hold the critics blameless. This reflects, along with other evidence,
believe, a growing gap between critical appraisal and public approval, and
find it worrisome.

—HOWARD LINDSAY

I feel that drama criticism is polluted by that poison which often exists ir
those who have been denied talent and teased with skill. I would like to add
that my reviews were 90 per cent favorable.

—BILL MANHOFF

The institution of drama criticism carries with it the dependence on the
subjective, personal tastes and opinions of the individual critics. I don't see
how you can alter this fact, and so I don't think you can improve the system
So long as the public sheepishly follows the major critics, our fates will be ir
the hands of Barnes, Kerr, et al. The fault lies not with the critics, who are
merely expressing "one man's opinion," but with a society in which indi-
viduality and boldness of thought lie dormant.

—WALTER MARKS

Let's examine the case of two fellows like Bob Fisher and myself, who hail from the West Coast and who have worked in television and the movies. The stamp of "pariah" is on us before we step off the plane to go into rehearsal. Evidently from the reviews not only our play received but also those of other plays that grew out of the minds of West Coast writers, a man who has worked in television or the movies has a hell of a nerve to perpetrate a play and try to get it on Broadway. How come the Civil Rights Bill doesn't protect West Coast authors against prejudice? Hardly a critic failed to note—and in a denigrating way—Mr. Fisher's and my TV experience. Not only is this sheer bigotry, but it isn't completely accurate. I have spent very little of my writing life in television. I've writen five books all published by major publishing houses. Two of them were big sellers and favorably reviewed (by even the New York *Times* and the *New Yorker*) and one was serialized in the *Saturday Evening Post*. I've also written many, many magazine articles and stories. Mr. Fisher, it's true, got his start in television, but then, so did Neil Simon, George Axelrod, Paddy Chayefsky and Frank Gilroy.

Arthur Marx

As a long-time member of the Dramatists Guild and as a practising critic of even longer experience (of motion pictures, to be sure, but hang on a moment; you'll see the connection), I was naturally profoundly interested in the assessment of my colleagues in one line of business by my more successful colleagues in the other. Any profession that stirs up such a storm and heat of passion can't be all that bad.

Almost all of the respondents seem to assume that drama criticism is a branch of the theater itself (or that movie criticism is a branch of the film industry) and that all those engaged in the practise thereof should have only one responsibility: to serve the better interests of stage and screen.

This, of course, is as fallacious as saying that a political columnist, a James Reston or a Walter Lippmann, must serve only the interests of the government, that a sports reporter must work only for the greater glory of boxing or baseball, that an art critic must be permitted only to tell Picasso how to improve his work, or what the museums should or should not show.

The plain fact is, of course, that the critic, the columnist, even the reporter serves no such purpose whatever. He is a journalist, a newspaperman, and his sole obligation is to the readers of his publication. You too will admit, I am sure, that many drama critics have been read, and are still being read, for the way they wrote, and not for any guidance on what the reader should see in the theater—Shaw, for one, Brooks Atkinson, for another; there must be many others. And in the current brouhaha I think you will also find numerous readers of the New York *Times* reading Walter Kerr for the sheer pleasure of the Kerr prose style, without any intention whatever of going to, or not going to, the theater.

—Leo Mishkin

Twenty years ago you could think of critics as a group, but you can't today, unless you want to throw in radio and television where they devote about sixty seconds to reviewing a show that has taken two years to produce. I suppose they are critics because they criticize.

—RICHARD RODGERS

The critics reflect the aspirations, the prejudices and the entertainment desires of the public, for which reasons they should be called "reviewers" rather than "critics." When they are unanimous for a show or against it, they correctly reflect the general ticket buyers and brokers. When they split, they indicate that the work is for a special audience, and the ticket buyer must beware.

—ROBERT WALLACE RUSSELL

Walter Kerr is tough but he loves talent, especially acting talent. No other reviewer currently on the scene seems quite as deeply and originally responsive to it, and the sheer amount of space and energy he devotes in his reviews to expressing his pleasure and admiration of it should be ample testament. The "inside" feel of his on-the-wing capsule profiles is probably unprecedented in contemporary theater reviews. Even more impressive than the profiles is his special gift for evocation. Whether positive or negative his antennae seem to be so sensitively in contact with the spirit and inner rhythm of a play that his verbal feedback may be often experienced by some readers as a re-creation.

While Mr. Kerr is also extremely discerning, however, and indeed often brilliant, this special vitality on occasion has been unable to resist being merely clever. In such circumstances, the cascading imagery and the vaulting metaphors of his style—though marvellously entertaining—have created, willy-nilly, a density of verbal plumage which, as distraction, was not above obscuring an author's central metaphor.

Understandably, it is difficult if not downright disagreeable to restrain virtuosity when one has already acquired it. The hazardous economic structure on which the Broadway theater so precariously tilts, however, would make it seem obligatory for all reviewers, particularly one of Mr. Kerr's stature, to rather err on the side of consideration.

—MILTON SCHAFER

Dramatists have long held pronounced if admittedly subjectively-colored views as to the derivation and make-up of critics—views often best not explored in journals nominally available to family audiences. Now the professionals have had at it, and a comparison of objective and subjective views might be instructive. Louis Harris and Associates were employed by the United Church of Christ's Office of Communication to prepare a survey entitled *Critics and Criticism in the Mass Media,* for reasons which seem at first glance to have been, well, subjective.

According to Louis Harris et al, a critic is likely to be male (81 per cent), working for a male editor (98 per cent), whose average age is 45, who considers his job to be relatively pink-slip-proof (the average critic has been on the job six years or more), more likely than not a Protestant (47 per cent), a political liberal (57 per cent), with a middle-of-the-road editor (48 per cent). He has a college degree (75 per cent), as an English or literature (51 per cent) or journalism (23 per cent) major. He had originally intended to be a journalist, and wound up as a critic as a matter of (50 per cent) chance.

Mr. Harris's average critic thinks that the basis for his critical proficiency is primarily his writing ability, and his grasp of journalism at a professional level. Generally (60 per cent), he has worked for his present medium in some other capacity before becoming its critic in one or another field of the arts. Most (percentage not admitted to) prove to be ambiguous as to defining the background or prerequisites for getting the job, or for planning a clear-cut strategy for performance as a critic. Of the critics surveyed, 98 per cent were working on a newspaper, when an editor assumed that a not-at-all-specific and generally some-years-ago-academic background, including some reference to the field to be appraised, constituted a proper criterion for selection for the job.

Once hired, the average critic receives no special training for the job, or, for that matter, supervision. He feels that he is responsible first to a general public, and only secondarily to an informed minority. He believes that the general nature of his readership dictates an avoidance of a too-intellectual approach. Most (66 per cent) of the critics responding to the Harris organization's inquiry admitted to too great an emphasis on manner of expression, or personal style, and too little attention to content. As to application of outside pressure, the critics identified the culprits as advertisers (21 per cent), employers (19 per cent), supervisors and editors (17 per cent), publicists and promoters (13 per cent) and personal threats (10 per cent). A careful re-perusal of the report discloses no amplification of, or breakdown regarding, that latter figure.

The critics' practise of leaving a show as the curtain call applause begins often seems inappropriate, particularly in the case of the reviewers with semi-weekly or monthly deadlines, who nonetheless follow the daily reviewers out in almost pecking-order fashion. But the ultimate may have been reached at the special afternoon critics' showing of Jean Genet's *The Screens* at the Chelsea Theater Center of the Brooklyn Academy of Music. Since normal night-performance curtain times for this five-hour-long show were up at 8:30 p.m., down at 1:30 a.m., critics were mercifully invited to a special 2 to 7 p.m. performance. Thus no reviewer had actually to rush to the office in order to get his copy into the Late City or equivalent edition. Moreover, the audience-stage physical set-up made it impossible for the actors to return to the stage for curtain calls if a mass exodus of critics occurred. The critics preferred tradition to the practicalities; and so, while some actors made it, the lead player, after five hours of unswerving effort, was blocked off from taking his bow. The hall was filled with applause, but the lead could only bow, unseen by most of the audience, to the backs of the departing file of reviewers.

—Robert Schroeder

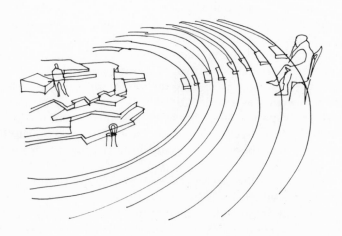

For *Variety*, Clive Barnes, New York *Times* drama critic, did a piece on the ineffectuality of critics, or rather their reviews, upon the theater as we know it. He detailed and rationalized this mishugas up and down several columns in sanctimonious but gorgeous haphazardry, and in the process propounded a method for revitalizing theater that is nothing short of astounding, and which merits the serious attention of anybody even remotely capable of being drawn into the orbit of a legitimate producer.

Contending the demise of a play can hardly be laid at the door of the critic (since it's none other than the producer who closes the show, says he) Barnes puts forward the suggestion, and it's really so cogent as to be outstanding, that no producer be allowed to put on a play *unless he guarantees to run it for a minimum of three months after opening.* Can we hear it for Mr. Barnes?

His justification for this compelling suggestion is simple though manifold. First says Mr. Barnes, and this is paraphrase, there have been umpteen presentations lambasted by critics which have weathered those tempests to achieve success merely by staying open and allowing audiences to find them. His suggested practise would give audiences that chance. Another round of applause for Mr. Barnes?

Second, adventurous legitimate producers would be driven out of habits which enable them to produce plays they don't wholly believe in. And third, vanity productions would be vastly curtailed if not eradicated entirely.

The ovation is a deserved one, Mr. Barnes. Take another bow.

Personally, however, I'll take a Clive Barnes rave to the suggested 90-day run any day, how about you?

—ROBERT SIMPSON

Drama critics are, for the most part, unable to express their general dissatisfaction in anything but general terms. Unable to discuss music and lyrics and unwilling to criticize acting and directing, they attack the libretto when the entire show fails to please.

—PETER STONE

Most people (including many who call themselves critics) don't know the difference between critic and reviewer, criticism and review. A reviewer is a person whose responsibility is to be a reliable consumer guide. You read what he says in order to decide whether or not you want to see something. He'll tell you a little bit about the plot, tell you who's in the cast, and toss a few qualitative adjectives around. "Fantastic!" "Repulsive!" "I cried till I laughed" or "I laughed till I wept" or "Sprint, don't jog to the box office" or "How did they let this one out of the crypt?" Etc.

That's all a reviewer is supposed to do. He's a good reviewer if his taste is pretty much yours; a bad reviewer if he encouraged you to waste your hard-earned on a musical whose every song was a dirge. Once you've seen the show in question, his opinion is worthless to you. He can tell you nothing you haven't found out for yourself.

A critic, on the other hand, does not have to agree with you to be a good critic. If he supports his thesis logically and intelligently, if he gives you a different perspective on the work in question, then he's a good critic. His function goes beyond a yea or a nay. A piece of criticism is a probe. How does this playwright's view of urban blight compare to Jules Feiffer's or Neil Simon's? How have Harold Prince and Stephen Sondheim advanced the boundaries of the musical theater this time? Why did John Guare choose this particular insane device to make his point? These are critical questions.

The critic's taste is his own. He doesn't ask you to take his word for things. He just asks you to consider his point of view and compare it with your own. Generally speaking, you cannot appreciate all that there is to be gotten out of a piece of criticism if you haven't seen the work being discussed.

To get down to cases—the gentlemen who give you reports from the stage on the 11 o'clock news are reviewers. They simply haven't the time to do more than tell you what genre the play fits into, flash a couple of stills from the production, and tell you in snappy journalese whether they think it's worth your while or not. The writers for the *News* are reviewers, Marilyn

Stasio's one-paragraph appraisals for *Cue* are reviews, etc. To a large degree it's a matter of restrictions.

Critics? Walter Kerr leaps to mind. His Sunday pieces tend to place the play in question into perspective, discussing what the creators have attempted in relation to similar attempts, presuming the reader's familiarity with theater history. Others who sometimes function as critics are Brendan Gill, Edith Oliver, Henry Hewes, Julius Novick, to mention a handful.

Clive Barnes?

Now here I find a paradox which I think is at the heart of the controversy that surrounds him. It is my opinion that his is the case of a writer of critical instincts placed in what is generally viewed as a reviewer's slot. Barnes's approach seems to be to have it both ways. Generally speaking, his lead and final paragraphs seem to be written for the consumer—filled with reviewers' phrases, adjectives, puns and wisecracks. In between these two paragraphs, his critical priorities take over. This is the real meat of his work, written for those who think of theater as something more than a night out. All manner of relevant background material and theories of interpretation are conveyed in a disarmingly conversational style. He seems determined to knock down the image of the critic as one who sits atop Mt. Olympus and hands down the only possible opinion. If he believes that a play for which he doesn't much care will genuinely please most of readers, as is the case of *Butterflies Are Free*, he will stress this fact, giving the press agents good quote material while still making his personal reservations clear.

—JEFF SWEET

I find most critics are frustrated performers, more interested in projection of their own personalities than in objective analysis and evaluation. By and large they are appalling point-missers, reflecting the vulgarity of the lowest-common-denominator audience. There is remarkably little scholarship or courage among them.

—DALE WASSERMAN

Cast and Credits.....

Identifying career highlights of contributors to this volume appear under their names in the index below.

aristophanes

BARRIE

ChEKhoV

GOETHE

H A M M E R S T E I N

IBSEN

Jonſon

KERN

LOPE de VEGA

MOLIÈRE

NASH

O'NEILL

RACINE

PORTER

STRINDBERG

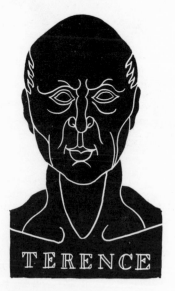

Voltaire

ALVERNO COLLEGE LIBRARY
Playwrights, lyricists, composers on the
792.0973G933

2 5050 00235775 0

110827

792.0973

G933

REMOVED FROM THE
ALVERNO COLLEGE LIBRARY

Alverno College Library
Milwaukee, Wisconsin